BESTSELLING BOOK SERIES

Paris For Dummies,
5th Edition

Cheat Sheet

Métro Stops for Paris Attractions

See the Métro map on the inside front cover and the RER map on the inside back cover to find the locations listed below.

Museums

Attraction	Métro Line Number: Stop
Centre Georges Pompidou	1: St-Paul
Musée d'Art et d'Histoire du Judaïsme	11: Rambuteau
Musée Carnavalet	1: St-Paul
Musée de Cluny	10: Cluny-La Sorbonne
Musée de l'Histoire de France	1,11: Hôtel-de-Ville
Musée Jacquemart-André	9: St-Philippe-du-Roule
Musée du Louvre	1: Louvre-Rivoli
Musée des Médailles	1, 7: Palais Royal
Musée d'Orsay	12: Solférino/RER Musée d'Orsay
Musée Picasso	1: St-Paul
Musée Rodin	13: Varenne

Churches

Attraction	Métro Line Number: Stop
Notre Dame	4: Cité
Sacré Cœur	12: Abbesses
Sainte-Chapelle	4: Cité

Parks

Attraction	Métro Line Number: Stop
Jardin du Palais-Royal	1, 7: Palais-Royal
Jardin des Tuileries	1, 8, 12: Concorde/1: Tuileries
Jardin et Palais du Luxembourg	4, 10: Odéon/RER Luxembourg/RER Port Royal
Place des Vosges	1: St-Paul

Monuments & Architecture

Attraction	Métro Line Number: Stop
Arc de Triomphe	1, 2, 6: Charles de Gaulle-Étoile
Champs-Elysées	1, 8, 12: Concorde/1, 13: Champs-Elysées Clémenceau/1, 9: Franklin D. Roosevelt/1: George V/1, 2, 6: Charles de Gaulle-Étoile
Conciergerie	4: Cité
La Crypte Archéologique	4: Cité/RER St-Michel-Notre-Dame
Eiffel Tower	8: École-Militaire/6: Bir-Hakeim/RER Luxembourg
Hotel des Invalides (Napoléon's Tomb)	8: Latour-Maubourg/13: Varenne/1, 13: Champs-Elysées Clémenceau/RER Invalides
Panthéon	10: Cardinal Lemoine/RER Luxembourg
Place de la Bastille	1, 5: Bastille

Cemetery

Attraction	Métro Line Number: Stop
Père Lachaise	2, 3: Père Lachaise

Kids

Attraction	Métro Line Number: Stop
Aquaboulevard	8: Balard
Les Catacombes	4, 6: Denfert-Rochereau
Cité des Sciences et de l'Industrie	7: Porte de la Villette
Les Égouts	9: Alma-Marceau/RER Pont-de l'Alma
Jardin d'Acclimation Bois de Boulogne	1: Les Sablons
Jardin des Plantes	5, 10: Gare d'Austerlitz/7, 10: Jussieu
Parc Zoologique de Paris	8: Porte Dorée

Historic Cafés & Bars

Attraction	Métro Line Number: Stop
Brasserie	7: Pont Marie
Brasserie Lipp	4: St-Germain-des-Prés
Café les Deux Magots	4: St-Germain-des-Prés
La Closerie de Lilas	RER Port-Royal
Harry's New York Bar	3, 7, 8: Opéra

FOR DUMMIES®

The fun and easy way™ to travel!

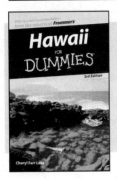 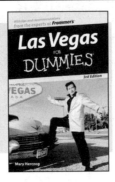
 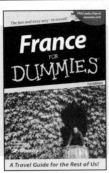
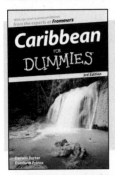 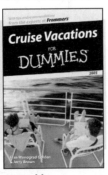

Paris
FOR
DUMMIES®
5TH EDITION

by Cheryl A. Pientka

WILEY

Wiley Publishing, Inc.

Paris For Dummies,® 5th Edition

Published by
Wiley Publishing, Inc.
111 River St.
Hoboken, NJ 07030-5774
www.wiley.com

WILEY

About the Author

Cheryl A. Pientka works in book publishing and has contributed to France For Dummies and Europe For Dummies. A graduate of Columbia University Graduate School of Journalism and the University of Delaware, she lives in New York City.

Dedication

To my mother, Mary Anne Pientka, to the memory of her husband and my father, Philip Pientka, and in honor of Francis LyHon Patterson III.

Acknowledgements

Thank you, thank you, and merci to Jamie Ehrlich; and once again, to the terrific Joseph Alexiou. To all my running buds, especially Kim, Brit, Jasmine, and Denny, to the dedicted people who have welcomed me into their volunteer fold, finding homes for so many cats and dogs, my relatives in PA, DE, FL, and Eire, and to you, the reader – I hope you'll find Paris everything you dreamed.

Publisher's Acknowledgments

We're proud of this book; please send us your comments through our Dummies online registration form located at www.dummies.com/register/.

Some of the people who helped bring this book to market include the following:

Editorial

Editors: Jamie Ehrlich, Development Editor; Michael Brumitt, Production Editor

Copy Editor: Doreen Russo

Cartographer: Roberta Stockwell

Editorial Assistant: Jessica Langan-Peck

Senior Photo Editor: Richard Fox

Cover Photos: Front Credit: © SIME s.a.s/eStock Photo. Description: Paris, Eiffel Tower and pink flowers. Back Credit: SIME s.a.s / eStock Photo. Description: Woman in bakery, baguettes in foreground.

Cartoons: Rich Tennant (www.the5thwave.com)

Composition Services

Project Coordinator: Erin Smith

Layout and Graphics: Reuben W. Davis, Julie Trippetti, Christine Williams

Proofreaders: Debbye Butler, Melissa Cossell

Indexer: Potomac Indexing, LLC

Publishing and Editorial for Consumer Dummies

Diane Graves Steele, Vice President and Publisher, Consumer Dummies

Kristin Ferguson-Wagstaffe, Product Development Director, Consumer Dummies

Kelly Regan, Editorial Director, Travel

Publishing for Technology Dummies

Andy Cummings, Vice President and Publisher, Dummies Technology/General User

Composition Services

Debbie Stailey, Director of Composition Services

Contents at a Glance

Maps at a Glance

Table of Contents

Introduction

*P*aris has been coveted since the Romans wrested away this settlement from a tribe of peaceful fishermen called the *Parisii* and named
it *Lutetia, Parisiorum*. A fascination with the city grew over nearly 2,000
years. It's not just the culture — though you can visit a different museum
every day for a year and still not hit all of the exhibits. Nor is it Paris's
breathtaking beauty — from the curved Beaux-Arts apartment buildings
to the graceful bridges arching over the Seine to the eye-pleasing formal
gardens balanced by natural parks to exquisite store windows and unexpected vistas.

If this is your first visit or if you haven't been to Paris in a decade or
more, you may just find your heart stolen by this legendary city.

You're also in for some changes. Parisians are trying mightily to over-
come the stereotype that they are collectively a rude bunch. Service at
stores and in restaurants can actually be downright warm, especially
when foreigners take the time to acknowledge storekeepers and waiters
with a pleasant smile and a simple, *"bonjour"* (hello).

I hope during your visit you will find, like I do, that Paris is an eternal
source of discovery. Even what looks to be a familiar walk will yield surprises — a passage that veers off the main road into a park; an unusual
building; a cluster of houses containing some half-forgotten history from
centuries past. Or maybe you'll discover the Parisian way of life where
relaxing in a cafe and watching the world go by is a natural part of every
day. It can be quite addictive!

Paris is more than a city; it's an encounter. Every visitor here experiences Paris's glory in an individual and unique way, and as always, I
hope the city grabs a hold of your heart so that once your time here is
finished, you'll itch to return.

About This Book

Consider this a textbook of sorts that you don't have to read from front
to back, with your visit to Paris your test (there are no failing grades,
however!). Basically *Paris For Dummies* presents you with to-the-point
information on Paris that's fun and easy to access. I explain very basic
information about the city for readers who have never visited and discuss points of interest for the seasoned traveler.

Please be advised that travel information is subject to change at any
time — and this is especially true of prices. Always write or call ahead

---

Dummies Post-it® Flags

As you read this book, you'll find information that you'll want to reference as you plan or enjoy your trip — whether it be a new hotel, a must-see attraction, or a must-try walking tour. Mark these pages with the handy Post-it® Flags included in this book to help make your trip planning easier!

---

for confirmation when making your travel plans. The author, editors, and publisher cannot be held responsible for the experiences of readers while traveling. Your safety is important to us, however, so we encourage you to stay alert and be aware of your surroundings. Keep a close eye on cameras, purses, and wallets, all favorite targets of thieves and pickpockets.

Conventions Used in This Book

Paris For Dummies is a reference book, meaning you may read the chapters in any order you want. We use some standard listings for hotels, restaurants, and sights. These listings enable you to open the book to any chapter and access the information you need quickly and easily.

In this book, we include lists of hotels, restaurants, and attractions. As we describe each, we often include abbreviations for commonly accepted credit cards. Take a look at the following list for an explanation of each.

> AE: American Express
>
> DC: Diners Club
>
> DISC: Discover
>
> MC: MasterCard
>
> V: Visa

Also included is some general pricing information to help you as you decide where to unpack your bags or dine on the local cuisine. We use a system of euros and dollar signs to show a range of costs for one night in a hotel (the price refers to a double-occupancy room) in Chapter 9 or a meal at a restaurant (included in the cost of each meal is soup or salad, an entree, dessert, and a nonalcoholic drink) in Chapter 10.

Always included are the Paris arrondissements, or administrative districts, in each address to give you a better idea of where each place is located. Paris is divided into 20 arrondissements, which spiral out like a snail shell from the first arrondissement in the very center of Paris (abbreviated *1er*), to the 20th on the outer edges of the city (abbreviated *20e*). The arrondissement number appears after the street address in each citation in this book. For example, "55 bd. St-Michel, 5e," indicates the building numbered 55 on the boulevard St-Michel is in the 5th arrondissement. To get an idea of where each arrondissement is located, consult the "Paris at a Glance" map in Chapter 1. Street abbreviations used throughout the book include not only *bd.* (boulevard), but also *rue* (street), *av.* (avenue), *place* (square), *bis* (an odd term generally meaning an address between two buildings), *ter* (terrace), or *quai* (quay or riverbank).

To help you orient yourself, we also give the nearest métro (subway) stop for all destinations (for example, Métro: Pont Marie).

Although exchange rates can and do fluctuate daily, the price conversions in this book were calculated at the rate of 1€ (the local currency, the euro) to $1.60 (U.S. dollars). For more information about the euro, see Chapter 4.

Foolish Assumptions

As we wrote this book, we made some assumptions about you and your needs as a traveler.

- ✔ You may be an experienced traveler who hasn't had much time to explore Paris and wants expert advice when you finally do get a chance to enjoy that particular locale.

- ✔ You may be an inexperienced traveler looking for guidance when determining whether to take a trip to Paris and how to plan for it.

- ✔ You're not looking for a book that provides all the information available about Paris or that lists every hotel, restaurant, or attraction available to you. Instead, you're looking for a book that focuses on the places that give you the best or most unique experience in Paris.

If you fit any of these criteria, *Paris For Dummies* gives you the information you're looking for!

How This Book Is Organized

Paris For Dummies is divided into seven parts with two appendixes. If you read the parts in sequential order, they can guide you through all the advance-planning aspects of your trip and then get you off and running while you're in the City of Light.

Part I: Introducing Paris

Provided here is a "best-of" overview of the city, some basic history and architecture, and the variety of events Paris offers at different times of the year.

Part II: Planning Your Trip to Paris

Should I use a travel agent or go it alone? Is travel insurance a good idea? These chapters touch on everything you need to consider before planning a trip, including hints on developing a realistic budget and what options are available to travelers with special needs or interests.

Part III: Settling into Paris

Some of the city's best moderately priced hotels (with a few super-budget and some deluxe resorts thrown in for good measure) are listed here, as well as advice on how to tie up those frustrating last-minute details that can unnerve the most seasoned of travelers. You'll learn in no time what kind of accommodations to choose in Paris and why you don't have to pay full price at hotel chains.

Tips on everything from navigating your way through Customs to getting to your hotel from the airport to discovering Paris neighborhood by neighborhood orient you to Paris in no time. You find out how to use the city's terrific transportation system, why you shouldn't rent a car here, and what to know when you hail a cab. You make sense of the euro, and find out where to turn if your wallet gets stolen.

Paris is known for its fine food, and Chapter 10 helps you choose some of the best restaurants for your taste and budget. Everything from moderately priced to haute cuisine restaurants is listed here, so you can discover that a fine meal is truly an art in itself. We also provide street food and light fare options for those occasions when you don't have the time, or the desire, for a full-course meal.

Part IV: Exploring Paris

How to get to Paris's top sights, how much they cost, how much time to devote to them, and handy indexes by sight, type, and neighborhood make Paris's most famous attractions (and some not so famous but just as good) easier to find. There are kid- and teen-specific sights, as well as information on orientation and other tours, a shopper's guide to Paris, three recommended itineraries, and five great day trips if you'd like to explore outside of the city.

Part V: Living It Up After Dark: Paris Nightlife

Part V gives you all the information you need about seeing plays, opera, ballet, and live music as well as which nightclubs and bars are the most fun. We are honest about whether the spectacles for which Paris has come to be known — the cabarets — are truly worth it. Uncover what's going on and where you can get reduced-rate tickets. Nothing is more beautiful than Paris at night, when the city's monuments are lit up like a stage. Anything can happen!

Part VI: The Part of Tens

What *For Dummies* book would be complete without a Part of Tens? Included is a quick collection of such fun tidbits as and great views of Paris without the lines and best places for a picnic — a quintessential Parisian pastime!

Appendixes

In the back of this book is Appendix A, a Quick Concierge that contains lots of handy information you may need when traveling in Paris: phone numbers and addresses of emergency personnel, area hospitals, and pharmacies; lists of local newspapers and magazines; protocol for sending mail and finding taxis; and more. Check out this appendix when searching for answers to lots of little questions that may come up as you travel. You can find the Quick Concierge easily because it's printed on yellow paper.

Appendix B is a glossary of English-to-French translations of basic vocabulary and health, travel, and (of course) shopping terms.

Icons Used in This Book

The following icons are scattered throughout the margins of this guide and are meant to draw your attention to especially useful text.

Keep an eye out for the Bargain Alert icon as you seek out money-saving tips and/or great deals.

The Best of the Best icon highlights the best Paris has to offer in all categories — hotels, restaurants, attractions, activities, shopping, and nightlife.

You see this icon whenever something needs your particular attention. When you need to be aware of a rip-off, an overrated sight, a dubious deal, or any other trap set for unsuspecting travelers, this icon alerts you to that fact. These hints also offer the lowdown on the quirks, etiquette, and unwritten rules of the area so you can avoid looking like a tourist and, instead, be treated more like a local.

This icon is a catchall for any special hint, tip, or bit of insider's advice that can help make your trip run more smoothly. Really, the point of a travel guide is to serve as one gigantic tip, but this icon singles out those nuggets of knowledge you may not have run across before or of which you can make immediate use.

This icon, in addition to flagging tips and resources of special interest to families, points out the most child-friendly hotels, restaurants, and attractions. If you need a baby sitter at your hotel, a welcoming relaxed atmosphere at a restaurant, or a dazzling site that delights your child, look for this icon. Information is included regarding larger, family-sized rooms at hotels and restaurants that serve meals that go easy on your little ones' tummies.

 Sometimes a great hotel, restaurant, or attraction may be a bit out of the center or require a bit of effort to get to. This icon alerts you to these secret finds, and you can rest assured, no spots are included that aren't truly worth the energy. This icon also signifies any resource that's particularly useful and worth the time to seek out.

Where to Go from Here

Where else? To Paris! *Paris For Dummies* shows you just how accessible this city can be. Included is a selective list of some of the best hotel, dining, and touring options along with insider info to help you make informed decisions. Follow the advice laid out here, and you'll want to return to Paris again and again.

Part I
Introducing Paris

The 5th Wave   By Rich Tennant

"I know it's a wedding present from your niece, I just don't know why you had to wear it to the Louvre."

In this part . . .

Are you a stranger to Paris? Or has it been a long time since you last visited? Then (re)introduce yourself to the city and whet your appetite to find out more about it. In Chapter 1, you get an overview of Paris and learn about the best the city has to offer. Chapter 2 gives you a crash course in Paris's history and architecture, briefly introduces you to French cuisine, soothes any worries you may have about the language, and recommends some great books and movies to enhance your understanding of the city. In Chapter 3, the pros and cons of the seasons as well as a Paris calendar of events helps you decide the perfect time for your visit.

Chapter 1

Discovering the Best of Paris

*T*he euro is devastating the dollar. Gas prices have never been so high. Airlines are charging for checked baggage. Planning a trip anywhere during these times may seem like an unaffordable luxury, and to Paris of all places — well, you may be hearing from all fronts how expensive it is. I'm here to tell you that, though prices are higher than they are at home, you don't have to break the bank to visit. *Paris For Dummies* is designed to give you an overview of all types of hotels, restaurants, and shopping in all price ranges. But I include tips, too, on how to save — and let you know when spending more is justified.

So, go ahead and visit one of the world's most beautiful and celebrated cities with what could be one of the best attractions of all — a way of life in which relaxing in a cafe and watching the world go by are natural parts of the day. Where you can, build into your itinerary time to linger and get lost — getting lost, after all, costs nothing. Discovering a tiny shop instead of a subway station or a pretty park around a bend can be more fun than a planned trip to a famous monument. And as for those famous monuments and museums: Yes, you'll discover that the **Louvre** is as incredible as its reputation, but did you know that the **Musée du quai Branly** has opened up near the Eiffel Tower and displays some of the Louvre's former treasures? And what a great time to visit — the **Orangerie,** closed for nearly a decade, has reopened, and Monet's *Water Lilies* here are spectacular! You'll find that taking a **motorboat tour of the Seine** is one of the best ways to see Paris, but why not rent a rowboat in the **Bois de Boulogne** and the **Bois de Vincennes,** two big, beautiful parks on each side of Paris that are a haven from the city's bustle? Whatever you do, you'll quickly discover that Paris (see map "Paris at a Glance") is more of an experience than merely a city, and each visitor experiences it in an entirely individual way.

Paris at a Glance

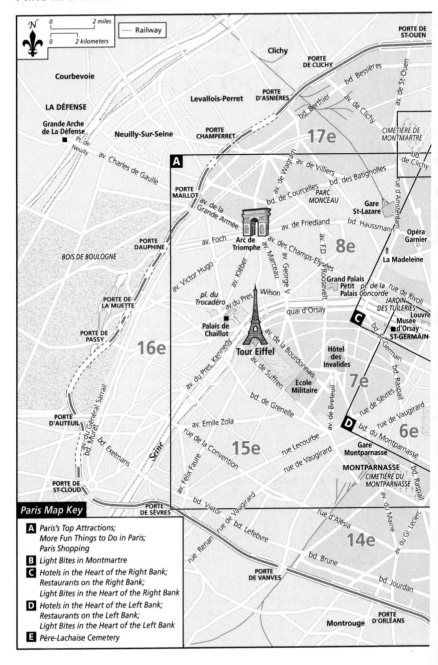

N

| 0 | 2 miles |
| 0 | 2 kilometers |

—— Railway

PORTE DE ST-OUEN

Clichy

PORTE DE CLICHY

Courbevoie

bd. Bessières

av. de St-Ouen

LA DÉFENSE

Levallois-Perret

PORTE D'ASNIÈRES

bd. Berthier

av. de Clichy

Grande Arche de La Défense

Neuilly-Sur-Seine

PORTE CHAMPERRET

17e

CIMETIÈRE DE MONTMARTRE

Pt. de Neuilly

av. Charles de Gaulle

A

av. de Wagram

av. de Villiers

bd. des Batignolles

bd. de Clichy

PORTE MAILLOT

PARC MONCEAU

bd. de Courcelles

Gare St-Lazare

bd. Haussmann

rue d'Amsterdam

Opéra Garnier

av. de la Grande Armée

av. de Friedland

8e

BOIS DE BOULOGNE

PORTE DAUPHINE

av. Foch

Arc de Triomphe

av. des Champs-Elysées

av. Marceau

av. George V

av. F.D. Roosevelt

La Madeleine

av. Victor Hugo

av. Kléber

Grand Palais

Petit Palais

pl. de la Concorde

rue de Rivoli

JARDIN DES TUILERIES

PORTE DE LA MUETTE

pl. du Trocadéro

Wilson

av. du Pres

quai d'Orsay

Louvre

Musée d'Orsay

ST-GERMAIN

C

bd. St-Germain

PORTE DE PASSY

16e

Palais de Chaillot

Tour Eiffel

av. de Suffren

av. de la Bourdonnais

Hôtel des Invalides

7e

rue de Sèvres

bd. Raspail

av. du Pres. Kennedy

Ecole Militaire

av. de Breteuil

rue de Vaugirard

6e

bd. du Montparnasse

av. du Gal Sarrail

bd. de Grenelle

D

PORTE D'AUTEUIL

av. Emile Zola

Gare Montparnasse

bd. Exelmans

bd. Murat

rue de la Convention

15e

rue Lecourbe

MONTPARNASSE

CIMETIÈRE DU MONTPARNASSE

bd. Raspail

Seine

rue de Vaugirard

av. Felix Faure

PORTE DE ST-CLOUD

PORTE DE SÈVRES

bd. Victor

rue de Vaugirard

rue d'Alésia

14e

av. du Gal Leclerc

av. du Maine

rue de bd. Lefebvre

rue Renan

bd. Brune

PORTE DE VANVES

bd. Jourdan

Montrouge

PORTE D'ORLÉANS

Paris Map Key

A *Paris's Top Attractions;*
More Fun Things to Do in Paris;
Paris Shopping

B *Light Bites in Montmartre*

C *Hotels in the Heart of the Right Bank;*
Restaurants on the Right Bank;
Light Bites in the Heart of the Right Bank

D *Hotels in the Heart of the Left Bank;*
Restaurants on the Left Bank;
Light Bites in the Heart of the Left Bank

E *Père-Lachaise Cemetery*

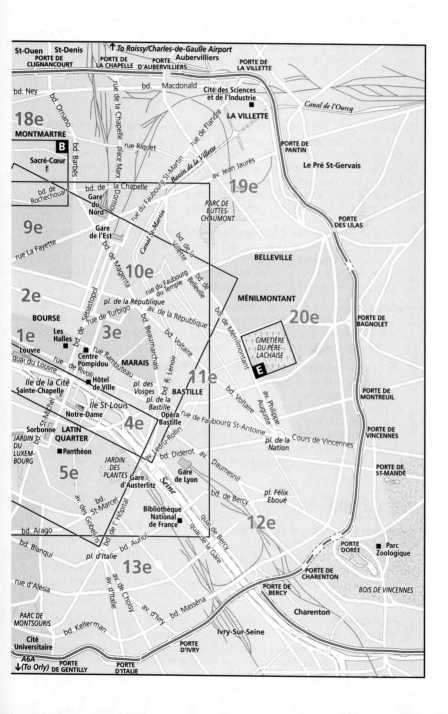

St-Ouen St-Denis ↑ To Roissy/Charles-de-Gaulle Airport
PORTE DE   PORTE DE   PORTE   Aubervilliers   PORTE DE
CLIGNANCOURT   LA CHAPELLE D'AUBERVILLIERS   LA VILLETTE

bd. Ney   bd. Macdonald   Cité des Sciences
                                      et de l'Industrie
                                                      Canal de l'Ourcq
18e   LA VILLETTE
MONTMARTRE

B
Sacré-Cœur   PORTE DE
                                                       PANTIN
                                           av. Jean Jaurès   Le Pré St-Gervais
bd. de   la Chapelle
Rochechouart   bd. de   **19e**
              Gare
              du   PARC DE
              Nord   BUTTES-   PORTE
9e   Gare   CHAUMONT   DES LILAS
              de l'Est
rue La Fayette   BELLEVILLE
              bd. de Magenta
2e   **10e**
              rue du Faubourg   MÉNILMONTANT
BOURSE   du temple
              pl. de la République   **20e**
1e Les   av. de la République   PORTE DE
        Halles rue de Turbigo   BAGNOLET
Louvre **3e** bd. Beaumarchais CIMETIÈRE
        Centre rue Rambuteau   DU PÈRE-
quai du Louvre Pompidou   LACHAISE
        Hôtel   MARAIS   **E**   PORTE DE
Ile de la Cité de Ville pl. des   MONTREUIL
Sainte-Chapelle Ile St-Louis Vosges **11e**
        Notre-Dame pl. de la BASTILLE
Sorbonne LATIN Bastille bd. Voltaire   PORTE DE
JARDIN QUARTER Opéra   VINCENNES
DU LUXEM- **4e** Bastille rue de Faubourg St-Antoine
BOURG   Panthéon   pl. de la Cours de Vincennes PORTE DE
5e   JARDIN   bd. Diderot Nation   ST-MANDÉ
          DES   Gare   av. Daumesnil
          PLANTES d'Austerlitz Gare
          bd.   Seine   de Lyon
          St-Marcel   bd. de Bercy pl. Félix
          Bibliothèque   Eboué   PORTE DE
bd. Arago National   **12e**   DORÉE Parc
bd. Blanqui de France pl. d'Italie   Zoologique
          13e   PORTE DE
rue d'Alésia av. de Choisy   CHARENTON BOIS DE VINCENNES
PARC DE   av. d'Italie bd. Masséna PORTE DE
MONTSOURIS bd. Kellerman   BERCY Charenton
Cité
Universitaire   Ivry-Sur-Seine
A6A   PORTE
↓(To Orly) PORTE PORTE   D'IVRY
         DE GENTILLY D'ITALIE

This chapter is designed as an at-a-glance reference to the absolute best — the best of the best in my opinion — that Paris has to offer. Each of these experiences and places is discussed in detail later in the book; you can find them in their indicated chapter, marked with a Best of the Best icon.

The Best Accommodations

With more than 2,200 chain hotels, deluxe palacelike accommodations, hotels that cater to business travelers, budget hotels, and mom-and-pop establishments, it's difficult to narrow things down to just a few. But the hotels here are the hotels that, in my opinion, you'll want to return to on your next visit (because no one can see Paris just once!). **I only list hotels in the first eight arrondissements, the most central locations in Paris.** See Chapter 9 for more information on the accommodations listed here.

- ✔ I love the **Hôtel de l'Abbaye Saint-Germain** (6e), a former convent on the Left Bank that is simply charming, with five-star service and beautiful tranquil surroundings. Rooftop suites and some first-floor rooms open onto vine-covered terraces, and the fabulous duplex apartment is terrific for honeymooners.

- ✔ In a city where accommodations range from the ultra-luxurious to the barely inhabitable, **Hôtel Verneuil** (7e) offers the elegance of a small boutique hotel at a reasonable price located just a short walk from St-Germain-des-Prés, the Louvre, the Musée D'Orsay, and the Seine.

- ✔ The impressive, airy **Hôtel du Jeu de Paume** on the exclusive Ile St-Louis was once a 17th century *jeu de paume* (the precursor to tennis) court, and you can still see the wooden skeleton rising from the open lobby. This is one of Paris's more unusual hotels, successfully combining sumptuous ancient and modern décor, and guests have their choice of staying in rooms or, for more than five days, private apartments. It's located right down the street from Notre-Dame and Left and Right Bank bridges.

The Best Food

No matter where you decide to dine or what kind of food you choose, you can count on having some of the most memorable meals of your life in Paris! The following list contains some of my favorite restaurants (the information in parentheses indicates the arrondissement in which each establishment is located). See Chapter 10 for more information on the restaurants listed here.

- ✔ **Le Cinq (8e):** Ah, to be able to dine here daily! This multi-Michelin-starred restaurant in the Four Seasons George V is truly extraordinary, from exquisite pull-out-all-the-stops food to its award winning sommelier and fantastic wine cellar. If you want a once-in-a-lifetime dining experience, you won't be disappointed.

✔ **Le 404 (3e):** You may join staff and patrons dancing on the bar at the end of your dinner at this hip and fun Moroccan restaurant not far from the heart of the Marais. You'll be talking to your neighbors over tasty *tajines,* couscous, and *pastilla* and toasting to new friendships with a crisp regional wine.

✔ **Le Potager du Marais (3e):** Vegetarians, rejoice! This tiny restaurant near the Centre Pompidou serves delicious French and other standards that happen to be meatless (there are also some options for vegans). Diners sit at a long communal table and the place is always packed (reservations for dinner are strongly suggested); there's such a friendly vibe, you almost won't be able to help talking to others around you.

The Best Sights

What's a visit to Paris without seeing the view from the Eiffel Tower (even though there are other great views that incorporate the famous landmark)? For most people, the real reason for visiting Paris is to see the quintessentially French attractions for which the city is known. Are the sights really as great as returning travelers say? *Mais oui!* Here are just a few of the best. See Chapter 11 for more information on the sights listed here.

✔ You can't miss the city's most famous landmark, the **Eiffel Tower,** which graces the city skyline with its lacy presence. At night for ten minutes each hour until it closes, the tower bursts into glittering light from 30,000 bulbs. Mail your postcards and letters from the tower's very own post office located the first level up; they'll get a special Tour Eiffel postmark.

✔ Take a **tour boat down the Seine** at night and see lights from bridges older than the United States cast reflections in the water. English-language commentary is included. (Even better: Take one of Fat Tire Bike's night bike tours around the city. Included in the price is a Seine boat ride.)

✔ The **Musée d'Orsay,** a former train station, has an unsurpassed collection of Impressionist masterpieces and beautiful displays of Art Nouveau furnishings. Much less overwhelming than the Louvre and well-located near the Seine and Eiffel Tower, this museum should make everyone's top five!

✔ Your first glimpse of the nearly 900-year-old **Cathédral de Notre-Dame** just may take your breath away. Flying buttresses lend a graceful air to what would otherwise be an imposing structure. Play Quasimodo and climb to the top of the bell tower (get there early — the lines grow huge from late morning through closing, especially in summer) or marvel at the gorgeous rose windows.

✔ The **Arc de Triomphe** was commissioned by Napoléon to honor his army and its 128 victorious battles, but the real reason people visit is for the view — one that takes in the Eiffel Tower. From the top,

49m (162 ft.) up, you can see in a straight line the Champs-Elysées, the obelisk in the place de la Concorde, the Louvre, and the Grande Arche de la Défense in St-Denis, a giant open cube built to be the modern equivalent to this arch.

✔ The **Musée Picasso** constantly rotates its exhibits that represent every phase of Picasso's prolific 75-year career. All of it is housed in a beautiful 17th-century mansion deep in the Marais, one of Paris's best and most interesting neighborhoods.

✔ The **Musée Nationale d'Auguste Rodin** is one of Paris's more relaxing museums. There are only 16 medium-sized rooms here, and after taking in the sensual sculptures, you can stroll through the gardens here to see more of the legendary artist's masterpieces such as *The Thinker* and *The Gates of Hell.*

✔ The **Musée de Cluny** is one of the jewels of Paris museums and is home to the famous tapestry series *The Lady and the Unicorn.* It houses ancient Roman hot and cold baths, the original statues pulled off Notre-Dame in 1790 by furious revolutionaries, and so, so much more, as well as a terrific gift shop to boot.

The Best Parks and Gardens

Paris has parks for every taste and interest offering flowers, rare plants, and views of the city and puppet shows, pony rides, and museums. Here are some of its best. Chapter 11 has more information.

✔ The **Jardin des Tuileries** (1er) is Paris's most visited park, where visitors to the Louvre next door like to revive in the fresh air and rest their feet on conveniently placed wrought-iron chairs surrounding the garden's fountains. In keeping with the French style of parks, trees are planted according to an orderly design and the sandy paths are arrow straight. During the summer, a carnival features an enormous Ferris wheel (with great views of the city) and some other thrill rides, a fun house, arcade-style games, and snacks.

✔ The **Jardin du Luxembourg** in the Latin Quarter is Parisians' most beloved park. Children love it for its playground, pony rides, puppet theater, and the Fontaine de Médicis where they can sail toy boats. Make use of the tennis and *boules* courts (*boules* is a French game similar to lawn bowling or the Italian *bocce* in which players try to be the first to roll their balls closest to the small object ball called the *cochonnet*), or appreciate the art exhibited on the wrought-iron fence at the garden's northwestern entrance near boulevard St-Michel and rue de Médicis. Courses are offered here in bee keeping, and the park's orchard grows apples and pears that end up on the plates of staff at the French Senate, which is housed in the garden's Palais du Luxembourg.

✔ **Parc de la Villette** (19e) is a modern park with a series of theme gardens, including an exotic bamboo garden and one featuring steam and water jets. Scattered throughout are playgrounds and other attractions — this is a must-visit if you've spent time at the huge children's science complex, **Cité des Sciences et l'Industrie.**

✔ Rock formations and grottoes in the tranquil **Parc de Belleville** (20e) are still around from the days when the hill was a strategic point for fighting Attila the Hun. Watch the sun set over western Paris and take in the wonderful (free!) views of the city. Topped by the **Maison de l'Air,** a museum with displays devoted to the air that we breathe, you can enjoy fountains, a children's play area, and an open-air theater that holds rock concerts during the summer.

The Best Shopping

Though the city has a well-deserved reputation as a bastion of over-the-top luxury (to understand why, head for the 8th arrondissement), discount, resale, and overstock stores also abound, as well as the wonderful Monoprix (see below). Whenever I'm in Paris, a visit to the following stores is a must. See Chapter 12 for more information on the stores listed here.

✔ **Monoprix,** a reasonably priced department store with branches around the city, has stylish clothing and is also great for accessories, low-priced cosmetics, lingerie, and house wares. Many locations also have large grocery stores good for gift buying. The one at 52 av. du Champs-Elysées, 8e, is chock-full of goodies and open until midnight.

✔ **Le Bon Marché** (6e) is elegant, but small enough to be manageable, and is the Left Bank's only department store. You can find the top designers here, as well as more affordable pieces, too, and the basement toy store has great gift selections. The third floor is particularly renowned for its large shoe selection and lingerie department (where dressing rooms have phones to summon your salesperson).

✔ Although it isn't cheap, Le Bon Marché's next-door grocery store, **Le Grand Épicerie** (6e) is one of the best luxury supermarkets in Paris and a great place to look for gourmet gifts such as olive oils, homemade chocolates, or wine. It makes for wonderful one-stop picnic shopping, too, offering a wide array of prepared foods and cheeses. If you're staying in an apartment or your hotel has a kitchen for guests, come here to purchase fixings for dinner.

The Best of Culture

Getting "cultured" is not a problem in Paris. There are more than 100 theaters, competing opera houses, and ballet and chamber music concerts in many churches. Even if your French is rusty or not up to par, many avant-garde productions and English-language theaters serve as alternatives to French-language plays. In this section, I list some of the best places to see theater, watch a ballet, or hear a symphony. See Chapter 15 for more information.

✔ You can see dazzling performances by the national opera and ballet troupes that perform at both the radiant **Palais Garnier** (9e) and the ultramodern **Opéra National de Bastille** (11e). The Palais Garnier conducts more ballet performances, and the Opéra Bastille puts on more opera.

✔ A good mix of modern and classic tragedies and comedies comes alive in wonderful performances in the **Salle Richelieu** of the **Comédie-Française,** 2 rue de Richelieu, 1er.

✔ For popular, contemporary plays, the **Théâtre National de Chaillot,** place du Trocadéro, 16e, is your place.

✔ Whatever your choice of the classic arts — opera, ballet, concerts, recitals — you'll find it performed at the **Châtelet, Théâtre Musical de Paris** (1er) by local and international performers of the highest caliber.

✔ More than a dozen Parisian churches regularly schedule relatively inexpensive organ recitals and concerts. The most glorious, where the music is nearly outdone by the glorious stained glass windows, is **Sainte-Chapelle** (4e).

The Best Clubs

Each neighborhood makes a different contribution to Paris's vibrant nightlife scene. Listed here are some of the best places to dance the night away. See Chapter 16 for more information.

✔ **Barrio Latino** (11e) has three bars on four floors, private areas where you can see (but not be seen), a second floor restaurant serving Latino food, a top-floor private club with a kitschy Che Guevara mural, and energetic Latin music that sets everyone to dancing. It's pure fun!

✔ **Batofar** (13e), an Irish light ship docked right in the Seine, is one hot, sweaty, and ultimately fun time right on the Seine, with all types of music represented, from drum-and-bass to British pop.

✔ Where else in Paris will you dance to the Hives and the Cure followed by some electro-pop spun by great DJs (and down some great beer, too)? It's at the unassuming **Le Truskel** (2e), an Irish pub with a basement "microclub" that has been drawing in crowds of 20-somethings since it opened in 2002.

✔ **Le Mix** (15e) boasts spinning provided by music gurus Ministry of Sound and David Guetta (a holy name among clubbers).

Chapter 2

Digging Deeper into Paris

- -

In This Chapter

▶ Discovering the rich history of Paris
▶ Admiring the city's architecture
▶ Enjoying the local cuisine
▶ Getting to know the local language
▶ Previewing the city in books and movies

- -

*T*his is Paris 101, a chapter that will fill you in on the city's history, the basics of French architecture, the art of the meal. With some key French phrases to help you get around and a glossary of food to order once you get there, you'll be ready to take on Paris in no time. An added bonus is your pretrip homework assignment where you'll never have to lift a pencil — reading wonderful books and watching great movies!

History 101: The Main Events

The ancient times

The Parisii tribe settled Paris in the third century B.C. on the **Ile de la Cité** (one of two islands in the Seine around Central Paris — these days, Notre-Dame sits on Ile de la Cité). They were peaceful fishermen who traded with other tribes along the river and with travelers on the main north-south trading road that connected the Mediterranean with northern Europe. Unfortunately, the road made attacking the Parisii all too convenient for invaders. The first and most successful were the Romans led by Julius Caesar in 52 B.C. During the Romans's 500-year stay, the settlement became known as Lutetia Parisiorum (*Lutèce* in French). You can still see the Roman public baths at the **Musée National du Moyen Age/Cluny Museum** in the **Latin Quarter.**

Years of barbarian invasions eventually weakened Rome's hold over the territory. Around A.D. 350, Attila the Hun, on his way to sack Paris, changed course at the last minute, purportedly due to the prayers of a young girl named **Geneviève.** She became the patron saint of Paris. In the 400s, Franks from the east successfully wrested control away from the Romans. In 508, Clovis, king of the Franks, chose Paris as his capital. It was abandoned as a capital 250 years later only to regain that status in

987 when Hugues Capet was proclaimed king of France. Celebrating the city's importance, two Gothic masterpieces, the cathedrals of **Notre-Dame** and **Sainte-Chapelle,** were built on the Ile de la Cité. Across the river, on the **Left Bank,** the **University of Paris** was founded in the mid–12th century, although now referred to as **La Sorbonne,** named after the **Collège de Sorbonne,** founded in 1257.

Revolutionary Paris

Under Louis XIV, who ruled for 72 years, the monarchy's power reached its height, supported by heavy taxes. Although he added monuments and splendor to the city, the Sun King moved his court to Versailles, alienating the citizenry and preparing the way for the French Revolution.

On July 14, 1789, a mob stormed the **Bastille** prison, which held many who were out of favor with French royalty. To most French citizens at the time, the Bastille was a sign of much that was wrong with the monarchy, and the attack on the Bastille came to represent the end of the monarchy. Three days later at the Hôtel de Ville, **Louis XVI** was forced to kiss the new French tricolor. On July 14, 1790, the Festival of the Federation was celebrated on the Champs de Mars, and an estimated 300,000 attended a Mass at which the king swore an oath of loyalty to the constitution. Still, radical factions grew. On August 10, 1792, revolutionary troops joined a Parisian mob storming the **Tuileries Palace,** where the king lived and took him prisoner. In 1793, he and **Queen Marie Antoinette** were beheaded in the place de la Concorde. At this time, Maximilien **Robespierre** was elected leader of the Committee of Public Safety, which conducted witch hunts for those it deemed counter-revolutionaries. This became known as the Reign of Terror. Between September 1793 and February 1794, 238 men and 31 women were tried and executed for crimes against the state. Nearly 5,500 more awaited trial in prisons until Robespierre's arrest in July 1794. He was executed the same month.

The era of Napoléons

During the last stage of the French Revolution, a directory of five men was ushered in to govern France. After four years, Napoléon staged a coup (1799), turning the country into a dictatorship. Five years later, (1804) at Notre-Dame, Napoléon crowned himself emperor and his wife, Joséphine, empress. After applying the Code Napoléon over all French territory, the Corsican general embarked on a series of military campaigns until his defeat at Waterloo in 1815. During his reign, he gave Paris many of its most grandiose monuments, notably the **Arc de Triomphe** and the **Bourse,** but his greatest gift was starting the **Louvre.** After the fall of Napoléon, the monarchy was restored through the **Bourbon Restoration,** placing **Charles X** on the throne. In 1830 the **July Monarchy** replaced Charles with King **Louis Philippe,** of the House of Orléans. His government lasted until the **Revolution of 1848,** which brought about the **Second Republic** and the 1851 election of **Louis Napoléon,** nephew of the original emperor. The first president of the

French republic, Louis was also known as **Napoléon III** after he established the **Second Empire** (1852–1870) and therefore also holds the distinction of being France's last monarch.

During the 19th century France experienced the intellectual and artistic developments that define it as a nation today. In Paris, the Second Empire was a time of architectural and urban evolution through the plans of **Baron Georges Haussmann.** Commissioned by Napoléon III to modernize the twisty, medieval city, it was Haussmann who created the wide boulevards and the wrought iron balconies that so clearly define the Paris of today.

Modern Paris

The **Eiffel Tower** (La Tour Eiffel), built only as a temporary structure for the 1889 World's Fair, was at one time the tallest structure in the world. Paris opened its first métro line in 1900, and by the turn of the 20th century, had thousands of restaurants and 27,000 cafes.

In the years that followed, Paris witnessed two world wars with more than ten million military casualties, nearly one million Jews losing their lives, and four years of German occupation. Tens of thousands of soldiers died fighting the end of French colonial rule around the world.

In 1968, students took to the streets of Paris, rebelling against France's antiquated educational system among a host of other causes, including the rights of workers (this period of time is known in France as *Mai 1968*). **Charles De Gaulle**'s government tried to quash the strikes with police action, but only succeeded in making the situation worse. Young people hurled paving stones at police in street battles, and ten million French workers throughout the country went on strike. This nearly led to the collapse of the government, and De Gaulle called for new elections. Almost as quickly as the student and worker revolution started, it was over by June 1968 when voters elected an even stronger De Gaulle administration. De Gaulle, himself, resigned in 1969. The government flirted unsuccessfully with socialism in the 1980s and ended the decade with a great celebration of democracy: the bicentennial of the French Revolution and the centennial of the Eiffel Tower.

Former Paris Mayor **Jacques Chirac** was elected president in 1995 on his promise to jump-start the economy, but growth remained stagnant, and the president was forced to share power with Prime Minister Lionel Jospin.

In 2005, as a result of the accidental electrocution of two teenagers of African and North African descent, riots broke out in Paris resulting in the burning of thousands of cars and trucks in the Ile-de-France region. The anger and violence turned into a months-long series of riots that spread throughout urban areas of France. The situation was not helped when former Interior Minister Nicolas Sarkozy referred to the suburban youth as *racaille,* meaning lowlife or scum. The year 2006 saw continual clashes between the citizenry and the French government when over a million people took part in student strikes opposing proposed changes to the basic layout of workers' rights in France, specifically changes that would allow employers to fire workers under the age of 26 without giving an officially stated reason.

In a very heated and publicly debated election, in 2007 **Nicolas Sarkozy** became the President of France. His presidency has proven to be controversial for a number of reasons. The French have been totally put off by his personality; supposedly he is often tactless and impulsive. The media frenzy covering his marriage to former model and singer-songwriter Carla Bruni, and the subsequent tabloid coverage of their life together, is regarded as unnecessary and distasteful. Politically and economically, his promise to totally revamp the nation's economy to a more American model (including a stronger work ethic) was met with equal welcome and disdain from various sectors of society. Implementing his proposed changes has proven to be less fruitful than many hoped (or feared), but since he has been elected France no longer has a maximum 35-hour workweek, and some taxes have been reduced.

Another cultural and political shift in France that may surprise return voyagers is the February 2007 legislation making it illegal to smoke in public places; this includes cafes, bars, restaurants, and other venues. The public has responded with polarized opinions about the ban, but most respect the new laws.

Building Blocks: Local Architecture

First-time visitors to Paris are struck by the graceful curves and balconies of the city's gorgeous apartment buildings, many of which were built during the reign of Napoléon III (mid-1800s) under Baron Haussmann, the appointed urban planner by the emperor. In addition to the mixture of styles associated with the 19th and 20th centuries, different architectural eras are represented in Paris, among them the Ancient Roman, Romanesque, Gothic, Renaissance, classical (classicism), and rococo periods. You can see artifacts from Paris's founding in the third century B.C. by a tribe of fishermen, as well as such modern-day projects as the guts-on-the-outside Centre Georges Pompidou and I.M. Pei's glass pyramid at the Louvre.

Paris's important architectural periods are outlined here.

- **Ancient Roman (125 B.C.–A.D. 450):** After Julius Caesar conquered the island of Lutétia, his legions began using bricks and concrete in building and introduced the load-bearing arch, which led to the construction of stronger bridges and doorways. You can see examples of excavated Roman ruins at the **Crypte Archéologique** (see Chapter 11), about 60m (200 ft.) directly in front of the entrance of Notre-Dame. Possibly the most important ancient ruins are the Roman baths in the cellar of the **Cluny Museum** (also in Chapter 11), a former private residence that was built around and on top of the ruins, and the Arènes de Lutèce, an amphitheater from the 1st century A.D. Unearthed during the construction of rue Monge in the 1860s, the public gathering place held gladiator competitions and could house up to 15,000 people.

✔ **Romanesque (800–1100):** This style is characterized by arches and curves, thick walls with small windows, huge piers to hold up the roof, simple geometric arrangements, and painting in decorative hues. The architects during this period built large churches; none survive intact in Paris; all were improved upon with different architectural styles or rebuilt. **St-Germain-des-Prés** is a Romanesque building with a Gothic interior. **St-Julien-le-Pauvre** was originally a Romanesque church, but later Gothic additions obscure the original details.

✔ **Gothic (1100–1500):** Known for its slender vertical piers and counterbalancing buttresses and for vaulting and pointed arches that allow for taller and thinner structures, the interiors of these buildings force the eyes upward. Windows with stained glass were constructed so that most of the illiterate population could understand the stories told in each pane. Gargoyles (drain spouts), spires, flying buttresses, rose windows, and choir screens were all features of the Gothic church. The best examples are **Notre-Dame,** of course, and the **Cathédrale de Notre-Dame de Chartres** (Chapter 14 describes this cathedral in more detail).

✔ **Renaissance (1500–1630):** This architectural style is characterized by harmonious form, mathematical proportion, and a unit of measurement based on the human scale. Roofs became steeply pitched, and dormer windows were built taller, using stone. The mansions surrounding the **Place des Vosges** are all Renaissance, as is the **Hôtel Carnavalet,** home to the **Musée Carnavalet.**

✔ **Classicism (1630–1800):** In this school, the emphasis was on form, simplicity, proportion, and restraint, influenced by the architecture of ancient Greece and Rome. Exteriors in the classical style may feature Doric, Corinthian, and Ionic columns, low and simple dormer windows, mansard roofs (having two slopes on all sides with the lower slope steeper than the upper, invented by François Mansard), and simple proportions; the interiors of classical buildings went over the top. This interior style is known as **rococo,** derived from the words *rocaille* (rock) and *coquille* (shell), delicate decorative motifs that appeared along with scrolls, branches of leaves, flowers, and bamboo stems. The best example of classicism and rococo is **Versailles** (see Chapter 14). The **Louvre** is also a classical tour de force.

✔ **Nineteenth century (1800–1889):** This style began with *neoclassicism,* a return to the majesty of past civilizations, and an adoption of classical forms and styles. Examples include the **Arc de Triomphe** and the **Madeleine.** The **Second Empire** brought wide boulevards lined with six-story apartment buildings with balconies and mansard roofs with dormer windows. The **Third Republic**'s industrial age produced glass and steel structures; the most famous are the **Eiffel Tower** and **Sacré-Coeur.**

✔ **Art Nouveau (1890–1914):** This period saw the end of the 19th century and continued into the 20th with beautiful renderings of plants and flowers in wrought iron **(Abbesses Métro station entrance)**, stained glass, wood, tile, and hand-painted wallpapers (for a wonderful introduction to Art Nouveau, visit the middle floor of the **Musée d'Orsay;** see Chapter 11).

✔ **Twentieth to twenty-first century (1900–):** Twentieth-century style may be defined by late President François Mitterand's *grands projets* (grand projects), most of which were controversial when completed. Richard Rogers's and Renzo Piano's **Centre Georges Pompidou** (see Chapter 11), with its "guts on the outside" architecture, horrified Parisians, as did I.M. Pei's glass pyramids at the Louvre, but residents have slowly come to accept them. The four looming towers shaped like open books that comprise Mitterand's last project, the Bibliothèque Nationale de France, are another story; the building, which is still suffering from the occasional technological glitch, has gotten little respect since its opening in the late 1990s.

The Grande Arche de la Défense in nearby St-Denis was designed to be a modern-day equivalent to the Arc de Triomphe. Mitterand commissioned the late Danish architect Johann Otto von Spreckelsen to build the Arche, which also completes the *axe historique* (a line of historic buildings and monuments extending west from its origin in the center of Paris; it includes the Arc de Triomphe and the obelisk in place de la Concorde); the Grande Arche looks like a floating square when seen from afar. Paris's "starchitect" Jean Nouvel, who used glass to great effect in the Fondation Cartier and Institut du Monde Arabe late in the 20th century, has given Paris the Musée du Quai Branly in the 21st, again making use of glass but also promoting a more ecological theme: a wall bursting with 15,000 live plants. The result was beautiful, although some locals complain that the plants suffer due to drainage problems. He will continue to be present in Paris as he was selected to design the upcoming Signal Tower in la Défense.

The new development there is part of a plan to expand Paris's population of skyscrapers, as the need for space has increased greatly. The expansion is greatly welcomed; however, the main opposition to it is part of the Parisian Green movement, who see the buildings as a waste of resources. The abandoned docks of the 13e just south of Gare d'Austerlitz are morphing into a gorgeous, green waterfront complex called Docks en Seine. Architects Jakob and Brendan MacFarlane are building a wood and metal construction over the warehouses to be covered with greenery, and located here will be the French Fashion Institute (Institut Français de la Mode) boutiques, a pool, restaurants, and a dance club.

A Taste of Paris: The Local Cuisine

Parisians have such wonderful meals from which to choose — regional French, three-star haute cuisine, North African *couscouseries,* tasty crêpes sold from street vendors, and more. During the last decade, the city witnessed the rise of *baby bistros,* restaurants opened by celebrity chefs and their talented young apprentices offering simpler and less-expensive meals than those served at their deluxe establishments. Also in vogue is a back-to-Grandmère's-kitchen approach featuring chefs turning out homey meals such as *blanquette de veau* (veal stew in white sauce), *cassoulet* (meat-and-vegetable casserole), and *confit de canard* (duck preserved and cooked in its own fat until it's so tender it falls off the bone). Asian influences are also in vogue; witness the success of L'Atelier de Joël Robuchon. I talk in more depth about dining in Paris in Chapter 10.

A glossary good enough to eat

Use this helpful guide when you're trying to decide what to order and how you want it cooked.

General Terms

compris (comb-*pree;* included)
déjeuner (*day-*zhu-nay; lunch)
dîner (*dee-*nay; dinner)
ménu dégustation (meh-*noo* day-goo-*stah-*sion; sampler, or tasting, menu)
petit déjeuner (pet-*tee day-*zhu-nay; breakfast)
prix fixe (pree feeks; set price)
supplément (sup-play-*mahn;* extra charge)

Les Entrées (layz ahn-trays; appetizers)

charcuterie (shar-koot-*ree;* assorted cold cuts)
crudités (kroo-dee-*tay;* assorted raw vegetables)
foie gras (fwah grah; gooseliver pâté)
salade composée (sa-*lad* com-poh-zay; mixed salad)
salade de chèvre chaud (sa-*lad* deh-shev-rah-*sho;* salad with warm goat cheese on croutons)
salade gesiers (sa-*lad* zheh-shee-*air;* salad with sautéed chicken gizzards)

salade landaise (sa-*lad* lahn-*dehs;* salad containing duck breast, duck liver, and duck gizzards)
salad niçoise (sa-*lad* nee-*shwahz;* salad with tuna, canned corn, anchovies, and potato)
saumon fumé (soh-*moh foo-*may; smoked salmon)
soupe à l'oignon (soop-ah-lowh-*yon;* onion soup)
soupe à pistou (soop-ah-pees-*too;* vegetable soup with pesto)
velouté (vay-loot-*ay;* cream-based soup)
vichyssoise (vee-shee-*swahz;* cold leek and potato soup)

Boeuf (bewf; beef)

bavette (bah-*vet;* flank steak)
chateaubriand (cha-tow-bree-*ahn;* porterhouse)
contre-filet (*kahn-*trah-fee-lay; filet steak)
côte de boeuf (cote dah bewf; T-bone)
entrecôte (ahn-trah-*cote;* rib-eye)
faux-filet (foe-fee-*lay;* sirloin)

filet mignon (fee-*lay* mee-*nyahn;* tenderloin)
langue de boeuf (lahng dah bewf; tongue)
onglet (ahn-*glay;* hanger steak)
pavé (pah-*vay;* thick steak; *literally:* paving stone)
queue de boeuf (kyew dah bewf; oxtail)
rôti de boeuf (*roe*-tee dah bewf; roast beef)
steak haché (stake *ha*-shay; minced meat or hamburger)
steak tartare (stake tar-*tar;* a lean cut of beef minced and served raw — a high-quality dish prepared by experts, people rarely get sick from eating this)
tournedo (*tor*-nay-doe; small tender filet usually grilled or sautéed)
veau (voe; veal)

Other Meats

agneau (ah-*nyoe;* lamb)
gigot (*gee*-joe; leg — usually of lamb)
jambon (zhahm-*bon;* ham)
médaillon (meh-dah-ee-*on;* medallions — beef, veal, lamb)
merguez (mare-*gay;* spicy sausage)
porc (pork; pork)
saucisses/saucisson (soh-*sees,* soh-see-*sohn;* sausage/little sausage)

Volailles (voe-lie; fowl)

blanc de volaille (blahn dah voe-*lai;* chicken breast)
caille (kaih; quail)
canard (kah-*nahr;* duck)
dinde (dand; turkey)
magret de canard (mah-*gret* dah kah-*nahr;* duck breast)
oie (wah; goose)
pigéon (pee-jee-*ohn;* game pigeon)
pintade (pan-*tahd;* guinea fowl)
poulet (*poo*-lay; chicken)

Fruits de Mer (free duh mair; seafood)

bar (bar; bass)
coquilles St-Jacques (*koe*-kee san-*jahk;* scallops)

crevettes (kreh-*vet;* shrimp)
daurade (doe-*rahd;* sea bream)
homard (oe-*mahr;* lobster)
huîtres (wee-*tra;* oysters)
langoustine (lang-oo-*steen;* crayfish)
morue/cabillaud (moh-*roo*/ka-bee-*oh;* cod)
moules (mool; mussels)
poissons (pwah-*son;* fish)
raie (ray; skate)
rascasse (ras-*kass;* scorpion fish)
rouget (roo-*zhay;* red mullet)
saumon (soh-*moh;* salmon)
thon (than; tuna)
truite (trweet; trout)

Les Légumes (lay lay-goom; vegetables)

artichault (ar-tee-*show;* artichoke)
asperge (as-*pearzh;* asparagus)
aubergine (oe-bur-*zheen;* eggplant)
champignons/cèpes/truffes/girolles (sham-pee-*nyahn*/sep/troof/*gee*-roll; mushrooms)
choucroute (shoo-*kroot;* sauerkraut)
choux (shoo; cabbage)
choux de bruxelles (shoo dah broo-*zells;* brussels sprouts)
courgette (kore-*zhette;* zucchini)
épinard (ay-pee-*nahr;* spinach)
haricots (ahr-ee-*koe;* beans)
haricots verts (*ahr*-ee-koe-vair; string beans)
oignons (wah-*nyoh;* onions)
petits pois (*pet*-tee pwah; peas)
poireaux (pwah-*roe;* leeks)
poivron rouge (pwah-vrah-*roozh;* red pepper)
poivron vert (pwah-vrah *vair;* green pepper)
pomme de terre (pum dah *tair;* potato)
pommes frites (*pum freet;* french fries)
riz (*ree;* rice)
tomate (toe-*maht;* tomato)

Les Fruits (lay free; fruit)

abricot (*ah*-bree-koh; apricot)
ananas (a-*na*-nas; pineapple)

banane (bah-*nan;* banana)
cerise (sair-*ees;* cherry)
citron (see-*troh;* lemon)
citron vert (see-troh-*vair;* lime)
fraise (frayz; strawberry)
framboise (frahm-*bwahz;* raspberry)
myrtille (meer-*teel;* blueberry)
pamplemousse (pahm-pull-*moos;* grapefruit)
pêche (pehsh; peach)
poire (pwahr; pear)
pomme (pum; apple)
prune (proon; plum)
pruneau (proo-*noh;* prune)
raisin (rah-*zeen;* grape)
raisin sec (rah-zeen-*sek;* raisin)

Les Desserts (lay day-sair; desserts)

Charlotte (shar-*lote;* molded cream ringed with a biscuit)
clafoutis (clah-foo-*tee;* thick batter filled with fruit and fried)
crème brûlée (krem broo-*lay;* creamy custard with caramel topping)
fromage blanc (froe-*mahzh* blahn; smooth cream cheese)
gâteau (gah-*toe;* cake)
glace (glahs; ice cream)
marquise (mar-*keez;* light, mousse-like cake)
mousse au chocolat (moos oh shok-*lah;* chocolate mousse)
tarte aux (tart oh; pie)
tarte tatin (tart ta-*ta;* caramelized upside-down apple pie)
vacherin (*vahsh*-reh; cake of layered meringue, fruit, and ice cream)

Preparation Methods

à l'ail (ah lai; with garlic)
à point (ah pwahn; medium)
au four (oh fore; baked)
béarnaise (bare-*nayse;* hollandaise sauce with tarragon, vinegar, and shallots)
bechamel (beh-sha-*mel;* white sauce made with onions and nutmeg)

beurre blanc (bur blahn; white sauce made with butter, white wine, and shallots)
bien cuit (byen kwee; well done)
bleu (bluh; very rare)
bordelaise (bore-dah-*lays;* brown meat stock made with red wine, mushrooms, shallots, and beef marrow)
bouilli (bwee-*ee;* boiled)
bourguignon (bore-gee-*nyoh;* brown meat stock flavored with red wine, mushrooms, and onions)
confit (kahn-*fee;* meat — usually duck or goose — cooked in its own fat)
consommé (kahn-soe-*may;* clear broth)
coulis (koo-*lee;* any nonflour sauce, purée, or juice)
cru (kroo; raw)
diable (dee-*ah*-blah; brown sauce flavored with cayenne pepper, white wine, and shallots)
en croûte (ahn *kroot;* in a pastry crust)
en papillote (ohn pah-pee-*oat;* cooked in parchment and opened at the table — usually fish)
estouffade (ay-too-*fahd;* meat that has been marinated, fried, and braised)
farci (fahr-*see;* stuffed)
feuilleté (fwee-eh-*tay;* in puff pastry)
fumé (*foo*-may; smoked)
gratiné (*grah*-tee-nay; topped with browned bread crumbs or cheese)
grillé (*gree*-ay; grilled)
hollandaise (ahl-lan-*dehs;* white sauce with butter, egg yolks, and lemon juice)
lyonnais (lee-ohn-*nay;* with onions)
marinière (mar-ee-*nyair;* steamed in garlicky wine stock)
meunière (moo-*nyur;* fish rolled in flour and sautéed)
parmentier (pahr-men-tee-*ay;* with potato)
Provençal (pro-ven-*saw;* tomato-based sauce, with garlic, olives, and onions)
rôti (*roe*-tee; roasted)
saignant (sen-*yahn;* rare)
terrine (tuh-*reen;* cooked in an earthenware dish)

Salivating over French cooking

Even with English translations, confronting a French menu can be a daunting experience. Dishes that have been familiar to French people since childhood are often unknown to outsiders. The following list is a user's guide to typical French dishes that you're likely to encounter.

- **Andouillette** (ahn-dwee-*et*): A sausage of pork organs encased in intestines. Andouillette has a strong flavor with a distinct aftertaste and is usually grilled and served with mustard and french fries. Look for the A.A.A.A.A. label — the Association Amicale des Authentiques Amateurs d'Andouillettes (Association of Real Andouillette Lovers) stamps it on the best andouillettes.

- **Blanquette de veau** (blahn-*ket* duh voe): Veal cooked in a white stew that includes eggs and cream.

- **Boeuf Bourguignon** (buhf bor-gee-*nyon*): Beef cooked with red burgundy wine, mushrooms, and onions.

- **Boudin** (boo-*dan*): A rich sausage made from pig's blood, usually combined with crème fraîche, onions, and eggs. More elaborate versions may feature a touch of garlic or chestnuts. The dish is often served with sautéed apples or mashed potatoes, which enhance the slightly sweet taste of the sausage.

- **Boudin blanc** (boo-*dan* blahn): A white sausage made from veal, chicken, or pork.

- **Bouillabaisse** (*bwee*-ah-bess): A fish stew from the Mediterranean that includes assorted shellfish and white fish accompanied by croutons, grated cheese, and *rouille,* a mayonnaise made with garlic.

- **Brandade** (brahn-*dahd*): Salt cod (*morue*) soaked in cold water, shredded, and cooked with garlic, olive oil, milk, and potato. It has the look and consistency of mashed potatoes but tastes like salted fish. A green salad makes a good accompaniment.

- **Carpaccio** (car-*pahsh*-shyow): Thinly sliced, cured raw beef or tuna.

- **Cassoulet** (cass-oo-*lay*): A rich stew made of white beans, dry sausage, onion, duck, prosciutto, herbs, carrots, and tomatoes. It's cooked slowly and usually served in a ceramic bowl or pot. Absolutely delicious, but heavy; don't plan any serious physical exertions after eating — digestion will be enough.

- **Cervelles** (suhr-vel): Pork or sheep brains.

- **Cheval** (sheh-vahl): Horse meat.

- **Choucroute** (shoo-*kroot*): Sauerkraut cooked with juniper berries and wine, served with an assortment of pork cuts, usually including brisket, pork shoulder, ham, frankfurters, or spicy sausage. It goes well with boiled potatoes and is served with mustard.

✓ **Confit de canard** (con-*fee* duh can-*ahr*): A duck leg cooked and preserved in its own fat. The fatty skin is usually salty, but the meat underneath is tender and juicy. Mashed potatoes make a good side dish.

✓ **Cuisses des grenouilles** (cwees day gren-*wee*): Frogs' legs.

✓ **Escargots** (es-car-*go*): Snails.

✓ **Foie** (fwah): Liver.

✓ **Gesiers** (jeh-*zyay*): Gizzards; very good in salads.

✓ **Lapin à la moutarde** (la-*pan* ah la moo-*tard*): Rabbit cooked with mustard, crème fraîche, and sometimes white wine. The mustard perks up the rabbit meat, which has a mild flavor.

✓ **Lièvre** (lee-*yevr*): Hare.

✓ **Magret de canard** (mah-*greh* duh can-*ahr*): The sliced breast of a fattened duck, sautéed and sometimes served with a green peppercorn sauce. The result more closely resembles red meat than poultry. As with any meat, specify how you want it cooked.

✓ **Pieds de cochon** (pyay duh coh-*shon*): Pig's feet.

✓ **Plateau de fruits de mer** (plah-*toe* duh free duh mair): A variety of raw and cooked seafood served on ice. You usually find two kinds of oysters — flat, round *belon,* and larger, crinkly *creuse.* Both types are cultivated, not harvested. The oysters are eaten with lemon or red-wine vinegar and accompanied by thin slices of buttered rye bread. In addition to various kinds of shrimp, clams, and mussels, you also see periwinkles (*bulots;* edible marine snails), which are eaten with mayonnaise.

✓ **Pot-au-feu** (*pot*-oh-fuh): A hearty dish of boiled vegetables and beef that sometimes includes the marrow bone. Scrape out the marrow, spread it on toast, and sprinkle it with salt. Sometimes the broth is served first, followed by the vegetables and beef. Mustard is the preferred condiment.

✓ **Ris de veau** (ree duh voe): The thymus gland of a calf (a white meat) sautéed in a butter and cream sauce. It has a delicate, pleasant taste but is high in cholesterol.

✓ **Rognons** (*ron*-yawn): Kidneys.

✓ **Tête de veau** (tet duh voe): Calf's head.

Words to the Wise: The Local Language

Parisians *do* speak English and yes, are willing to speak it — especially with visitors who do them the courtesy of trying to speak a few phrases of French. You often find that you can't even complete a sentence in French before you're answered in English. Don't be afraid of saying you don't understand French (*Je ne comprends pas;* juh neh cohm-*pren* pah); you will save yourself, and the person with whom you are conversing, a lot of time, and get help that much faster.

Phrases to remember are the essential *Parlez-vous anglais* (par-*lay* voo ahn-*glay;* do you speak English?); the common courtesy phrase of *Bonjour madame/monsieur* (bohn-*joor* mad-*am,* mis-*yoo*) when you enter a store or place of business; and *au revoir madame/monsieur* (oh-*vwah*) when you leave. This book, too, has an extensive glossary of words and phrases (See Appendix B for "A Glossary of French Words and Phrases") that anticipate nearly every situation.

Background Check: Books and Movies

Compiled here are lists of books and movies to help prepare you for your trip.

Books

There are so many books about the experiences of travelers who fell under the city's spell, or the doings of a particular French person, or the efforts of those who try to figure out just what it is that makes France such a peculiar culture but such a wonderful place to visit. The following list provides just a sample.

- ✔ *C'est La Vie: An American Conquers the City of Light, Begins a New Life, and Becomes — Zut Alors — Almost French* by Suzy Gershman (Viking). Frommer's *Born to Shop* author Gershman had long planned to retire in France with her husband. But when he died of an unexpected illness, she moved to Paris alone to try to work through her grief. A deliciously chatty chronicle of her first year in Paris.

- ✔ *The Flâneur* by Edmund White (Bloomsbury). Edmund White, who lived in Paris for 16 years, wanders through the streets and avenues and along the quays, taking readers into parts of Paris virtually unknown to visitors — and to many Parisians.

- ✔ *French Toast: An American in Paris Celebrates the Maddening Mysteries of the French* by Harriet Welty Rochefort (Thomas Dunne Books). Part memoir, part guide by an Iowan who picked up and moved to Paris more than 20 years ago, this book sheds light on why the French do things the way they do, and how you can, too, while you're there.

- ✔ *A Moveable Feast* by Ernest Hemingway is the memoir of this Lost Generation writer's life in Paris during the '20s and '30s. Beautifully written, the book is full of anecdotes about life in the city during the period and of course the expatriate writing community that thrived.

✔ *Paris to the Moon* by Adam Gopnik (Random House). The often humorous and tender account of the five years *New Yorker*–writer Gopnik spent in Paris with his wife and young son.

✔ *The Piano Shop on the Left Bank: Discovering a Forgotten Passion in a Paris Atelier* by Thad Carhart (Random House). Carhart notices an unassuming piano shop while walking his children to school one day. He eventually gains entry into a new world of the piano and its French fans as well as its art and history — and rediscovers the forgotten joys of playing the piano.

✔ *Savoir Flair* by Polly Platt (Culture Crossings Ltd.) details cultural do's and don'ts by an American who has lived in Paris since 1967. This guide is simply essential!

✔ *Seven Ages of Paris* by Alistair Horne (Vintage) is a colorful narrative history of Paris and, due to its designation as the center of the French world, the history of France, as well. Interesting and informative, it is a great unintimidating introduction to a city with a whole lot of history.

✔ *Sixty Million Frenchmen Can't Be Wrong* by Jean-Benoit Nadeau and Julie Barlow (Sourcebooks). Two Canadian journalists who move to France on a two-year fellowship deconstruct French ideas about land, food, privacy, and language.

✔ *A Year in the Merde* and *Talk to the Snail* by Stephen Clarke (Bloomsbury USA). In the first, Clarke describes how he, an Englishman, arrives in Paris to set up some English tearooms in Paris, giving a laugh-out-loud account of the pleasures and perils of being a Brit in France. In his follow-up, Clarke gives us his hilarious 11 commandments for understanding the French, with a great section on the typical tourist experience.

Movies

It's difficult to cull this down into a small list because there are so many terrific films about France. Most here take place in Paris, and their shots of this beautiful city will only increase your anticipation of visiting.

✔ *À Bout de Souffle (Breathless):* In this classic by Jean-Luc Godard, a small-time gangster kills a cop and then flees to Paris to get enough money together to leave the country with his girlfriend. Wonderful shots of Paris in the late 1950s.

✔ *Before Sunset:* In this sequel to the 1995 film *Before Sunrise,* the two main characters, who had met in Vienna and spent a memorable night together, reunite after one gives a reading from his new book at Shakespeare and Company.

✔ *Gigi:* This 1958 Lerner and Loewe musical set in Paris at the turn of the 20th century follows a young girl as she is groomed into a would-be courtesan (based on a story by the French author Colette).

✔ *Jules et Jim:* In this François Truffaut classic, two best friends fall in love with the same woman in 1912 Paris. Breathtaking!

✔ *The Fabulous Destiny of Amélie Poulain:* It's hard to tell who the star is in this movie about a young woman trying to do good, actress Audrey Tautou or the city of Paris.

✔ *La Vie en Rose:* Marion Cotillard won an Oscar and César in 2007 for best actress portraying Édith Piaf in this biographical film of the singer's tumultuous life.

✔ *Paris, je t'aime:* This 2006 collaboration of 18 short films, all named after different Parisian neighborhoods, is a beautiful collection of humorous, dramatic, and heart-wrenching oeuvres. It gives some great insight to the diversity of Parisian life while featuring the architecture and character in the City of Light.

✔ *The Triplets of Belleville:* This animated film is about a Tour de France racer kidnapped by gangsters and the grandmother who goes in search of him with the help of a musical trio — the Triplets of Belleville. Though it doesn't take place in Paris, it's a terrific introduction to the country and fun to watch with your kids. (There isn't much talking, so not a lot of subtitles to decipher.)

✔ *Zazie Dans le Metro:* In Louis Malle's very funny 1962 film, a young girl is foisted on her unwilling transvestite uncle, and they have a series of madcap adventures in Paris.

✔ **Les 400 Coups:** Truffaut's tale of a neglected Parisian teen who commits petty crimes but gets in trouble for trying to do right is set in a dingy, seedy version of Paris.

Chapter 3

Deciding When to Go

The pros and cons of each season are listed here to help you decide when you can make the most of your visit to Paris. Also compiled is a calendar of the most memorable events in Paris; you may want to consider planning your trip to coincide with one of the festivals, sporting events, or celebrations.

Revealing the Secret of the Seasons

Residents and visitors alike find Paris ideal in spring and autumn, when weather is kind, crowds are reasonably sized, and Parisian life runs at a steady hum. Winter can be gray and bone-chillingly damp, but there are plenty of things to do inside: You can fill an entire trip with visits just to the Louvre, and January has its own joy — two to three weeks of shopping the twice yearly government mandated sales. In summer, you can bask in daylight that lasts until 10 p.m.

Table 3-1 presents average temperature by month in Paris to help you plan your trip. (In Paris, temperatures are reported in Celsius.)

Table 3-1	Average Daytime Temperatures for Paris											
	Jan	Feb	Mar	Apr	May	June	July	Aug	Sept	Oct	Nov	Dec
Fahrenheit (F)	38°	39°	46°	51°	58°	64°	74°	76°	61°	53°	45°	40°
Celsius (C)	3°	4°	8°	11°	14°	18°	28°	29°	16°	12°	7°	6°

Paris in the springtime

In 2008, spring came early to Paris with some flowers blooming in February, an unusual occurrence. Spring generally arrives in Paris around April and brings some beautifully clear, fresh days. The parks and gardens of Paris — and those at Versailles, Fontainebleau, and Giverny (see Chapter 14) — burst with colorful, fragrant blooms. Crowds of visitors don't kick in until July summer vacation (except during the spring fashion shows in Mar), so lines are relatively short at the top sightseeing attractions, and airfares have yet to reach their summertime highs.

But keep in mind that April in Paris is *not* as temperate as Cole Porter would have you believe. In fact, Paris weather can be very similar to that in London: It's fickle. Pack for warm, cold, wet, dry, and every other eventuality; in other words, bring layers and don't even *think* about coming without an umbrella. Also, nearly every Monday in May is a holiday in France — stores and many museums are closed, the métro runs on a holiday schedule, and other venues are affected.

Paris is a beach

Long and sultry days make visiting Paris in summer ideal — 6 a.m. sunrises and 10 p.m. sunsets — so you're afforded additional hours to wander and discover. You can find discounts of 30 percent to 50 percent in most stores during July, one of the two big months for shopping sales (the other is Jan). Hotel room rates are less expensive in July and August. Also during August, parking is free in some areas of the city.

But remember that an influx of tourists during the summer means long lines at museums and other sites. The weather also is capricious: You may have a week of rain and 55-degree temperatures, followed by days of cloudless skies and high temperatures, and much of the city is without air-conditioning.

Because most Parisians take their vacations in August, the city is wonderfully tranquil in some places and devoid of life in others. Although the entire city doesn't exactly shut down in August, some shops and restaurants close for the entire month. The city's cultural calendar slows down, too, and you may have to walk an extra block or two to find an open shop or newsstand. And if you go to Paris in August with thoughts of practicing your French, think again. French may be the language you're least likely to hear.

Fabulous festive fall

Paris bursts into life starting the first week of September, a time typically known as *la rentrée* (the return). This season is one of the most exciting times of the year, when important art exhibitions open along with trendy new restaurants, shops, and cafes. By the middle of September, airfares drop from summertime highs. And with daytime temperatures in the 60s and 70s and nights in the 50s, the weather is pleasant.

Keep in mind, however, that finding a hotel at the last minute in the fall can be difficult due to the number of business conventions and trade shows that take place in the city, including the October fashion shows. Be sure to book ahead.

Transportation strikes of varying intensities traditionally occur during the fall. Some go virtually unnoticed by the average traveler, but others can be giant hassles.

Winter wonderland

You can find great airfare deals during the winter; airlines and tour operators often offer unbeatable prices on flights and package tours. Lines at museums and other sights are mercifully short. You can ice skate in front of the Hôtel de Ville. And, if shopping is your bag, you can save up to 50 percent during the sales in January.

But remember that although Paris winters may appear mild on paper, in reality, residents know that they are gray (sometimes the sun doesn't shine for weeks), dreary, and bone-chillingly damp (there's a reason French women wear scarves!). And look out for those winds that lash up and down the city's grand boulevards. Bring a warm, preferably waterproof, coat and umbrella.

A Paris Calendar

When you arrive, check with the **Paris Convention and Visitors Bureau** (☎ **08-92-68-30-00** [at a charge of .35€/55¢ per minute]; www.parisinfo. com) and buy *Pariscope, L'Officiel des Spectacles* for dates, places, and other up-to-date information. Or, if you pass by an English-language bookstore or bar, pick up a copy of the English-language *Paris Free Voice*. For a refresher course in the ways and means of Paris addresses, see the Introduction.

Below are Paris's month by month attractions.

January

A big, noisy parade on New Year's Day makes Paris more Rose Bowl than City of Light. **La Grande Parade de Montmartre** is fun and flashy with majorettes, high school bands, and elaborate floats that traverse the city streets. The parade begins at 2 p.m. (so you *can* sleep in) in the place Pigalle, 18e (the 18th arrondissement, or neighborhood), and ends at the place Jules-Joffrin, 18e. January 1.

The **Fête des Rois** is a holiday kids love, the celebration of the Feast of the Three Kings, and custom dictates the wearing of gold paper crowns to celebrate. The main object of celebration is a flaky, almond-paste-filled pie that conceals a ceramic charm (so watch your teeth). According to custom, whoever finds the charm becomes king or queen for the day, is entitled to wear the crown, and has free reign, as it were, in his or her choice of a consort. The pie with the charm is available at all *pâtisseries* (dessert shops). January 6.

La Mairie de Paris Vous Invite au Concert features a two-week, two-people-for-the-price-of-one special admission to a variety of jazz and classical concerts across the city. Mid-January.

An annual **Commemorative Mass for Louis XVI** attracts a full turnout of aristocrats, royalists, and even some far-right types. At the Chapelle Expiatoire, 29 rue Pasquier, 8e. Sunday closest to January 21.

Residents go all out for the **Chinese New Year Festival,** which, depending on the Chinese calendar, falls between January 21 and February 19. Celebratory events take place in Chinatown (13e). A parade features dragons, dancers, and fireworks. Plan on grabbing a bite to eat in one of the many excellent Chinese restaurants in the area.

Twice a year, in January and September, more than 40,000 buyers make their way to the **Ready-to-Wear Fashion Shows** in the Salon International de Prêt-à-Porter (Parc des Expositions, 15e; Métro: Balard or Porte de Versailles). The exposition hall at the Porte de Versailles hosts shows of the new clothing lines from some 1,200 designers. Admission for non-trade visitors is around 23€ ($28). Invitation-only fashion shows are also held at the major design houses. End of January.

February

Foire à la Feraille de Paris is one big upscale flea market. This yearly antiques and secondhand fair takes place in the Parc Floral de Paris in the Bois de Vincennes (12e). Contact one of the branches of the **Office de Tourisme et des Congrès de Paris** for exact dates.

- The Welcome kiosk beneath the glass roofed terminal of the Gare du Nord, 18 rue Dunkerque, 10e; open 7 days a week from 8 a.m. to 6 p.m. (Métro and RER: Gare du Nord)

- The Gare de Lyon Welcome Center, 20 bd. Diderot, 12e; open Monday to Saturday 8 a.m. to 6 p.m. (Métro and RER: Gare de Lyon)

- 21 place du Tertre, 18e; open daily 10 a.m. to 7 p.m. (Métro: Abbesses)

- On the median strip facing 72 bd. Rochechouart, Montmartre, 18e; open daily 10 a.m. to 6 p.m. (Métro: Anvers)

- Carrousel du Louvre, beneath the Pyramide, 99 rue de Rivoli, 1er; open daily 10 a.m. to 7 p.m. (Métro: Palais Royal/Musée du Louvre)

Hundreds of farmers display animals and produce and win prizes for the biggest and best at **Salon de l'Agriculture,** a country fair in the heart of the city. Regional food stands offer tastes from all parts of France, and the atmosphere is friendly and quintessentially French at the Parc des Expositions de Paris, Porte de Versailles, 15e. For more information, call the Parc des Expositions information line at ☎ **01-43-95-37-00** or the Paris Convention and Visitors Bureau. Admission is 10€ ($12) adults; 6€ ($7.20) children and students. Last week of February to first week of March.

March

Professional actors and residents of the neighborhood perform in **La Passion à Ménilmontant,** the Passion play (the events leading up to and including the Crucifixion of Christ), for a month around Easter. The play is staged at the Théâtre de Ménilmontant (20e). The event is a local tradition that's been observed since 1932. Admission is around 9€ to 20€ ($11–$24). Call ☎ **01-46-36-98-60** or 01-46-36-03-43 for the schedule. Mid-March to mid-April.

When the **Foire du Trône,** a tacky and fun annual carnival, comes to town, spring is just around the corner. Take a trip up on the Ferris wheel and other rides, try your hand at games, buy hokey souvenirs, and sample fairground food. The fair is located at the Pelouse de Reuilly in the Bois de Vincennes (Métro: Porte Dorée, Porte de Charenton, or Liberté). Late March to end of May.

April

Follow Paris's archbishop as he performs **Le Chemin de la Croix (the Stations of the Cross)** from the square Willette in Montmartre up the steps to the basilica of Sacré-Coeur where he leads prayers to commemorate the Passion and Crucifixion of Jesus Christ. Good Friday, 12:30 p.m. March or April.

One of the most popular athletic events of the year, the **Paris Marathon** has runners sprinting past a variety of the city's most beautiful monuments. The 42km (26-mile) event attracts enthusiastic crowds. April 5, 2009.

The huge annual fair, **Foire de Paris,** is a great place to bargain hunt and people-watch, and signals the start of spring with hundreds of stands selling good-priced food and wine, and a variety of clothing and household goods. The fair takes place at the Parc des Expositions, Porte de Versailles. Late April to early May.

The **Grandes Eaux Musicales** and **les Fêtes de Nuit de Versailles** bring the sounds of classical music to life at the magnificent fountains in the gardens of the Château de Versailles every Sunday from mid-April to mid-October, and every Saturday and national holiday from June through August. Even better are the Grandes Fêtes, spectacular sound-and-light shows with fireworks that take place one Saturday in June, three Saturdays in July, one Saturday in August, and two Saturdays in September. These events are held at the Château de Versailles, Versailles. Log on to www.chateauversailles.fr for more information. (See Chapter 14 for tour companies that go to Versailles.)

May

May is a month of one holiday after the next in France. Banks, post offices, and most museums are closed for **May Day,** May 1, the French version of

Labor Day, but you can watch a workers' parade that traditionally ends at the place de la Bastille. May 1.

Museums around the country stay open late with special exhibits and entertainment during **La Nuit des Musées.** Mid-May.

Montmartre's **Vintage Car Rally** is an array of antique cars that makes its way through the streets of Montmartre starting at 10 a.m. in rue Lépic and ending at the place du Tertre. Sunday closest to May 15.

The weather is usually beautiful during **Les Cinq Jours Extraordinaire** (five extraordinary days), when the shops in the rue du Bac, de Lille, de Beaune, des St-Pères, and de l'Université, and on the quai Voltaire, feature a free open house focusing on a special object chosen according to the annual theme. The whole quarter takes on a festive ambience, red carpets line the streets, and plants and flowers decorate shop fronts. Third week of May.

If you are lucky enough to procure hard-to-find tickets to the **French Open,** Paris's biggest tennis event, you'll find yourself watching the red-clay matches in the Stade Roland Garros in the Bois de Boulogne on the western edge of the city. Unsold tickets — those not reserved for corporate sponsors — go on sale two weeks before the competition starts. The stadium is at 2 av. Gordon Bennett, 16e. Call the French Federation of Tennis at the stadium for more information (☎ 01-47-43-48-00) or visit the Web site at www.frenchopen.com. Last week in May and first week in June.

June

The other Orangerie, this one in the beautiful Bagatelle gardens on the edge of the Bois de Boulogne, is the backdrop for the **Festival Chopin à Paris,** a much-loved annual series of daily piano recitals. Mid-June to mid-July (Métro: Porte Maillot, then take bus 244).

The celebration of the summer solstice has never been louder! The entire country becomes a concert venue in celebration of the first day of summer, and this musical day is called the **Fête de la Musique.** You can hear everything from classical to hip-hop for free in squares and streets around Paris. A big rock concert usually happens in the place de la République, and a fine classical concert generally takes place in the gardens of the Palais-Royal. June.

World-renowned jazz acts play weekends in the Bois de Vincennes' lovely Parc Floral during the **Paris Jazz Festival,** now a fixture on the international jazz circuit. Check out www.parisinfo.com/shows-exhibitions-paris/5397-paris-jazz-festival for more information. Middle of June until the end of July.

One of the most distinguished aviation events in the world is the **Paris Air Show,** which takes place in odd-numbered years at Le Bourget

Airport just outside Paris. Visitors can check out the latest aeronautic technology on display. Call the Paris Convention and Visitors Bureau for more information.

Art exhibits, concerts, and a fantastic parade are staged in the Marais, the boulevard St-Michel, and in other Paris streets to celebrate **Gay Pride.** Call the Centre Gai et Lesbien for dates at ☎ **01-43-57-21-47.** Late June.

July and August

French independence day, **Bastille Day,** is July 14, but the festivities actually begin the night before on July 13, with free *bals* (dances) open to everyone at fire stations all over the city. (Some of the best *bals* are in the fire stations on the rue du Vieux-Colombier near the place St-Sulpice, 6e; the rue Sévigné, 4e; and the rue Blanche, near place Pigalle, 9e.) Although the *bals* are free, drinks cost. On July 14, be sure to get to the Champs-Elysées waaay before the 10 a.m. start of the Bastille Day military parade if you hope to see anything. Later that night a sound-and-light show with terrific fireworks can be seen at the Trocadéro. Rather than face the crowds, many people watch the fireworks from the Champs de Mars across the river, from hotel rooms with views, or even from the hill on rue Soufflot, in front of the Panthéon. July 13 and 14.

The **Paris, Quartier d'Été** (Paris, summer neighborhood) celebration has contemporary music, dance, and film as the bills of fare at outside venues around the city. The outdoor movies shown on a giant screen at Parc de la Villette (Métro: Porte de la Villette) are particularly popular. July 14 to August 15.

If you plan to be in Paris in July, bring your beach clothes! **Paris Plage,** a month-long festival, turns a bit of the Right Bank into the Riviera. From mid-July to mid-August, the city closes off 3.5km (2 miles) of its quays between the Pont Henri IV and the quai des Tuileries so that people can enjoy the same activities they would at the beach — all but swimming in the swift and dangerous Seine (a pool was added between pont Marie and pont Sully in 2004). There are three "beaches" made from sand, grass, or wooden planks; palm trees and wooden lounge chairs; snack bars and cafes; a climbing wall, trampolines, an area to play *boules;* and even old-time dance halls known as *guinguettes.* Concerts are organized by the electronics store Fnac, and there are dance and comedy performances as well.

The final day of the three-week-long **Tour de France** is the third Sunday of July. The winner is crowned at the Champs-Elysées. If you plan to attend the celebration, be sure to arrive very early because the crowds are tremendous. You need a special invitation for a seat in the stands near place de la Concorde, but you can see the cyclists farther up the Champs-Elysées and, depending on the route (which changes each year), elsewhere in the city, too. Check the newspapers the day before or log on to www.letour.com.

The **Fête de l'Assomption** celebrates the journey of Mary, Jesus's mother, to Heaven after her death. Church services at Notre-Dame are the most popular and colorful on this important French holiday (many stores are closed, and transportation runs on a holiday schedule), and banners are draped over the church's towers to celebrate the day. August 15.

September
One of the largest and most prestigious antiques shows in the world, the **Biennale des Antiquaires,** opens to the public in even-numbered years in the Cour Carée du Louvre, the underground exhibition space connected to the museum. For more information, contact the Paris Convention and Visitors Bureau. Early September.

Planning your trip to Paris around September 15? Then be sure to visit the off-limits palaces, churches, and other official buildings that throw open their doors to the public for two days during **Les Journées de Patrimoine** (the days of Patrimony). Long lines can put a damper on your sightseeing, so plan what you want to see and show up early (with a good book, just in case). Get a list and a map of all the open buildings from the Paris Convention and Visitors Bureau. Weekend closest to September 15.

The annual arts festival, the **Festival d'Automne,** is recognized throughout Europe for its innovative programming and the high quality of its artists and performers. Check the Paris Convention and Visitors Bureau for more information.

The second of two annual **Ready-to-Wear Fashion Shows** takes place in September (see the previous entry under "January").

This street party cum parade gets bigger every year, and at press time, the mid-September Paris **Techno Parade** was expecting 300,000 viewers to turn out to celebrate musical freedom with a conscience. The parade teamed up with an NGO to fight hunger in 2006 and began eco-friendly initiatives in 2007.

October
More than a half million people visit museums, libraries, swimming pools, churches, and bars and restaurants during **Nuit Blanche.** Open very late or all night for one night, parts of the city become a nighttime art installation. Early October.

The wine might not taste that great, but it's all about the celebration of the harvest at Montmartre's one remaining vineyard, Clos Montmartre. Watch as the wine is auctioned off at high prices to benefit local charities during the **Fêtes des Vendanges à Montmartre** here. Locals dress in period costumes, and the streets come alive with music. First or second Saturday of October.

As interesting for browsing as for buying is the FIAC **(Foire Internationale d'Art Contemporain),** one of the largest contemporary art fairs in the world. With stands from more than 150 galleries, half of them foreign, the fair takes place at the Parc des Expositions, Porte de Versailles, 15e (Métro: Balard or Porte de Versailles). Admission is 14€ ($16). For more information, call ☎ **08-92-69-26-94.** Mid- to late October.

November

Many of the city's major museums celebrate the art of photography during **Mois de la Photo** (the month of the photo) with shows. Check listings in the weekly guide *Pariscope.* All month.

The French commemorate those who died fighting in both World Wars with a wreath-laying ceremony at the Arc de Triomphe, and veterans sell poppy corsages in memory of **Armistice Day.** November 11.

November in Paris can be awfully gray and chilly, but you'll warm up quickly just after midnight on the third Thursday (technically Fri) of November for the annual celebration of the public release of **Beaujolais Nouveau** — a lightweight red wine that is bottled after the fall harvest and meant for immediate consumption as it has a short shelf life. (You can find it in the States as well, right around Thanksgiving.) Wine bars and cafes are packed just for the event.

The annual **Lancement des Illuminations des Champs-Elysées** (lighting of the avenue's Christmas lights) makes for a festive evening, with jazz concerts and an international star to push the button that lights up the avenue. For more information, call the Paris Convention and Visitors Bureau. Late November.

December

Each year a different foreign city installs a life-size Christmas manger scene (**La Crèche sur le Parvis**) in the plaza in front of the Hôtel de Ville (City Hall). The crèche is open daily from 10 a.m. to 8 p.m. December 1 to January 3.

Part II
Planning Your Trip to Paris

The 5th Wave   By Rich Tennant

"And how shall I book your flight to Paris -First Class, Coach, or Medieval?"

In this part . . .

Look no further than these chapters to help you plan everything for your trip — from where to stay and how much to spend on traveling successfully with children to what to do if your wallet has been stolen. Chapter 4 tells you what to expect in each price category so you can plan a workable budget. Chapter 5 gets you to Paris, whether it be by plane, train, automobile, or hovercraft and discusses the pros and cons of package tours. Chapter 6 takes into account special interests and gives advice to families, seniors, disabled persons, and gay men and lesbians. And in Chapter 7, you get some advice about those last-minute details that can frustrate even the most frequent flier.

Chapter 4

Managing Your Money

* *

In This Chapter

▶ Developing a workable budget
▶ Cutting costs — but not the fun
▶ Handling your money
▶ Dealing with a lost or stolen wallet

* *

A good way to budget your trip to Paris is to mentally walk through the journey, from the moment you leave to the minute you get back home, and don't forget to figure in your transportation to and from the airport. Then add in the flight cost (see Chapter 5 on how to fly to Paris for less), the price of getting from the Charles-de-Gaulle or Orly airports to your hotel, your hotel rate per day, meals, public transportation costs, admission prices to museums and the theater, and other entertainment expenses. Add another 25 percent to the total for good measure. You never know when you might stumble across a cute boutique or a *brocante* (a flea market with one-of-a-kind items).

Planning Your Budget

Cities rarely are cheap or expensive across the board; Paris tends to be pricey for dining but more reasonable for accommodations, so booking a good hotel shouldn't be a problem. The following list offers guidelines for what you're likely to spend while in Paris. The rate of exchange at press time was 1€ = $1.60.

> ✔ **Lodging:** Before you start shelling out money for lodging, think about how much time you'll actually spend in your room. For between 80€ and 100€ ($128–$160), you can rent a clean, functionally furnished hotel room with a private bathroom and cable TV. This type of budget room is comfortable, has the basic furnishings and décor; the drawbacks are thin yet serviceable towels and thin bars of packaged soap (Hint: You can buy better soaps in the grocery store or at chain store Monoprix for just a few euros).
>
> If you're feeling extravagant and willing to spend 200€ ($320) or more, luxury, upper-tier hotels offer more services, such as room service, air-conditioning, and toiletries.

✔ **Transportation:** The Paris métro, the model for subways around the world since its inauguration in 1900, is one of the best transit systems around in terms of price and efficiency. Getting across town in less than a half-hour is no problem, and the cost is lower when you purchase one of several available discount tickets or a *carnet* (booklet) of ten tickets. (See Chapter 8 for options and prices.)

If you thrive on labyrinthine one-way streets, a dearth of parking spaces, hellish traffic, and driving among what are statistically the worst drivers in Europe, then renting a car in Paris is for you, but I strongly discourage it! If you want to rent a car to see other parts of France or make a day trip outside of Paris, rent on your way out of the city. (See Chapter 7 for addresses and phone numbers of car rental agencies in Paris.)

✔ **Restaurants:** The French consider dining out one of the finer joys in life, and they pay for it. You can expect to do the same. An average Parisian dining experience — a three-course dinner in a popular upscale restaurant — runs about 60€ to 80€ ($72–$96) per person.

You can find establishments serving satisfying two-course meals for as little as 14€ ($22) and ethnic eateries and sandwich shops that help you save even more money. Dining reasonably in Paris isn't impossible when you know where to look. Chapter 10 helps you discover just that.

✔ **Attractions:** Entry fees to museums and other sights can add up quickly; find money-saving advice in Chapter 11, after which making a list of must-dos will give you a feel for how much money to set aside.

✔ **Shopping:** Paris is one of the world's best places to shop. Store owners arrange their wares in such enticing window displays (with prices) that they'll have you *faites du leche-vitrines* (licking the windows) in no time. You can find some great deals during the semiannual sales in January and July, but remember that a steep 19.6 percent tax (value-added tax, abbreviated VAT or TVA) is added to most goods. If you live outside the European Union, you're usually entitled to get back part of the tax, if you meet certain requirements. See Chapter 12 for more information.

✔ **Nightlife:** Don't forgo the spectacles at the Lido or Moulin Rouge if you've always wanted to see them — just know beforehand that you'll be charged a small fortune for entry and alcoholic beverages. Plan on seeing the show without dinner, and exit with a wallet that isn't quite as light as it otherwise would be. Budget big, too, especially when you plan to visit clubs and other nightspots; nightclubs usually have covers (though the first drink is generally included) and bars are not cheap. You can save money for ballet, opera, and plays at the national theaters by buying half-price or same-day tickets. See Chapter 15 and 16 for more information.

Table 4-1 gives you approximate prices for some common expenses, listed in euro, U.S. dollars, and British pounds.

Table 4-1	What Things Cost in Paris		
Expense	Euro	U.S. Dollars	Pounds Sterling
Taxi from Charles-de-Gaulle Airport to the city center (depending on traffic)	50€	$80	£40
Taxi from Orly Airport to the city center	45€	$72	£36
Public transportation for an average trip on the métro within the city (from a métro carnet of 10)	1.50€	$2.40	£1.20
Glass of wine	5€	$9	£4.50
Coca-Cola (at a cafe)	3.50€	$5.60	£2.30
Cup of coffee	2€	$3.20	£1.60
Admission to the Louvre	9€	$14	£7
Movie ticket	8.30€	$13	£6.50
Concert ticket (at the Opera Garnier)	5€–150€	$8–$240	£4–£170

Cutting Costs

One of the primary ways to save money at the outset is by booking a package tour. For many destinations, you can book airfare, hotel, ground transportation, and even some sightseeing just by making one call to a travel agent or searching the Internet, for a lot less than if you tried to put the trip together yourself. (See Chapter 5 for specific companies to call.)

I can't repeat it enough: Always ask for discount rates. Membership in AAA, frequent-flyer plans, trade unions, AARP, or other groups may qualify you for savings on car rentals, plane tickets, hotel rooms, even meals. Ask about everything; you may be pleasantly surprised.

The following list offers additional cost-cutting strategies for various expenses.

✔ **Food and drink**

- Make lunch your main meal. Many restaurants offer great deals on a fixed-price (prix fixe) lunch or offer a daily formule (day's special) of appetizer, main course, and dessert that can often be cheaper than ordering off the regular menu. After two or three courses at midday, you won't want a big dinner.

- Try the ethnic neighborhoods. You can get terrific Chinese and Vietnamese foods in the 13th arrondissement between the place d'Italie and the Porte de Choisy; and the 10e, 18e, and 20e have restaurants with North African, Turkish, Vietnamese, and Thai menus. Couscous is on the menu at many restaurants and usually is an inexpensive offering, and falafel stands abound in the Marais.

- Keep in mind that the *plat du jour* (daily entree special) usually is the cheapest main dish at a budget restaurant.

- Remember that wine is cheaper than soda. Some mineral waters, likewise, are less expensive than others. Ask for tap water (*une carafe d'eau,* oon kar-*ahf* doh), which is free.

- If you're just having drinks or coffee, do it standing at the bar. You pay twice as much when you're seated at a table.

- Know the tipping rules. Most restaurants include the gratuity in the bill. Look for *service compris* on your bill, which means 15 percent has been added already. It is customary to leave extra; 5 percent if the service was good.

✔ **Lodging**

- Book your hotel room early. Rooms at the best prices fill up quickly, especially in the fall.

- Negotiate the room price, especially in the low season. It never hurts to ask for discounts, either: Ask for a discount if you're a student or older than 60; ask for a discount when you're staying three days or more.

- Check the Web for online specials. Most Parisian hotels have their own Web sites and offer promotions, especially for stays of three days or longer.

- Reserve a room with a kitchen. It may not seem like much of a vacation if you cook your own meals and wash your own dishes, but you can save a lot of money by not eating in restaurants three times a day. Even if you make only breakfast and pack an occasional bag lunch, you can save a little extra cash for souvenirs and gifts for your family and friends back home. Shopping the open-air markets and grocery stores offers a fun peek into the French way of life.

- Try renting an apartment instead of staying in a hotel. Renting a Paris apartment can be surprisingly cheap, and apartment rental services flourish online. You save money by eating more meals in the apartment, and you experience a little of what it's like to live like a resident of Paris. (See Chapter 9 for specific rental agencies.)

- Consider a housing swap. If you have a house in a desirable locale for French tourists (big cities or near national parks) you may just be able to arrange a mutually beneficial arrangement — for free. (See Chapter 9 for details.)

✔ **Shopping and entertainment**

- For discounts on fashion, try the rue St-Placide in the 6e arrondissement. You find plenty of overstock and *dégriffe* (clothes with labels removed) items on this street near Le Bon Marché department store (where clothes are decidedly *not* cheap). Stylish inexpensive clothing also can be found at Monoprix stores located all over the city.

- If you plan to visit two or three museums a day for multiple days, buy the Paris Museum Pass. It's offered in three versions: a two-consecutive-day pass (30€/$48), a four-consecutive-day pass (45€/$72), and a six-consecutive-day pass (60€/$96). It's a great deal if you plan to visit a lot of museums. See Chapter 11 for more information.

- Take advantage of the reduced admission fees at museums. The reduced prices usually apply after 3 p.m. (at the Louvre, it's after 6 p.m.) and all day Sunday. Remember that on the first Sunday of every month, admission to national museums is free.

- Buy half-price theater and other performance tickets. You can find same-day half-price tickets at one of the kiosks by the Madeleine or at the Gare Montparnasse. The kiosks are little huts with panels indicating whether the performance is sold out (symbolized by a little red man) or if tickets are still available (a little green man). (See Chapter 15 for more information.)

- Avoid going to clubs on weekends. Some clubs are cheaper than others, and some are cheaper during the week. Many clubs allow women in free until a certain time (usually 11 p.m.).

✔ **Transportation**

- Fly during the week rather than on weekends. Many airlines charge slightly less if you fly on weekdays.

- Travel during the *off season* (also called the *low season*), the period from approximately October to April.

- Pack light so that you can take the cheapest way into the city from the airport and won't have to worry about lugging around heavy bags. You can save around 38€ ($61) by taking a train or bus instead of a cab from Roissy-Charles-de-Gaulle Airport and about 33€ ($53) from Orly.

- While in Paris, use the bus or métro or walk.

- Buy a carnet of ten métro tickets at a time. A single ticket costs 1.50€ ($1.70), but if you plan on staying a few days, a carnet (pack of ten) costs only 11€ ($13). Better yet, if you know you're going to be in Paris one to two days, buy a **Paris Visite pass,** which is good for unlimited subway and bus travel. At 8.50€ ($14) for one day or 14€ ($22) for two days (kids 4–11 pay half price; kids under four ride free), it's a good deal. If you'll be in Paris longer than three days, your best bet is the **Carte Orange**. It costs 16€ ($26) for zones 1 and 2 (Paris and some of the suburbs) and 22€ ($35) for zones 1 to 3 (Paris and suburbs including Disneyland). You'll need to provide a passport-size photo (or snap one at photo booths in major train and métro stations). (See Chapter 8 for more details.)

Handling Money

The euro, the single European currency for much of the European Union, became the official currency of France and 11 other participating countries on January 1, 1999, but it didn't go into general circulation until January 1, 2002. The old currency, the French franc, disappeared into history on March 1, 2002. Exchange rates of participating countries are locked into a common currency fluctuated against the dollar.

Converting to euro

In converting prices to U.S. dollars, the conversion rate used here is 1€ = $1.60. For up-to-the-minute exchange rates between the euro and the dollar, check the currency converter Web site at www.xe.com/ucc.

At this writing the U.S. dollar rate to the £ equals approximately US$2. These were the rates of exchange used to calculate the values in Table 4-1.

You can withdraw euro at any ATM in Paris, and ATMs are everywhere and open 24 hours. Find them outside nearly every bank, in major department stores, airports, and train stations. MasterCard and/or Cirrus cards can be used at any ATM that displays the MasterCard and/or Cirrus marks. Visa and/or PLUS can also be used at ATMs displaying Visa and PLUS signs.

Keep in mind you won't be able to check your balance or transfer funds, so keep track of your withdrawals while you travel.

Remember that every time you withdraw cash from an ATM, your bank hits you with a fee, sometimes as much as $5. Check how much your bank charges before leaving home. On top of this fee, the bank from which you withdraw cash may also include its own fee. Thus, taking out larger amounts of money every two to three days makes more sense than more frequent withdrawals of smaller denominations. Likewise, remember that your bank places a limit on the amount of money you can take out per day, usually between 300€ and 500€ ($500–$1,000).

If you need to withdraw more than your bank's limit, visit any Parisian bank where a teller can swipe your ATM card for the amount you need, as long as the amount doesn't surpass the Parisian bank's own limit. Approach the bank's information desk first to explain in English what you need done.

Pulling out your plastic: Using credit cards

MasterCard and Visa are accepted at nearly any establishment that takes credit cards in Paris. But American Express and Diners Club aren't widely accepted at small restaurants, shops, or budget hotels in Paris or the rest of the country.

Remember that you pay interest on cash advances on your credit card from the moment you receive the cash. And, many credit card companies now tack on additional fees for foreign currency transactions — sometimes up to 4 percent, on top of the 1 percent service charge that MasterCard and Visa charge. If you don't know how much your credit card charges for currency conversion, contact a company representative.

Going the way of the dinosaur: The extinction of traveler's checks

These days, there's no need to waste valuable time standing in long lines at the American Express office or in search of *bureaux de change* to cash traveler's checks. Simply use your ATM card to withdraw the money you need. Relatively few banks in Paris exchange currency or cash traveler's checks, preferring to send visitors to *bureaux de change* in touristy areas that charge a hefty fee.

If you want the safety of the traveler's check without the hassle, check out American Express's Traveler's Cheque Card. It's a reuseable, reloadable card that is not linked to your bank account. You can even add more funds when you're out of the country by calling American Express collect at ☎ 801-945-9450. To learn more, consult the Web site at www.americanexpress.com.

You can cash traveler's checks at **American Express,** 11 rue Scribe, 9e, ☎ 01-47-77-70-00 (Métro: Auber or Opéra); **Travelex,** 194 rue de Rivoli, 1er, ☎ 01-42-60-37-61 (Métro: Tuileries); or **Global Change,** 240 rue de Rivoli, 1er, ☎ 01-42-36-14-82.

Dealing with a Lost or Stolen Wallet

Every credit card company has an emergency international number that you can call if your wallet or purse is stolen. In the unlikely event that this happens, be sure to block charges against your credit card account immediately. Your credit card company may be able to wire you a cash advance off your credit card immediately, and in many places, can deliver an emergency credit card in a day or two. Call ☎ **0-800-90-11-79** if you've lost or had your **Visa** card stolen. **American Express** card and traveler's check holders in France can call collect ☎ **336-393-1111** for money and lost card emergencies. For **MasterCard,** call ☎ **0800-90-13-87.**

If your traveler's checks are lost or stolen, you need to be able to report exactly which checks are gone in order to get them replaced. The check issuer can tell you where to pick up the new checks.

Here's what to do if your pocket has been picked: First, make a police report as soon as possible. There are three or four police stations (*commissariats*) in each arrondissement (the train stations also have small police stations). Go to the station closest to where the crime took place. If you were robbed in the subway, however, you can go to any police station. You will receive a *Récépissé de Déclaration de Perte ou de Vol* (receipt for declaration of loss or theft). If you have lost your passport, identification documents, and/or valuables, you are given separate receipts — one for your papers (*pièces d'identité*) and one for your valuables. The police receipts are sometimes necessary in applying for the replacement of airline tickets, **INTERAIL** passes (Europass and Eurail), passports, and traveler's checks or for supporting insurance claims.

The report must be made in person and most police stations have English-speaking personnel. Call the U.S. Embassy (☎ **01-43-12-22-22**) for assistance in interpreting if you have difficulty being understood.

Though it's unlikely the police will recover your lost or stolen items, contact the police and file a police report anyway — you may need it for credit card or insurance purposes later.

Finally, you can visit the lost and found office, run by the French police, to verify whether your belongings were returned: **Centre des Objets trouvés de la Prefecture de Police de Paris,** 36 rue des Morillons, 75015 (☎ **08-21-00-25-25** [.10€/20¢ per minute]; Métro: Convention), open Monday to Thursday 8:30 a.m. to 5 p.m., and Friday 8 a.m. to 4:30 p.m.

Chapter 5

Getting to Paris

. . . .

In This Chapter

▶ Identifying which airlines fly to Paris
▶ Finding the best fare
▶ Arriving by train or ferry
▶ Choosing a package tour

. . . .

*T*hough the Internet has drastically changed travel planning, you still need to decide what kind of travel best suits you. This chapter will make you an expert in no time and well able to get yourself to Paris simply and easily.

Flying to Paris

Though Paris has two major airports: Charles de Gaulle and Orly, most non-European visitors will probably land at the larger, busier, and more modern Charles de Gaulle. Known as CDG, and sometimes called Roissy-Charles de Gaulle, it's located 23km (15 miles) northeast of downtown Paris. Orly Airport is located 14km (8½ miles) south of the city. Web sites and phone numbers for the major airlines serving Paris are in the list that follows. These sites offer schedules, flight bookings, and package tours. Most have Web pages where you can sign up for e-mail alerts that list weekend deals and other late-breaking bargains.

Airlines that fly there from the United States and Canada:

- ✔ **Air Canada** (☎ 888-247-2262; www.aircanada.ca) flies direct to Paris from Montréal and Toronto.

- ✔ **Air France** (☎ 800-237-2747; www.airfrance.com) flies direct from Atlanta, Boston, Chicago, Cincinnati, Houston, Los Angeles, Miami, Newark, New York, Philadelphia, and Washington, D.C.

- ✔ **Air Tahiti Nui** (☎ 877-824-4846; www.airtahitinui-usa.com) flies from Los Angeles.

- ✔ **American Airlines** (☎ 800-433-7300; www.aa.com) flies direct from Boston, Chicago, Dallas, New York, and Miami.

✔ **British Airways** (☎ 800-247-9297; www.ba.com) flies to Paris with a layover in London from Atlanta, Baltimore, Boston, Chicago, Houston, Los Angeles, Miami, Orlando, Philadelphia, Phoenix, Newark, New York, San Francisco, Tampa, and Dulles.

✔ **Continental Airlines** (☎ 800-523-3273; www.continental.com) flies direct to Paris from Houston, Cleveland, and Newark.

✔ **Delta Air Lines** (☎ 800-221-1212; www.delta.com) flies direct from Atlanta, Cincinnati, and New York and shares flights with Air France from Boston, Chicago, Cincinnati, Detroit, Dulles, Houston, Los Angeles, Philadelphia, San Francisco, Salt Lake City, and Seattle.

✔ **Iceland Air** (☎ 800-223-5500; www.icelandair.com) flies to Paris with a layover in Reykjavik from Boston, Minneapolis, Orlando, and New York.

✔ **Northwest/KLM** (☎ 800-225-2525; www.nwa.com) flies direct to Paris from Detroit; KLM flies from other cities including Los Angeles, Memphis, Minneapolis, New York, and Seattle with a layover in Amsterdam.

✔ **United Airlines** (☎ 800-864-8331; www.united.com) flies direct from Chicago, Los Angeles, San Francisco, and Washington, D.C.

✔ **US Airways** (☎ 800-428-4322; www.usairways.com) flies from Philadelphia.

Airlines that fly there from the United Kingdom:

✔ **Air France** (☎ 0870-142-4-343; www.airfrance.co/uk) flies from cities including Aberdeen, Birmingham, Bristol, Cardiff, Edinburgh, Glasgow, Leeds, London, and Manchester.

✔ **British Airways** (☎ 0870-850-9-850; www.ba.com) flies direct to Paris from London and with a layover in London from Edinburgh, Glasgow, and Manchester.

✔ **easyJet** (☎ 0871-244-2366; www.easyjet.com) flies from Belfast, Bristol, Glasgow, Edinburgh, New Castle, Liverpool, London, and Luton.

Airlines that fly there from Australia and New Zealand:

✔ **Qantas** (☎ 13-13-13 anywhere in Australia; www.qantas.com.au) flies from Sydney.

✔ **Singapore Airlines** (check the Web site for phone booking from your particular city; www.singaporeairlines.com) flies from Sydney and Auckland.

Getting the best deal on your airfare

Though every airline offers virtually the same product, prices can vary by hundreds of dollars. Competition among the major U.S. airlines is unlike that of any other industry.

Business travelers who need the flexibility to buy their tickets at the last minute and change their itineraries at a moment's notice — and who want to get home before the weekend — pay the premium rate, known as the *full fare*. If you're lucky enough to fly to Paris this way, more power to you. It was certainly not cheap! But if you can book your ticket far in advance, stay over Saturday night, and are willing to travel midweek (Tues–Thurs), you can qualify for the least expensive price — usually a fraction of the full fare. On most flights, even the shortest hops within the United States, the full fare is close to $1,000 or more, but a 7- or 14-day advance purchase ticket may cost a good bit less. Obviously, planning ahead pays.

The airlines also periodically hold sales, in which they lower the prices on their most popular routes. These fares have advance purchase requirements and date-of-travel restrictions and may be nonrefundable, but you can't beat the prices. As you plan your vacation, keep your eyes open for these sales, which tend to take place in seasons of low travel volume — November 1 to December 1 and January to April. You almost never see a sale around the peak summer vacation months of July and August, or around Thanksgiving or Christmas, when many people fly, regardless of the fare they have to pay.

Consolidators, also known as *bucket shops,* negotiate bulk quantities of airline tickets and sell them at a discount. They are great sources for international tickets, although they usually can't beat the Internet on fares within North America. Start by looking in Sunday newspaper travel sections; their ads are usually formatted to look like classified ads. U.S. travelers should focus on the *New York Times, Los Angeles Times,* and *Miami Herald.*

Bucket-shop tickets are usually nonrefundable or rigged with stiff cancellation penalties, often as high as 50 percent to 75 percent of the ticket price, and some put you on charter airlines with questionable safety records (I know one person who flew a rickety charter to Paris through a thunderstorm and swears he will never fly charter again).

Several reliable consolidators are worldwide and available on the Web. **STA Travel** (☎ 800-781-4040; www.statravel.com), the world's leader in student travel, offers good fares for travelers no matter your age. **ELTExpress** (☎ 201-541-3826 for air travel originating in the U.S. and Canada; www.flights.com) started in Europe and has excellent fares worldwide, particularly to Europe. **LowestFare.com** (☎ 800-FLY-CHEAP; www.lowestfare.com) is owned by priceline.com. Montreal-based **Air Tickets Direct** (☎ 888-858-8884; www.airticketsdirect.com) has been operating since 1991.

Booking your ticket online

The big three online travel agencies, **Expedia** (www.expedia.com), **Travelocity** (www.travelocity.com), and **Orbitz** (www.orbitz.com), sell most of the air tickets bought on the Internet. (Canadian travelers should try www.expedia.ca and www.travelocity.ca; U.K. residents can go for expedia.co.uk and opodo.co.uk.) Each has different business deals with the airlines and may offer different fares on the same flights, so shopping around is wise. Expedia, Orbitz, and Travelocity will also send you an **e-mail notification** when a cheap fare becomes available to your favorite destination.

Of the smaller travel agency Web sites, **SideStep** (www.sidestep.com) recently merged with kayak.com to search more than 140 sites at once. It's a browser add-on that in reality beats competitors' fares about as often as other sites do.

Great **last-minute deals** are available through free weekly e-mail services provided directly by the airlines. Most of these deals are announced on Tuesday or Wednesday and must be purchased online. Most are only valid for travel that weekend, but some (such as Southwest's) can be booked weeks or months in advance. Sign up for weekly e-mail alerts at airline Web sites or check megasites that compile comprehensive lists of last-minute specials, such as **Smarter Travel** (www.smartertravel.com). For last-minute trips, **www.lastminute.com** often has better deals than the major-label sites.

If you're willing to give up some control over your flight details, use Priceline's (www.priceline.com) *opaque* fare service. I say opaque because it offers rock-bottom prices in exchange for travel on a mystery airline at a mysterious time of day, often with a mysterious change of planes en route, sometimes more than one change of planes. The mystery airlines are all major, well-known carriers, but your chances of getting a 6 a.m. or 11 p.m. flight are pretty high. Priceline also has nonopaque service; you can pick exact flights, times, and airlines from a list of offers.

 Great last-minute deals are also available directly from the airlines themselves through a free e-mail service called *E-savers.* Each week, the airline sends you a list of discounted flights, usually leaving the upcoming Friday or Saturday and returning the following Monday or Tuesday. Airline sites also offer schedules, flight booking, and information on late-breaking bargains.

Arriving by Other Means

If you're arriving in Paris by **train** from northern Germany, Belgium, or London, you disembark in the **Gare du Nord.** Trains from Normandy come into the **Gare St-Lazare,** in Northwest Paris near Galeries Lafayette and Opéra Garnier. Trains from western France (Brittany, Chartres, Versailles, Bordeaux) head to the **Gare de Montparnasse** in the 14e; those from the southwest (the Loire Valley, Pyrénées, Spain) arrive at the **Gare d'Austerlitz** near the Jardin des Plantes, in the 13th arrondissement. Those from the south and southeast (the Riviera, Lyon, Italy,

Geneva) pull in at the **Gare de Lyon.** Trains coming from Alsace and eastern France, Luxembourg, southern Germany, and Zurich arrive at the **Gare de l'Est.** All train stations connect to métro stations with the same name. All Paris train stations are located within the first 15 arrondissements, and are easily accessible.

Buses connect Paris to most major European cities and the most well-known of the companies are **Eurolines.** There are no American offices, so you must make bus transportation arrangements after arriving in Europe. In Great Britain, contact Eurolines (☎ 08-705-14-32-19). In Paris, contact Eurolines (at their Latin Quarter agency at 55 rue St. Jacques, 5e; ☎ 43-54-11-99). International buses pull into the **Gare Routière Internationale** (International Bus Terminal) in the suburb of Bagnolet, just across the *périphérique* (ring road) from the Galliéni Métro station. To get into Paris proper, take Line 3 and change buses according to your final destination.

If you are arriving in Paris from the U.K., about a dozen companies run **hydrofoil, ferry,** and **hovercraft** across the English Channel, or *La Manche* (pronounced la mahnsh; "the sleeve"), as the French say. Services operate daily and most carry cars. Hovercraft and hydrofoils make the trip across the Channel in about 40 minutes; the shortest ferry route between Dover and Calais is about one and a half hours. The major routes are between Dover and Calais and Folkestone and Boulogne (about 12 trips a day). Depending on weather conditions, prices and timetables can vary. This is not the best way to get to Paris from the U.K.; the entire trip from London to Dover by train, then from Dover to Calais by ferry, and Calais to Paris by train takes about 11 hours. You can check schedules and reserve space on ferries on **Ferrybooker.com** (www.ferrybooker.com). Special fares at press time included Dover to Calais for 70€ ($112) per car with up to five passengers.

It's important to make reservations because ferries are crowded.

The **Channel Tunnel** (Chunnel) opened in 1994, and the popularity of its Eurostar train service has had the happy effect of driving down prices on all cross-channel transport. This remarkable engineering feat means that if you hop aboard Le Shuttle in Britain, you can be eating a meal in France two to four hours later. You can purchase tickets in advance or at the station. Eurostar tickets start around 63€ ($100) one way off season if you book seven days in advance. Prices rise in April and in June. Eurostar transports *passengers only* (no vehicles) between London or Ashford in Kent and Paris, Brussels, Lille, and beyond. For more information on Eurostar, including online booking, go to www.eurostar.com. For special packages information in the U.S., visit RailEurope (www.raileurope.com) or the TravelPro Network (www.travelpro.net).

A separate company known as **Eurotunnel** (☎ 08-705-35-35-35 in the U.K.; www.eurotunnel.com) can transport passengers with their cars between Folkestone in the United Kingdom and Calais in France. Car prices start at £22 ($44) for a round-trip day trip and can rise to £199 ($399) for a round-trip journey longer than five days. One-way prices start at £49 ($98).

Joining an Escorted Tour

On escorted tours, the tour company takes care of all the details, and tells you what to expect at each leg of your journey. You know your costs up front, and you don't get many surprises. Escorted tours can take you to the maximum number of sights in the minimum amount of time with the least amount of hassle.

It's the least independent way to travel, but some travelers find escorted tours liberating — no hassles with public transportation, no deciphering maps, and the comfort of knowing what you're getting. Others fervently despise escorted group tours, because they feel as if they're being herded from one sight to the next, missing the element of surprise and individuality that independent travel affords.

If you decide to go with an escorted tour, I *strongly* recommend purchasing travel insurance, especially if the tour operator requires payment up front. But don't buy insurance from the tour operator! If the tour operator doesn't fulfill its obligation to provide you with the vacation you paid for, there's no reason to think that it'll fulfill the insurance obligations either. Get travel insurance through an independent agency. (For more about the ins and outs of travel insurance, see Chapter 7.)

When choosing an escorted tour, along with finding out whether you have to put down a deposit and when final payment is due, ask a few simple questions before you buy.

- ✔ **What is the cancellation policy?** Can they cancel the trip if they don't get enough people? How late can you cancel if you are unable to go? Do you get a refund if you cancel? If they cancel?

- ✔ **How jam-packed is the schedule?** Does the tour schedule try to fit 25 hours into a 24-hour day, or does it give you ample time to relax by the pool or shop? If getting up at 7 a.m. every day and not returning to your hotel until 6 or 7 p.m. at night sounds like a grind, certain escorted tours may not be for you.

- ✔ **How large is the group?** The smaller the group, the less time you spend waiting for people to get on and off the bus. Tour operators may be evasive about this, because they may not know the exact size of the group until everybody has made reservations, but they should be able to give you a rough estimate.

- ✔ **Is there a minimum group size?** Some tours have a minimum group size, and may cancel the tour if they don't book enough people. If a quota exists, find out what it is and how close they are to reaching it. Again, tour operators may be evasive in their answers, but the information may help you select a tour that's sure to happen.

✔ **What exactly is included?** Don't assume anything. You may have to pay to get yourself to and from the airport. A box lunch may be included in an excursion but drinks may be extra. Beer may be included but not wine. Find out how much flexibility you have: Can you opt out of certain activities, or does the bus leave once a day, with no exceptions? Are all your meals planned in advance? Can you choose your entree at dinner, or does everybody get the same chicken cutlet?

Depending on your recreational passions, I recommend one of the following tour companies.

✔ **The French Experience** (☎ 800-283-7262; www.frenchexperience. com) has been around since 1983 and offers several fly/drive programs through different regions of France (the quoted price includes airfare and a rental car). You can specify the type and price level of hotels you want. The agency arranges the car rental in advance, and the rest is up to you.

✔ Perhaps the most instantly recognizable tour operator in the world, **American Express Vacations** (☎ 800-335-3342; www.american expressvacations.com) has more comprehensive offerings than those of other companies and includes package tours and independent stays.

Choosing a Package Tour

For lots of destinations, package tours can be a smart way to go. In many cases, a package tour that includes airfare, hotel, and transportation to and from the airport costs less than the hotel alone on a tour you book yourself. That's because packages are sold in bulk to tour operators who then resell them to the public. It's a bit like buying your vacation at a Costco or Sam's Club — except the tour operator is the one who buys the 1,000-count box of garbage bags and resells them ten at a time.

Package tours can vary as much as those garbage bags, too. Some offer a better class of hotels than others; others provide the same hotels for lower prices, others exclude children. Some book flights on scheduled airlines; others sell charters. In some packages, your choice of accommodations and travel days may be limited. Some let you choose between escorted vacations and independent vacations; others allow you to add on just a few excursions or escorted day trips (also at discounted prices) without booking an entirely escorted tour.

To find package tours, check out the travel section of your local Sunday newspaper or the ads in the back of national travel magazines such as

Travel + Leisure, National Geographic Traveler, and *Condé Nast Traveler.*
Air France Holidays (☎ **800-2-FRANCE;** www.airfranceholidays.
com) has France-specific package tours; their six-night Paris Affair
special starts at $1,149 and includes air and hotel fare, breakfast, a
Seine River cruise, and a performance of the Paradis Latin cabaret.
Liberty Travel (call ☎ **888-271-1584** to find the store nearest you; www.
libertytravel.com) is one of the biggest packagers in the Northeast,
and usually boasts a full-page ad in Sunday papers.

Another good source of package deals is the airlines themselves. Most
major airlines offer air/land packages, including **American Airlines
Vacations** (☎ **800-321-2121;** www.aavacations.com), **Delta Vacations**
(☎ **800-654-6559;** www.deltavacations.com), **Continental Airlines
Vacations** (☎ **800-301-3800;** www.covacations.com), and **United
Vacations** (☎ **888-854-3899;** www.unitedvacations.com). Several big
online travel agencies — Expedia, Travelocity, Orbitz, and Lastminute.
com — also do a brisk business in packages. If you're unsure about the
pedigree of a smaller packager, check with the Better Business Bureau
in the city where the company is based, or go online at www.bbb.org. If
a packager won't tell you where it's based, don't fly with them.

Chapter 6

Catering to Special Travel Needs or Interests

● ●

In This Chapter

▶ Taking the family along

▶ Getting discounts for seniors

▶ Locating wheelchair-accessible attractions and accommodations

▶ Identifying resources for gay and lesbian travelers

● ●

*I*t seems unimaginable that there once was a time when people dressed up for a trip through the air and walked onto a plane unhindered (pleasant flight attendants brought free and copious drinks and snacks, though rampant cigarette smoke made breathing a challenge). These days, no one finds traveling a piece of cake, but for some people it poses more challenges. If you're bringing your family to Paris, or have a disability and are wondering how to pilot yourself down cobblestone streets and winding métro corridors, if you're a senior citizen, or you want to see the gay side of Paris, this is the chapter for you.

Taking the Family Along

Parks and playgrounds are plentiful in Paris, as are kid-specific sights and museums, interesting boat rides, and bike tours *and* the French welcome children, making Paris one of the best places to travel with kids in the world. In addition, you're less than an hour away from Disneyland Paris in the suburb of Marne la Valée. Paris is just as safe as, if not safer than, most big American cities. Though taking your children thousands of miles away may seem at times like an insurmountable challenge, it can be immensely rewarding, giving you new ways of seeing the world through smaller pairs of eyes.

Look for good family-oriented vacation advice on the Internet from sites like the **Family Travel Forum** (www.familytravelforum.com), a comprehensive site with customized trip planning and discussion boards; the award winning **Family Travel Network** (www.familytravel network.com), which offers travel features, deals, and tips; **Traveling**

Internationally with Your Kids (www.travelwithyourkids.com), started by parents whose daughters were born abroad and is a clearinghouse for information on traveling (and even moving abroad) with your children from those who have been there; and **FamilyTravelFiles.com** (www.thefamilytravelfiles.com), which provides an online magazine and a directory of off-the-beaten-path tours and tour operators for families.

If you plan your trip well in advance, your kids may get a kick out of learning the language from one of the many French-language instructional videotapes on the market.

Such books as Ludwig Bemelmans's *Madeline* series, Albert Lamorisse's *The Red Balloon,* and Kay Thompson's *Eloise in Paris* are great for kids under eight years of age. Older teens may appreciate Ernest Hemingway's *A Moveable Feast* (Scribner paperback reissue), Victor Hugo's *Les Misérables,* Mark Twain's *Innocents Abroad,* and Rose Tremain's *The Way I Found Her* (Washington Square Press paperback reprint). All will probably like the popular French comic book series *The Adventures of Asterix,* by René Goscinny and Albert Uderzo. Translated into English and available at bookstores, there's also an English-language site: www.gb.asterix.com.

Children younger than 18 are admitted free to France's national museums (although not necessarily to Paris's city museums), and some attractions offer a lower rate for families of four or more. When purchasing tickets, ask if there is a family rate (*carte famille nombreux,* pronounced kart fam-*ee* nohm-*brooz*).

The following bargains will require some skill in the French language. If you don't understand it, you may want to recruit someone who does because these are terrific bargains. Children younger than 12 traveling by rail through France, can use the **Carte Enfant Plus,** a children's rail pass. It's available at any SNCF (French National Railroads) station or, for non-Americans, online at www.sncf-voyages.com (if you scroll all the way to the bottom of the home page, you will see a tiny British flag; click on this for English). Unfortunately, SNCF does not sell directly to North Americans who have to purchase these cards at a French train station. The pass offers up to a 50 percent discount for the child and one to four adult travel companions on non-TGV (Train Grand Vitesse, France's high-speed train) mainline trains in off-peak periods, and 25 percent off on TGV trains (except overnight trains) and mainline trains during peak travel times. The pass costs 78€ ($125), and you can reserve it online right before you leave, and pick it up at any Paris train station within the time limit (usually two days). Similarly, a discount travel card is available for those ages 12 to 25 called **Carte 12-25.** For 49€ ($79), a cardholder is entitled to up to 60 percent discounts on all TGV and non-TGV rail services and couchette (sleeping car) berths. A guaranteed 25 percent reduction is available on all TGV rail services and couchette berths on non-TGV mainline services at all times where no seats are available at the 50 percent reduction rate. A passport photo must be presented when applying for these cards. *Note:* To find out where to buy or pick up these passes in any of Paris's major train stations, go to their *Acceuil* (Welcome) information kiosk and have an English-speaking representative direct you.

 When traveling with a baby, you can arrange ahead of time for such necessities as a crib and bottle warmer at your hotel, and, if you're driving, a car seat (small children are prohibited from riding in the front seat). Find out whether your hotel stocks baby food; if not, take some with you for your first day, but then plan to buy some. Plenty of choices are available, from Nestlé to Naturalia.

Transportation in Paris isn't as stroller-friendly as in the United States. Be prepared to lift your child out of the stroller when boarding buses, climbing up and down stairs, and/or walking long distances in some métro subway stations. The upside of all of this is that once you get to your destination, you and your child can stroll and play in some of the world's prettiest parks and gardens.

And when you need some kid-free time, consider visiting the **American Church**'s basement bulletin board where English-speaking (often American) students post notices offering baby-sitting services. The church is located at 65 quai d'Orsay, 7e (☎ **01-45-62-05-00;** Métro: Invalides). Or try one of the following agencies that employ some English-speaking baby sitters: **Allo Maman Dépannage** (☎ **01-34-05-00-47**), or **Kid Services** (☎ **08-20-00-02-30** [.10€/20¢ per minute]). Specify when calling that you need a sitter who speaks English.

The books *Travels With Baby: The Ultimate Guide for Planning Trips with Babies, Toddlers, and Pre-school Age Children* by Shelly Rivoli (Travels With Baby Books), *How to Take Great Trips with Your Kids* by Sanford Portnoy (The Harvard Common Press), and *Trouble-Free Travel With Children: Over 700 Helpful Hints for Parents on the Go* by Vicki Lansky (The Book Peddlers) are full of good, general advice that can apply to travel anywhere. Another reliable tome with a worldwide focus is *Adventuring with Children* (Foghorn Press).

You can also check out *Family Travel Times,* published six times a year by **Travel with Your Children,** 40 Fifth Ave., New York, NY 10011 (☎ **212-477-5524;** www.familytraveltimes.com). Subscriptions are $39 for one year, $49 for two years. A free publication list and a sample issue are available on request.

 Finally, a word of advice: Although French people love kids and welcome them just about anywhere, they expect them to be well mannered. Proper behavior is expected everywhere, but especially in restaurants and museums. French children are taught at an early age to behave appropriately in these settings, and French adults expect the same from your kids.

Making Age Work for You: Tips for Seniors

 Mention that you're a senior citizen when you first make your travel reservations; you may be entitled to some discounts before you even get to Paris. When you arrive in Paris, don't be shy about asking for senior discounts, and always carry a form of identification that shows your date of birth.

 People over the age of 60 qualify for reduced admission to theaters, museums, and other attractions and for other travel bargains like the **Carte Senior,** which entitles holders up to 50 percent discounts on TGV rail services and couchette berths on non-TGV mainline services, subject to seating availabilities. There is 25 percent off all TGV rail services and couchette berths on non-TGV mainline services at all times, where no seats are available at the 50 percent reduction. The Carte Senior also triggers some discounts on admissions to museums and historic sites. It's valid for one year, costs 85€ ($136), and you can buy it at any SNCF (train) station. You have to present a passport photo when applying for these cards. *Note:* To find out where to buy these passes within the train station, go to the *Acceuil* (Welcome) information kiosk, where an English-speaking representative will direct you.

Membership in certain organizations can qualify you for some discounts. Be sure to bring whatever membership card the organization issues. If you're older than 50, consider joining **AARP** (☎ **888-687-2277;** www.aarp.org), for discounts on hotels, airfares, and car rentals. As a member, you're eligible for a wide range of special benefits, including *AARP The Magazine.*

Hundreds of travel agencies specialize in senior travel, and although many of the vacations are of the tour-bus variety, which may cramp the style of an independent senior, one bonus is that free trips are often thrown in for organizers of groups of 20 or more. Obtain travel information from **SAGA International Holidays,** 222 Berkeley St., Boston, MA 02116 (☎ **800-343-0273**).

Recommended publications offering travel resources and discounts for seniors include the quarterly magazine *Travel 50 & Beyond* (www.travel50andbeyond.com); *101 Tips,* available from Grand Circle Travel (☎ **800-959-0405;** www.gct.com); and *Unbelievably Good Deals and Great Adventures That You Absolutely Can't Get Unless You're Over 50* (McGraw-Hill), by Joan Rattner Heilman.

Accessing Paris: Advice for Travelers with Disabilities

Unfortunately, those features that make Paris so beautiful — uneven cobblestone streets, quaint buildings with high doorsills from the

Middle Ages, and twisting lanes too narrow and traffic-clogged to simultaneously admit pedestrians and autos — also make using a walker or a wheelchair a nightmare. According to French law, newer hotels with three stars or more are required to have at least one wheelchair-accessible guest room. Most of the city's older, budget hotels, which are exempt from the law, occupy buildings with winding staircases, or elevators smaller than phone booths, and generally aren't good choices for travelers with disabilities.

Slowly, but surely, however, Paris is becoming more accessible. There is now space for wheelchairs in the first class cars of France's high-speed trains (le Train Grand Vitesse or TGV) — for the price of a second-class ticket. For more information in English about traveling through France by train go to www.voyages-sncf.fr.

Few métro stations have elevators, most feature long tunnels, and some have wheelchair-unfriendly moving sidewalks and staircases. Escalators often lead to flights of stairs, and many times when you climb a flight of stairs, you're faced with another set of stairs leading down. However, line 14 of the métro is wheelchair accessible, and so are the stations at Nanterre-Université, Vincennes, Noisiel, Saint-Maur-Créteil, Torcy, Auber, Cité-Universitaire, Saint-Germain-en-Laye, Charles-de-Gaulle-Étoile, Nanterre-Ville, and several others. The RER's Line E is also wheelchair accessible.

Wheelchair lifts or kneeling stairs are standard equipment on more than 50 city buses. Bus 91, which links the Bastille with Montparnasse, is wheelchair accessible, and so are Bus 20, which runs from Gare St-Lazare near Galeries Lafayette to Gare de Lyon, and Bus 31 from Charles de Gaulle Étoile near the Arc de Triomphe to Gare de l'Est. Some high-speed and intercity trains are equipped for wheelchair access, and a special space is available in first class (at the price of a second-class ticket) for wheelchairs, although you must reserve well in advance.

Don't let inconveniences change your mind about visiting Paris. Before your trip, go to the **Paris Convention and Visitor's Bureau Web site,** which provides an overview of facilities for people with disabilities in the French transportation system and at monuments and museums in Paris and the provinces (http://en.parisinfo.com/guide_paris/rub5978.html&id_article=14572). This list contains everything from tour guides to accessible parks to organizations for persons with disabilities to specialized transport.

L'Association des Paralysés de France (The Association of the Paralyzed of France), 17 bd. Auguste-Blanqui (☎ **01-40-78-69-00;** Web site in French: www.apf.asso.fr), publishes (in French only, unfortunately) *Le Guide Vacances (The Vacation Guide),* which lists accessible hotels as well as cultural and sporting activities taking place all over France.

Click on www.ratp.info/informer/reseau_ferre.php and scroll down for a list of métro and RER stops that offer elevator access to the platforms, either with the assistance of an attendant *(avec agent)* or free service *(service libre).*

If you speak French, contact the **Groupement pour l'Insertion des Personnes Handicapées Physiques** (Help for the Physically Handicapped), Paris Office, 10 rue de Georges de Porto Riche (☎ **01-43-95-66-36**), and **Les Compagnons du Voyage** of the RATP (Paris public transportation; ☎ **01-58-76-08-33**; Web site in French: www.ratp.fr) for an actual trained "companion" to help navigate the city's public transportation system.

An excellent English-language resource is the U.K. organization, RADAR. A new version of their thoroughly researched guidebook for people with disabilities, *Access in Paris,* hit presses in 2008 and includes such information as maps of all the curbs in Paris and good public toilet facilities (www.accessinparis.org/index.php).

Check out www.miusa.org, the Web site of **Mobility International USA** (☎ **541-343-1284** voice and TTY), which promotes international exchange. Another place to try is **Access-Able Travel Source** (www.access-able.com), a comprehensive database of travel agents who specialize in travel for people with disabilities and a clearinghouse for information about accessible destinations around the world.

Many travel agencies offer customized tours and itineraries for travelers with disabilities. **Flying Wheels Travel** (☎ **877-451-5006**; www.flyingwheelstravel.com) is a full-service travel agency for people with disabilities and offers escorted tours and cruises and private tours in minivans with lifts. **Access-Able Travel Source** (www.access-able.com) has extensive access information and advice for traveling around the world with disabilities. **Accessible Journeys** (☎ **800-846-4537** or 610-521-0339; www.disabilitytravel.com) addresses the needs of wheelchair travelers and slow walkers and their families and friends.

Organizations that offer assistance to travelers with disabilities include **MossRehab** (www.mossresourcenet.org), with a library of accessible-travel resources online; **SATH (Society for Accessible Travel and Hospitality;** ☎ **212-447-7284**; www.sath.org; annual membership fees are $49 adults, $29 seniors and students), an educational nonprofit membership organization whose mission is to raise awareness of the needs of all travelers with disabilities, remove physical and attitudinal barriers to free access, and expand travel opportunities in the United States and abroad. SATH has travel resources for all types of disabilities and informed recommendations on destinations, access guides, travel agents, tour operators, vehicle rentals, and companion services, and includes *Open World Magazine* online; and the **American Foundation for the Blind** (AFB; ☎ **800-232-5463**; www.afb.org), a referral resource for the blind or visually impaired that includes information on traveling with guide dogs.

For more information specifically targeted to travelers with disabilities, check out the quarterly magazine *Emerging Horizons* ($17 per year, $22 outside the United States; www.emerginghorizons.com).

Following the Rainbow: Resources for Gay and Lesbian Travelers

France is one of the world's most tolerant countries toward gays, transgender, bi, and lesbians and has no laws that discriminate. Technically, sexual relations are legal for consenting partners ages 16 and older. A casual indifference to their lifestyles led many to settle here: Oscar Wilde and James Baldwin lived in Paris, as did Gertrude Stein and Alice B. Toklas.

The biggest concentration of gay bookstores, cafes, bars, and clothing boutiques is in the Marais, which stretches from the Hôtel de Ville to the Bastille. The best source of information on Parisian gay and lesbian life is the **Centre Gai et Lesbien,** 63 rue Beaubourg, 3e (☎ 01-43-57-21-47; www.centrelgbtparis.org; Métro: Rambuteau), open Monday 6 p.m. until 8 p.m., Tuesday 4 to 8 p.m., Wednesday, Friday, and Saturday 12:30 to 8 p.m., Thursday 3 to 8 p.m., Sunday 4 to 7 p.m. The center is a source of information, and members of its staff coordinate the activities and meetings of gay people around the world. Another helpful source is **La Maison des Femmes,** 163 rue Charenton, 12e (☎ 01-43-43-41-13; maisondesfemmes.free.fr; Métro: Reuilly-Diderot), which has a cafe and a feminist library for lesbians and bisexual women. Meetings about everything from sexism to working rights and informal dinners and get-togethers all take place here.

Gay magazines that focus mainly on cultural events include *Illico* (free in gay bars) and *Tetu,* available at almost all newspaper stands. This magazine is similar to the U.S. publications *Out* and *The Advocate,* and each issue has a separate pull-out section with cultural and nightlife events in Paris and every major city in France. *Lesbia* is available for women. You can find these and others at Paris's largest and best-stocked gay bookstore, **Les Mots à la Bouche,** 6 rue Ste-Croix-la-Bretonnerie, 4e (☎ 01-42-78-88-30; www.motsbouche.com; Métro: Hôtel-de-Ville). Open 11 a.m. to 11 p.m. Monday through Saturday and 1 to 9 p.m. Sunday.

The **International Gay and Lesbian Travel Association** (IGLTA; ☎ 800-448-8550 or 954-776-2626; www.iglta.org) is the trade association for the gay and lesbian travel industry. It offers an online directory of gay- and lesbian-friendly travel businesses.

Many agencies offer tours and travel itineraries specifically for gay and lesbian travelers. **Now, Voyager** (☎ 800-255-6951; www.nowvoyager.com) is a well-known San Francisco–based gay-owned and -operated travel service. Canada's GayTraveler (www.gaytraveler.ca) is a Web site dedicated to travel for the gay, lesbian, bisexual, and transgendered communities. The site has discussion boards and a free monthly newsletter in addition to lists of all-gay cruises, tours, packages, and other holiday events.

The following travel guides are available at most bookstores: ***Frommer's Gay & Lesbian Europe*** (Wiley), an excellent travel resource (www.frommers.com); ***Out and About*** (www.outandabout.com), which offers such guidebooks as *Three Days in Paris* packed with solid information on the global gay and lesbian scene; ***Spartacus International Gay Guide*** (Bruno Gmünder Verlag; www.spartacusworld.com/gayguide) and ***Odysseus*** (Odysseus Enterprises; www.odyusa.com/html/trvlguide.html), both good, annual English-language guidebooks focused on gay men; and the Damron guides (www.damron.com), with separate annual books for gay men and lesbians.

Chapter 7

Taking Care of the Remaining Details

- -

- -

*P*lanning a trip to Paris can be half the fun. This chapter helps you organize those inevitable last-minute loose ends and details.

Getting a Passport

A valid passport is the only legal form of identification accepted around the world. You can't cross an international border without it. Getting a passport is easy, but the process takes some time.

Applying for a U.S. passport

If you're applying for a first-time passport, follow these steps.

1. Complete a **passport application** in person at a U.S. passport office; a federal, state, or probate court; or a major post office. To find your regional passport office, either check the **U.S. Department of State** Web site, http://travel.state.gov/passport/passport_1738.html, or call the **National Passport Information Center** (☎ 877-487-2778) for automated information.

2. Present a **certified birth certificate** as proof of citizenship. (Bringing along your driver's license, state or military ID, or social security card is also a good idea.)

3. Submit **two identical color passport-sized photos,** measuring 2-x-2 inches in size. You often find businesses that take these photos

near a passport office. *Note:* You can't use a strip from a photo-vending machine because the pictures aren't identical.

4. Pay a **fee.** For people 17 and over, a passport is valid for ten years and costs $100. For those 16 and under, a passport is valid for five years and costs $85.

Allow plenty of time before your trip to apply for a passport; processing normally takes three weeks but can take longer during busy periods (especially spring).

If you have a passport in your current name that was issued within the past 15 years (and you were over age 16 when it was issued), you can renew the passport by mail for $75.

Applying for other passports

The following list offers more information for citizens of Australia, Canada, New Zealand, and the United Kingdom.

- ✔ **Australians** can visit a local post office or passport office, call the **Australia Passport Information Service** (☎ **131-232** toll-free from Australia), or log on to www.passports.gov.au for details on how and where to apply. The fee for Australian passports is AU$208 for adults, and AU$104 for children and seniors.

- ✔ **Canadians** can pick up applications at passport offices throughout Canada and post offices (☎ **800-567-6868;** www.ppt.gc.ca). Applications must be accompanied by two identical passport-sized photographs and proof of Canadian citizenship. Processing takes 10 to 18 days if you apply in person, or about three weeks by mail. The cost is C$87 for adults; C$37 for children.

- ✔ **New Zealanders** can pick up a passport application at any New Zealand Passports Office or download it from its Web site. For information, contact the **Passports Office** or check out its Web site. Contact the **Passports Office** at ☎ **0800-225-050** in New Zealand or log on to www.passports.govt.nz. The cost for an adult passport is NZ$150; NZ$80 for a child's passport. Processing takes ten business days.

- ✔ **United Kingdom** residents can pick up applications for a standard ten-year passport (five-year passport for children under 16) at passport offices and Check & Send post offices. For information, contact the **United Kingdom Passport Service** (☎ **0870-521-0410;** www.passport.gov.uk/index.asp). An adult passport is £72; a child's passport costs £46.

Always keep a photocopy of the inside page of your passport with your picture packed separately from your wallet or purse. In the event your passport is lost or stolen, the photocopy can help speed up the replacement process. When traveling in a group, never let one person carry all the passports. If the passports are stolen, obtaining new ones can be much more difficult, because at least one person in a group needs to be able to prove his or her identity to identify the others.

If you're a U.S. citizen and either lose or have your passport stolen in Paris, go to the Office of American Services, Embassy of the United States between 9 a.m. and noon Monday to Friday at 4 av. Gabriel, 8e (☎ 01-43-12-22-22; http://france.usembassy.gov/pass-lost.html; Métro: Concorde). Canadians in the same circumstances need to visit the Consulate of the Canadian Embassy, 35 av. Montaigne, 8e (☎ 01-44-43-29-00; Métro: Franklin-D-Roosevelt or Alma Marceau). Australians must go to the Ambassade d'Australie at 4 rue Jean Rey, 15e (☎ 01-40-59-33-00; Métro: Bir-Hakeim). New Zealanders need to visit the New Zealand Embassy, 7 Ter rue Léonard de Vinci, 16e (☎ 01-45-01-43-43; Métro: Victor-Hugo).

Why Not to Rent a Car in Paris

Gas is expensive. This should be reason enough to make use of France's excellent national train system, but if you are an extreme sports aficionado, driving in Paris is for you. Parisian drivers are ruthlessly aggressive. Traffic is dense. Roundabouts pop up everywhere, and cars seem to hurtle at you from the left — no better example than the Étoile circle that surrounds the Arc de Triomphe, where cars enter and exit from *12 different locations* at high speeds. Parking is difficult, both in terms of finding a space and the size of the spaces available. Most hotels, except luxury ones, don't have garages. And if you drive to Paris from somewhere else and get on the limited-access roadway called the *périphérique* that circles the city, you'll find that its exits aren't numbered. Because the Paris métro is one of the world's best urban transportation systems, having a car in Paris seems highly unnecessary. Even the day trips described in Chapter 14 are easily accessible by public transportation.

If you must drive in Paris, make sure that you have a copilot helping you navigate the streets. Children, by law, are required to sit in the back, and front and backseat passengers must wear seat belts. And remember that the majority of rentals available in France (and, indeed, most of Europe) have manual (stick-shift) transmissions. In fact, if you request an automatic transmission, you'll probably end up paying more for the car, if a car is even available.

When you rent a car, try doing so for three days or more because the cost usually works out to be less per day than renting for one day, and unlimited mileage is thrown in. Reserve before you leave home (make sure to print out your reservation!), and keep in mind that government taxes are calculated at about 20.6 percent of the total contract, collision damage insurance tacks on 15€ to 20€ ($24–$32) per day, gas is very expensive, and a surcharge of about 15€ ($24) is assessed if you pick up the car at the airport.

Car rental agencies in Paris include:

- ✔ **Avis,** gare d'Austerlitz, arrivals gate, 13e (☎ **01-45-84-22-10;** www.avis.com). A compact car, such as a Renault Clio, that seats four runs about 165€ ($264) per day unlimited mileage before tax.

- ✔ **Europcar,** 60 bd. Diderot, 12e (☎ **08-25-35-23-52** [.20€/30¢ per minute]; www.europcar.fr). A compact two-door with air-conditioning, such as the Volkswagen Golf, costs 190€ ($304) per day with unlimited miles before tax.

- ✔ **Hertz France,** gare de l'Est (2, rue du 8 Mai 1945), 10e (☎ **01-42-05-50-43;** www.hertz.com). A compact car such as a Fiat Panda costs about 196€ ($314) per day with limited mileage.

- ✔ **National,** Charles de Gaulle Airport, Terminal One (☎ **01-48-62-65-81;** www.nationalcar.com). A compact five-door car that seats four, such as a Citröen C4 1.6, costs 107€ ($171) per day unlimited mileage before tax.

The major highways *(autoroutes)* to Paris are the **A1** from the north (the United Kingdom and Belgium); the **A13** from Normandy and other points in northwest France; the **A109** from Spain and the southwest; the **A7** from the Alps, the Riviera, and Italy; and the **A4** from eastern France. At the beginning and end of long weekends, school breaks, and August summer vacations, these roads become parking lots.

Playing It Safe with Travel and Medical Insurance

Three kinds of travel insurance are available: trip-cancellation insurance, medical insurance, and lost luggage insurance. The cost of travel insurance varies widely, depending on the cost and length of your trip, your age and health, and the type of trip you're taking, but expect to pay between 5 percent and 8 percent of the vacation itself.

- ✔ **Trip-cancellation insurance** helps you get your money back if you have to back out of a trip, if you have to go home early, or if your travel supplier goes bankrupt. Allowed reasons for cancellation can range from sickness to natural disasters to the Department of State declaring your destination unsafe for travel. Protect yourself by paying for the insurance with a credit card — by law, consumers can get their money back on goods and services not received if they report the loss within 60 days after the charge is listed on their credit card statement.

  Note: Many tour operators, particularly those offering trips to remote or high-risk areas, include insurance in the cost of the trip or can arrange insurance policies through a partnering provider, a convenient and often cost-effective way for the traveler to obtain insurance. Make sure the tour company is a reputable one, however: Some experts suggest you avoid buying insurance from the tour or cruise company you're traveling with, saying it's better to buy from a third-party insurer than to put all your money in one place.

✔ Most health plans (including Medicare and Medicaid) do not provide **medical insurance** coverage for travel overseas, and the ones that do often require you to pay for services up front and reimburse you only after you return home. Even if your plan does cover overseas treatment, most out-of-country hospitals make you pay your bills up front and send you a refund only after you return home and file the necessary paperwork with your insurance company. As a safety net, you may want to buy travel medical insurance, particularly if you're traveling to a remote or high-risk area where emergency evacuation is a possible scenario. If you require additional medical insurance, try **MEDEX Assistance** (☎ **800-537-2029;** www.medexassist.com) or **Travel Assistance International** (☎ **800-821-2828;** www.travelassistance.com).

✔ **Lost luggage insurance** is not necessary for most travelers. On international flights (including U.S. portions of international trips), baggage coverage is limited to approximately $9.07 per pound, up to approximately $635 per checked bag. If you plan to check items more valuable than the standard liability, see if your valuables are covered by your homeowner's policy, or get baggage insurance as part of your comprehensive travel-insurance package; the BagTrak product is included in Travel Guard International's travel insurance packages (☎ **800-826-1300;** www.travelguard.com). Don't buy insurance at the airport, as it's usually overpriced. Be sure to take any valuables or irreplaceable items with you in your carry-on luggage, as many valuables (including books, money, and electronics) aren't covered by airline policies.

If your luggage is lost, immediately file a lost-luggage claim at the airport, detailing the luggage contents. For most airlines, you must report delayed, damaged, or lost baggage within four hours of arrival. The airlines are required to deliver luggage, once found, directly to your house or destination free of charge.

For more information on travel insurance, contact one of the following recommended insurers: **Access America** (☎ **800-284-8300;** www.accessamerica.com); **Travel Insured International** (☎ **800-243-3174;** www.travelinsured.com); **Travelex Insurance Services** (☎ **800-228-9792;** Mon–Fri 8 a.m.–8 p.m. Central time; www.travelex-insurance.com); and **InsuranceToGo.com** (☎ **877-598-8646;** www.insurancetogo.com).

Staying Healthy when You Travel

I know you're not going to get sick on this vacation, so feel free to skip over this section! Of course, the last time I checked, those nasty flu bugs weren't listening to me any more than they probably listen to you, so just in case you're bitten . . .

The French government pays 70 percent of the cost of doctor visits, and its national health insurance covers 99 percent of France's population. Visitors needing medical care in France find that same-day appointments are easily made, and patient fees are relatively inexpensive. Patients almost always have to pay up front, unless they're citizens of European Union countries with reciprocal medical arrangements. Some U.S. health insurance companies reimburse you for the cost of treating illnesses in foreign countries; make sure to keep all your receipts.

If you do get sick, ask the concierge at your hotel to recommend a local doctor — even his or her own doctor, if necessary. You can also call **SOS Medecins** (☎ 01-47-07-77-77), a 24-hour service. Ask for an English-speaking doctor. The **Centre Médicale Europe,** 44 rue d'Amsterdam, 9e (☎ 01-42-81-93-33; www.centre-medical-europe.com), is another good and efficient option. It has a host of specialists, and foreigners pay around 30€ ($48) for a consultation. If you're in urgent need of a dentist, try **SOS Urgences Stomatologiques et Dentaires,** 87 bd. Port-Royal (☎ 01-43-36-36-00).

Talk to your doctor before leaving on a trip if you have a serious and/or chronic illness. For conditions such as epilepsy, diabetes, or heart problems, wear a **MedicAlert identification tag** (☎ 888-633-4298; www.medicalert.org), which immediately alerts doctors to your condition and gives them access to your records through MedicAlert's 24-hour hotline. Contact the **International Association for Medical Assistance to Travelers** (IAMAT; ☎ 519-836-0102; www.iamat.org) for tips on travel and health concerns in the countries you're visiting, and lists of local, English-speaking doctors. The United States **Centers for Disease Control and Prevention** (☎ 800-232-4636; www.cdc.gov) provides up-to-date information on health hazards by region or country and offers tips on food safety.

Staying Connected by Cellphone or E-mail

The three letters that define much of the world's **wireless capabilities** are GSM (Global System for Mobiles), a big, seamless network that makes for easy cross-border cellphone use throughout Europe and dozens of other countries worldwide. In the United States, T-Mobile, AT&T Wireless, and Verizon use this quasi-universal system; in Canada, Microcell uses GSM, and all Europeans and most Australians use GSM.

If your cellphone is on a GSM system, you can make and receive calls across civilized areas on much of the globe, from Andorra to Uganda. Just call your wireless operator and activate *international roaming* on your account. Unfortunately, per-minute charges can be high — usually $1 to $1.50 in Western Europe and up to $5 in such places as Russia and Indonesia.

That's why it's important to buy an *unlocked* world phone from the get-go. Many cellphone operators sell *locked* phones that restrict you from using any other removable computer memory phone chip card (called a **SIM card**) other than the ones they supply. Having an unlocked phone allows you to install a cheap, prepaid SIM card (found at a local retailer) in your destination country. (Show your phone to the salesperson; not all phones work on all networks.) You get a local phone number — and much, much lower calling rates. Getting an already locked phone unlocked can be a complicated process, but it can be done; just call your cellular operator and say you're going abroad for several months and want to use the phone with a local provider.

For many, **renting** a phone is a good idea. (Even owners of cellphones with international calling capabilities have to rent new phones if they're traveling to non-GSM regions, such as Japan or Korea.) Although you can rent a phone from any number of overseas sites, including kiosks at airports and at car rental agencies, I suggest renting the phone before you leave home. One good place is www.roadpost.com. You can rent a phone from them that starts at $59 for basic service (plus $1.45 per minute) in France. The phone comes with your own number, voice mail, call forwarding, adaptors and accessories for your travel destinations, and free 24/7 technical support. When you return home, just ship the phone back to Road Post in the prepaid envelope they provide. You can give loved ones and business associates your new number, make sure the phone works, and take the phone wherever you go — especially helpful for overseas trips through several countries, where local phone-rental agencies often bill in local currency and may not let you take the phone to another country.

In France, phone rental isn't cheap. You usually pay $40 to $50 per week, plus airtime fees of at least a dollar a minute. One option is www.mobirent.fr, a French company that specializes in phone rental and will deliver to your lodging. The phone and its accessories are accompanied by one of three pricing plans: first class, business class, or economy. Economy rates are 52€ ($83) for 90 minutes of calling in France, 162€ ($260) for 90 minutes of calls to North America, and 243€ ($389) for 90 minutes of calls to the rest of the world. With rates like this, it may be more prudent to just buy a cellphone in France. For under $100, you get a phone and accessories, and some free minutes — don't forget that unlike mobile phone services in the States, receiving calls and text messages in France is free, and you can still call most places in Europe or America at somewhat reasonable rates. Cellphone stores abound in Paris: the biggest are **SFR** (there's a branch at 125 rue de Rennes, 6e;

Métro: St-Placide), **France Télécom** (a central location is 46 bis rue de Louvre, 1e; Métro: Les Halles), and **Bouygues Télécom** (33 rue de Rivoli, 4e; Métro: Hôtel de Ville). The first two companies provide better quality service and less blackout periods, while Bouygues Télécom is generally cheaper. You can also ask about rental policies at these stores; however, at the time of this writing, these companies are ceasing to offer this service.

Accessing the Internet Away from Home

Travelers have any number of ways to check their e-mail and access the Internet on the road. Of course, using your own laptop — or even a PDA (personal digital assistant) or electronic organizer with a modem — gives you the most flexibility. But even if you don't have a computer, you can still access your e-mail and even your office computer from cybercafes.

It's hard nowadays to find a city that *doesn't* have a few cybercafes. Although there's no definitive directory for cybercafes — they are independent businesses, after all — two places to start looking are at www.cybercaptive.com and www.cybercafe.com.

Aside from formal cybercafes, most **youth hostels** nowadays have at least one computer you can use to get on the Internet. And most **public libraries** across the world offer Internet access free or for a small charge. You can always find a cybercafe near a college; in France the Latin Quarter abounds with them around rue des Écoles and boulevard St-Michel. Try Luxembourg Micro, 81 bd. St-Michel, 5e (☎ 01-46-33-27-98; Métro: St-Michel). Avoid **hotel business centers** unless you're willing to pay exorbitant rates.

If you plan to take a laptop to Paris, ask if your hotel has free or cheap wireless access. **T-Mobile Hotspot** (www.t-mobile.com/hotspot) serves up wireless connections at more than 1,000 Starbucks coffee shops nationwide and at the Starbucks locations in Paris. **Boingo** (www.boingo.com) and **Wayport** (www.wayport.com) have networks in airports and high-class hotel lobbies. **iPass** (www.ipass.com) providers also give you access to a few hundred wireless hotel lobby setups, in such Parisian hotels as Le Meridien Montparnasse and Holiday Inn Tour Eiffel. The companies' pricing policies can be complicated, with a variety of monthly, per-connection, and per-minute plans, but in general you pay around $30 a month for limited access — and as more and more companies jump on the wireless bandwagon, prices are likely to get more competitive.

If Wi-Fi is not available at your destination, most business-class hotels throughout the world offer dataports for laptop modems, and a few thousand hotels in the United States and Europe offer free high-speed Internet access using an Ethernet network cable. You can bring your own cables, but most hotels rent them for around $10. **Call your hotel in advance** to see what your options are.

Keeping Up with Airline Security Measures

Today security procedures at airports around the world mean longer waits in lines and getting to the airport earlier, especially for an international flight. Generally, you'll be fine if you arrive at the airport **one and a half hours** before a domestic flight and **three hours** before an international flight.

Bring a **current, government-issued photo ID** such as a driver's license or passport (of course you will need your passport if you are traveling to France). Keep your ID at the ready to show at check-in, the security checkpoint, and sometimes even the gate. (Children under 18 do not need government-issued photo IDs for domestic flights, but they do for international flights to most countries.)

Speed up security by not wearing metal objects such as big belt buckles and make sure to pack all liquids (this includes makeup, toothpaste, and so on) in your check-in baggage. If you have metallic body parts, a note from your doctor can prevent a long chat with the security screeners. Keep in mind that only ticketed passengers are allowed past security, except for folks escorting passengers or children with disabilities.

Travelers in the U.S. are allowed one carry-on bag, plus a "personal item" such as a purse, briefcase, or laptop bag. The Transportation Security Administration (TSA) has stabilized **what you can carry on** and what you can't. The general rule for carry-on luggage is that sharp things are out as are all liquids, including water bottles, gels, lotions, and any similar items (makeup, lipstick, and toothpaste, and so forth). Be sure to pack any of these items in your checked baggage or they will be confiscated. Baby formula, breast milk, and prescriptions are some of the exceptions to the rule (the name on the prescription must match the name of the passenger). To be safe, visit the TSA Web site at www.tsa.gov for a current list of restricted items.

Part III
Settling into Paris

The 5th Wave   By Rich Tennant

"Welcome to the Hotel de Notre-Dame. If there's anything else I can do for you, please don't hesitate to ring."

In this part . . .

*T*his section helps you get from point A to point B without wasting time and money. Better yet, it suggests great places to stay and tells you all you want to know about eating French-style and then directs you to some memorable eateries. Chapter 8 guides you from the airport to your hotel, describes the most popular neighborhoods, and tells you where to go for information once you're in Paris. Read Chapter 9 for reviews of the best accommodations in Paris — for all budgets. Chapter 10 proves that Paris is indeed a feast with an overview of the local dining scene, advice on how to trim the fat from your food budget, and recommendations for some of the best restaurants, brasseries, cafes, wine bars, tea salons, and sandwich places in the city. A handy index cross-references all the dining establishments by neighborhood, price, and type.

Chapter 8

Arriving and Getting Oriented

*T*he Paris experience begins for most on the plane, where announcements are made in English and French. For others it begins at the airport — with bi- and trilingual signs directing you to passport control and baggage claim. The airports are now mostly nonsmoking, but the smell of cigarettes remains, though faintly. Luggage carts are free! Depending on when you travel, you might experience long lines at passport control. People dress more formally than at home. It all may seem a little astonishing. But, the important thing is you've arrived! Now you can move on to the first item of the day — getting from the airport to your hotel.

Navigating Your Way through Passport Control and Customs

Most visitors to Paris land at Charles de Gaulle Airport. It's known as CDG and sometimes called Roissy-Charles de Gaulle. Nearly all direct flights from North America land at Charles de Gaulle. Bilevel Terminal 1 (Aérogare 1) is the older and smaller of the two terminals and is used by foreign airlines. Narrow escalators and moving sidewalks connect its podlike cement terminals. The bright and spacious Terminal 2 (Aérogare 2) is divided into halls A through F and is used by Air France, domestic and intra-European airlines, and some foreign airlines, including Air Canada.

A free shuttle bus *(navette)* connects Terminals 1 and 2. Signs in French and English in both terminals direct you to Customs, baggage claim, and transportation to the city. Staff at information desks are also on hand to answer questions.

Two lines are set up for passport control, one for European Union nationals and the other for everyone else. These lines can move quite quickly or horrendously slowly; it usually depends on the clerk checking your passport.

When passing through Customs, keep in mind that restrictions are different for citizens of the European Union than they are for citizens of non-E.U. countries. As a non-E.U. national, you can bring in 200 cigarettes or 100 cigarillos or 50 cigars or 250 grams of smoking tobacco duty-free. You can also bring in two liters of wine and one liter of alcohol of more than 80 proof. In addition, you can bring in 50 grams of perfume, and a quarter-liter of eau de toilette. Travelers can also bring in 175€ ($280) in other goods. (See Chapter 12 for what you're allowed to bring home.) Because you probably aren't going to need to make a claim, you should be waved through by an officer pretty quickly. Customs officers do, however, pull random travelers over to check luggage. Whenever that happens to you, don't be offended; be polite and as helpful as you can, and if you don't speak French, let them know by saying, *"Je ne parle pas français"* (zhe ne *parl* pah frahn-*say*).

 Regardless of the terminal, you need euro to get from the airport into Paris. You can find ATMs in the arrival areas of the airports along with *bureaux de change,* where you can exchange dollars for euro, but you're better off buying and bringing 300€ ($480) from your bank at home. Airport ATMs are notorious for being broken when you need them most, and the airport *bureaux de change* are just as notorious for their bad rates of exchange.

Making Your Way to Your Hotel

You can travel to and from the airports by several different means, and the amount of text here notwithstanding, they're all easy!

If you fly into Charles de Gaulle

Charles de Gaulle Airport (CDG) is located 23km (15 miles) northeast of downtown Paris. Transportation into the city is plentiful.

Taking a taxi

Probably the easiest, but certainly not the cheapest, mode of transportation to your hotel from the airport is by **taxi.** A cab into town from Charles de Gaulle takes 40 to 50 minutes, depending on traffic. The initial fare for up to three passengers is 2.20€ ($3.50) and rises .85€ ($1.35) for each kilometer between 10 a.m. and 5 p.m. Between 5 p.m. and 10 a.m., the standing charge remains the same, but the per-kilometer charge rises to 1.10€ ($1.80). An additional fee of 1€ ($1.60) is imposed for luggage weighing more than 5kg (11 lb.) or for an extra bag. If your French is poor or nonexistent, write down the name and full address of your hotel. The five-digit postal code is the most important morsel of information, because it tells the driver the arrondissement where to take you. Look up the code and check the meter before you pay — rip-offs of arriving tourists are not uncommon. Whenever you strongly think that you may have been overcharged, demand a receipt (*un reçu, ray-*soo), which drivers are obligated to provide, and contact the **Paris Préfecture of Police (☎ 01-53-71-53-71).**

The taxi stands at Charles de Gaulle are located at:

✔ **CDG Terminal 1:** Exit 20, arrivals level

✔ **CDG Terminals 2A and 2C:** Exit 6

✔ **CDG Terminals 2B and 2D:** Exit 7

✔ **CDG Terminal 2e and 2F:** Exit 1

✔ **CDG Terminal 3:** Arrivals level

Taking a shuttle

If you don't want to schlep your bags through Paris's streets and métro stations, taking an airport shuttle is definitely the way to go. Although more expensive than airport buses and trains, shuttles are much cheaper and roomier than taxis. And you can reserve a seat in advance and pay by credit card. **World Shuttle,** 13 rue Voltaire, 94400 Vitry-sur-Seine (☎ 01-46-80-14-67; www.world-shuttles.com), costs 26€ ($42) for one person, 17€ ($27) per person for two or more from Charles de Gaulle and Orly. The price per van (before 5:30 a.m.) is 70€ ($112) for two to four people.

PariShuttle (☎ 01-53-39-18-18; www.parishuttle.com) offers a similar service. You're picked up in a minivan at Orly or Charles de Gaulle and taken to your hotel for 27€ ($43) for one person, 20€ ($32) per person for groups of two to four people, and 17€ ($27) per person for five to eight people. The cost for children up to ten years is 10€ ($16).

Riding the rails

A good option when you're not overloaded with baggage and want to keep your expenses down is to take the suburban commuter train to the métro. **RER** (Réseau Express Régional) **Line B** stops near Terminals 1 and 2. Easy, cheap, and convenient, you can ride both to and from the airport from 5 a.m. to midnight Monday through Friday and 7 a.m. to 9 p.m. weekends.

Free shuttle buses connect terminals CDG 1 to the RER train station. You can pick up the free shuttle bus in CDG Terminal 1 by following the RER

Paris Neighborhoods

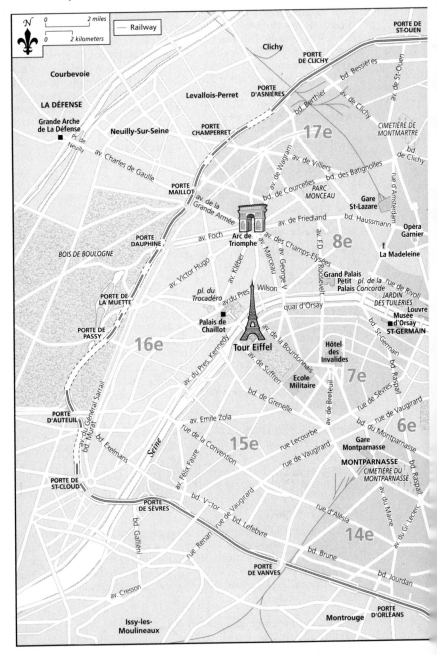

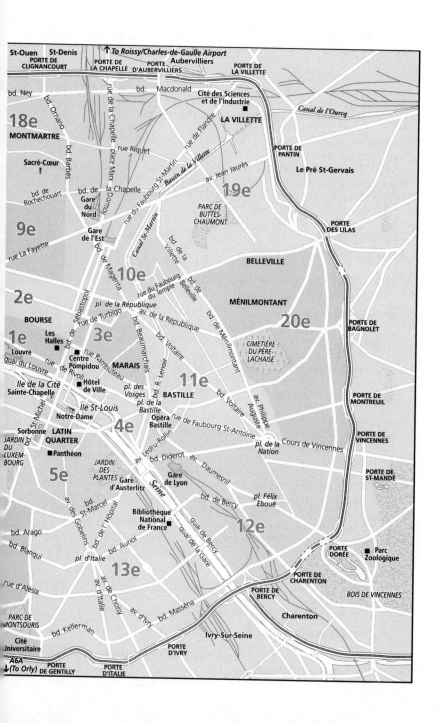

B logos (with a picture of a bus alongside) to the exit on the arrivals level. CDG 2 has direct access to the RER station; follow the round RER B logos.

Buy the **RER** ticket, which costs 8.40€ ($13) at the RER ticket counter and hang onto it in case of ticket inspection. (You can be fined if you can't produce your ticket for an inspector.) You will need your ticket later to get off the RER system and onto the métro.

Depending where your hotel is located, you exit either on the Right or the Left Bank. From the airport station, trains depart about every 15 minutes for the 40- to 50-minute trip into town and stop on the **Right Bank** at Gare du Nord and Châtelet-Les Halles, and on the **Left Bank** at St-Michel, Luxembourg, Port-Royal, and Denfert-Rochereau, before heading south out of the city.

Boarding the bus

A bus is better than the RER if:

- ✔ You're heading into Paris during off-peak driving hours, and you're not in a hurry.

- ✔ Your hotel is located near one of the drop-off points. *Note:* The bus is most convenient for the hotels I recommend in the 2e and 8e arrondissements. If you're staying outside these arrondissements, you can take a taxi from the shuttle drop-off point or board the closest subway if you aren't loaded down with luggage. If a bus isn't convenient, check out the door-to-door airport shuttle services in the earlier "Taking a shuttle" section.

If your hotel is located on the **Right Bank**, in the **8e, 16e,** or **17e** arrondissements, take Les Cars **Air France coach Line 2,** which stops at rue Gouvion Saint-Cyr at Porte Maillot before ending up at 1 av. Carnot at place Charles de Gaulle-Étoile, the name for the huge traffic roundabout at the Arc de Triomphe. The bus costs 14€ ($22) one-way and runs every 15 minutes from 5:45 a.m. to 11 p.m. You do not have to be a passenger on an Air France flight to use the service, and tickets are available in a small office next to the bus or from the bus driver. The trip from the airport into the city and vice versa takes about 40 minutes in light traffic, such as on weekend mornings. During weekday morning rush hour, however, the same trip can take twice as long. Pick up the coach from:

- ✔ **CDG Terminal 1:** Gate 34, arrivals level

- ✔ **CDG Terminals 2B and 2D:** Gate 6

- ✔ **CDG Terminal 2E and 2F:** Gate 3, arrivals level

If your hotel is located on the **Right Bank** near the **Bastille** (11e or 12e) or on the **Left Bank** in **Montparnasse** (14e), take the **Air France Line 4** coach, which stops at boulevard Diderot in front of the Gare de Lyon before ending up on rue du Commandant Mouchotte near the back of the Gare de Montparnasse. The bus costs 10€ ($16) one-way and runs every 30 minutes from 5:55 a.m. to 10:55 p.m. both to and from the airport. It takes about 50 minutes to get from the airport into the city in light traffic. Catch this coach from:

- ✔ **CDG Terminal 1:** Gate 34, arrivals level

- ✔ **CDG Terminals 2B and 2D:** Exit 6

- ✔ **CDG Terminal 2E and 2F:** Gate 3, arrivals level

Take the **Roissybus** if your hotel is on the **Right Bank** near the **Opéra** (2e or 9e). It costs 8.90€ ($14) and leaves every 15 minutes from the airport between 6 a.m. and 7 p.m. and every 20 minutes between 7 p.m. and 11 p.m. The drop-off point is on rue Scribe, a block from the **Opéra Garnier** near American Express. You can get to your destination in 45 to 60 minutes in regular traffic. Buy your tickets in the small office next to where the bus is parked or on the bus. Pick up this coach from:

- ✔ **CDG Terminal 1:** Gate 30, Arrivals

- ✔ **CDG Terminals 2A and 2C:** Gate 9 from Terminal 2A

- ✔ **CDG Terminal 2B and 2D:** Gate 11

- ✔ **CDG Terminal 2E and 2F:** Arrivals level

If you fly into Orly

Orly Airport, 14km (8½ miles) south of the city, has two terminals — **Ouest** (West) and **Sud** (South) — and English speakers find the terminals easy to navigate. French domestic flights land at Orly Ouest, and intra-European and intercontinental flights land at Orly Sud. Shuttle buses connect these terminals, and other shuttles connect them to Charles de Gaulle every 30 minutes or so. A tourist information desk is conveniently located on the arrivals level of both terminals.

Like Charles de Gaulle Airport, two lines are set up for passport control; one for European Union nationals, one for visitors carrying passports from all other countries, and you should be waved through Customs. (See the previous section, "Navigating Your Way through Passport Control and Customs" for information about what you can bring into France.)

Taking a taxi

A cab from Orly into Paris costs about 40€ ($64), depending on traffic, and takes anywhere from 25 minutes to an hour. The taxi stand at Orly Sud is just outside Exit M; at Orly Ouest it's at Exit I. The same advice as when taking a taxi from Charles de Gaulle holds true here: Write down the full name and address of your hotel for the driver. And remember that cabs charge 1€ ($1.60) for each piece of luggage put in the trunk.

Busing is best — sometimes

Take the Les Cars **Air France coach Line 1** if your hotel is located on the **Left Bank** near Les Invalides (7e). Buses leave Orly Sud at Gate L, and Orly Ouest at Gate H, arrivals level, every 15 minutes from 6:15 a.m. to 11:15 p.m. The trip takes about 30 minutes and costs 10€ ($16). You can request that the bus stop at Montparnasse-Duroc (14e).

The cheapest trip into town is on the **Jetbus.** You take this bus from Orly to Métro station Villejuif-Louis Aragon in south Paris (13e). It costs 6.40€ ($10) for the 15-minute journey. Beginning at 6:34 a.m., the bus leaves every 15 minutes from Orly Sud, Gate H, and from Orly Ouest at Gate C on the arrivals level. The bus departs Paris for Orly from 6:15 a.m. to 10:15 p.m.

Taking the train

If you're staying on the **Left Bank,** take the **RER C line** by catching a free shuttle bus from Gate Orly Sud and Gate G at Orly Ouest to the **Rungis** station, where RER C trains leave every 15 minutes for **Gare d'Austerlitz** (13e). A one-way fare is 6€ ($8) for the train for adults and 4.25€ ($5.68) for children. The trip into the city takes about 30 minutes, making various stops along the Seine on the **Left Bank.**

If you're staying on the **Right Bank,** you can take the **Orlyval/RER B line** to **Antony** Métro station (from Gate K in Orly South and Gate W in Orly West). You connect at the **Antony** RER station where you board the RER B train to Paris. Hold on to the ticket because you will need it to get into the métro/RER system. A trip to the Châtelet station on the Right Bank takes about 30 minutes and costs 6.10€ ($9.75) for the RER train and 7.40€ ($12) for Orlyval. Once in Paris, the train stops at **Denfert-Rochereau, Port-Royal, Luxembourg,** and **St-Michel** on the Left Bank, and then crosses to the Right Bank for stops at **Châtelet** and **Gare du Nord.**

Figuring Out the Neighborhoods

You arrive at your hotel, check in, and maybe unpack a little. But taking a nap prolongs your jet lag. So, go out and act like a Parisian by having a cup of coffee at a cafe before getting ready to explore.

The Seine River divides Paris into two halves: the **Right Bank** *(Rive Droite)* on the north side of the river and the **Left Bank** *(Rive Gauche)* on the south side of the river. The larger Right Bank is where you find the city's business sector, stately monuments, and high-fashion industry. The Left Bank has the publishing houses, universities, and a reputation as bohemian because students, philosophers, and creative types have been congregating here for centuries. Two of the city's tallest monuments are on the Left Bank — the **Tour Montparnasse** (that lonely tall black building hovering on the edge of the city) and the **Eiffel Tower.**

The city is divided into 20 numbered *arrondissements* (municipal districts). The layout of these districts follows a distinct pattern. The first (abbreviated 1er for *premiere*) arrondissement is the dead center of Paris, comprising an area around Notre-Dame and the Louvre. From there, the rest of the districts spiral outward, clockwise, in ascending order. The lower the arrondissement number, the more central the location. To get a better idea, consult the "Paris Neighborhoods" map.

Arrondissement numbers are key to locating an address in Paris. And this book lists addresses the way they appear in Paris, with the arrondissement number following the specific street address (for instance, 29 rue de Rivoli, 4e, is in the fourth arrondissement). Arrondissement numbers are noted on street signs and are indicated by the last two digits of the postal code. An address with a postal code of 75007 is located in the seventh arrondissement. Once you know the arrondissement in which an address is located, finding that spot is much easier. Numbers on buildings running parallel to the Seine usually follow the course of the river east to west. On north-south streets, numbering begins at the river.

Neighborhoods in the following sections are listed first by arrondissement, and then by neighborhood name. Only the better-known arrondissements — meaning the ones that you're most likely to stay in or visit — are mentioned here.

On the Right Bank

The following are the neighborhoods you're likely to visit on the Right Bank.

1er: Musée du Louvre/Palais-Royal/ Les Halles/Ile de la Cité

Traditionally, people consider the Right Bank to be more upscale, with Paris's main boulevards, such as **Champs-Elysées,** and museums such as the **Louvre.** One of the world's greatest art museums (some say *the* greatest), the **Louvre,** still lures visitors to Paris to the 1er arrondissement. You can see the contrast between many of the city's elegant addresses along the rue de Rivoli and arched arcades under which all kinds of touristy junk is sold. Walk through the **Jardin des Tuileries,** the most formal garden of Paris, and take in the classic beauty, opulence, and wealth of the **place Vendôme,** which is home to the Ritz Hotel. Browse the arcaded shops and view the striped columns and seasonal art on display in the garden of the **Palais Royal,** once the home to Cardinal Richelieu. The slightly seedy **Forum des Halles,** an above- and below-ground shopping and entertainment center, is also here.

This arrondissement tends to be crowded, and hotel prices are higher during Paris's high tourist season (in early fall) because the area is so convenient. Aristocratic town houses, courtyards, and antiques shops, flower markets, the **Palais de Justice, Notre-Dame Cathedral,** and **Sainte-Chapelle** (the chapel built in 1243 for St. Louis, famous for its gorgeous stained-glass windows) are also part of the 1er on Ile de la Cité, an island in the Seine. This is one of Paris's prettiest and most crowded neighborhoods, as is its sister island, Ile St-Louis (see "4e: Ile St-Louis/Centre Pompidou" below).

2e: La Bourse

Often overlooked by tourists, the 2e houses the **Bourse** (stock exchange), and some of the pretty 19th-century covered shopping passageways. The district, lying between the Grands Boulevards and the rue Etienne Marcel, is also home to the up-and-coming **Sentier** area, where the garment trade is located, and wholesale fashion outlets abound. Sex shops and prostitutes line parts of the rue St-Denis, but the nearby area known as Montorgueil has lined former seedy streets with upscale and trendy cafes and boutiques, turning the area into a desirable location and a nice tourist destination.

3e: Le Marais

Le Marais (translated as "the swamp") is one of Paris's hippest neighborhoods, and one of the city's most popular attractions, the **Musée Picasso,** and one of the more interesting museums, **Musée Carnavalet,** are located here. Paris's old Jewish neighborhood is located around the rue des Rosiers, and the rue Vieille-du-Temple is home to numerous gay bars and boutiques. Sadly, the hip boutiques that can pay the area's extremely high rents are beginning to crowd out the old stalwarts. Jo Goldenberg, the venerable Jewish deli, closed its doors in 2007.

4e: Ile St-Louis/Centre Pompidou

Aristocratic town houses, courtyards, and antiques shops, the **Brasserie Ile-St-Louis** (a historic brasserie with literary associations), **Berthillon** (reputed to be Paris's best ice cream), the **Centre Georges Pompidou museum,** and the **place des Vosges** make up the 4e arrondissement, which is located partly on the Ile St-Louis and partly in the Marais district. The area around the Centre Pompidou is one of Paris's more eclectic; you see everyone from pierced and Goth-style art students to chic Parisians walking their children to school to tourists buying football shirts from one of the many souvenir stores.

8e: Champs-Elysées/Madeleine

The 8e is the heart of the Right Bank, and its showcase is the **Champs-Elysées.** The Champs stretches from the **Arc de Triomphe** to the city's oldest monument, the Egyptian obelisk on **place de la Concorde.** The fashion houses, the most elegant hotels, expensive restaurants and shops, and the most fashionably attired Parisians are here.

9e: Opéra Garnier/Pigalle

Everything from the **Quartier de l'Opéra** (the neighborhood around the Opéra Garnier) to the strip joints of **Pigalle** falls within the 9e, which was radically altered by Baron Haussmann's 19th-century redevelopment projects; his Grands Boulevards radiate through the district. You'll probably pay a visit to the 9e to shop at its famous department stores **Au Printemps** and **Galeries Lafayette.** Try to visit the **Opéra Garnier** (Paris Opera House), if only to see the gorgeous ceiling by Marc Chagall.

10e: Gare du Nord/Gare de l'Est

In the movie *Amélie,* the young heroine likes to skip stones on the Canal St-Martin in the hip neighborhood of the same name with a burgeoning night scene, located here. Though most of this arrondissement is dreary (**Gare du Nord** and **Gare de l'Est** are two of the city's four main train stations), the canal's **quai de Valmy** and **quai de Jemmapes** are scenic, tree-lined promenades. The classic movie *Hotel du Nord* was also filmed here.

11e: Opéra Bastille

The 11e has few landmarks (though its Bastille monument is one of France's most well-known) or famous museums, but the area has become a mecca for hordes of young Parisians looking for casual, inexpensive nightlife. Always crowded on weekends and in summer, the overflow retires to the steps of the **Opéra Bastille,** where inline skaters and skateboarders skate and teens flirt. A market on the weekends on Boulevard Richard Lenoir across from the Bastille monument features the creations of more than 200 artists.

16e: Trocadéro/Bois de Boulogne

This area of Paris is where the moneyed live. Highlights include the **Bois de Boulogne** (the huge wooded park on Paris's western edge), the **Jardin du Trocadéro** (known for its famous fountains bordering the Eiffel Tower), the **Musée de Balzac,** the **Musée Guimet** (famous for its Asian collections), and the **Cimetière de Passy,** resting place of Manet, Talleyrand, Giraudoux, and Debussy. One of the largest arrondissements, the 16e is known today for its exclusivity, its BCBG residents (*Bon Chic Bon Genre,* or yuppie), its upscale rents, and some rather posh (and, according to its critics, rather smug) residential boulevards. The arrondissement includes what some visitors consider the best place in Paris from which to view the Eiffel Tower, the **place du Trocadéro.**

18e: Montmartre

The **Moulin Rouge,** the **Basilica of Sacré-Coeur** (the white domed structure on a hill overlooking Paris), and the **place du Tertre** (the square filled with restaurants behind it) are only some of the attractions in this outer arrondissement. Take a walk through the winding old streets here, and you feel transported into another era. The **Bateau-Lavoir,** Picasso's first studio in Paris, is also here. The city's most famous flea market, **Marché aux Puces de la Porte de St-Ouen,** is nearby in the 20e.

On the Left Bank

The following are neighborhoods you're likely to visit on the Left Bank.

5e: Latin Quarter

Bookstores, schools, churches, nightclubs, student dives, Roman ruins, publishing houses, and expensive boutiques characterize this district, which is called *Latin* because students and professors at the Sorbonne, located here, once spoke Latin exclusively. Stroll along **quai de Montebello,** inspecting the inventories of the *bouquinistes* (booksellers), and wander the shops in the old streets of rue de la Huchette and rue de la Harpe (but don't eat here; you can find much better places). The 5e also stretches down to the **Panthéon** and to the steep cobblestone rue Mouffetard behind it, where you can visit one of the city's best produce markets, eat at a variety of ethnic restaurants, or raise a glass in *très* cool Café Contrescarpe.

6e: St-Germain and the Luxembourg Gardens

The art school that turned away Rodin, the **École des Beaux-Arts,** is here, and so are some of the chicest designers around. But the secret of the district lies in discovering its narrow streets and hidden squares. Everywhere you turn here, you encounter famous historical and literary associations. For instance, the restaurant **Brasserie Lipp** is where Hemingway lovingly recalls eating potato salad in *A Moveable Feast,* and the **Café les Deux Magots** is depicted in the movie adaptation of Hemingway's *The Sun Also Rises.* The 6e takes in the **rue de Fleurus** where Gertrude Stein lived with Alice B. Toklas, and down the street is the wonderful **Luxembourg Gardens,** probably local residents' most loved park. (Try to find the Statue of Liberty in the garden.)

7e: Near the Eiffel Tower and Musée d'Orsay

The city's most famous symbol, the **Eiffel Tower,** dominates the 7e, and part of the **St-Germain** neighborhood is here, too. The **Hôtel des Invalides,** which contains **Napoléon's Tomb** and the **Musée de l'Armée,** are in the 7e, in addition to the **Musée Rodin** and the **Musée d'Orsay,** the world's premier showcase of 19th-century French art and culture. The Left Bank's only department store, **Le Bon Marché,** is also located here, and so is a warren of streets along which beautiful shoes, clothing, and household objects are sold.

13e: Butte-aux-Cailles and Chinatown

Although high-rises dominate much of 13e, a nightlife scene emerged around 2000 on barges along the **quai Tolbiac** (where the **Bibliothèque François Mitterand** sits) and in the cozy network of winding streets that make up the **Butte-aux-Cailles** (literally "hill of pebbles") neighborhood. The 13e is a lively hub for Paris's Asian community with Vietnamese and Chinese restaurants along **avenue d'Ivry** and **avenue de Choisy** next to stores selling all kinds of items from France's former colonies in Southeast Asia. The Chinese New Year Parade takes place here in late January or February.

14e: Montparnasse

Montparnasse is the former stomping ground of the *lost generation* — writers Gertrude Stein, Ernest Hemingway, Edna St. Vincent Millay, Ford Madox Ford, and other American expatriates gathered here in the 1920s. After World War II, it ceased to be the center of intellectual life in Paris, but the memories linger. Some of the world's most famous literary cafes, including **La Rotonde, Le Select, Le Dôme,** and **La Coupole,** are in the northern end of this large arrondissement, near the Rodin statue of Balzac at the junction of boulevard Montparnasse and boulevard Raspail. Some of those same literary giants (most notably Jean-Paul Sartre and Simone de Beauvoir) are buried nearby, in the Cimitière du Montparnasse. At its southern end, the arrondissement contains pleasant residential neighborhoods filled with well-designed apartment buildings, many built between 1910 and 1940.

Finding Information after You Arrive

The **Office de Tourisme et des Congrès de Paris** (www.parisinfo.com) has branches throughout the city at the following locations. *Note:* These centers are closed on May 1.

- ✔ **The welcome kiosk beneath the glass roofed terminal of the Gare du Nord,** 18 rue Dunkerque, 10e; open seven days a week from 8 a.m. to 6 p.m. (Métro and RER: Gare du Nord)

- ✔ **The Gare de Lyon Welcome Center,** 20 bd. Diderot, 12e; open Monday to Saturday 8 a.m. to 6 p.m. (Métro and RER: Gare de Lyon)

- ✔ **21 place du Tertre,** 18e; open daily 10 a.m. to 7 p.m. (Métro: Abbesses)

- ✔ **On the median strip facing 72 bd. Rochechouart,** Montmartre, 18e; open daily 10 a.m. to 6 p.m. (Métro: Anvers)

- ✔ **Carrousel du Louvre, beneath the Pyramide,** 99 rue de Rivoli, 1er; open daily 10 a.m. to 6 p.m. (Métro: Palais Royal/Musée du Louvre)

- ✔ **25 rue des Pyramides,** 1er; open daily from 9 a.m. to 7 p.m. from June 1 to October 31, 10 a.m. to 6 p.m. the rest of the year (Métro: Pyramides)

Getting around Paris

Probably your best introduction to Paris, and to the way the city is laid out, is from the north tower at Notre-Dame. You can see the magnificent cathedral from many parts of the city, and a visit helps you get oriented.

By métro

The best way to get around Paris is to walk, but for longer distances the
métro, or subway, rules. The **Métropolitain** is fast, safe, and easy to navigate. Open from 5:45 a.m. to 12:45 a.m., it's an efficient and cheap way
to get around. You may want to avoid it during rush hour, between 7 to
10 a.m. and 6 to 8 p.m. Operated by the RATP (Régie Autonome des
Transports Parisiens), the métro has a total of 16 lines and more than
360 stations, making it likely that one is near your destination. The
métro is connected to the suburban commuter train, the **Réseau
Express Régional** (RER), which connects downtown Paris with its airports and suburbs.

You can recognize a métro station either by an elegant Art Nouveau gate-
way reading *Métropolitain* or by a big yellow *M* sign. Unless otherwise
marked, all métro stations have a ticket booth, where a single ticket costs
1.45€ ($2.40) or a group of ten tickets called a *carnet* (kar-*nay*) is 11€
($18). You can buy them from an attendant or, in most stations, from a
machine. Every métro stop has maps of the system; you can get portable
maps by asking at a ticket booth for *une carte* (oon *kart*). Near the exits,
you can find a *plan du quartier,* a very detailed pictorial map of the streets
and buildings surrounding the station, with all exits marked. A good idea
is to consult the *plan du quartier* before you exit the system, especially at
very large stations. You may want to use a different exit to reach the other
side of a busy street or wind up closer to your destination.

Navigating the métro is easy, and you'll be a pro in no time. Here's what
you do.

1. **Use the métro map on the inside front cover of this book to
   figure out which station is closest to you.**

   For example, if you want to go to the Louvre and are in your hotel
   in the Latin Quarter, say the Familia, check this book's hotel listing
   for its nearest métro station. That station, or your starting point, is
   Jussieu. Look at the métro map on the Cheat Sheet at the front of
   this book for the line containing the Jussieu station. (Each end of
   the lines on the métro map is marked with the number of the line.)
   The Jussieu station is on Line 7.

2. **Look for your destination station.**

   Look for your destination station, in this case the Louvre. You see
   that the Louvre has two stops: the Palais-Royal Musée du Louvre
   station on Line 7 and the Louvre Rivoli station on Line 14. Choose
   the Palais-Royal Musée du Louvre station, and you won't have to
   change trains.

3. **Enter the métro system through a turnstile with two ticket slots.**

   With the magnetic strip facing down, insert your ticket into the
   nearer slot. Your ticket pops out of the second slot. Remove it, and

either walk through a set of rubberized doors that briskly open on each side or push through a turnstile.

Keep your ticket with you until you exit the station. At any point while you're in the métro, an inspector may ask to see your ticket again. If you fail to produce it, you may have to pay a steep fine. When you ride the RER, or suburban rail, you must keep your ticket because you have to insert it into a turnstile when you exit the station.

4. **Make sure you're going in the right direction.**

   When you're past the entrance, look at your subway map and trace the line past your destination to its end. The station's name at the end of the line is the name of the subway train on which you'll be traveling; in the case of Line 7 the train is La Corneuve. To get back to your hotel from the Louvre, you take the train going in the opposite direction, marked Villejuif Louis Aragon and exit at the Jussieu station.

5. **Enter the train and exit at the station you want.**

   Blue signs reading *Sortie* mark all exits.

It's pretty easy. Suppose, however, that the métro line nearest to you doesn't directly go to your destination. For example, you want to go to the Arc de Triomphe from Jussieu, and the stop is Charles de Gaulle-Étoile. Find the Charles de Gaulle-Étoile stop on the métro map. You see that you can reach Charles de Gaulle-Étoile on Line 6 or Line 1. But you're on Line 7. You have to change trains. Changing trains is called a *correspondance,* or transfer.

To make a **transfer** *(correspondance),* follow these steps.

1. **Figure out which transfer station you need.**

   On your map, blank white circles indicate where a number of lines intersect. These circles denote *transfer stations,* where you can change subway trains.

   To figure out where you need to change from the 7 train to Line 1 or Line 6 (to get from Jussieu to the Arc de Triomphe), use the map to see where Line 7 intersects with Line 1 and with Line 6. Line 7 and Line 6 intersect at Stalingrad, opposite from where you want to go. But Line 7 and Line 1 intersect at Concorde, very close to Charles de Gaulle-Étoile. This is the train you want to take. To make sure you go in the right direction on Line 1, look on your map for the name of the station at the very end past Charles de Gaulle-Étoile. It's called Grande Arche de la Défense, and this is the name of the train you want to ride.

2. **Look for a bright orange *Correspondance* sign above the platform at the transfer station.**

Beneath it is a white sign that has the number of the line you can transfer to in a circle (in the example, Line 1).

3. Follow the direction the sign indicates for the line you want.

You eventually come to two stairwells leading to the platforms. Navy blue signs mark this area, indicating the train's direction and listing all the stops the train makes. Make sure you choose the stairwell leading to the train going in the direction you want — in the example, you want the train to Grande Arche de la Défense, so that you can exit at Charles de Gaulle-Étoile.

 The distances between platforms at the *correspondance* (transfer) stations can be very long. You may climb stairs, walk a short distance, only to descend stairs to walk some more. Châtelet is particularly long. Some lines are connected by moving sidewalks that seem to do nothing but make a very long walk a little less long. For those with limited mobility, take the bus or a cab.

The métro connects with the suburban commuter train, the RER, in several stations in the city. The RER operates on a zone fare system, but métro tickets are valid on it in the city. You probably won't go past the first two zones, unless you visit Disneyland on the A4 or Versailles on the C5. When you ride the RER, keep your ticket because you need to insert it into a turnstile to leave the station.

 The doors on most métro cars don't open automatically. You must lift a door handle or press a button to get on and off.

 Anyone who has ever been crushed on a Paris subway at rush hour can attest that commuters don't easily give up their places. If you step out of the train to let someone off, you may just be giving others on the platform the chance to squeeze in before you. Be polite, but stand your ground.

After the subway shuts down around 1 a.m., the RATP operates **Noctambuses** that run on the hour from 1:30 a.m. to 5:30 a.m. from Châtelet-Hôtel de Ville, but they don't cover every arrondissement. Check the maps at the entrance to métro stations to determine if a Noctambus services your destination. The bus has a distinctive yellow-and-black owl symbol, and tickets cost 2.70€ ($3.10).

 A ten-ticket carnet good for the métro and on buses is a good deal for 11€ ($18) because a single ticket costs 1.45€ ($2.40). You can purchase a carnet at all métro stations as well as *tabacs* (cafes and kiosks that sell tobacco products). The heavily publicized **Paris Visite** card offers free or reduced entry to some minor attractions and free souvenirs from others in addition to unlimited travel on métro and buses, but make sure the attractions that interest you are included on the list (ask for it at the ticket window first). Buy the **Paris Visite** (the regular pass covers zones 1 through 3, which include all of central Paris and many of its suburbs) if you're in Paris for only a day or two. At 8.50€ ($14) for one day or 14€ ($22) for two days (kids 4–11 pay half price; kids under four ride free), it's a good deal. However, the three-day 19€ ($30) and the five-day 28€ ($44) Paris Visites are a waste of money. Instead, purchase the Carte Orange (see below).

How long do you plan to be in Paris? If you plan to use public transportation frequently, consider buying the **Carte Orange.** It costs 16€ ($26) for zones 1 and 2 and 22€ ($35) for zones 1 to 3. You'll need to provide a passport-size photo. Bring one from home or visit a photo booth at one of the many Monoprix stores, major métro stations, department stores, or train stations, where you can get four black-and-white pictures for less than 5€ ($8). Make sure you buy the weekly Carte Orange, called *coupon hebdomadaire* (koo-*poh* eb-*doh*-muh-dare) and not the monthly *coupon mensuel* (koo-*poh men*-soo-ell). The card is valid Monday through Sunday and on sale Monday through Wednesday of the same week, and Friday through Sunday for the following week.

The weekly passes don't last exactly seven days from the date of purchase; they begin Monday mornings and end Sunday night. So if you pay for a full weekly pass on Saturday, it will only last two full days and you won't get your money's worth. Don't buy the Carte Orange *hebdomidaire* if you find yourself in Paris toward the end of the week.

Paris l'Open Tour is good for one or two days of unlimited travel around Paris on special open-air buses. It offers three hop-on/hop-off routes for 29€ ($46) for a one-day pass and or 32€ ($51) for a two-day ticket. Use your Paris Visite card to get the one-day ticket for 22€ ($35).

For more information on the city's public transportation, call the RATP's English information line (☎ **08-92-69-32-46** or 08-92-68-41-14 [.35€/55¢ per minute]; www.ratp.fr).

By bus

The bus system is convenient and can be an inexpensive way to sightsee without wearing out your feet. Most Parisian buses run from 6:30 a.m. to 8:30 p.m.; a few run until 12:30 a.m. Each bus shelter has a route map, which you want to check carefully. Because of the number of one-way streets, the bus is likely to make different stops depending on its direction. Main stops are written on the side of the buses with the endpoint shown on the front above the driver. Furthermore, the back of every bus shelter has posted large bus maps and smaller maps inside the shelter showing the specific bus route. Métro tickets are valid for bus travel, and although you can buy single tickets from the conductor, you can't buy ticket packages (carnets) on the bus.

Board at the front of the bus. If you have a single-trip ticket, insert it into the slot in the small machine right behind the driver. The machine punches your ticket and pops it back out. If you have a pass, show it to the driver. To get off at the next stop, press one of the red buttons on the safety poles; the *arrêt demandé* (stop requested) sign above the driver lights up.

Keeping the picks out of your pockets

Over the past few years, petty crime has been making a comeback in Paris, a city that is otherwise relatively safe. Anywhere you find a high concentration of tourists, you also find pickpockets — including in the métro, hovering around the lines outside the Eiffel Tower and Notre-Dame, and in the church and its bell tower. Keep an eye out for little bands of scruffy children, who often surround you, distract you, and make off with your belongings.

Your best bet is to use common sense. Be aware of the people around you at all times. Get a money belt. Women wear purses diagonally across the body with the flap facing the body. Make sure zipper purses are closed at all times. (In fact, zippered purses aren't recommended.) See Chapter 4 for what to do if you get pickpocketed.

The downside of taking the bus is that it often gets mired in heavy Parisian traffic, so I don't recommend it if you're in a hurry. And, like the métro, avoid the bus during rush hours when it seems *le monde* (the world) is sharing the bus with you.

Bus routes great for sightseeing include:

- ✔ **Bus 69:** Eiffel Tower, Invalides, Louvre, Hôtel de Ville, place des Vosges, Bastille, Père-Lachaise Cemetery

- ✔ **Bus 80:** Department stores on boulevard Haussmann, Champs-Elysées, avenue Montaigne *haute couture* shopping, Eiffel Tower

- ✔ **Bus 96:** St-Germain-des-Prés, Musée de Cluny, Hôtel de Ville, place des Vosges

By taxi

You have three ways to get a taxi in Paris, and I rank them in order of how successful they are.

- ✔ The best way to find a cab is by **phoning Alpha Taxis** (☎ 01-53 60 63 50) or **Taxis G7** (☎ 01-47-39-47-39). Keep in mind, however, that phoning ahead is more expensive because the meter starts running as soon as the driver commences the journey to get you.

- ✔ You can also **wait at a taxi stand** *(station de taxis)* marked by a blue Taxi sign. Depending on the time of day, however, you may wait in a long line of people, or a very limited number of cabs stop.

- ✔ Finally, you can **hail a cab,** as long as you're not within 60m (200 ft.) of a taxi stand. Look for a taxi with its white light illuminated, which means the cab is available. An orange light means the cab is occupied or on the way to a pickup. You may get a cab driver who refuses to take you to your destination; by law, a driver can do this only during his or her last half-hour at work. Be prepared, as well, for the selective vision of drivers, especially when you hail a cab. Don't be surprised to see a free taxi or two pass you by.

The initial fare for up to three passengers is 2.20€ ($3.50) and rises .85€ ($1.35) for each kilometer between 10 a.m. and 5 p.m. Between 5 p.m. and 10 a.m., the standing charge remains the same, but the per-kilometer charge rises to 1.10€ ($1.80). An additional fee of 1€ ($1.60) is imposed for luggage weighing more than 5kg (11 lb.) or for an extra bag. A fourth passenger incurs a 2.85€ ($4.55) charge. Common practice is to tip your driver 10 percent to 15 percent on longer journeys when the fare exceeds 15€ ($24); otherwise round up the charge and give the driver the change.

By car

Streets are narrow, parking is next to impossible, and nerve, skill, ruthlessness, and a knowledgeable copilot are required if you insist on driving in Paris. I *strongly* recommend that you don't. (If you must drive in Paris, do it in Aug when residents are away on vacation, and traffic is lighter.)

A few tips: Get an excellent street map and ride with another person; traffic moves so lightning-fast you don't have time to think at intersections. You must pay to park Monday to Saturday, 9 a.m. to 7 p.m. Parking is free on Sundays and public holidays; during August certain streets offer free parking (look for yellow stickers on the parking meters). Street parking is limited to two hours and fees start at 1€ ($1.60) an hour on Paris's outskirts, to 3€ ($4.80) in central Paris. Note that meters do not accept coins and only take the Paris Carte card, available in *tabacs* for 10€ ($16) to 30€ ($48). After inserting the Paris Carte, the meter issues a ticket to be placed on the windshield.

Drivers and all passengers must wear seat belts. Children under 12 must ride in the back seat. Drivers are supposed to yield to the car on the right, except where signs indicate otherwise, as at traffic circles.

 Watch for the *gendarmes* (police officers), who lack patience and who consistently contradict the traffic lights. Horn blowing is frowned upon except in emergencies. Flash your headlights instead.

By bicycle

The banks of the Seine are closed to cars and open to pedestrians and cyclists March to November each Sunday from 10 a.m. to 5 p.m. It may not make much of a dent in the air quality, but bicycling is a fun and healthy way to spend a Sunday afternoon.

Paris Mayor Bertrand Delanoe scored a huge hit in 2007 with the introduction of Velib', the low-cost bike rental program. Over 20,000 bikes are available for as little as 1€ per hour ($1.60) in an effort to encourage more cycling and less pollution. Bike rental stands are located all over the city, pedallers use a credit card or buy a Velib' pass to rent the bikes which can be returned to any stand around the city. The Paris Respire (Paris Breathes) campaign shuts off certain streets every Sunday all year long for bikers, runners, strollers, and inline skaters. The main routes run north-south from the Bassin de La Villette along the Canal St-Martin through the Left Bank and east-west from Château de Vincennes to the Bois de Boulogne and its miles of bike lanes.

For more information and a bike map, pick up the *Plan Vert* from the tourist office. (For bike tours of the city, see Chapter 11.)

Paris à pied (on foot)

Paris is one of the prettiest cities in the world for strolling, and getting around on foot is probably the best way to really appreciate the city's character. The best walking neighborhoods are **St-Germain-des-Prés** on the Left Bank and the **Marais** on the Right Bank, both of which are filled with romantic little courtyards, wonderful boutiques, and congenial cafes and watering holes. The **quays of the Seine,** as well as its bridges, are also lovely, especially at sunset when the sun fills the sky with a pink glow that's reflected on the water. And try not to miss the pretty Canal St-Martin with its arched bridges and locks in the 10e, featured in the movies *Amélie* and *Hôtel du Nord* or the tiny streets off the Montmartre *butte* (hill).

 Take special care when crossing streets, even when you have the right of way. The number-one rule of the road in France is that whoever is coming from the right side has the right of way. Drivers often make right turns without looking, even when faced with pedestrians at crosswalks. And don't ever attempt to cross a traffic circle if you're not on a crosswalk. The larger roundabouts, such as the one at the Arc de Triomphe, have pedestrian tunnels.

Chapter 9

Checking in at Paris's Best Hotels

*P*art of the fun of traveling is waking up in a new place with unlimited opportunities for exploring! If this is your first trip to Paris, your expectations about what a hotel room should look like may be based on what you have seen in your own country. For those visiting from North America, one important thing to know is that rooms in Paris tend to be on the smaller side, even in expensive places (unless you opt for a modern chain hotel, which can lack charm, or ultra-deluxe lodgings). Parisian doubles are almost never big enough to hold two queen-size beds, and the space around the bed usually isn't big enough for more than a desk and perhaps a chest of drawers. The story is the same in London, Rome, and most other continental capitals where buildings date back two, three, four, or more centuries, when everything was smaller.

Parisian hotels also vary widely in their plumbing arrangements. Some units come equipped with only a sink; others may also have a toilet and either a shower or tub. Private bathrooms with tubs often have hand-held shower devices, and some shower stalls don't have curtains (the water often drains into a grate in the floor). The trend is toward renovating small hotels by installing a small shower, toilet, and sink in each room, but don't count on having *all* these amenities in your room unless you're in a pricier hotel.

Acoustics tend to be unpredictable in old Parisian hotels. Your quarreling neighbors may compete with street noise for the prize of most annoying, so bring earplugs for the neighbors, or ask for a room in the rear of the hotel to avoid the street noise. Another point to remember: Most budget hotels in Paris don't have air-conditioning, so consider this if you're visiting in July or August.

Getting to Know Your Options

More than 2,200 hotels are located in Paris — chain hotels, deluxe palacelike accommodations, hotels that cater to business travelers, budget hotels, and mom-and-pop establishments.

The French government grades hotels with a star system, ranging from one star for a simple motel or inn to four stars for a deluxe hotel. Moderately priced hotels usually get two or three stars. This system is based on a complex formula of room sizes, facilities, plumbing, elevators, dining options, renovations, and so on.

To find the hotel that's right for you, you need to weigh five variables: price, location, room size, amenities, and — the least tangible, but perhaps most desired of them all — a charming Parisian ambience. If the first variable, price, poses no problem, then you can have it all: great location, huge room, super perks, and sumptuous surroundings. Most travelers, however, need to make some compromises.

Before committing to a hotel, keep in mind that Paris offers additional options for lodging — renting an apartment, for example. Nothing beats living in Paris as a Parisian. In your own **apartment,** you can cook with fresh and unusual ingredients from the local green markets, taste fine wines that would be too expensive in a restaurant, and entertain new friends. Although the daily rate can be higher than a budget hotel, the room will be larger, you can save money on meals, and in the end, you may end up paying the same rate you would for room and board at a hotel — or less.

The most practical way to rent an apartment is through an agency. Most agencies require a seven-day minimum stay and offer discounts for longer stays. I've found that apartments vary quite a bit in size, location, and amenities. At the bottom end — for about 100€ ($160) per day — you'll find yourself in either a small, centrally located studio, or a larger studio in a neighborhood a bit far from the center of Paris. Studio apartments usually feature a convertible couch; an armchair or two; a bathroom with a tub or shower; and a tiny kitchenette with a refrigerator, stove, coffeemaker, and maybe a microwave. Dishes, cutlery, pots and pans, telephone, TV, iron, vacuum cleaner, linens, and sometimes a washing machine are also provided. Pay a bit more — around 200€ ($320) per day — and you get a more centrally located one-bedroom apartment. As with anything else, higher prices pay for larger, more luxurious spaces.

You can find many rental agencies online and comparison shop among them. Companies offering attractive apartments at reasonable prices are **Apartment Living in Paris** (www.apartment-living.com) which, at press time, advertised a 135m (450-ft.) two-room rental in the Latin Quarter for 100€ ($160) a night, and **Lodgis Solutions** (www.lodgis.com), which also rents apartments in New York, the French Riviera, and Marrakech, and at press time advertised a stylish one-bedroom in the upscale fourth for 750€ a week ($1,200). **Paris Vacation Rentals** (www.rentals-paris.com) is an agency that deals in short-term rental of upscale apartments at very good prices (a good-sized one bedroom near the Louvre was renting for 1,000€/$1,600 a week). A little more expensive is **New York Habitats** (www.newyorkhabitat.com), a New York real estate brokerage that rents flats in Paris and elsewhere as a sideline (a cozy Marais studio was renting for 370€/$590 per week). Check out **Bonjour Paris** (www.bonjourparis.com) for reviews and information about apartment rental agencies.

Keep in mind that this is a short-term apartment rental. You have to sign a contract and put down a security deposit, which may not be refunded if you damage the apartment in any way.

If the agency offers optional gift baskets or transportation to and from the airport, refuse them. The gift basket usually contains items you can buy more cheaply at the grocery store, and the transportation is usually twice as much as a cab.

If you bring the kids with you to Paris, your best option may be the *aparthotel*, a hybrid between an apartment and a hotel where you can have the autonomy of an apartment with some of the amenities of a hotel. You book an aparthotel just like you do any other hotel, through its Web site or phone number. And, like hotels, they have 24-hour reception desks, satellite TV, housekeeping services, kitchenettes, and laundry. For a family of four, a one-bedroom apartment is a good-value alternative to two double rooms in a cheap hotel. And if you use your kitchenette to prepare even half of your own meals in Paris, you can reap huge savings on your dining bill.

If you don't mind opening your house or apartment to others during your vacation, you might find that an **apartment swap** is your best bet. Several agencies will work with you for a small fee to advertise your residence and find a place for you to stay abroad. Check out **Home Xchange Vacation** (www.homexchangevacation.com) or **Home Base Holidays** (www.homebase-hols.com). It's almost always better to do an apartment swap through an agency which screens members so that you are protected from problems.

Finding the Best Room at the Best Rate

The *rack rate* is the maximum rate a hotel charges for a room. It's the rate you get if you walk in off the street and ask for a room for the night. But you often don't have to pay it! This section gives tips on finding the best rooms in Paris at the best rate.

Finding the best rate

At chain hotels (especially the American ones) and other luxury hotels, you can often get a good deal simply by asking for a discounted rate. Your odds of getting a reduced rate improve drastically if you're staying for more than a few nights.

Keep in mind that bartering for a cheaper room isn't the norm at Paris's budget hotels. Small and privately owned, owners post their rates in the reception area and are not willing to negotiate. To be fair, they may not be able to afford to let rooms go for less.

Room rates change with the seasons as occupancy rates rise and fall. In Paris, summer is low season. Yes, you're reading that correctly: Room rates tend to be lower in July and August, which is typically when the French flee the big cities for the beaches and the mountains. November and December are also low season, but early fall is high season, with October, in particular, heavy with conventioneers, making it difficult to find a room. If a hotel is close to full, it's less likely to extend discount rates.

Prices for the hotels recommended here are designated with dollar signs; Table 9-1 explains how this works. In a nutshell, the more dollar signs you see, the more expensive the hotel. The number of dollar signs corresponds to the hotel's rack rates (full rate), from the cheapest double room in low season to the most expensive in high season. The most noticeable difference between budget hotels and the most expensive hotels is better amenities and services, followed by a more luxurious décor. None of the recommended hotels listed in this chapter is a dump; the places are decent and reputable. Naturally, the luxury level in a 1,000€ ($1,200) room is substantially higher than in a 100€ one ($160).

Table 9-1: Key to Hotel Prices

Dollar Sign(s)	Price Range	What to Expect
$	Less than 100€ ($160)	These accommodations are relatively simple and inexpensive. Rooms are likely to be small, and televisions are not necessarily provided. Parking is not provided but is rather catch-as-you-can on the street.
$$	101€–150€ ($162–$240)	A bit classier, these midrange accommodations offer more room, more extras (such as irons, hair dryers, a trouser press, cable or satellite TV, and Wi-Fi access), and a more convenient location than the preceding category.

Dollar Sign(s)	Price Range	What to Expect
$$$	151€–300€ ($242–$480)	Higher-class still, these accommodations are on the plush side with chocolates on your pillow, a classy restaurant, room service, good-quality toiletries, and maybe a view of the Eiffel Tower or another landmark.
$$$$	Above 300€ ($480+)	These top-rated accommodations come with luxury amenities such as on-premise spas, deluxe toiletries, stereo and DVD players, multi-starred gourmet restaurants with room service, views, robes — frankly nearly every luxury you can imagine but you pay for them.

Room prices are subject to change without notice, so the rates quoted in this book may be different from the actual rate you receive when you make your reservation. Be sure to mention membership in AAA, AARP, frequent-flier programs, and any other corporate rewards programs you belong to when making your reservation at a chain hotel. You never know when it may be worth a few dollars off your room rate. Family-run establishments rarely have arrangements with large organizations.

Keep this advice in mind when you're trying to save money on a room.

✔ A **travel agent** may be able to negotiate a better price at top hotels than you can get yourself. (The hotel gives the agent a discount for steering business its way.)

✔ Always ask if the hotel offers any **weekend specials,** which typically require you to stay two nights (either Fri–Sat or Sat–Sun). In Paris, you can find this kind of deal from September through March at almost all price levels.

✔ A *forfait* (fohr-feh) is a discount that requires you to stay a certain number of nights — perhaps a minimum of three or five. Sometimes something else is thrown in (like a bottle of champagne) to sweeten the deal. If you're going to be in Paris for more than three days, always ask if there's a *forfait,* and then pick the hotel with the best deal.

✔ Don't forget about **package deals** (see Chapter 5) that include airfare, hotel, and transportation to and from the airport.

✔ Look on the **Internet** for deals (see below).

Surfing the Web for hotel deals

Although the major travel booking sites (such as Travelocity, Orbitz, Expedia, and Cheap Tickets; see Chapter 5 for details) offer hotel booking, using a site devoted primarily to lodging can be best because you may find properties that aren't listed on more general online travel agencies. The **Paris Convention and Visitors Bureau** (www.parisinfo.com) gives detailed information on hotels and other lodging they sanction and provides links to accommodations reservation centers (but the Web site doesn't tell you about special rates). Some lodging sites specialize in a particular type of accommodation, such as bed-and-breakfast accommodations, which you won't find on the more mainstream booking services. Others offer weekend deals on major chain properties that cater to business travelers and have more empty rooms on weekends. And finally, some individual hotels will offer an "Internet bonus" for a reservation made on their personal Web site. Therefore, checking out some of the online lodging sites, many of which offer discounts, is in your best interest.

Hotel Discounts (www.hoteldiscounts.com) offers bargain room rates at hotels in more than two dozen U.S. and international cities. The service prebooks blocks of rooms in advance, so sometimes it has rooms — at discount rates — at hotels that otherwise are considered sold out. **TravelWeb** (www.travelweb.com) lists more than 16,000 hotels worldwide, focusing on chains such as Hyatt and Hilton, and you can book almost 90 percent of these online. **France Hotels Online** (www.france-hotel-online.com) offers detailed listings of independent hotels, apartments, and bed-and-breakfasts according to budget and neighborhood. **All Hotels** (www.all-hotels.com) lists 140,000 lodgings throughout the world. (The hotels on this site pay a fee to be listed.) **Places to Stay** (www.placestostay.com) lists inns, B&Bs, resorts, hotels, and properties you may not find anywhere else. **Hostelworld** (www.hostelworld.com) lists youth hostels and cheap hotel deals in Paris and major cities around the world and offers ratings written by former clients of the various accommodations. Budget travelers can find excellent deals here.

Arriving Without a Reservation

If you arrive in Paris without a reservation, you have two choices. You can pick up a phone and start dialing (after you purchase a phone card for public phones at the nearest *tabac,* a cafe or kiosk that sells tobacco products). Or you can walk into one of the branches of the **Paris Convention and Visitors Bureau** and let the multilingual staff make you a reservation. The main switchboard for any branch is ☎ **08-92-68-30-00** (.35€/55¢ per minute). Only the staff at three of the office's six branches offer reservations services, so call before you go. (*Note:* These centers are closed on May 1 and Dec 25.)

✔ The **Anvers** welcome center, on the median strip facing 72 bd. Rochechouart; open daily 10 a.m. to 6 p.m. (Métro: Anvers)

✔ The welcome kiosk beneath the modern glass roofed terminal of the **Gare du Nord,** 18 rue Dunkerque, 10e; open daily from 8 a.m. to 6 p.m. (Métro and RER: Gare du Nord

✔ The welcome kiosk at the **Gare de Lyon,** 20 bd. Diderot, 12e; open Monday through Saturday 8 a.m. to 6 p.m. (Métro and RER: Gare de Lyon)

Hotels with unsold rooms offer them through the Paris Convention and Visitors Bureau at rock-bottom prices, so you may get a three-star hotel at a two-star price. The staff will make a reservation for you on the same day that you want a room, free of charge, but it must be on a credit card or check card (which will act as a credit card while in a foreign country).

Note that during the summer season, you'll have to wait in a long line, and you aren't guaranteed a room.

Paris's Best Hotels

The thousands of hotels in Paris range from small alcove singles in historic buildings to the historic and palatial that anticipate a traveler's every need. But only around 50 are described here. The reason? You don't need an overwhelming, encyclopedic list of all the hotels, just ones that are right for you, and an equally right backup in case your first choice is booked solid. In compiling this list, the first step was considering the typical traveler's wish list. And for most of you, the main priority is location. Thus, the first criterion, though ruthless, was simple. **If a hotel isn't located in the first eight arrondissements, it isn't recommended in this book.**

The second concern was price. The most expensive category listed here, $$$$, contains hotels that cost more than 300€ ($480) a night, which is expensive by nearly anyone's standards. Only a few hotels described here fall into the $$$$ category because most travelers are on a budget. (For a complete rundown on the $ system, see Table 9-1.) Three-quarters of the hotels in this chapter rent doubles for less than 150€ ($240) night but nevertheless give you comfort, some nice amenities, and that *frisson* of Parisian character for which the city's hotels are known. And none of the hotels listed here is a dive.

Finally, a variety of neighborhoods between the first and eighth arrondissements is represented here with a nice range of styles from conservative to trendy. The aim? I want to make sure that everyone is accounted for, regardless of budget, taste, or style of travel.

In this chapter, two maps pinpoint the locations of the hotels: "Hotels in the Heart of the Right Bank" and "Hotels in the Heart of the Left Bank." Reviews are arranged alphabetically for easy reference. Hotels that are

Hotels in the Heart of the Right Bank (1–4, 8–12, and 16–18)

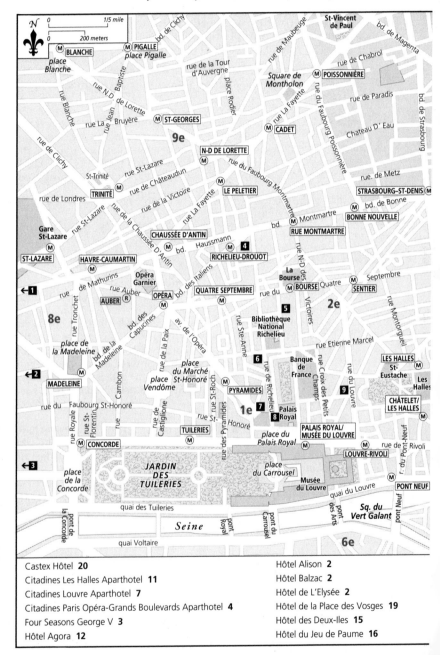

Castex Hôtel **20**

Citadines Les Halles Aparthotel **11**

Citadines Louvre Aparthotel **7**

Citadines Paris Opéra-Grands Boulevards Aparthotel **4**

Four Seasons George V **3**

Hôtel Agora **12**

Hôtel Alison **2**

Hôtel Balzac **2**

Hôtel de L'Elysée **2**

Hôtel de la Place des Vosges **19**

Hôtel des Deux-Iles **15**

Hôtel du Jeu de Paume **16**

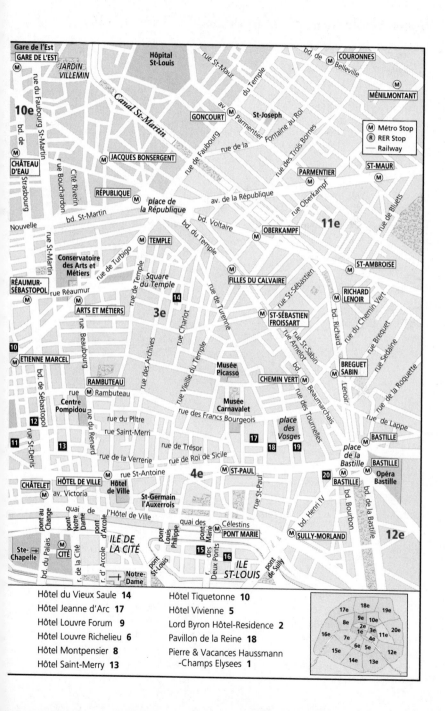

Gare de l'Est
GARE DE L'EST
Ⓜ
JARDIN VILLEMIN
Hôpital St-Louis
rue St-Maur
du Temple
bd. de Ⓜ Belleville
COURONNES
MÉNILMONTANT Ⓜ

rue du Faubourg St-Martin
Canal St-Martin
10e
bd. de
Strasbourg
CHÂTEAU D'EAU Ⓜ
rue Bouchardon
Cité Rivérin
JACQUES BONSERGENT Ⓜ
GONCOURT Ⓜ
av. Parmentier
St-Joseph
Fontaine au Roi
rue des Trois Bornes
rue de Faubourg
rue de la

Ⓜ Métro Stop
Ⓡ RER Stop
— Railway

RÉPUBLIQUE Ⓜ
place de la République
av. de la République
PARMENTIER Ⓜ
ST-MAUR Ⓜ
rue Oberkampf
rue de Bluets

Nouvelle
bd. St-Martin
bd. St-Martin
bd. Voltaire
OBERKAMPF Ⓜ
11e

rue St-Martin
RÉAUMUR-SÉBASTOPOL Ⓜ
Conservatoire des Arts et Métiers
rue Réaumur
rue de Turbigo
Square du Temple
TEMPLE Ⓜ
bd. du Temple
FILLES DU CALVAIRE
rue St-Sébastien
ST-AMBROISE Ⓜ
RICHARD LENOIR Ⓜ
rue du Chemin Vert
rue Bréguet

ARTS ET MÉTIERS Ⓜ
3e
rue de Temple
14
rue Charlot
rue de Turenne
ST-SÉBASTIEN FROISSART Ⓜ
rue St-Sabin
rue Amelot
bd. Richard
rue Sedaine

10
ETIENNE MARCEL Ⓜ
rue Beaubourg
rue des Archives
rue Vieille du Temple
Musée Picasso
CHEMIN VERT Ⓜ
bd. Beaumarchais
BREGUET SABIN Ⓜ
rue de la Roquette

bd. de Sébastopol
RAMBUTEAU Ⓜ
rue Ⓜ Rambuteau
Centre Pompidou
rue du Renard
rue du Plître
rue Saint-Merri
rue des Francs Bourgeois
Musée Carnavalet
place des Vosges
rue des Tournelles
rue de Lappe
BASTILLE Ⓜ

12
11
13
rue de la Verrerie
rue de Trésor
rue de Roi de Sicile
17
18
19
place de la Bastille
BASTILLE Ⓜ

CHÂTELET Ⓜ
HÔTEL DE VILLE Ⓜ
Hôtel de Ville
av. Victoria
rue St-Antoine
4e
ST-PAUL Ⓜ
rue St-Paul
20
BASTILLE Ⓜ
Opéra Bastille
bd. de la Bastille

quai de
l'Hôtel de Ville
St-Germain l'Auxerrois
quai des Célestins
PONT MARIE
bd. Henri IV
bd. Bourbon
SULLY-MORLAND Ⓜ
12e

Ste-Chapelle
CITÉ Ⓜ
pont au Change
pont Notre Dame
pont d'Arcole
r. de la Cité
r. d' Arcole
ÎLE DE LA CITÉ
Notre-Dame
pont Louis Philippe
pont St-Louis
pont Marie
des Deux Ponts
15
16
ÎLE ST-LOUIS
pont de Sully

Hôtel du Vieux Saule **14**
Hôtel Jeanne d'Arc **17**
Hôtel Louvre Forum **9**
Hôtel Louvre Richelieu **6**
Hôtel Montpensier **8**
Hôtel Saint-Merry **13**

Hôtel Tiquetonne **10**
Hôtel Vivienne **5**
Lord Byron Hôtel-Residence **2**
Pavillon de la Reine **18**
Pierre & Vacances Haussmann -Champs Elysees **1**

17e 18e 19e
8e 9e 10e
16e 2e 20e
1e 3e 11e
7e 4e
6e 5e 12e
15e
14e 13e

Hotels in the Heart of the Left Bank (5–7 and 13–14)

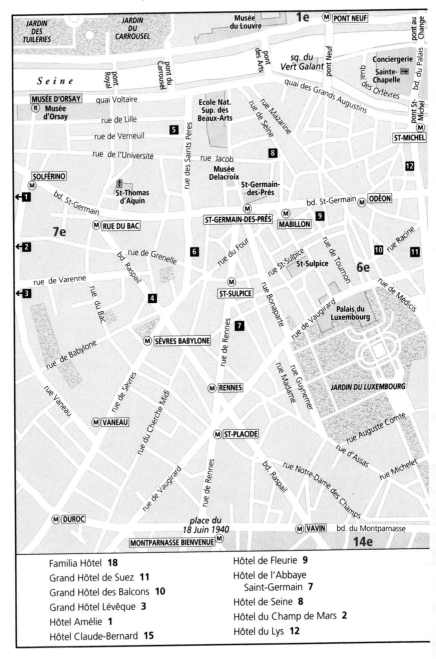

Familia Hôtel **18**
Grand Hôtel de Suez **11**
Grand Hôtel des Balcons **10**
Grand Hôtel Lévêque **3**
Hôtel Amélie **1**
Hôtel Claude-Bernard **15**

Hôtel de Fleurie **9**
Hôtel de l'Abbaye
Saint-Germain **7**
Hôtel de Seine **8**
Hôtel du Champ de Mars **2**
Hôtel du Lys **12**

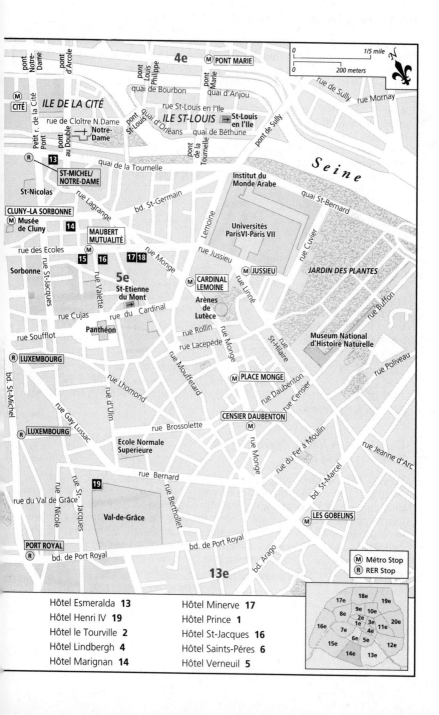

Hôtel Esmeralda **13**
Hôtel Henri IV **19**
Hôtel le Tourville **2**
Hôtel Lindbergh **4**
Hôtel Marignan **14**
Hôtel Minerve **17**
Hôtel Prince **1**
Hôtel St-Jacques **16**
Hôtel Saints-Péres **6**
Hôtel Verneuil **5**

especially good for families are designated with the kid-friendly icon. Listed immediately beneath the name of the hotel is the neighborhood in which it's located and the number of dollar signs corresponding to the hotel's rack rates, from the cheapest double room in low season to the most expensive in high season. At chapter's end are indexes of accommodations by price and neighborhood for easy reference.

Almost all hotels serve breakfast in some form. Note that a normal *petit déjeuner* (breakfast), also referred to as *continental,* will usually include coffee or tea, juice, a croissant, *pain au chocolat* (a croissant with a thin thread of chocolate filling) or similar pastry, and toast with various *confitures* (jams). If a hotel also offers *un petit déjeuner Américain* (American breakfast), it means they offer a buffet with eggs and meats — but you will pay for it.

Castex Hôtel
$$ Le Marais (4e)

The Castex is a popular budget classic, near *everything* in the eastern part of the Marais and the staff is friendly. Each large room has a writing table or a desk and chair; some have views overlooking the courtyard. The entryway opens onto to a wide and comfortable wood-beamed lobby with newspapers and seating for guests. Rooms have televisions, some are also wood-beamed. Reserve at least a month in advance. The rue St-Antoine is a half-block away and offers some good cheap shopping and a variety of places to eat.

See map p.106. 5 rue Castex. ☎ *01-42-72-31-52. Fax: 01-42-72-57-91.* www.castex-paris-hotel.com. *Métro: Bastille or Sully-Morland. Rates: 120€ ($198) single; 150€ ($240) double or twin; 220€ ($350) triple. Breakfast 10€ ($16). AE, MC, V. Check Web site for promotions.*

Citadines Les Halles Aparthotel
$$–$$$ Louvre (1er)

Staying here is like living in your own quiet high-rise apartment in the middle of Paris. With more than 85 rooms, visitors can choose from studios and one-bedrooms that have fully equipped kitchenettes, and services include a 24-hour reception desk, satellite TV, air-conditioning, housekeeping, baby-equipment rental, and laundry facilities. Located in the middle of a large pedestrian zone, this neighborhood is a bit dicey late at night, so if you're a single traveler, this hotel may not be the best bet.

See map p. 106. 4 rue des Innocents (91m/299 ft. from the Forum des Halles). ☎ *01-40-39-26-50.* www.citadines.com. *Métro: Les Halles. Rates: 140€–260€ ($224–$416). AE, MC, V.*

Citadines Louvre Aparthotel
$$$ Louvre (1er)

This seven-story aparthotel is in a terrific location in an upscale and pretty neighborhood just opposite the Comédie-Française and next to the Jardin du Palais-Royal. Once a students' residence, it has several studios (each with a double fold-out sofa) and apartments equipped for travelers with disabilities. Studios and one-bedrooms (a separate bedroom with two single beds and pull-out double sofa) have fully equipped kitchenettes, and services include a 24-hour reception desk, satellite TV, air-conditioning, housekeeping, baby-equipment rental, and laundry facilities. Book well in advance.

See map p. 106. 8 rue de Richelieu (1 block north of the Louvre). ☎ **01-55-35-28-00.** www.citadines.com. *Métro: Palais-Royal or Pyramides. Rates: 195€–315€ ($312–$504). AE, MC, V.*

Citadines Paris Opéra-Grands Boulevards Aparthotel
$$$–$$$$ Opéra (2e)

Around the corner from the Opéra Comique, the Musée Jacquemart-André, and the Comédie-Française and near the Grands Boulevards, this five-story aparthotel is the most central in the Citadines chain. It's located in a peaceful passage, and rooms come with fully equipped kitchenettes; available services include a 24-hour reception desk, satellite TV, Internet, air-conditioning, baby-equipment rental, dry cleaning, laundry facilities, housekeeping, bar, billiard table, and fitness center. A one-bedroom apartment here (two single beds in the bedroom, a double pull-out couch) can be a good alternative to renting two rooms in a cheap hotel because cooking in the kitchenette saves on your dining costs.

See map p. 106. 18 rue Favart. ☎ **01-40-15-14-00.** www.citadines.fr. *Métro: Richelieu-Drouot. Rates: 125€–145€ ($200–$231) per night one–six days, for a two-person studio; 260€–290€ ($416–$464) one–six days, for a three-person duplex (one bedroom) apartment; 295€–315€ ($472–$504) per night one–six days, four-person (one bedroom) apartment. AE, MC, V.*

Familia Hôtel
$–$$ Latin Quarter (5e)

This hotel has many repeat visitors and no wonder — the rooms have been painstakingly restored with either provincial-inspired wallpaper or frescoes painted by students from l'École des Beaux-Arts (Paris's best art school). The cozy lobby exudes the atmosphere of a tiny castle with rich tapestries, a winding staircase, and frescoed walls. Some rooms have balconies (numbers 22, 23, 52, 53, 61, 62, 65) with captivating views of the Latin Quarter. From the fifth and sixth floors, you can see Notre-Dame. Bathrooms are small but modern and tiled. All rooms have cable TV and hair dryers. The staff provides kid-friendly services (such as bottle heating) and larger rooms for the weary traveler who requests ahead. Take note that most rooms in the hotel are on the small side, and the least expensive doubles in the corners are tiny. No air-conditioning is provided — remember that it can get hot in Paris heat waves.

See map p. 108. 11 rue des Écoles. ☎ *01-43-54-55-27. Fax: 01-43-29-61-77.* www. hotel-paris-familia.com. *Métro: Cardinal Lemoine or Jussieu. Parking: 20€ ($32). Rates: 81€–92€ ($130–$147) single; 92€–104€ ($147–$166) double; 144€ ($230) triple; 161€ ($258) quad; 112€ ($179) single or double with balcony. Breakfast 6€ ($9.60). AE, DC, MC, V.*

Four Seasons George V
$$$$ Champs-Elysées (8e)

This is one of Paris's truly legendary palace hotels combining the old (Murano chandeliers and Louis XIV tapestries) with a sleek, light-wood-and-marble lobby opening onto an outside marble courtyard decorated with bright blue awnings and umbrellas. A team of concierges greet guests staying in 245 large rooms, separated from the public corridors by their own hallways for more peace and quiet. Louis XVI–style furniture, marble bathrooms, stereo systems, DVD players, and wireless Internet access are the norm. The Honeymoon Suite has three terraces, and other suites offer a stone's-throw view of the Eiffel Tower — some from their bathtubs. Amenities include the signature Four Season mattresses (930 coils instead of the industry-standard 800), a spa (with its own elevator) offering 24-hour massages and a huge pool, an American bar, and multi-starred restaurant, Le Cinq (reviewed in Chapter 10). Check online for package deals.

See map p. 106. 31 av. George V, 1½ blocks from the Champs-Elysées. ☎ *01-49-52-70-00. Fax: 01-49-52-70-10. Métro: George V. Rates: 695€–990€ ($1,112–$1,584) double; 1,450€–11,000€ ($2,320–$17,600) suite. Continental breakfast at Le Cinq 36€ ($58); American breakfast 48€ ($77). AE, DC, MC, V.*

Grand Hôtel des Balcons
$$–$$$ St-Germain-des-Prés (6e)

Steps from Théâtre de l'Odéon is this gracious and comfortable hotel with balconied rooms, modern light oak furnishings, bright fabrics, 19th-century stained-glass windows, and Art Nouveau lobby furnishings (look for the voluptuous statue of Venus in the breakfast room). Although most rooms and their wrought-iron balconies are small and basic, clever use of space allows for full-length mirrors and some rooms have closets on the larger side. Bathrooms are small to miniscule but well-designed. The higher-priced doubles, triples, and quads are bigger and luxurious; some have double-sink bathrooms. All rooms have satellite television and Internet access. If you opt to have breakfast here, it's a sumptuous and filling breakfast buffet. The Jardin du Luxembourg is a five-minute walk south.

See map p. 108. 3 rue Casimir Delavigne. ☎ *01-46-34-78-50. Fax: 01-46-34-06-27.* www.balcons.com. *Métro: Odéon. RER: Luxembourg. Rates: 65–85€ ($89–$116) single; 80–110€ ($110-$150) double; 160–200€ ($219–$274) triple. Buffet breakfast 10€ ($16). AE, DC, MC, V.*

Grand Hôtel Lévêque
$ Eiffel Tower (7e)

This 1930s-era hotel is just three blocks from the Eiffel Tower on a colorful pedestrian street bustling with the rue Cler market, bakeries, restaurants, a terrific crêpe stand, wine shops, and florists. The newly renovated lobby has a comfortable lounge area with a bar and fireplace and a brand-new breakfast room The snug rooms have new chic décor with small bathrooms in excellent condition, satellite TV, hair dryer, Internet access, and ceiling fan. Staff members are very friendly and helpful, and if you ask, they may be able to give you a higher-priced room on the fifth floor with a balcony and partial view of the Eiffel Tower. This hotel fills up fast, so book well in advance. Street-side rooms (which have good views) cost a little more than interior rooms; as always, check online for deals. *Note:* At press time, staff reported that the hotel was about to be wired for Wi-Fi.

See map p. 108. 29 rue Cler (where rue Cler meets rue de Grenelle). ☎ **01-47-05-49-15.** *Fax: 01-45-50-49-36.* www.hotel-leveque.com. *Métro: École-Militaire or Latour-Maubourg. Rates: 67€–72€ ($107–$115) single room without bathroom; 97€–120€ ($155–$192) double bed with bathroom; 97€–130€ ($155–$208) twin beds with bathroom; 137€–142€ ($219–$227) triple with bathroom. Breakfast 9€ ($14). AE, MC, V.*

Hôtel Agora
$–$$ Louvre (1er)

This is a very good find on a busy pedestrian street near Les Halles and has a traditional French air once you mount a curved staircase (after the initial climb, an elevator leads from reception to upper floors) to its eclectic reception area. Rooms have antique furniture, marble mantelpieces, floral prints, and old-fashioned wallpapers. If you want a room on the larger side, ask for 1, 2, or 6. The windows are double-glazed, thankfully, which helps muffle the outside noise. The bathrooms are decently sized; some have bathtubs and even bidets, an often confusing French charm, which is rarely offered at hotels with such reasonable prices. Fifth-floor rooms have balconies with views of the impressive St-Eustache Church.

See map p. 106. 7 rue de la Cossonnerie. ☎ **01-42-33-46-02.** *Fax: 01-42-33-80-99. Métro: Châtelet. Rates: 105€–134€ ($168–$214) single; 132€–157€ ($192–$251) double; 170€ ($272) triple. Breakfast 12€ ($19). AE, MC, V.*

Hôtel Alison
$$ Madeleine (8e)

This hotel has a retro 1970s ambience that somehow manages to be perfectly in tune with the classy neighborhood. The large, well-appointed rooms are furnished in modern style, with black furniture and light walls, and have plenty of storage space, a safe, minibar, trouser press, satellite TV, Internet access, and double-glazed windows. Hair dryers and upscale toiletries grace gleaming, tiled bathrooms with wall-mounted showers. You can relax on low, orange-leather couches in the plush lobby or enjoy a drink in the vaulted brick lounge. Breakfast is served under a vaulted stone ceiling. The hotel is located between the Madeleine and the Elysée Palace and near the Champs-Elysées and rue Faubourg St-Honoré

See map p. 106. 21 rue de Surène. ☎ **01-42-65-54-00.** *Fax: 01-42-65-08-17.* www. hotel-alison.com. *Métro: Madeleine or Concorde. Rates: 82€–94€ ($131–$150) single; 115€–168€ ($184–$269) double; 169€–188€ ($270–$301) triple; 209€–296€ ($334–$474) for two adjoining rooms. Breakfast 9€ ($14). AE, DC, MC, V.*

Hôtel Amélie
$ Eiffel Tower (7e)

This is a modest 16-room hotel bedecked with overflowing flower pots at each window. The rooms are small and basic with tiny closets, writing desks, minibars, and a downscale décor, but the tiled bathrooms offer hair dryers and good-quality toiletries. The location is excellent for seeing such seventh arrondissement sights as the Eiffel Tower and Napoléon's Tomb, yet the atmosphere is peaceful, almost serene. Stroll down nearby rue Cler for some great fruit and veggie markets or for an expert crêpe made by a lovely Greek *vendeur* who has been there for years. There is no elevator. The owners often have seasonal promotions; check the Web site for specials.

See map p. 108. 5 rue Amélie. ☎ **01-45-51-74-75.** *Fax: 01-45-56-93-55.* www.hotel amelie-paris.com. *Métro: Latour-Maubourg. Rates: 90€–115€ ($144–$184) single; 110€–130€ ($176–$208) double; 115€–130€ ($184–$208) twin beds. Breakfast 9€ ($14). Check Web site for special offers. AE, DC, MC, V.*

Hôtel Balzac
$$$$ Champs-Elysées (8e)

Just one quiet street from the Arc de Triomphe is this gorgeous jewel box of a hotel. Luxuriously renovated for 11 million€ in 2007, this is the place to stay if you want all the amenities of a palace hotel in a more intimate setting. Enjoy butler service; a bar, lounge, and tearoom; 24-hour room service; Molton Brown toiletries; in-room entertainment systems that include a wall mounted flatscreen TV, CD, and DVD player; ADSL and Wi-Fi; minibar; thick high-quality duvets and high-thread-count linens. The 278-sq.-m (3,000-sq.-ft.) Suite Royale (2,500€/$3,137) is the hotel's best, with its own 265m (883-ft.) terrace where one can dine with a beautiful view of the Eiffel Tower and soak in a Jacuzzi bath after a busy day of sightseeing.

See map p. 106. 6 rue Balzac. ☎ **866-672-2496** *in the U.S. or 01-44-35-18-00 in France. Fax: 01-44-35-18-05.* www.hotelbalzac.com. *Métro: Charles de Gaulle-Étoile. Rates: 420€ ($672) classic room; 470€ ($752) superior room; 520€ ($832) deluxe room; 790€ ($1,264) suite; 2,000€ ($3,200) Presidential Suite. Breakfast 28€ ($45), buffet breakfast 38€ ($61). AE, MC, V.*

Hôtel Claude-Bernard
$$–$$$ Latin Quarter (5e)

This is one of my highly recommended hotels because it keeps very high standards while keeping costs down. The inside features a lobby bar (but it's not manned by a regular bartender; you have to ask at reception if you want to be served), a lounge area with comfortable banquettes, and a two-person elevator. The decently sized rooms have warm and tasteful wallpaper, sleek bathrooms, minibars, Wi-Fi, satellite TV, decorative balconies with flowers, and often a well-preserved piece of antique furniture. Some particularly attractive suites come with couches and armchairs. A sauna is available for guests to use, and all rooms are air-conditioned. Nearby are the Panthéon, the Sorbonne, and the fantastic Cluny Museum. Check the Web site for promotions.

See map p. 108. 43 rue des Écoles. ☎ **01-43-26-32-52.** *Fax: 01-43-26-80-56.* www. paris-hotel-booking.com. *Métro: Maubert-Mutualité. Rates: 138€–168€ ($221–$269) single; 168€–208€ ($269–$333) double; 208€–288€ ($333–$461) triple; 258€–358€ ($413–$573) quad. Buffet breakfast 9.80€ ($16).*

Hôtel de Fleurie
$$$–$$$$ St-Germain-des-Prés (6e)

Just off place Odéon, the pretty Fleurie has every comfort, including air-conditioning, marble bathrooms with heated towel racks, quality toiletries, Oriental carpets, Wi-Fi, and satellite TV. The jewel-toned rooms are small but comfortable, and all are furnished in a modern or classic style with such touches as fresh flowers, pretty gingham curtains, and wood-paneled accents. Book at least six weeks in advance for one of the *chambres familiales* — two connecting rooms with two large beds in each room. Continental breakfast is served in the cozy vaulted stone cellar dining room; the homemade jams are sure to please. Located near the church of St-Germain-des-Prés, the historic Café de Flore, Les Deux Magots, and Brasserie Lipp, it's also a few blocks from the Seine and the Jardin du Luxembourg. Check the Web site for specials.

See map p. 108. 32-34 rue de Grégoire-de-Tours. ☎ **01-53-73-70-00.** *Fax: 01-53-73-70-20.* www.hotel-de-fleurie.com. *Métro: Odéon. Rates: 160€–200€ single ($256–$320); 210€–250€ ($336–$400) double with queen-size bed; 280€–350€ ($448–$560) deluxe rooms (large room with two twin beds or one king-size bed); 395€–450€ ($632–$653) family suite. Breakfast 13€ ($21); 7.50€ ($12) for children under 12. AE, DC, MC, V.*

Hôtel de l'Abbaye Saint-Germain
$$$–$$$$ St-Germain-des-Prés (6e)

This former convent on the Left Bank is a wonderful choice for travelers who aren't willing to spend deluxe hotel prices but still want elegance, tranquillity, and deluxe-quality service. Some of the 42 rooms and two- and four-bedroom suites have their original exposed oak ceiling beams, 19th-century-style furnishings, and damask upholstery; all are air-conditioned, with hair dryers and satellite TV. The rooms are a good size by Paris standards, and the suites are absolutely spacious. The style of décor is modern with funky bedspreads and framed drawings and prints of famous Andy Warhol creations. Some first-floor rooms open onto a vine-covered terrace. Rooftop suites also have terraces, and there is one fabulous duplex terrific for honeymooners. You can eat breakfast — included in the price of your room — in the flower-filled courtyard.

See map p. 108. 10 rue Cassette, four short blocks from the northwest corner of the Jardin du Luxembourg. ☎ 01-45-44-38-11. Fax: 01-45-48-07-86. www.hotel-abbaye.com. *Métro: St-Sulpice. Rates: 215€–251€ ($246–$366) standard double; 315€–367€ ($456–$587) large room; 395€–461€ ($504–$738) suite; 455€–519€ ($728–$830) duplex suite. Rates include breakfast. AE, MC, V.*

Hôtel de la Place des Vosges
$$–$$ Le Marais (4e)

The entrance to the place des Vosges is only steps away from this hotel which used to be the stables of King Henri IV. Now the exposed stone walls and beamed ceilings complement a somewhat dark and dusty, antiques-filled lobby. The small rooms have beamed ceilings, satin-cotton blend bed sheets with anti-allergen spreads, and tiled bathrooms. All rooms have satellite TVs, free Wi-Fi, safes, desks, and hair dryers, but there is a lack of storage space. The larger top-floor room (no. 10) has a pretty view over the Right Bank and a Jacuzzi, but the elevator stops a floor down, which is a consideration if you have a lot of luggage.

See map p. 106. 12 rue de Birague. ☎ 01-42-72-60-46. Fax: 01-42-72-02-64. www.hotelplacedesvosges.com. *Métro: Bastille. Rates: 90€ ($128) single, double, or twin beds with shower or tub; 95€ ($152) room with large bed and massaging shower head; 150€ ($240) top-floor room with loft, shower, and Jacuzzi. Breakfast 8€ ($13). MC, V.*

Hôtel de L'Elysée
$$$ Champs-Elysées (8e)

The Costes brothers bought this hotel in 2007, and at press time, hotel staff said everything was "up in the air." When I visited, I saw rooms with patterned wallpaper, built-in closets, half-headboards, and stucco ceilings. The wonderful, but small mansard suite no. 60 features wood beams overhead and skylights set into the low, sloping ceilings that provide peek-a-boo vistas of Parisian rooftops, including a perfectly framed view of the Eiffel Tower. All fifth- and sixth-floor rooms enjoy at least rooftop views, the former from small balconies (nos. 50–53 offer glimpses of the Eiffel Tower). (Take note that there are 15 steep steps from where the elevator stops to the top floor.) A pretty sitting room off the lobby welcomes guests with a small bar and fireplace, arched ceilings and period reproduction furniture give the hotel an air of charm.

See map p. 106. 12 rue des Saussaies. ☎ 01-42-65-29-25. Fax: 01-42-65-64-28. www.france-hotel-guide.com/h75008efsh.htm. *Métro: Champs-Elysées-Clemenceau or Miromesnil. Rates: 110€–225€ ($176–$360) double; 205€–245€ junior suite ($328–$392). Breakfast 12€ ($19). AE, DC, MC, V.*

Hôtel des Deux-Îles
$$$ **Île St-Louis (4e)**

This appealing jewel box of a hotel is superbly located on the Île St-Louis (practically in Notre-Dame's backyard). The owners are interior decorators, and it shows; the 17 rooms have exposed oak ceiling beams and provincial upholstery, and the lobby is a warm and cozy gem with fresh flowers and bamboo furniture. Off the lobby is a rock garden that some of the rooms overlook and a basement breakfast room with a fireplace. Although amenities include completely renovated bathrooms with hair dryers, cable TV, Wi-Fi, minibars, and air-conditioning, rooms are small, so if you have a large amount of luggage, you may want to look elsewhere. Paris's best ice cream shop, Berthillon (closed in Aug), is just around the corner, and you can find Berthillon ice cream in neighborhood brasseries, too. So much is nearby — the Memorial de la DéportationSainte-Chapelle; the Conciergerie; and the bird and flower markets on Île de la Cité, to name only a few — you may not know where to begin, so start early in the morning with Notre-Dame.

See map p. 106. 59 rue St-Louis-en-l'Île. ☎ **01-43-26-13-35.** *Fax: 01-43-29-60-25.* www. deuxiles-paris-hotel.com. *Métro: Pont Marie. Rates: 159€ ($254) single with shower; 189€ ($290) double or twin beds. Breakfast 12€ ($19). AE, V.*

Hôtel de Seine
$$$ **St-Germain-des- Prés (6e)**

The Hôtel de Seine is centrally located on a street full of art galleries in St-Germain-des-Prés, between boulevard St-Germain and rue Jacob. It's a few blocks from the Seine and the pedestrian bridge Pont des Arts that leads to the Louvre. Each room is distinctly decorated with either French provincial furniture and flowered wallpaper or Provence-inspired jewel-toned paint and Louis XVI reproductions. Rooms have satellite TV, marble bathrooms, hair dryers. Check the Web site for specials and promotions.

See map p. 108. 52 rue de Seine. ☎ **01-46-34-22-80.** *Fax: 01-46-34-04-74.* www. paris-hotel-seine-river.com. *Métro: St-Germain-des-Prés, Mabillon. Rates: 153€–173€ ($245–$277) single; 173€–185€ ($277–$296) double; 183€–195€ ($293–$312) twin; 218€–230€ ($349–$368) triple. Breakfast 12€ ($19). V.*

Hôtel de Suez
$–$$ **Latin Quarter (5e)**

Ask for rooms at the back of this hotel in a great Latin Quarter location; those that face boulevard St-Michel are quite loud late into the night on weekends. The rooms in this hotel are a good size, beds are firm, storage space is ample, and the modern bathrooms have hair dryers. Décor is typical modern hotel: a comfortable mirrored lobby furnished with couches and Art Nouveau lamps, rooms with striped or flowered bedspreads, and curtains with color-coordinated artwork and blonde furniture. Each room has satellite TV with numerous channels and Wi-Fi is available throughout the building. The hotel is near Musée de Cluny, Jardin du Luxembourg, and the Panthéon. The Seine and Notre-Dame are a ten-minute walk away.

31 bd. St-Michel. ☎ **01-53-10-34-00.** *Fax: 01-40-51-79-44.* www.hoteldesuez.fr. *Métro: St-Michel. Rates: 85€–150€ ($136–$240) single; 95€–150€ ($152–$240) double; 130€–175€ ($208–$298) triple. Breakfast 7€ ($11). AE, MC, V.*

Hôtel du Champ de Mars
$–$$ Eiffel Tower (7e)

Canelle, the proprietors' cocker spaniel, will welcome you to this 25-room hotel that resembles a country house tucked away on a colorful street near the Eiffel Tower. It's also a terrific bargain. Rooms are decorated with flowered drapes, fabric-covered headboards, throw pillows, and cushioned high-backed seats, and each is unique. Along with the countryside feel are modern urban amenities: satellite TV and bathrooms with hair dryers, large towels, and good lighting; those with tubs have wall-mounted showers. A cozy breakfast room is located in the remodeled basement. Reserve at least four months in advance. In the summer, the two best rooms are on the ground floor and open onto the leafy courtyard; they stay cool despite the lack of air-conditioning. A grocery store is two doors down for travelers needing provisions at 27 rue Cler, and the rue Cler outdoor market (open Tues–Sun mornings) is right around the corner.

7 rue du Champ de Mars. ☎ **01-45-51-52-30.** *Fax: 01-45-51-64-36.* www.hotel duchampdemars.com. *Métro: École-Militaire. RER: Pont de l'Alma. Rates: 84€–90€ ($134–$144) single with shower; 90€ ($144) double with tub; 94€ ($150) twin beds with tub; 112€ ($179) triple. Breakfast 8€ ($13). AE, MC, V.*

Hôtel du Jeu de Paume
$$$$ Ile Saint-Louis (4e)

Madame Elyane Prache and her golden retriever, Scoop, will give you a friendly greeting at this impressive, airy hotel on the exclusive Ile St-Louis. The wooden skeleton of a 17th-century *jeu de paume* (precursor to tennis) court rises from the open lobby two stories above a stone and wood entry with a fireplace, couches, glassed-in elevator, and spiral staircases. Most accommodations are snug to medium, but the simple stylish décor under hewn beams keeps rooms from feeling cramped. Eat breakfast in the plant-filled garden or indoors in the inviting lobby. The three standard duplexes with spiral stairs are roomier (and don't cost any more than a double), but if you are staying five days or longer and want true bliss, check into the three-bedroom 900€ ($1,300) duplex apartment with a private terrace. A 600€ ($840) two-bedroom apartment is also available for stays of five days or longer.

54 rue Saint-Louis-en-L'Ile. ☎ **01-43-26-14-18.** *Fax: 01-40-46-02-76.* www.jeude paumehotel.com. *Métro: Pont-Marie. Rates: 180€–255€ ($288–$408) single; 275€–350€ ($440–$560) double; 395€–545€ ($632–$872) suite. Breakfast 18€ ($29), pets 10€ ($16). AE.*

Hôtel du Lys
$$ St-Germain-des-Prés (6e)

Housed in a 17th-century mansion on a street that dates back to 1180, this hotel, with original tall casement windows and homey, intimate rooms decorated in floral wallpaper with exposed-beam high ceilings, is a haven from the bustling neighborhood. Rooms feature double glazing to keep out the noise, and rooms 19 and 22 have balconies. People with disabilities need to heed the lack of an elevator, and the staircase, although historic, is narrow. The Lys is just a few blocks from the Seine and Notre-Dame in an area that gets quite crowded in summer. Breakfast is included.

See map p. 108. 23 rue Serpente. ☎ *01-43-26-97-57. Fax: 01-44-07-34-90.* www. hoteldulys.com. *Métro: St-Michel or Odéon. Rates: 100€ ($160) single; 105€– 120€ ($168–$192) double; 140€ ($224) triple. Rates include breakfast. MC, V.*

Hôtel du Vieux Saule
$$–$$$ Le Marais/Bastille (3e)

This is not our typical Parisian hotel. With a giant display of cacti and other desert plants in the woody lobby, you will think you've arrived in a hotel in the middle of Arizona. The cheerful, but small, rooms have a modern décor and tiled bathrooms, hair dryers, safes, double-glazed windows, luggage racks, Wi-Fi, satellite TV, trouser presses, and even small irons and ironing boards. The rooms on the fifth floor tend to be bigger. Breakfast is a buffet served in the original 16th-century cozy vaulted cellar accessed by a winding staircase (no elevator). For those worn out by the day's sightseeing, check out the sauna — again, an unusual perk for Paris. Promotions are often offered online.

See map p. 106. 6 rue de Picardie. ☎ *01-42-72-01-14. Fax: 01-40-27-88-21.* www. hotelvieuxsaule.com. *Métro: République. Parking: 12€ ($19) for 12 hours. Rates: 120€–140€ ($192–$224) single with shower or shower and tub; 140€–160€ ($224–$256) double with shower or tub or superior double; 180€–200€ ($288–$320) deluxe double or triple. Buffet breakfast 10€ ($16). AE, DC, MC, V.*

Hôtel Esmeralda
$–$$ Latin Quarter (5e)

This off-beat and ramshackle hotel is a favorite with budget travelers, so you'll want to book at least three months in advance. Its creaky wood floors and cramped and sometimes dusty hallways pale in comparison to its superior location just steps away from the Seine and Notre-Dame. If you prefer hotels with such amenities as satellite TV, free toiletries, or space, then the Esmeralda is probably not for you. There is an old, winding wooden staircase (no elevator) and outstanding views of Notre-Dame and the Seine from the hotel's front rooms (make sure to specify these rooms when you reserve). East rooms overlook St-Julien-le-Pauvre and square Viviani. Shabby-chic velvet coverings and antique furniture create homey warmth that almost makes up for the disappointingly dark rear rooms. The front rooms with a view have modern bathrooms with tubs, and some are exceptionally large for the location and relative size of this hotel, making them perfect for travelers with children. The hotel is just steps away from the landmark Shakespeare & Company bookstore.

See map p. 108. 4 rue St-Julien-le-Pauvre. ☎ *01-43-54-19-20. Fax: 01-40-51-00-68. Métro: St-Michel. Rates: 32€–61€ ($51–$98) single; 61€–95€ ($98–$152) double; 110€ ($176) triple; 120€ ($192) quad. Breakfast 6€ ($9.60). Shower 2€ ($3.20) per person. No credit cards.*

Hôtel Henri IV
$ Louvre (1er)

This hotel doesn't have an elevator; only five rooms have showers or tubs, only two have toilets, and none have phones. The stairs are creaky, and no matter how old you may be, this place will make you feel young in comparison. But this super-budget Henri IV is one of Europe's most famous hotels and nearly always is full. It occupies a dramatic location on place Dauphine — the northernmost tip of Ile de la Cité, across the river from St-Germain and the Louvre and a few steps from Pont-Neuf. The 17th-century building houses cozy rooms that are past their prime, though many find them romantically evocative (others think they're just run down). Each room has a sink, but guests share the spotless toilets and showers on each of the five floors. One of the communal bathrooms has an enormous tub, and a few rooms have beautiful views of place Dauphine. Rooms 19 and 20 have a shower, toilet, and a terrace for 65€ ($82). All in all, staying here is an adventure. Book far in advance.

See map p. 108. 25 place Dauphine. ☎ *01-43-54-44-53. Métro: Pont Neuf. Rates: 42€ ($67) single with sink; 65€ ($104) single with shower and toilet; 47€ ($75) double with sink; 52€ ($83) double with shower but no toilet; 74€ ($118) double with toilet and tub or shower. Rates include breakfast. MC, V.*

Hôtel Jeanne d'Arc
$–$$ Le Marais (4e)

Reserve well in advance for this great budget hotel on a pretty little street just off the place St-Catherine. The place is full of eccentric furniture and countryside touches, like soft tangerine-colored wallpaper decorating the halls of the ground floor and a plant-filled dining room. Reception is through a door on the right which features the hotel's signature mosaic mirror, a tribute to French pride. Rooms are small to decent-sized with large windows, card-key access, and large bathrooms, but storage space is a bit cramped. Other room features include direct-dial telephones, cable TV, and bedside tables. If a view is important, make sure you request a room at the top or facing the street because some rooms don't have one. The hotel is in the center of the Marais, and it can be a little noisy, but you're near the Musée Picasso, place des Vosges, and the Bastille, and the fabulous Au Bistro de la Place cafe is in the square next door.

See map p. 106. 3 rue de Jarente. ☎ *01-48-87-62-11. Fax: 01-48-87-37-31.* www.hotel jeannedarc.com. *Métro: St-Paul or Bastille. Rates: 62€ ($99) single; 89€–116€ ($142–$186) double; 146€ ($234) triple; 160€ ($256) quad. Breakfast 6€ ($9.60). MC, V.*

Hôtel le Tourville
$$$ Eiffel Tower (7e)

This splendid restored mansion, located just steps behind Les Invalides, boasts a four-star rating: You receive almost all the amenities of a pricier hotel — a lobby bar, with TV and newspapers, good-quality toiletries, hair dryers, air-conditioning, chic décor with antiques — for rates miraculously below four-star prices. Rooms are decorated in soft yellows, pink, or sand, with crisp white damask curtains, antique bureaus and lamps, fabulously mismatched old mirrors, marble bathrooms, and satellite TV. Three superior rooms have been renovated in a chic somewhat masculine style and boast impressive bathrooms. You may want to ask for one of the four rooms with walk-out vine-draped terraces or a junior suite with whirlpool bath. The staff is wonderfully helpful and polite. A grocery store a few doors down is open until 10 p.m., and a *tabac* is right next door.

See map p. 108. 16 av. de Tourville. ☎ **01-47-05-62-62.** *Fax: 01-47-05-43-90. Métro: École-Militaire. Rates: 180€ ($288) standard double; 240€ ($384) superior double; 270€ ($432) double with private terrace; 350€–450€ ($560–$720) suites. Breakfast 15€ ($24). AE, DC.*

Hôtel Lindbergh
$$ St-Germain-des-Prés (7e)

This pretty aviation-themed hotel is in a terrific St-Germain-des-Prés location. Photos of the hotel's namesake, Charles Lindbergh in his plane, standing with Louis Blériot, the first man to fly across the English Channel, and with Antoine St-Exupéry, author of *The Little Prince,* add a nice touch to the taupe-colored lobby. The standard rooms are simple with colorful bedspreads and matching bathrooms. Deluxe rooms have floor-length draperies, fabric headboards, and color-coordinated cushioned seating. The hotel is right at the edge of the St-Germain-des-Prés shopping district, and Le Bon Marché department store, with its terrific L'Épicerie supermarket, is at the end of the block. The Musée Rodin is within walking distance. Those with energy can hoof the distance over to the Eiffel Tower; otherwise catch bus 69 from nearby rue du Bac to the Champ du Mars.

See map p. 108. 5 rue Chomel. ☎ **01-45-48-35-53.** *Fax: 01-45-49-31-48.* www.hotel lindbergh.com. *Métro: Sévres-Babylone. Rates: 98€–108€ ($157–$261) smaller double with shower; 136€–160€ ($218–$256) double (or twin beds) with shower and tub; 156€–180€ ($250–$288) triple; 190€ ($304) quad. Breakfast 8€ ($13). AE, MC, V.*

Hôtel Louvre Forum
$ Louvre (1er)

If very basic accommodations don't do it for you, you'll want to go elsewhere, but you will miss out on a great deal. This is a truly central, reasonably priced hotel (with air-conditioning!) just steps from the Louvre. The brightly colored rooms with '70s-style furnishings have small tiled bathrooms (with hair dryers) and writing tables with lamps, and somewhat uncomfortable chairs. Each room has a small armoire with hanging space and shelves; the rooms on the lower floors are a bit cramped. The lobby features a mural of the neighborhood, which is only a short walk from the elegant Palais Royal and the Louvre.

See map p. 106. 25 rue du Bouloi. ☎ *01-42-36-54-19. Fax: 01-42-36-66-31.* www.paris-hotel-louvre-forum.com. *Métro: Louvre-Rivoli. Rates: 90€ ($144) single with shower; 100€ ($160) double with shower; 110€ ($176) double or twin beds with full bathroom. Continental breakfast 10€ ($16). AE, DC, MC, V.*

Hôtel Louvre Richelieu
$–$$ Louvre (1er)

I have included this very basic hotel with good-sized rooms and a great location — halfway between the Louvre and the Opéra — because of its great value. I repeat, however, that it is very basic. Enter through a corridor with restored stone walls and climb the stairs to the second-floor lobby. The two-bed double rooms are dark, but spacious with high ceilings. Each room has a writing table, a small closet, and a suitcase rack. The lack of an elevator here means that you may want to book elsewhere if you're loaded down with luggage. Reserve at least two weeks in advance for summer. A bakery is right next door.

See map p. 106. 51 rue de Richelieu. ☎ *01-42-97-46-20. Fax: 01-47-03-94-13.* www.louvre-richelieu.com. *Métro: Palais-Royal-Musée du Louvre, Pyramides. Rates: 102€ ($163) single or double with bathroom; 75€ ($120) single with bathroom down the hall; 88€ ($141) double with bathroom down the hall; 122€ ($195) twin with bathroom; 132€ ($211) triple with bathroom; 156€ ($250) quad with bathroom. Breakfast 6€ ($9.60). MC, V.*

Hôtel Marignan
$–$$ Latin Quarter (5e)

Paul Keniger is the third generation of his family to care for this very warm establishment that first opened in the 1930s. The Kenigers welcome families, don't mind if you bring your own food into the dining room, and they even make the kitchen available during the low season. A washer/dryer and iron are at your disposal. Signs in English recommend neighborhoods to visit and tours to take, and you can always ask one of the Kenigers for recommendations. The hotel is very close to the Sorbonne — it's around the corner from the Panthéon, near the outdoor green market on rue Mouffetard — and its good rates attract students. One of the best organized Web sites for a hotel I've seen, check it out for individual floor plans of each room, as well as the ever-present promotions. Rooms fill up quickly in July and August, so if you plan to travel then, book well in advance.

See map p. 108. 13 rue du Sommerard. ☎ *01-43-54-63-81. Fax: 01-43-25-16-69.* www.hotel-marignan.com. *Métro: Maubert-Mutualité or St-Michel. Rates: 49€ ($78) single with shared toilet; 60€ ($96) single with toilet; 68€ ($109) double with toilet in the hall; 80€ ($128) double with toilet; 90€ ($144) double with shower and toilet; 90€–125€ ($144–$200) three–five persons with toilet; 115€–155€ ($184–$248) three–five persons with shower and toilet. Rates include continental breakfast. MC, V.*

Hôtel Minerve
$$ Latin Quarter (5e)

Owners of the Familia Hôtel (reviewed earlier in this chapter), Eric and Sylvie Gaucheron, also own this pretty and more upscale hotel next door. Rooms are large and romantic with wood-beamed ceilings, exposed stone walls, carved mahogany wood furnishings, and expensive hand-painted sepia frescos can be found in several of the rooms, as well as provincial fabrics. All have modern bathrooms with hair dryers, satellite TV, Internet access via Wi-Fi, and air-conditioning. Ten rooms have large balconies with tables and chairs overlooking the street. The Minerve is as welcoming to kids as the Familia. If you're craving an American breakfast, head just a few blocks down to the delicious Breakfast in America at 73 rue des Écoles. The Minerve offers airport transportation using Parishuttle (www.parishuttle.com), a van-transportation service.

See map p. 108. 13 rue des Écoles. ☎ **01-43-26-26-04.** *Fax: 01-44-07-01-96.* www.hotel-paris-minerve.com. *Métro: Cardinal Lemoine or Jussieu. Rates: 90€–123€ ($144–$197) single; 106€–136€ ($170–$218) double; 156€ ($250) triple; 156€ ($250) large double with balcony or patio; 289€ ($462) family suite. Breakfast 8€ ($13). AE, MC, V.*

Hôtel Montpensier
$–$$ Louvre (1er)

Supposedly the former residence of Mademoiselle de Montpensier, cousin of Louis XIV, this hotel's high ceilings and windows, the stained-glass ceiling in its lounge, and its grand staircase all work together to create a sense of faded grandeur. Many rooms on the first two floors, which date from the 17th century, are serviceable with a budget-hotel décor, while rooms on the fifth floor (an elevator is available) have attractive slanted ceilings and good views over the rooftops. They are smaller than the first- and second-floor rooms, but all the sizes here are quite impressive given the rates. Most rooms are comfortably outfitted with easy chairs, ample closet space, and modern bathrooms with hair dryers. Reserve at least a month in advance for July. The prices are terrific for this location, just two blocks from the Jardin du Palais Royal and right down the street from the Louvre and the Jardin des Tuileries. Service was downright icy when I visited in the off season; hopefully staff have thawed since.

See map p. 106. 12 rue Richelieu. ☎ **01-42-96-28-50.** *Fax: 01-42-86-02-70.* www.hotel-paris-montpensier.com. *Métro: Palais-Royal-Musée du Louvre. Rates: 67€–71€ ($107–$114) single with shared toilet and shower; 71€–79€ ($114–$126) double with shared toilet and shower; 95€–103€ ($152–$165) double or twin with shower; 109€–129€ ($174–$206) double or twin with bath; 129€–139€ ($206–$222) triple; 149€–159€ ($238–$254) quad. Ask about special promotions when booking or check the Web site. Breakfast 8€–9€ ($13–$14). AE, MC, V.*

Hôtel Prince
$–$$ Eiffel Tower (7e)

Just a ten-minute walk from the Eiffel Tower, the Prince is a good value for the location. Rooms are modern, soundproof, and have exposed stone walls, matching curtains and bedspreads, and big bathrooms with fluffy towels. Although they vary in size, all rooms are pleasant, comfortable, and well kept, with double-glazed windows, suitcase racks, TV, minibar, air-conditioning, and ample closets, and even hair dryers and safes. If you're too worn out from sightseeing to stagger out the door to the two downstairs cafes (not a part of the hotel), the hotel can arrange for a local restaurant to deliver a meal. Room 001 on the ground floor next to reception is available with facilities for travelers with disabilities.

See map p. 108. 66 av. Bosquet. ☎ **01-47-05-40-90.** *Fax: 01-47-53-06-62.* www.hotel-paris-prince.com. *Métro: École-Militaire. Rates: 79€ ($126) single with shower; 99€–117€ ($158–$187) double; 101€–119€ ($161–$190) twin; 125€ ($200) triple (comes with tub). Buffet breakfast 10€ ($16). AE, MC, V.*

Hôtel Saint-Merry
$$$ Le Marais (4e)

This unique hotel located on a pedestrian-only street in the Maraisand was formerly the presbytery of the Church of Saint-Merry next door. It was also once a brothel, but no matter what its history, it retains an almost spooky medieval atmosphere. In fact, the bed in room no. 9 has flying buttresses on either side (easy to trip over in the dark). The rooms have beamed ceilings, stone walls, wrought-iron chandeliers, and candelabras. Fabrics are sumptuous; bathrooms are fully tiled, and equipped with hair dryers. Staff is very helpful. Higher prices are for larger rooms with views. In keeping with its medieval feeling you won't find an elevator in the building (***Note:*** 21 winding steps lead to the second-floor reception area). TVs are in suites only. The hotel is a few short blocks from the Seine and Hôtel de Ville. The Louvre is about a 15-minute walk away.

See map p. 106. 78 rue de la Verrerie. ☎ **01-42-78-14-15.** *Fax: 01-40-29-06-82.* www.hotelmarais.com *(for booking only). Métro: Hôtel-de-Ville or Châtelet. Rates: 160€–230€ ($256–$368) double or twin; 205€–275€ ($328–$440) triple; 335€–407€ ($536–$651) suite. In-room breakfast 11€ ($18). AE, V.*

Hôtel Saints-Pères
$$$ St-Germain-des-Prés (6e)

Travelers have made this romantic hotel one of the Left Bank's most popular. Designed in the 17th century, this was the residence of Louis XIV's architect, and the hotel looks the part, furnished with antiques, old paintings, tapestries, and gilt mirrors. Many of its 39 rooms overlook an interior courtyard where breakfast and drinks are served. Rooms have modern amenities such as air-conditioning, satellite TVs, and minibars. The most requested is the magnificent *chambre à la fresque* where guests sleep beneath a 17th-century painted ceiling. The hotel is a stone's throw from celebrated Brasserie Lipp, Café de Flore, and the Deux Magots. Check Web site for special offers.

See map p. 108. 65 rue des St-Pères. ☎ *01-45-44-50-00. Fax: 01-45-44-90-83.* www. esprit-de-france.com *(booking only). Métro: St-Germain-des-Prés or Sèvres-Babylone. Rates: 170€–225€ ($272–$360) double; 300€–320€ ($480–$510) suite; 295€–315€ ($472–$504) duplex suite; 365€–380€ ($584–$608) for the chambre à la fresque. Buffet breakfast 14€ ($22). AE, MC, V.*

Hôtel St-Jacques
$$ Latin Quarter (5e)

Not only was this hotel designed by Baron Haussman (architect of Paris and its grand boulevards), it also had a cameo in the Cary Grant–Audrey Hepburn film *Charade.* Several of its rooms have restored 19th-century ceiling murals, and most of the high ceilings have elaborate plasterwork, giving the décor an old-Paris feel that is accentuated with traditional furniture and fabric-covered walls. The owners have added their own touches in the hallways, with stenciling on the walls and *trompe l'oeil* painting. Modern comforts include generally spacious rooms, an elevator, tiled bathrooms with hair dryers and toiletries, double-glazed windows, ample closet space, fax and computer outlets, safes, and satellite TV. Although they aren't accessible by elevator (which stops a floor down), the rooms on the top floor are less expensive and have great views (be sure to ask for them specifically).

See map p. 108. 35 rue des Écoles (at rue des Carmes). ☎ *01-44-07-45-45. Fax: 01-43-25-65-50.* www.hotel-saintjacques.com. *Métro: Maubert-Mutualité. Rates: 92€ ($147) single with bathroom; 105€–137€ ($168–$219) double; 168€ ($269) triple. Breakfast 9.50€–11€ ($15–$18). AE, DC, MC, V.*

Hôtel Tiquetonne
$ Opéra (2e)

Though the happening neighborhood of Montorgeuil is quickly losing its last vestiges of seediness, the somewhat shabby, though terrific bargain Tiquetonne still remains. If a view is more important than space, ask for one of the top rooms boasting views of the Eiffel Tower or Sacré-Coeur. Each room has the basics: a bed with a wall-mounted wooden headboard, table, and comfortable chairs and adequate storage space. Walls tend to be thin. The Tiquetonne is located just off the busy pedestrian street rue Montorgueil and is a stone's throw from the red-light district of rue St-Denis and a five-minute walk to the Marais and the Georges Pompidou center. Ask for rooms facing the quieter rue Tiquetonne. Note: The hotel is closed in August.

See map p. 106. 6 rue Tiquetonne. ☎ *01-42-36-94-58. Fax: 01-42-36-02-94. Métro: Etienne Marcel or Réamur-Sébastopol. Rates: 35€ ($56) single with toilet; 45€ ($72) single with shower; 55€ ($88) double with shower or tub. Shower 6€ ($9.60) per person. Breakfast, ordered directly to the room, is 7€ ($11). V.*

Hôtel Verneuil
$$$ St-Germain-des-Prés-Eiffel Tower (7e)

In a city where accommodations range from the ultra-luxurious to the barely inhabitable, Hotel Verneuil offers the elegance of a small boutique hotel at a reasonable price. Located in the 7th arrondissement just a short walk from St-Germain-des-Prés, the Louvre, the Musée D'Orsay, and the Seine, Hotel Verneuil provides the location, quiet, and value that any visitor to Paris can appreciate. The 17th-century building's sedate, classically decorated lobby contrasts with the 26 small, quirky rooms upstairs, all with reasonably sized, en suite bathrooms. Original wood beams grace many of the guest rooms, and breakfast (an additional charge) is served in a whitewashed cellar with vaulted ceilings. Art galleries, antique dealers, and more than a few good cafes, including the legendary Café de Flore and Les Deux Magots, line the streets around the hotel. It's an intimate, charming place that's nice to come home to after a day of sightseeing.

See map p. 108. 8 rue de Verneuil. ☎ *01-42-60-82-14. Fax: 01-42-61-40-38. Métro: Rue du Bac. Rates: 140€ ($224) single with bathroom; 170€ ($272) double with bathroom; 220€ ($352) deluxe double with bathroom. Extra bed 23€ ($37). Continental breakfast 13€ ($21). MC, V.*

Hôtel Vivienne
$-$$ Opéra (2e)

Hôtel Vivienne is well located between the Louvre and the Opéra and offers comfortable, simply decorated rooms at a good price. They have the traditional molding found in classic Parisian apartments, and have soundproofing — something lacking in most Parisian lodgings. The bathrooms vary in size from adequate to huge, and all have hair dryers and wall-mounted showers in the tubs. Some of the rooms have adjoining doors, perfect for families; others have small terraces. A few have views of the Eiffel Tower. Before venturing from the neighborhood, explore the Galeries Vivienne and Colbert, gorgeous historic covered passageways with pretty shops, intimate restaurants, and art galleries. Also of note, the French restaurant scene in the Diane Keaton–Jack Nicholson film, *Something's Gotta Give,* was filmed at Le Grand Colbert restaurant right down the street.

See map p. 106. 40 rue Vivienne. ☎ *01-42-33-13-26. Fax: 01-40-41-98-19.* www. hotel-vivienne.com. *Métro: Bourse, Richelieu-Drouot, Grands Boulevards. Rates: 60€–75€ ($96–$120) single or double with shower, shared toilet; 87€–114€ ($139–$182) double with shower, shared toilet; 83€–110€ ($133–$176) double with toilet and bath; 114€ ($183) twin with toilet and a tub. Breakfast 9€ ($14), and 10€ ($16) in room. MC, V.*

Lord Byron Hôtel Residence
$$$ Champs-Elysées (8e)

Located just off the Champs-Elysées on a narrow street lined with town houses, the Lord Byron is one of the best values in the neighborhood, which is calm and not subject to the bustle of France's widest avenue. Exuding a sense of luxury and peacefulness, draperies filter the sun in the Lord Byron's lobby, the reception desk is under an arch, and a pleasant little garden makes you feel miles away from the hubbub. An elevator will whisk you to rooms furnished with antique reproductions, Provençal and classic French fabrics, and framed landscapes. They also feature minibars, satellite TVs, hair dryers, and full bathrooms. Staff is warm and friendly.

See map p. 106. 5 rue de Chateaubrand. ☎ *01-43-59-89-98. Fax: 42-89-46-04. Métro: George V, walk down rue Washington for one block, turn left. Rates: 155€ ($248) single with bathroom; 195€–215€ ($312–$346) double or twin; 280€ ($448) apt/suite. An extra bed is 28€ ($45). Breakfast 12€ ($19). AE, MC, V.*

Pavillon de la Reine
$$$$ Le Marais (3e)

Translated as "The Queen's Pavilion," this is more a French country house than a castle in the middle of Paris, just off the Place des Vosges. Enter through wrought-iron gates and pass through the pretty flowered courtyard and on into a cozy wood-beamed and flagstone-floored lobby where in winter, a fire burns in the marble fireplace in the antique-filled lounge. The large standard rooms are decorated with such country touches as gingham wallpaper and Louis XIII–style furniture, the superior duplex rooms have modern beds (some decorated in velvets and taffeta) located in a loft above a cozy sitting room with comfortable chairs and couches. Rooms overlook the courtyard or a flowered patio and have all the amenities: air-conditioning, cable TV, Internet, room service, minibar, and laundry service. Breakfast is served in the vaulted cellar, amidst tapestries; pastries are made at the *boulangerie* next door. You will definitely be treated like a queen (or king) here.

See map p. 106. 28 place des Vosges. ☎ *01-40-29-19-19. Fax: 01-40-29-19-20.* www. pavillon-de-la-reine.com. *Métro: St-Paul. Rates: 370€ ($592) standard room; 430€ ($688) superior room; 460€ ($736) deluxe room; 520€–660€ ($832–$1,056) duplex room; 570€–830 ($912–$1,328) suite. Continental breakfast 25€–26€ ($40–$42), buffet breakfast 30€–32€ ($48–$51). AE, DC, MC, V.*

Pierre & Vacances City Aparthôtel
$$$$ Champs-Elysées (8e)

Located near Galeries Lafayette and Au Printemps and in walking distance of the Champs-Elysées, the Madeleine Church, parc Monceau, and a lot of public transportation, this seven-story hotel is quite luxurious. Studios and apartments are spacious and beautiful — featuring rare wood furnishings and granite bathrooms. Services and amenities include satellite TV, Internet access, baby-equipment rental, dry cleaning, laundry facilities, housekeeping every day, bar, and fitness center

See map p. 106. 129-131 bd. Haussmann. ☎ *01-5645-58-87-00.* www.pierreet vacances-city.com. *Métro: Miromesnil. Rates: 219€ ($350) per night two-person studio; 334€ ($534) per night one-bedroom apartment that sleeps four; 375€ ($600) per night one-bedroom superior apartment that sleeps four. AE, MC, V.*

Index of Accommodations by Neighborhood

Louvre (1er)

Citadines Les Halles Aparthotel $$-$$$
Citadines Louvre Aparthotel $$$
Hôtel Agora $-$$
Hôtel Henri IV $
Hôtel Louvre Forum $
Hôtel Louvre Richelieu $-$$
Hôtel Montpensier $-$$

Opéra (2e)

Citadines Paris Opéra-Grands
Boulevards Aparthotel $$$-$$$$
Hôtel Tiquetonne $
Hôtel Vivienne $-$$

Le Marais (3e, 4e)

Castex Hôtel $$
Hôtel de la Place des Vosges $$-$$$
Hôtel des Deux-Iles $$$
Hôtel du Jeu de Paume $$$$
Hôtel du Vieux Saule $$-$$$
Hôtel Jeanne d'Arc $-$$
Hôtel Saint-Merry $$$
Pavillon de la Reine $$$$

Latin Quarter (5e)

Familia Hôtel $-$$
Hôtel Claude-Bernard $$-$$$
Hôtel de Suez $-$$
Hôtel Esmeralda $-$$

Hôtel Marignan $-$$
Hôtel Minerve $$
Hôtel St-Jacques $$

St-Germain-des-Prés (6e)

Grand Hôtel des Balcons $$-$$$
Hôtel de Fleurie $$$-$$$$
Hôtel de l'Abbaye Saint-Germain $$$-$$$$
Hôtel de Seine $$$
Hôtel du Lys $$
Hôtel Saints-Pères $$$

Eiffel Tower (7e)

Grand Hôtel Lévêque $
Hôtel Amélie $
Hôtel du Champ de Mars $-$$
Hôtel le Tourville $$$
Hôtel Lindbergh $$
Hôtel Prince $-$$
Hôtel Verneuil $$$

Champs-Elysées–Madeleine (8e)

Four Seasons George V $$$$
Hôtel Alison $$
Hôtel Balzac $$$$
Hôtel de l'Elysée $$$
Lord Byron Hôtel Residence $$$
Pierre & Vacances City Aparthôtel $$$$

Index of Accommodations by Price

$

Familia Hôtel (5e)
Grand Hôtel Lévêque (7e)
Hôtel Agora (1er)
Hôtel Amélie (7e)
Hôtel de Suez (5e)
Hôtel du Champ de Mars (7e)
Hôtel Esmeralda (5e)
Hôtel Henri IV (1er)
Hôtel Jeanne d'Arc (4e)
Hôtel Louvre Forum (1er)

Hôtel Louvre Richelieu (1er)
Hôtel Marignan (5e)
Hôtel Montpensier (1er)
Hôtel Prince (7e)
Hôtel Tiquetonne (2e)
Hôtel Vivienne (2e)

$$

Castex Hôtel (4e)
Citadines Les Halles Aparthotel (1er)
Familia Hôtel (5e)

Grand Hôtel des Balcons (6e)
Hôtel Agora (1er)
Hôtel Alison (8e)
Hôtel Claude-Bernard (5e)
Hôtel de la Place des Vosges (4e)
Hôtel de Suez (5e)
Hôtel du Champ de Mars (7e)
Hôtel du Lys (6e)
Hôtel du Vieux Saule (3e)
Hôtel Esmeralda (5e)
Hôtel Jeanne d'Arc (4e)
Hôtel Lindbergh (7e)
Hôtel Louvre Richelieu (1er)
Hôtel Marignan (5e)
Hôtel Minerve (5e)
Hôtel Montpensier (1er)
Hôtel Prince (7e)
Hôtel St-Jacques (5e)
Hôtel Vivienne (2e)

$$$

Citadines Les Halles Aparthotel (1er)
Citadines Louvre Aparthotel (1er)
Citadines Paris Opéra-Grands
Boulevards Aparthotel (2e)

Grand Hôtel des Balcons (6e)
Hôtel Claude-Bernard (5e)
Hôtel de Fleurie (6e)
Hôtel de l'Abbaye Saint-Germain (6e)
Hôtel de la Place des Vosges (4e)
Hôtel de l'Elysée (8e)
Hôtel des Deux-Iles (4e)
Hôtel de Seine (6e)
Hôtel du Vieux Saule (3e)
Hôtel le Tourville (7e)
Hôtel Saint-Merry (4e)
Hôtel Saints-Pères (6e)
Hôtel Verneuil (7e)
Lord Byron Hôtel Residence (8e)

$$$$

Citadines Paris Opéra-Grands
Boulevards Aparthotel (2e)
Four Seasons Georges V (8e)
Hôtel Balzac (8e)
Hôtel de Fleurie (6e)
Hôtel de l'Abbaye Saint-Germain (6e)
Hôtel du Jeu de Paume (4e)
Pavillon de la Reine (3e)
Pierre & Vacances City Aparthôtel (8e)

Chapter 10

Dining and Snacking in Paris

. . . .

In This Chapter

▶ Getting the inside scoop on Paris's dining scene

▶ Eating well without breaking the bank

▶ Grabbing something on the go

▶ Discovering the best bakeries, cafes, wine bars, and tea salons

▶ Finding a restaurant by location, cuisine, and price

. . . .

*P*aris, and the rest of the country, is a feast. Traditional haute cuisine — a delicate balance of flavors, sauces, and ingredients blended with a studied technique — includes such classics as *blanquette de veau* (veal in an eggy cream sauce), *pot-au-feu* (an excellent stew of fatty beef and vegetables), *coq au vin* (chicken braised in red wine with onions and mushrooms), *bouillabaisse* (seafood soup), and that hearty staple *boeuf bourguignon* (beef stew with red wine).

But when people started thinking healthy a few decades back, buttery, creamy, saucy French cuisine quickly found itself on the outs. So the French invented *nouvelle cuisine,* which gave chefs an excuse to concoct new dishes — still French, mind you, but less fattening because they use fewer heavy creams and less butter and serve (much) smaller portions. When the nouvelle trend lost steam (in part because of the miniscule portions), people began spinning off more-healthful and/or more-creative cooking styles. (In fact, these days, that American staple and butt of many French jokes — the hamburger — has finally become chic! Served in a variety of inventive ways, it's not what you'll find back home — and it's eaten with knife and fork!) Add to these styles the mix of French regional restaurants and the many ethnic dining rooms, and you'll never want for variety.

This chapter is designed to make you feel comfortable about dining in Parisian restaurants and have at least one experience of a true French meal that stretches over several incredible courses. Each restaurant listed has all the ingredients of an excellent dining spot — fantastic cooking, reasonable prices, and great atmosphere — and creates the kind of experience that lingers on in your memory after the last dish is cleared away. Then, when you just can't sit down to another multiple-course meal, you can choose other options, from street and ethnic food, to cafeterias, tea salons, and cafes.

For detailed culinary information, see Chapter 2, where I give a brief run-down on French cuisine, a useful glossary of French culinary terms, and a user's guide to typical French dishes.

Getting the Dish on the Local Scene

Making reservations for dinner

The vast majority of French restaurants are very small establishments with limited seating, and tables are scrupulously saved for folks who book. Always try to make at least a same-day reservation, even for a modest neighborhood bistro. If you are concerned about your language skills, you can always visit the establishment before service starts to make a same-day or next-day reservation. Or, ask the concierge in your hotel, or the hotel's desk clerk to make a reservation for you. Some top restaurants require several weeks' notice. Remember to call if you're going to be more than 20 minutes late. Showing up late is considered bad form.

If you're staying at a hotel with a staff concierge, phone or fax ahead and ask the concierge to make a reservation if you'd like to eat at a sought-after restaurant. Make the call as early as possible, specifying your preferred date with a back-up date or two. Don't forget to tip the concierge (slip 10€/$16 into an envelope and discreetly present it when checking out).

Dressing to dine

Only the most expensive restaurants enforce dress codes (suit and tie), and in theory, you can dress up or down as you like. Parisians, however, are a pretty stylish lot (how do Frenchwomen get their scarves to *do* that?), even when dressing informally in jeans. Relaxed dressing doesn't mean sloppy jeans and sneakers — *especially* sneakers. The look to aim for is casual but upscale. You can't go wrong if you dress in neutrals — think black, beige, cream, navy, and chocolate. If you wear jeans, pair them with a nice jacket, sweater, or shirt and good shoes and nice accessories. Go a notch dressier than what you'd wear at home.

Knowing the difference between a cafe and a bistro

Eateries go by various names in France, and in theory at least, these labels give you some clue to how much a meal costs. From most expensive to least expensive, the lineup generally goes like this: restaurant, bistro, brasserie, cafe. The key word is *generally*. Never rely on the name of an establishment as the sole price indicator; some of the city's most expensive places call themselves cafes. Furthermore, the awnings above quintessential cafes often claim the labels of restaurant, cafe, brasserie, or some other combination. The only way to be sure of the price is to read the menu, which by law is posted outside.

The following is a list of the different types of establishments and what you should expect.

- **Restaurants** are where you go to savor French cuisine in all its glory. At their best, classic dishes are excellent, and new dishes are inventive. Dining is usually more formal than in bistros or brasseries, and service is slower. You may also have more than one server. Generally, restaurants serve lunch between noon and 2:30 p.m. and dinner between 7 and 10 p.m. You must be seated for lunch no later than 2 p.m., if you want a full meal.

Between 3 and 7 p.m., you may find it nearly impossible to have a sit-down meal in a Paris restaurant or bistro. During this swing shift, your best bet is to head to a cafe, tearoom, or wine bar. Dining at 7 p.m. is considered very early for dinner in Paris; most Parisians wouldn't think about sitting down before 8 p.m. But starting too late — 10 p.m. is getting dangerous — can also leave you without many options.

Restaurant critics are divided about the *menu dégustation* (meh-*noo* day-goo-*stah*-see-oh; sampler, or tasting, menu), featured in many of the city's top restaurants. Made up of small portions of the chef's signature dishes, it offers tremendous value because you have the opportunity to try more dishes. But some say there are too many portions for a customer to get a sense of the chef's artistry, and the mixture of so many flavors just confuses, instead of enriches, the palate.

- The typical **bistro** used to be a mom-and-pop operation with a menu confined to such Parisian standbys as *boeuf bourguignon* (braised beef in red wine sauce), and *tarte tatin* (caramelized upside-down apple pie). Today, many bistros have expanded upon the old classics but retain the tradition of offering hearty, relatively low-priced dishes in a convivial, intimate atmosphere. Think crush of elbows and the sounds of corks popping, glasses clinking, multitudes of conversations, and people having a good time. Bistros are where Parisians come to dine most often.

- Literally, the word **brasserie** means "brewery" and refers to the Alsatian menu specialties that include staples such as beer, Riesling wine, and *choucroute* (a sauerkraut-based dish, usually topped by cuts of ham). Most brasseries are large, cheerful, brightly lit places that open early and close late (some are open 24 hours a day), and have an immense selection of dishes on the menu, although many no longer specialize in Alsatian fare. At brasseries, you can usually get a meal at any time of day, even in hours when restaurants and bistros are closed, and the food is relatively inexpensive.

Sadly, brasseries began to fall to corporate acquisition in the 1970s, and today most are part of one all-encompassing chain. Although this fact shouldn't stop you from visiting some of Paris's legendary eateries, look out for places that list mundane and repetitive food on their menus — they're more numerous than you think. Your best bet is to get a look at the menus of brasseries that interest you and compare costs, as well as listings. If *poulet rôti* (rotisserie chicken), *steak frites* (steak and fries), and omelets seem to be highlights, you may want to try eating somewhere else.

✔ **Cafes** are typically open from about 8 a.m. to 1 a.m. They serve drinks and food all day from a short menu that often includes salads, sandwiches, steak, mussels, and french fries. Prime locations or famous literary cafes carry higher price tags. Most cafes offer reasonably priced omelets, *croques* (see later), sandwiches, soups, or salads. Omelets come plain with just a sprinkling of herbs or filled with cheese, ham, or other hearty additions. Onion soup *(soupe à l'oignon)* is a traditional Parisian dish, and you may see *soupe de poisson* (fish soup) on the menu. Another cafe favorite is the *croque monsieur,* a grilled ham sandwich covered with melted cheese (which often comes open-faced), or a *croque madame,* the same dish topped with an egg. Or try a *salade niçoise,* a huge bowl filled with lettuce, boiled potatoes, tuna, hard-boiled eggs, capers, tomatoes, olives, and anchovies or a *salade de chèvre chaude,* fresh greens topped with warm goat cheese on croutons. These dishes make a light, pleasant meal for 6€ to 12€ ($9.60–$19).

Parisians use cafes the way the British use pubs — as extensions of their living rooms. They're places where you meet friends before heading to the movies or a party, read your newspaper, write in your journal, or just hang out and people-watch. Regardless of whether you order a cup of coffee or the most expensive cognac in the house, no one will ask you to leave. Coffee, of course, is the chief drink. It comes black in a small cup, often with a thin wrapped square of dark chocolate, unless you order a *café crème* or *café au lait* (coffee with steamed milk, which Parisians usually have at breakfast). *Thé* (tay; tea) is also fairly popular but generally isn't high quality (check on the menu for mentions of a specific brand — "Thé Mariages Frères," for example, will be very good). *Chocolat chaud* (shock-o-*lah*-shoh; hot chocolate), on the other hand, is absolutely superb and made from real ground chocolate. The result is a thick, rich, yet not too sweet taste of heaven.

✔ **Tearooms,** or *salons de thé,* usually open midmorning and close by early evening. Some serve light lunches, but most are at their best in the afternoon for desserts with coffee or tea.

✔ **Wine bars** operate from midmorning to late evening when you can order wine by the glass and munch on snacks such as *tartines* (open-faced sandwiches), olives, and cheese. Some offer simple lunch menus, but like cafes and tearooms, they're generally better for light bites.

To tip or not to tip

In France, waiting tables is a profession with benefits and retirement security, and waiters are treated with respect (even though you may come across some who do not return the sensibility). When it comes to tipping them, you may have heard not to leave anything since a gratuity is already included in the bill. It's true that an 18 percent service charge, which appears on the bill as *service compris*, is added. But waiters never get the full 18 percent. Thus, it's customary to leave a few euro, or about 5 percent of the bill after a meal, unless the service was truly terrible.

Understanding the order of a meal

A proper meal consists of three, or sometimes four, courses, so portions are usually moderate. Be aware of the traditional way French restaurants serve food.

- An *apéritif* is a light drink that precedes the meal. The French don't like to start a meal by numbing the palate with strong liquor. They usually stick to such offerings as a *kir*, a mixture of white wine and *crème de cassis* (black currant liqueur), which is light and the most common premeal drink.

- You're always served bread with your meal, but you must request butter.

- Water isn't placed on the table automatically — you must ask for it. To get regular tap water (which is perfectly fine to drink), as opposed to the pricey equivalent in a bottle, simply ask for *une carafe d'eau* (oon kar-*aff* doh).

- Cheese comes after the main course and is usually accompanied by a red wine.

- Dessert comes after the cheese course, but dessert and cheese can be served at the same time at your request.

- Diners traditionally don't drink coffee during the meal. Black coffee is served after dessert in a demitasse cup with sugar cubes on the side. If you want milk with your coffee, you must ask for a *café au lait* (ka-*fay* oh lay) or *café crème* (ka-*fay* krem).

- After the meal is finished, it is possible to order a *digestif*, or a small glass of liquor or fortified wine, thought to aid the digestion. Some classic *digestifs* are cognac, Calvados (an apple brandy from Normandy), sherry, and port.

- If you have food left on your plate, don't ask for a doggie bag. Restaurants are not accustomed to handling these types of requests.

The *menu du jour* at many establishments includes red or white wine. The standard measure is *un quart* (a quarter-liter carafe), sometimes served in *un pot* or *un pichet* (a pitcher). If wine isn't included, you can order *vin ordinaire* (house wine) or a Beaujolais (a light, fruity red wine), a Côtes du Rhône (a dry red wine), or a Chardonnay (a light white wine), which are very reasonably priced. And you can always opt for soda, juice, or water instead (*l'eau plat* is still water; *l'eau gazeuse* is carbonated water). Cocktails are available but discouraged because they're thought to numb the palate. Note that soda is often more expensive than a glass of wine at many establishments.

 In France, as anywhere, you should never underestimate the importance of good manners. Your meal will be much smoother if you remember essential but basic phrases such as *"Bonjour, monsieur"* (hello, sir) and *"Merci, madame"* (thank you, madam). Keep in mind, too, that French table manners require that all food, even fruit, be eaten with a knife and fork.

 Contrary to what you may have seen in the movies, *never, **ever*** refer to the waiter as *"garçon,"* (boy) and don't snap your fingers at him or her. Instead, say, *"Monsieur, s'il vous plaît!"* or *"Madame/Mademoiselle, s'il vous plaît!"* (Sir/Madam/Miss, if you please!).

Trimming the Fat from Your Budget

If you're watching your pocketbook when it comes to dining out, following a few of these simple tips can go a long way toward making the bill as appealing as the food.

- **Order prix-fixe (set-price) meals.** These set-price meals are up to 30 percent cheaper than ordering the same dishes à la carte. What's the trade-off? Your options are more limited than if you order from the main menu. Review the prix-fixe option carefully to determine what you're getting at that price. Does the meal come with wine, and if so, how much — a glass or a half-bottle? Is dessert or coffee included?

- **Make lunch your main meal.** Many restaurants offer great deals on a fixed-price lunch. You probably won't be hungry for a full meal at dinnertime after two or three courses at lunch.

- **Try the crêperies.** Crêperies (many are off the boulevard du Montparnasse around the square Délambre) offer a great value. Try savory meat- or vegetable-filled crêpes, called *galettes,* with a bowl of cider for your main meal and honey, jam, *chantilly* (whipped cream), chocolate, or fruit-filled crêpes for dessert. Surroundings are usually Brittany-inspired with red-checked tablecloths, wooden beams, maritime souvenirs, and pictures of Bretagnons in native dress.

✔ **Try the falafel stands.** If your day's plans include a trip to the Marais (Picasso Museum, Place des Vosges, Maison de Victor Hugo, and shopping; see Chapters 11 and 13 for information on guided tours), have for lunch a delicious and cheap falafel or other Middle Eastern food from one of the storefronts on and around rue des Rosiers.

✔ **Try chain restaurants or sandwich shops.** Chez Clément, Léon de Bruxelles, and Bistro Romain offer some good-value, though not inspired, meals. Pomme de Pain, Cosi, and Lina's have fresh and tasty sandwiches.

✔ **Pay attention to the menu's details.** On most menus, the cheaper dishes are made of cheaper cuts of meat or the organs of animals, such as brains, tripe, and the like (often appearing on menus are *cervelles,* which are pork or sheep brains, *tête de veau,* calf's head, *rognons,* kidneys).

✔ **Don't eat breakfast at your hotel.** Doing so adds, at the very least, $5 more per person to your hotel bill. Grab a croissant or a *pain au chocolat* (chocolate-filled pastry) from a *boulangerie* (bakery).

✔ **Know the tipping rules.** Service is usually included at restaurants but it's customary to leave about 5 percent extra for your server.

Paris's Best Restaurants

Restaurants are listed alphabetically for easy reference, followed by the price range, neighborhood, and type of cuisine for each. Price ranges reflect the cost of a three-course meal for one person ordered à la carte, featuring an appetizer, main dish, dessert, and coffee — alcohol is not included.

The number of dollar signs used to describe each restaurant gives you a general idea of how much a meal costs at dinner, but don't make price your only criteria for choosing a restaurant. Most establishments offer fixed-price menus (also called *formules* or *prix fixe*) that can bring the cost down one whole price category. Likewise, if you're dying to try a place that's above your budget, visit it at lunch when meals are cheaper. See Table 10-1 for a key to the restaurant prices.

Table 10-1	Key to Restaurant Prices
Dollar Sign(s)	*Price Range*
$	Less than 20€ ($32)
$$	21€–50€ ($34–$80)
$$$	51€–100€ ($82–$160)
$$$$	Over 101€ ($162)

The restaurants listed here range from moderately priced establishments to homey neighborhood favorites to chic "in" spots. Also included are some bargain eateries and a few of the city's most sumptuous restaurants where haute cuisine is an art form.

See the "Restaurants on the Right Bank" and "Restaurants on the Left Bank" maps for locations of restaurants in this section.

A La Petite Chaise
$$ St-Germain-des-Prés (7e)   CLASSIC FRENCH

Founded in 1680, this small gem is alleged to be the oldest restaurant in Paris, and its roster of historic diners is quite impressive: Heir to the throne Philip d'Orléans and his priest, Cardinal Dubois, George Sand, Toulouse-Lautrec, Colette and François Mitterand, are just a few. The entryway, adorned with a smoky antique mirror from the early 18th century, leads to a softly illuminated, cozy dining room reminiscent of an old country inn, which it once was. Start with *assiette nordique et son sorbet de citron vert* (a plate of salmon with a side of lime sorbet). Main courses may include a *parmentier de poissons à l'échalote et sa salade verte* (thinly sliced fish in a shallot sauce served with a green salad) or leg of lamb cooked in its own juices. The house special dessert is *gateau au chocolat* — a rich chocolate cake topped with English cream.

See map p. 140. 36 rue de Grenelle. ☎ *01-42-22-13-35. Métro: Sèvres-Babylone. (Exit the station on bd. Raspail and walk one block north to rue de la Chaise. Follow the street to the end, where it intersects rue de Grenelle.) Prix-fixe lunch menu comes with a glass of wine and a café: 19€, 25€, or 29€ ($30, $40, or $46); dinner prix fixe (main course with appetizer and dessert): 33€ ($53). AE, MC, V. Open: Daily noon–2 p.m. and 7–11 p.m.*

Au Bascou
$$ Le Marais (3e)   BASQUE/SOUTHWEST

Located in a simple and softly lit rustic interior, some of the best Basque dishes in Paris can be found here. (The Basque region is the corner of southwestern France resting along the Spanish border and is known for its distinct dialect and the excellent culinary skills of its citizens.) Consider starting with a *pipérade basquaise* (a light terrine of eggs, tomatoes, and spices) before moving on to roast wild duck or rabbit in a red-wine sauce. A bottle of Irouléguy, a smooth red Basque wine, makes a nice accompaniment to meals, and the service, though friendly, at times can leave a lot to be desired. You may want to save this place for a night when you don't want to linger over dinner.

See map p. 138. 38 rue Réaumur. ☎ *01-42-72-69-25. Métro: Arts et Métiers. (Exit the station at rue de Turbigo and cross over it to rue Réamur. Head east one block; the restaurant is on the corner of rue Réamur and rue Volta.) Main courses: 18€ ($29). AE, MC, V. Open: Mon–Fri noon to 2 p.m. and 8–10:30 p.m.*

Restaurants on the Right Bank

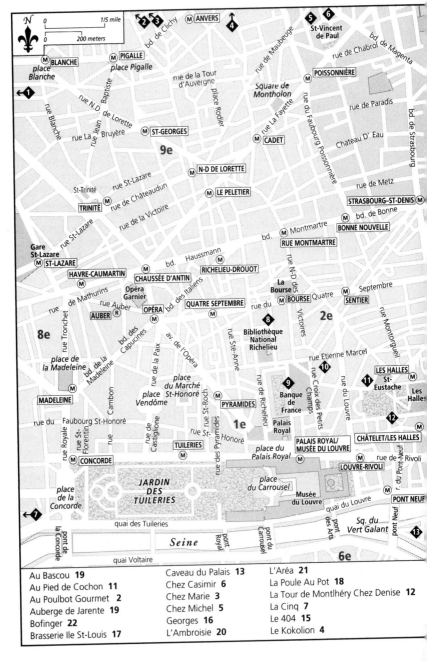

Au Bascou **19**	Caveau du Palais **13**	L'Aréa **21**
Au Pied de Cochon **11**	Chez Casimir **6**	La Poule Au Pot **18**
Au Poulbot Gourmet **2**	Chez Marie **3**	La Tour de Montlhéry Chez Denise **12**
Auberge de Jarente **19**	Chez Michel **5**	La Cinq **7**
Bofinger **22**	Georges **16**	Le 404 **15**
Brasserie Ile St-Louis **17**	L'Ambroisie **20**	Le Kokolion **4**

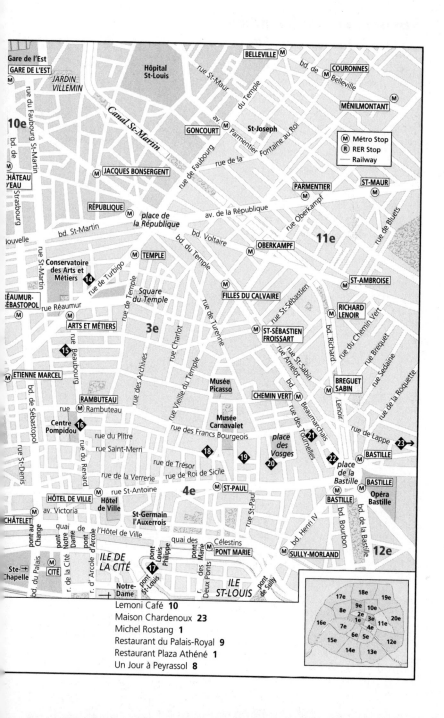

Gare de l'Est
GARE DE L'EST
JARDIN
VILLEMIN
Hôpital
St-Louis
BELLEVILLE
bd. de
COURONNES
Belleville
MÉNILMONTANT
rue St-Maur
rue du Temple
rue du Faubourg St-Martin
Canal St-Martin
10e
av. Parmentier
GONCOURT
St-Joseph
St-Joseph
Fontaine au Roi
bd. de
CHÂTEAU
D'EAU
Strasbourg
rue de Faubourg
rue de la
JACQUES BONSERGENT
PARMENTIER
ST-MAUR
M Métro Stop
R RER Stop
---- Railway
RÉPUBLIQUE
place de
la République
av. de la République
rue Oberkampf
rue des Bluets
Nouvelle
bd. St-Martin
bd. Voltaire
11e
rue St-Martin
Conservatoire
des Arts et
Métiers
TEMPLE
bd. du Temple
OBERKAMPF
RÉAUMUR-
SÉBASTOPOL
rue Réaumur
rue de Turbigo
Square
du Temple
FILLES DU CALVAIRE
ST-AMBROISE
ARTS ET MÉTIERS
3e
rue de Temple
rue de Turenne
rue St-Sébastien
RICHARD
LENOIR
ST-SÉBASTIEN
FROISSART
rue St-Sabin
rue du Chemin Vert
rue Brequet
ETIENNE MARCEL
rue Beaubourg
rue Charlot
rue de l'Amelot
bd. Richard
rue Sedaine
Musée
Picasso
rue Vieille du Temple
bd. de Beaumarchais
BREGUET
SABIN
rue de la Roquette
bd. de Sébastopol
RAMBUTEAU
rue des Archives
CHEMIN VERT
rue Rambuteau
Musée
Carnavalet
rue des Francs Bourgeois
place
des
Vosges
rue de Lappe
Centre
Pompidou
rue du Plître
rue des Tournelles
BASTILLE
rue St-Denis
rue Saint-Merri
18
19
20
21
22
place
de la
Bastille
23
rue du Renard
rue de Trésor
rue de Roi de Sicile
BASTILLE
HÔTEL DE VILLE
rue de la Verrerie
rue St-Antoine
4e
ST-PAUL
BASTILLE
Opéra
Bastille
CHÂTELET
av. Victoria
Hôtel
de Ville
St-Germain
l'Auxerrois
rue St-Paul
bd. Henri IV
bd. Bourbon
bd. de la Bastille
Ste-
Chapelle
quai de
l'Hôtel de Ville
quai des
Célestins
PONT MARIE
SULLY-MORLAND
12e
pont au Change
pont Notre Dame
pont d'Arcole
ILE DE
LA CITÉ
pont Louis Philippe
pont Marie
r. de la Cité
CITÉ
r. d' Arcole
pont St-Louis
rue des Deux Ponts
ILE
ST-LOUIS
pont de Sully
bd. du Palais
Notre-
Dame

Lemoni Café **10**
Maison Chardenoux **23**
Michel Rostang **1**
Restaurant du Palais-Royal **9**
Restaurant Plaza Athéné **1**
Un Jour à Peyrassol **8**

17e 18e 19e
8e 9e 10e
2e 1e 3e 11e 20e
16e 7e 4e
15e 6e 5e 12e
14e 13e

Restaurants on the Left Bank

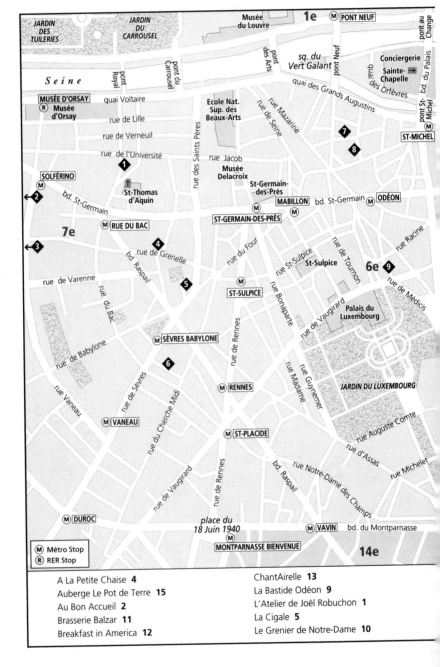

A La Petite Chaise **4**
Auberge Le Pot de Terre **15**
Au Bon Accueil **2**
Brasserie Balzar **11**
Breakfast in America **12**

ChantAirelle **13**
La Bastide Odéon **9**
L'Atelier de Joël Robuchon **1**
La Cigale **5**
Le Grenier de Notre-Dame **10**

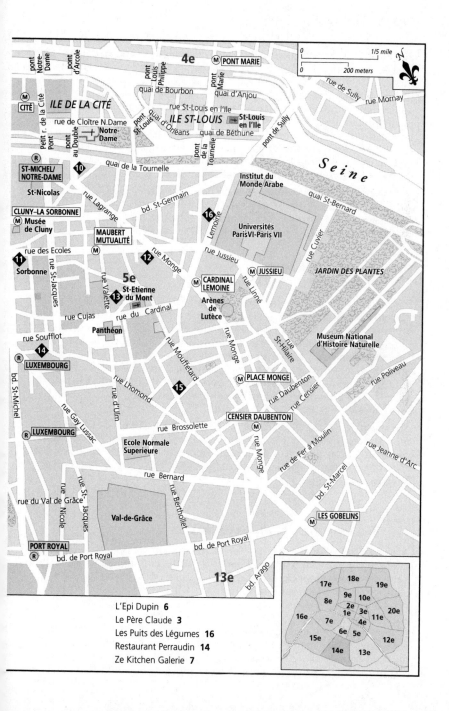

L'Epi Dupin **6**
Le Père Claude **3**
Les Puits des Légumes **16**
Restaurant Perraudin **14**
Ze Kitchen Galerie **7**

Auberge de Jarente
$$ **Le Marais (4e)** BASQUE

Since 1964, cooks have been using olive oil, tomatoes, and all kinds of peppers to create mouth-watering Basque fare here. The 23€ ($37) menu may include starters of fish soup or *terrine de lapin à la confiture d'oignons* (rabbit terrine served with onions, chutney style). Or try the house cassoulet (white bean casserole with meat), and for a main course, such Basque-influenced dishes as sliced duck breast in a barely sweet honey lemon sauce and potatoes. Top it off with a massive crème brûlée and sheep's cheese with jam. Order this menu because a half-bottle of wine is included — this is rare! The rustic décor includes a cavelike, cozy downstairs, and service is downright familial.

See map p. 138. 7 rue de Jarente (between rue de Sevigné and rue de Turenne, just west of place des Vosges). ☎ *01-42-77-49-35. Métro: Bastille or St-Paul. (Take rue de Turenne and follow it one block to rue de Jarente.) Prix-fixe lunch: 14€ ($22); prix fixe: 23€ ($37). AE, V. Open: Tues–Sat noon–2:30 p.m. and 7:30–10:30 p.m.*

Auberge Le Pot de Terre
$ **Latin Quarter (5e)** CLASSIC FRENCH

Parisians in the know relish this restaurant's quality fresh food at dirt cheap (for Paris) prices. Served in a rustic dining room with stone walls and exposed wooden ceiling beams, the classic market fare served by charming waitstaff includes such starters as a fantastic onion soup, mussels cooked in white wine with onions, and a duck liver salad. Main courses could be duck confit with parsleyed potatoes, roast leg of lamb with garlic, sautéed salmon with sorrel. You couldn't say that the food is terribly unique for a French restaurant, but it is well prepared and, at 16€ ($26) for a three-course menu, worth a visit.

See map p. 140. 22 rue du Pot de Fer. ☎ *01-43-31-15-51. Métro: Place Monge. (Exit the station and walk up the place to Rue Ortolan. Cross rue Mouffetard and continue on rue du Pot de Terre, just before rue Tournefort.) Main courses: 9.50€–16€ ($15–$26); prix fixe: 16€ ($26). MC, V. Open: Tues–Fri noon–2:30 p.m., Mon 7–11 p.m., Sat–Sun noon–11:30 p.m.*

Au Bon Accueil
$$ **Eiffel Tower (7e)** MODERN BISTRO

A stone's throw from the Eiffel Tower, the elegant Au Bon Accueil's daily-changing, green market–based menu is simple and delicious. Tables are set with chewy grainy bread and a small plate of *saucisson* (thinly sliced sausage) in an unpretentious dining room with sand and wood colors and slate floors. If you're ordering from the prix-fixe menu, you may start with a green salad with raspberry vinegar, fresh Parmesan, and smoked bacon followed by *aile de raie, radis noirs confits et salade de pourpier* (wing of ray with black radish confit and wild dandelion salad). Main dishes are divine and can include *poulet de Bresse poché puis rôti, gnocchis de pommes de terre et salsifs à la truffe noire* (Bresse chicken poached then roasted served with potato gnocchi and the root vegetable salsify with black truffles) or whole lobster tail from Brittany in its own juices served with white and green asparagus. Fantastic desserts include raspberry macaroons served with lime cream. The dining room only seats 25, so reserve in advance.

See map p. 140. 14 rue de Monttessuy. ☎ *01-47-05-46-11. Reservations strongly recommended. Métro: Alma Marceau. (Exit the station, cross the Pont I'Alma and the quai Branly, and turn onto av. Rapp; follow av. Rapp two blocks to rue de Monttessuy and turn right.) Main courses: 17€ ($27); three-course prix fixe: 31€ ($50). MC, V. Open: Mon–Fri noon–2:30 p.m. and 7:30–10:30 p.m.*

Au Pied de Cochon
$$ Les Halles (1er)   CLASSIC FRENCH

With marble, murals, elaborate sconces, chandeliers, an excess of tourists and some of the most patient waiters around, Au Pied de Cochon opened in 1946 and has played a vibrant part in the history of this old market neighborhood. Specialties here are platters of fish and of course, pork, specifically andouillette AAAAA (a strong-tasting regional tripe sausage) which you can get grilled with béarnaise sauce. There's also the namesake dish, *pied de cochon* (pigs' feet). Or, if you're daring — and hungry — have the *plateau rouge:* half a Canadian lobster, crayfish, shrimp, crabs, and other red fish served on a towering pile of shaved ice. Finish with melt-in-your-mouth *profiteroles* (cream puffs).

See map p. 138. 6 rue Coquillière (between rue du Jour and rue Jean-Jacques Rousseau on the northwest side of the garden of the Forum des Halles shopping center). ☎ *01-40-13-77-00. Métro: Châtelet-Les Halles. Main courses: 17€–30€ ($26–$48). AE, DC, V. Open: Daily 24 hours.*

Au Poulbot Gourmet
$–$$ Montmartre (18e)   CLASSIC FRENCH

This is a reliable old standard a bit off the tourist track in Montmartre and well worth the trek. Its chic burgundy leather banquettes are usually filled with a local crowd savoring moderately priced classic cuisine that may include stewed lamb shoulder from Corrèze, and *pot au feu os à moelle crème de Raifort* (tender beef boiled with vegetables and served with marrow and horseradish). As an appetizer, try the *crépinette de pied de cochon* (pork sausage patty). Desserts are made on the premises and the selection changes often, but you can count on a *moelleux aux chocolat* (chocolate cake with a wonderfully liquid center) served with an orange purée, or a light custard cream.

See map p. 138. 37 rue Lamarck. ☎ *01-46-06-86-00. Métro: Lamarck-Caulincourt. (Follow rue Lamarck from Sacré-Coeur; the restaurant is about a third of the way down the hill.) Three-course dinner: 34€ ($54). MC, V. Open: Mon–Sat noon–2 p.m. and 7:30–10 p.m.; lunch served Sun between Oct–May noon–1:30 p.m.*

Bofinger
$$ Bastille (4e) ALSATIAN/BRASSERIE

Parisians like to joke that the clientele at this famous restaurant near the Bastille is made up of tourists and the elderly. But Bofinger, which first opened in 1864, continues to pack them in, with waiters in long white aprons delivering hearty cuisine, much of it based on the Franco-Germanic cooking of the Alsace region — lots of *choucroute* (sauerkraut, usually served with sausages or other cuts of pork). The downstairs dining room is ornately decorated with Art Nouveau flourishes and a glass-domed ceiling. Upstairs is cozier with wood paneling. It's owned by the Flo brasserie chain, which means that you'll see similar menus in the chain's other restaurants, which include Julien and Brasserie Flo. Service can be whirlwind. Brasseries are good for off-hours dining, tending to stay open until 1 a.m.

See map p. 138. 5-7 rue de la Bastille. ☎ *01-42-72-87-82. Métro: Bastille. (Exit the station at bd. Beaumarchais and turn left at rue de la Bastille.) Fixed-price menus: 32€ ($50), with half-bottle of wine, dinner daily and lunch Sat–Sun; 24€ ($38) lunch weekdays. AE, DC, MC, V. Open: Mon–Fri noon–3 p.m. and 6:30 p.m.–1 a.m.; Sat–Sun noon–1 a.m.*

Brasserie Balzar
$$ Latin Quarter (5e) ALSATIAN/BRASSERIE

Though it's now owned by the brasserie-buying titan Flo Group, locals still count this brasserie that opened in 1898 as a favorite and can regularly be seen in off hours sipping coffee and nibbling pastries. Choose from such hearty French classics (served by twinkly-eyed waiters) as *steak tartare avec frites* (raw minced beef with french fries and salad) or roast leg of Quercy lamb. You can also get a good veal liver *(foie de veau)*, steak au poivre (steak with crushed peppercorns), and a few fresh fish dishes. Portions are copious, french fries are crunchy, perfectly salted, and among the best in Paris.

See map p. 140. 49 rue des Écoles (on the corner of rue de la Sorbonne and rue des Écoles, less than a block south of the Musée de Cluny). ☎ *01-43-54-13-67.* www. brasseriebalzar.com. *Métro: Cluny-Sorbonne. Main courses: 16€–34€ ($25–$54). AE, MC, V. Open: Daily noon–midnight. Closed Aug.*

Brasserie de l'Île St-Louis
$$ Ile St-Louis (4e) ALSATIAN/BRASSERIE

Brasserie de l'Ile St-Louis is loud and bustling. Its outdoor tables have an unparalleled view of the eastern tip of Ile de la Cité, the back of Notre-Dame, the Seine, and the Panthéon. The food is quintessentially Alsatian — including *choucroute* (heaps of tender, biting sauerkraut and meaty slices of ham); the hearty cassoulet, laden with rich beans and tender pieces of lamb and pork; and ham shank atop a bed of lentils. Although the food is not all that it used to be, the location is worth the trip.

See map p. 138. 55 quai de Bourbon. ☎ *01-43-54-02-59. Métro: Pont Marie. Main courses: 18€–30€ ($28–$48) lunch and dinner. V. Open: Thurs–Tues noon–midnight.*

Breakfast in America
$ Latin Quarter (5e) AMERICAN

Connecticut-born filmmaker Craig Carlson opened this diner in 2003 after years as an expat craving American-style big breakfasts. The food here is even better than what you get in the roadside spots back home, and it's been discovered by the locals: American travelers in need of a fix are often outnumbered by Parisians who pack the place for fluffy pancakes, crispy bacon, omelets, and a 2.10€ ($3.35) "bottomless mug o' joe." Breakfast is served all day every day except Sundays, but the menu also includes burgers, nachos, chicken wings, and sandwiches. A 9.95€ ($16) combo of burger, fries, and coffee is a good deal for Paris. Sunday's 16€ ($25) brunch is, of course, particularly busy. Service is efficient and friendly and in English; you may even be seated by Craig himself. There is another location in the Marais at 4 rue Malher, Métro: Saint-Paul. *Note:* Tip is *not* included in the final tab here. The restaurants are very small and fill up quickly.

See map p. 140. 17 rue des Ecoles, 5e. ☎ *01-43-54-50-28.* www.breakfast-in-america.com. *Métro: Cardinal Lemoine or Jussieu. Main courses: 7€–11€ ($11–$18). MC, V. Open: Daily 8:30 a.m.–11 p.m.; Mon–Sat lunch and dinner menu noon–closing; Sun brunch menu all day, lunch/dinner 4pm–closing.*

Caveau du Palais
$$ Ile de la Cité (4e) CLASSIC FRENCH

It's quieter at night at this restaurant where Yves Montand and Simone Signoret were regulars. Artist André Renoux painted the interior *(Interior Restaurant Caveau du Palais)* and the cozy wood-beamed place bustles at lunch; it's a favorite of lawyers from the nearby Palais de Justice. It's located in the heart of the serene, tree-lined place Dauphine, a secluded cobblestoned park nestled off Pont Neuf near the tip of Isle de la Cité. Start with the peppery house pâté or save your meat cravings for the house's special *côte de boeuf,* a kilo of grilled giant ribs prepared for two. Finish it off with a classic crème brûlée or a few *boules* of ice cream. The owners display the work of up-and-coming artists and their big dog is a friendly presence.

See map p. 138 19 place Dauphine. ☎ *01-43-26-04-28. Métro: Pont Neuf. Main courses: 27€–50€ ($43–$80). AE, DC, MC, V. Open: Mon–Sat noon–2:30 p.m. and 7–10:30 p.m.*

ChantAirelle
$$ Latin Quarter (5e) AUVERGNE

One of my favorite places to take people in Paris, ChantAirelle has delicious peasant food, an outdoor high-walled garden, products for sale from the Auvergne region of France, and an enormous and friendly black cat. The door "moos" when opened and other wildlife sounds can be heard beneath the happy chatter of diners. Food is presented in good-sized portions, and appetizers may include *ardoise de salaisons de Haute-Loire* (a terrine served with regional meats including a variety of saucissons and country ham) or *oeuf pochés à la fourme d'Ambert artisanale* (poached eggs with regional cheese made by artisans). Main courses include a tender *magret de canard au miel de Montagne et à la fleur de thym* (duck filet cooked in mountain honey and thyme blossom) or a *truffade* (a casserole of thinly sliced potatoes cooked in cream, with smoked ham in the center). The best Auvergne wine is the Chateauguay, a fine fruity red. The restaurant is a block from the Panthéon.

See map p. 140. 17 rue Laplace. ☎ *01-46-33-18-59. Métro: Maubert-Mutualité. (Take the street behind the Panthéon, rue Valette, and turn right onto rue Laplace.) Main courses: 14€–17€ ($24–$27); three-course prix fixe: lunch, 23€ ($37) with glass of wine included. MC, V. Open: Mon–Fri noon–2 p.m., Mon–Sat 7–10:30 p.m.*

Chez Casimir
$$ Gare du Nord (10e)   CLASSIC FRENCH

If you're arriving (or leaving) Paris via the Gare du Nord, schedule a lunch or dinner at this terrific restaurant not too far from the station. It's owned by Thierry Breton and on the same street as its sister restaurant, Chez Michel (reviewed later in this list). Both are well worth the trip and reservations are strongly suggested. The menu here consists of ingredients from the green market found that morning or the night before. Start with the refreshing *carpaccio de haddock* (marinated sliced raw haddock), then have *onglet de boeuf poêlé, choux de bruxelles et carottes* (pan-fried beef served with Brussels sprouts and carrots), or be almost-too-adventurous and try the *tete de veau*, a French comfort-food classic — meat from the head and neck region of a young calf. For dessert, indulge in *clafoutis aux prunes rouges* (a pancake made from crepe batter dotted with bits of red plums).

See map p. 138. 6 rue Belzunce. ☎ *01-48-78-28-80. Métro: Gare du Nord. (Exit the station on rue de Dunkerque and look for rue de Compiegne. Follow rue de Compiegne across bd. Magenta, turn left on Magenta and walk a few steps to the corner. This is rue Belzunce. Make a right here, and walk a block to the top of the street. The restaurant is on your right.) Main courses: 14€–20€ ($22–$32). MC, V. Open: Lunch Tues–Fri noon–2 p.m., dinner Mon–Sat 7–11:30 p.m.*

Chez Marie
$$ Montmartre (18e)   CLASSIC FRENCH

At the base of the rue du Calvaire steps heading to the place de Tertre, is a cozy restaurant with some of the cheapest eats in this neighborhood, which isn't exactly known for bargain dining. Food is hearty, and the proprietor, M. Rajha, is charming and friendly. The dining room is decorated with wood benches, red-and-white picnic tablecloths, and a collage of Toulouse-Lautrec period posters and kitschy Lautrec-style paintings of cats dining. Stick to such basics as onion soup, cassoulet, or *poulet rôti avec frites* (roast chicken with french fries) and you're guaranteed to leave full and content and still have money in your wallet.

See map p. 138. 27 rue Gabrielle. ☎ *01-42-62-06-26. Métro: Abbesses. A 10€ ($16) three-course menu is served nightly until 9:30 p.m., other prix fixe are 15€ ($24) and 19€ ($30). Main courses: 8.50€–19€ ($14–$30). AE, DC, MC, V. Open: Daily noon–3 p.m. and 6–11:30 p.m. Closed Jan.*

Chez Michel
$$ Gare du Nord (10e)   BRETON

Crowds of Parisians come here to the sister restaurant of Chez Casimir for excellent, unusual food at very fair prices served in twin dining rooms. The succulent scallops are hand-picked by scuba divers, served with truffles in the winter. The menu may include *crème d'homard Bréton* (cream of lobster soup topped with shaved Parmesan cheese) or the regional *kig ha farz* (a stew made with veal and pork flavored with herbs and served with bacon bits and vegetables) or it may venture south to Nîmes with such local specialties as a *brandade de morue legerment gratinée au parmesan* (a salt-cod casserole, baked lightly with Parmesan cheese). For dessert, ask if they have *kouign amann* (a Breton pastry made of layers of brioche dough, butter, and caramelized sugar). The cellar is more casual with wooden tables. Choose from more than 100 different wines at retail cost, a truly dizzying experience.

See map p. 138. 10 rue Belzunce. ☎ *01-44-53-06-20. Métro: Gare du Nord. (Exit the station on rue de Dunkerque and look for rue de Compiegne. Follow rue de Compiegne across bd. Magenta, turn left on Magenta and walk a few steps to the corner. This is rue Belzunce. Make a right onto Belzunce, walk a block to the top of the street. Make another right, passing restaurant Chez Casimir, and walk to the corner of rue Belzunce and rue St-Vincent de Paul. Chez Michel is here.) Three-course prix fixe: 30€ ($48). MC, V. Open: Tues–Fri noon–2 p.m.; Mon–Fri 7 p.m.–midnight. Closed last week of July and first three weeks of Aug.*

Georges
$$–$$$ Les Halles (4e)   MODERN BISTRO

Perched atop the Centre Pompidou, Georges boasts a 360-degree view of Paris from its windows and outside terrace; come here at sunset for the lovely light and watch the lights of Paris twinkle on below. Owned by the famed Costes brothers, who have ultrahip restaurants across the city and the Hotel Costes, the décor is made of up of white plastic tables and chairs and large silver and white abstract sculptures. The waitresses could understudy as models — rail thin, six feet tall, and radiant. The menu changes every month, but modern French food is fused with Asian-inspired creations. You might find a starter of avocado-stuffed king crab, or gazpacho. Move on to turbot grilled in béarnaise sauce, *mandarina* crispy duck (a play perhaps on the French purse company?), or the mysterious *tigre qui pleure* (crying tiger — you'll just have to ask). Desserts usually combine inseason fruits in French-inspired tarts and cakes. Dress chic, in black or something as funky as this place is.

See map p. 138. 27 rue Gabrielle. ☎ *01-44-78-47-99. Reservations required. Métro: Rambuteau. Main courses: 22€–150€ ($35–$240). AE, MC, V. Open: Daily noon–2 a.m. (kitchen closes at 11 p.m.).*

La Bastide Odéon
$$ St-Germain-des-Prés (6e) PROVENÇAL

Gilles Ajuelos has been serving delicious Provençal cooking since 1994 in a lovely cream-colored dining room accented with weathered wood and Provençal fabrics in shades of red. The menu changes regularly, but the dynamic creations may include starters of Paimpol coco beans prepared in poached eggs and a fincly chopped Bilboa cod cooked in olive oil, or a warm grilled eggplant layered pastry with tomato and ricotta cheese. Main dishes may include roast quail in its own juices, served with a mushroom and Reggiano-Parmesan risotto, or a grilled, thick tuna steak served with a spicy purée of yellow tomatoes. For dessert, try a *millefeuille* (multilayered pastry) with bourbon vanilla ice cream, or roasted figs in a confit of *"fruit rouges"* or strawberries, raspberries, and red currant; all accompanied by an almond *financier* and ice cream. There's a nice, slightly pricey selection of wine. The restaurant is located on a narrow stretch of sidewalk next to the Théâtre de l'Odéon and a short walk from the Jardins du Luxembourg's place Edmond Rostand/boulevard St-Michel entrance.

See map p. 140. 7 rue Corneille. ☎ *01-43-26-03-65.* www.bastide-odeon.com. *Métro: Odéon. (Exit the station and take rue de l'Odéon south to place de l'Odéon, where the Théâtre de l'Odéon is located. To the left of the theater is rue Corneille; take this about 45m/150 ft. to the restaurant.) Main courses: 10€–19€ ($16–$30). Lunch menu at 26€ ($42). AE, MC, V. Open: Tues–Sat 12:30–2 p.m. and 7:30–10:30 p.m. Closed first three weeks in Aug and Dec 25–Jan 1.*

La Cigale Récamier
$$ Invalides (7e) CLASSIC BISTRO

Located on rue Récamier, a stone-paved garden square, La Cigale has elegant outdoor dining during warm weather with some of the best food you can get in Paris for these prices. Though the original owner retired after 30 years, you can still get the delicious house specialty, delicate soufflés, beaten high and brimming with Camembert or tarragon cream. Try the Camembert and morels, a seasonal luxury. If you're not in the mood for a soufflé, other tempting entrees include steak au poivre (steak with coarsely ground peppercorns) or *filet de dorade* (filet of sea bream). For dessert try — you got it! — a soufflé made with, among other things, pistachios or melt-in-your-mouth chocolate (with a chocolate fondue!) or Grand Marnier or almonds with rhubarb marmalade.

See map p. 140. 4 rue Récamier. ☎ *01-45-48-86-58. Reservations recommended. Métro: Sèvres-Babylone. (Exit the station at rue de Sèvres and cross over bd. Raspail to the Hôtel Lutétia. Rue Récamier is the street just behind the hotel. The restaurant is about 24m/80 ft. down.) Main courses: 19€–23€ ($30–$37). DC, MC, V. Open: Mon–Sat noon–2 p.m. and 7:30–11 p.m.*

L'Ambroisie
$$$$ Le Marais (4e) HAUTE CUISINE

This gorgeous, three Michelin-starred, spare-no-expense restaurant located in a 17th-century town house has been rated one of the best in France but has slipped a bit, and service is snobby. It counts among its diners former U.S. President Bill Clinton, who ate here as a guest of Jacques Chirac. Served in two mirrored and frescoed high-ceilinged dining rooms and a cozy back room (in summer there is an outdoor terrace), the seasonal specialties created by Chef Bernard Pacaud may include an anise-flavored cold fennel soup with crawfish, or *civet de homard* (lobster stew), or a whole *poulet Bresse* (tender roasted chicken from Bresse) carved at the table and served with gnocchi. For dessert, try the *tarte fine,* which has won awards: It's a chocolate pie served with bitter chocolate and mocha ice cream. If you can afford it, this restaurant just begs to be the setting for marriage proposals, anniversaries, and other special and romantic events.

See map p. 138. 9 place des Vosges. ☎ 01-42-78-51-45. Reserve at least four weeks ahead. Métro: St-Paul. (Exit the station on rue St-Antoine and head east to rue de Birague, which leads into the place des Vosges. Turn left at the place des Vosges and follow the arcade around the corner to the restaurant.) Jacket and tie advised. Main courses: 86€–200€ ($165–$320). AE, MC, V. Open: Tues–Sat noon–1:30 p.m. and 8–9:30 p.m. Closed two weeks in Feb and three weeks in Aug.

La Poule au Pot
$$ Les Halles (1er)   CLASSIC BISTRO

When Les Halles still was Paris's marketplace, its workers came to La Poule au Pot to share this signature dish, an old French recipe of chicken stewed with broth and vegetables, which has been served here since 1935 with much success — if the *livre d'or* (a gold book filled with the names of visiting celebrities) means anything. After the market's demise, visits from such celebrities as Maurice Chevalier, the Rolling Stones, and Prince kept this Parisian bistro on the map. The atmosphere created by the long zinc bar, *pots* of wine, red leather banquettes, a blackboard with the day's market specials, wood paneling, and waiters in long aprons transports you to another era, and traditional French fare is the name of the game here. Begin with a dozen escargot cooked Burgundy style with butter, garlic, and parsley or *oeufs cocotte à la crème* (eggs baked with cream), then try a filet of salmon cooked in a saffron cream sauce, or the succulent house *poule au pot* with a tureen of the broth on the side. Finish with a velvety crème brûlée.

See map p. 138. 9 rue Vauvilliers. ☎ 01-42-36-32-96. Métro: Louvre-Rivoli. (Exit the station on rue de Rivoli and cross the street to rue du Louvre. Walk two blocks to rue St-Honoré and make a right. Proceed two blocks to rue Vauvilliers. The restaurant is near the end of the street, close to the gardens of the Forum des Halles.) Main courses: 24€–36€ ($38–$58); prix fixe: 33€ ($53). MC, V. Open: Mon–Sat 7 p.m.–5 a.m.

L'Aréa
$$ Le Marais/Bastille (4e)   MIDDLE EASTERN/BRAZILIAN

Trendy artist types, musicians, and locals have been packing the house for Brazilian–Middle Eastern food at this inexpensive hip joint with a happening vibe near the place Bastille for 17 years. Owner Edward Chuaka was born in Brazil to Lebanese parents, and his menu not only shows it but attracts a big crowd of regulars. Choose such starters from either Brazil or Liban as *filezinho à Carioca* (ground beef marinated in red wine) or a *mezzé* plate of hummus, tabbouleh, and other assorted Lebanese salads, main courses like *Moqueca de peixe* (filet of dorade served in a sauce of coconut milk, tomato, peppers, and palm over rice) and *Grillades Libanaises* (skewers of Lebanese sausage, beef, lamb, and chicken served with tabbouleh and potatoes). Go early to get a seat; the place gets full later in the evening, with people waiting at the bar and spilling into the quiet rue des Tournelles.

See map p. 138. 10 rue des Tournelles. ☎ *01-42-72-96-50. Métro: Bastille. Main courses: 13€–19€ ($21–$30); fixed-price lunch menu: 15€ ($24), fixed-price dinner menu: 28€ ($45). AE, MC, V. Open: Tues–Sun noon–3p.m., 6 p.m.–2am.*

L'Atelier de Joël Robuchon
$$–$$$ Eiffel Tower (7e) MODERN BISTRO

This Michelin-starred place is still a *bonne addresse* among the dining chic. Joël Robuchon, arguably the most famous chef in France when he retired in the 1990s, came out of retirement in 2003 to open this chic red-and-black lacquered restaurant that serves simple French and Asian fusion food in which the ingredients are the real stars. Seating is at a 36-person counter that wraps around the open kitchen. The idea is to give diners a "behind the line" experience, so you may see Robuchon giving orders, sous-chefs saucing main dishes, or a pig being roasted on a spit. The menu continually changes. Robuchon offers tapaslike tasting plates that diners are encouraged to share. Main dishes can include tournedos of beef flavored with Malabar black pepper, cutlets of milk-fed lamb with thyme, or bass cooked in its own juices with lemon grass. Robuchon has a no-reservations policy after the first lunch seating, so get here early.

See map p. 140. In the Hôtel du Port-Royal, 5-7 rue de Montalembert. ☎ *01-42-22-56-56. Reservations only accepted for the first seating. Métro: Rue du Bac. Main courses: 17€–65€ ($20–$78); prix fixe: 80€ ($96). AE, DC, MC, V. Open: Daily. First seating 11:30 a.m.–12:30 p.m., second seating 2–3:30 p.m. Dinner 6:30 p.m.*

La Tour de Montlhéry Chez Denise
$$–$$$ Les Halles (1er) CLASSIC FRENCH

If you don't eat meat, this is not the place for you. This is a meat lover's paradise, and evidence is everywhere: Hams and sausages dangle from the wood beams and efficient waiters whisk enormous plates of food such as lamb's brains to appreciative customers. This is an old Parisian restaurant with a zinc bar graced by wine barrels; seating is quite close (you'll probably become friends with the diners on each side of you by the end of the night). The less expensive items on the menu tend to be dishes like tripe Calvados, stuffed with potatoes, and stuffed cabbage and kidneys, though the proprietors do pay a nod to fish lovers with a tasty seafood terrine and *tuna tartare*. Other typical dishes are grilled lamb chops, *steak-frites* (beef filet and french fries), and, for those who want to try truly authentic, reputably delicious French fare, *steak tartare* (marinated raw beef topped by a raw egg). *Bon courage!*

See map p. 138. 5 rue des Prouvaires. ☎ *01-42-36-21-82. Reservations required. Métro: Louvre-Rivoli. (Exit the station on rue de Rivoli and head east to rue du Roule. Follow rue du Roule to rue St-Honoré, where Roule becomes rue des Prouvaires. The restaurant is near the corner of Prouvaires and St-Honoré.) Main courses: 23€–38€ ($37–$61). V. Open: Mon–Fri noon–5 a.m. Closed mid-July to mid-Aug.*

Le Cinq
$$$$ Champs-Elysées (8e)   HAUTE CUISINE

Chef Phillippe Legendre has earned two Michelin stars for this restaurant in the Four Seasons Georges V, and I've been raving about it since 2000. This is a true temple to *haute cuisine* from the gray-and-gold dining room with its high ceilings and overstuffed chairs to the Limoges porcelain and Riedel stemware created for the restaurant. The sumptuous and inventive cuisine is served by the perfect waitstaff. Diners may start with an eggplant risotto with a carpaccio of *cèpes* (mushrooms) from Sologne served with black truffles and continue with milk-fed Pyrénées lamb roasted in sesame and mint cream. For dessert, a Manjari chocolate soufflé flavored with orange or the chef's choice of assorted chocolate desserts may be on the menu. The wine list here is magnificent; if he has time, chief sommelier Thierry Hamon may even give you a tour of the cellar.

See map p. 138. 31 av. George V (in the Four Seasons George V Hotel). ☎ *01-49-52-71-54. Reservations required. Métro: George V. Light tasting menu: 135€ ($216), gourmet tasting menu (without beverage): 210€ ($336); main courses: 80€–260€ ($128–$416). AE, MC, V. Open: Daily noon–2:30 p.m. and 6:30–11 p.m.*

Le 404
$$ Le Marais (3e)   MOROCCAN

This is one happening place where patrons and staff may dance on the bar or in the aisles and the vibe is high energy and downright fun. Named for the Peugot 404, one of the most popular models of car in Morocco in the 1960s, the restaurant is known as much for its fashionable clientele as its tasty *tajines,* couscous, and other North African dishes, all eaten in a dining room that simply evokes another place with carved wooden screens in front of tall windows, low (and close-to-your-neighbor) seating, and exposed stone walls. You may start the evening with a meze tasting plate of hummus and other regional appetizers and continue on to a flaky and tender chicken *tajine* stewed in lemon and olives (*tajine* is the clay pot in which everything is cooked) or couscous with seven vegetables.

See map p. 138. 69 rue des Gravilliers. ☎ *01-42-74-57-81. Reservations required. Métro: Arts et Métiers. Main courses: 17€–24€ ($27–$38). AE, MC, V. Open: Mon–Sun noon–3 p.m., nightly 8 p.m.–midnight.*

Fast French food zones

When you're short on time or money, the following streets have many restaurants with fast service at low prices.

- ✔ **Avenue d'Ivry** and **Avenue de Choisy, 13e:** Far off the tourist track, the Vietnamese, Chinese, and Thai restaurants along these wide avenues cater to the local Southeast Asian population. Prices are low and quality is high, and you can eat like the locals.

- ✔ **Boulevard de Belleville, 11e:** This street features many *couscouseries* (couscous restaurants) that are reasonably priced and satisfactory, if not outstanding. Middle Eastern snacks, pastries, and a glass of mint tea make an exotic and inexpensive meal.

- ✔ **Boulevard du Montparnasse, 14e:** It's not fast food, but it's still worth a mention. The block between rue Vavin and boulevard Raspail has four cafes with literary associations (early-20th-century writers such as Hemingway, Fitzgerald, Joyce, and St-Vincent Millay spent a lot of time at La Coupole, Le Dôme, Le Select, and La Rotonde) as well as high and moderately priced seafood restaurants, crêperies, sandwich shops, and ethnic eateries.

- ✔ **Métro Belleville, 11e:** The streets radiating out from this station are the northern headquarters for Asian cuisine. You can usually slurp down noodle soup at any hour of the day and well into the night.

- ✔ **Rue des Rosiers, in the Marais, 3e:** People have been known to trudge across town for the huge pita-bread sandwiches sold on this street. Stuffed with falafel (deep-fried chickpea balls), eggplant, and salad, and then topped with your choice of sauce, this must be the best 5€ ($8) meal in town.

- ✔ **Rue du Montparnasse, 14e:** The street between boulevard Edgar Quinet and boulevard du Montparnasse is a crêperie row of inexpensive Breton eateries. Whether the crêpes are sugared up with syrups and jam or stuffed with vegetables and meat (these are often called *galettes*), they make a tasty light meal for less than 11€ ($18).

- ✔ **Rue Sainte-Anne, 2e:** Sushi usually is expensive in Paris, but because this street lies within the same neighborhood as many Japanese businesses, you find the freshest fish and most authentic Japanese dishes at moderate prices.

Le Grenier de Notre-Dame
$–$$ Latin Quarter (5e)   VEGETARIAN

This cozy, two-level plant-filled restaurant near Notre-Dame opened in 1978 on a street that once was home to butcher shops. The food, which can be inconsistent, is generally good, filling, and nearly all vegetarian, but vegans take note: Eggs, cheese, and some fish are used here. Especially recommended is the miso soup with tofu and seaweed and the vegetable pâté served with warm toast; a white bean cassoulet filled with tofu, *seitan*, and vegetables; and the enormous portions of lentil moussaka made with lentils, white cheese, egg, tomatoes, and eggplant. For dessert try the homemade chocolate cake with orange sauce. The wine list includes a variety of organic offerings. Service varies from downright warm to grumpy.

See map p. 140. 18 rue de la Bûcherie. ☎ *01-43-29-98-29. RER: St-Michel/Notre-Dame. (Exit onto quai de Montebello; turn right onto rue d'Arcole, then left onto rue de la Bûcherie.) Three courses at lunch: 16€ ($26), dinner 18€ ($29); main courses: 15€–17€ ($24–$27). MC, V. Open: Mon–Fri noon–2:30 p.m. and 6:30–10:30 p.m., Sat and Sun noon–11 p.m.*

Le Kokolion
$–$$ Montmartre (18e)   CLASSIC FRENCH

A red facade and colored lights illuminate the entrance of this small and adorable little French "resto." Atmosphere is key here: Funky glass spheres hang from the ceiling and provide some dim lighting, posters of old movies and recent plays in the quarter are also displayed, along with the occasional kitschy photograph. Open only for dinner, service can be slow once it gets crowded. The food quality is even higher than the prices you pay. A 24€ ($40) dinner menu can start out with an *os à moelle gratiné avec sel du cuve ronde et toast* (a beef bone-marrow casserole made with reservoir salt) or *aubergine grillé au chevre et tomates confits, sauce pistou* (eggplant grilled with goat's cheese and preserved tomatoes in a basil, garlic, and olive oil sauce); dinner could be a half a rooster roasted in tarragon gravy served with homemade potato purée or rack of lamb roasted in an herbed crust. Their wine list is great and inexpensive: Ask the Kevin Spacey look-alike waiter for recommendations (he may be the only one present). The desserts will unfortunately leave something to be desired (at these low prices you can't have everything!) so think about that before you decide on a prix-fixe menu that includes dessert. The Kokolion closes late, as it serves dinner to the after-theater crowd from the nearby Théâtre de l'Atelier. You can start dining as late as midnight, but be warned that by 10 p.m., waiters can be slow.

See map p. 138. 62 rue d'Orsel. ☎ *01-42-58-24-41. Reservations suggested. Métro: Abbesses or Anvers. Dinner menu: 25€ ($40); main courses: 16€–24€ ($26–$38). MC, V. Open: Tues–Sat 7:30 p.m.–12:30 a.m.*

Le Père Claude
$$ Eiffel Tower (5e)   CLASSIC BISTRO

The family that runs Le Père Claude does it with much love as evidenced by the thoughtfully rustic outside (empty champagne barrels, a wagon wheel, birch branches, and a bench) and the brown and cream interior where pictures of waitstaff through the years adorn some of the walls. (The restaurant even has its own jazz band with the names of its members on the front door.) Expect to tuck into enormous portions of red meat dishes here. Starters may include warm sausage with pistachios and apples, duck liver pan fried with tortellini and morel mushrooms, and yes, *cuisses de grenouilles* (frogs' legs). The *panaché de viandes* is an assortment of perfectly roasted meats served with a comforting heap of mashed potatoes. Make sure you specify how you want the beef cooked, or it will be served the way the French like it — *bleu,* which means very, very rare (refer to Chapter 2 for more about how meat is cooked). *Bouillabaisse* is the house special Thursday and Friday nights. President Jacques Chirac and Don King have been spotted (separately) chowing down here, but it's usually home to families and, to a lesser extent, tourists with big appetites. After dinner, you can stroll up the avenue de La Motte-Picquet and take in a view of the spectacular illuminated Eiffel Tower.

See map p. 140. 51 av. de La Motte-Picquet. ☎ *01-47-34-03-05. Métro: La-Motte-Picquet-Grenelle. (Exit the station on av. de La Motte-Picquet and head northeast about .4km/¼ mile, toward the Champ de Mars.) Main courses: 18€–62€ ($29–$99). AE, MC, V. Open: Daily noon–2:30 p.m. and 7–11:30 p.m.*

L'Epi Dupin
$$ St-Germain-des-Prés (6e)   FRENCH

L'Epi Dupin is still perhaps the best of the bistros (see "Knowing the difference between a cafe and a bistro" earlier) and a good value as well. Chef François Pasteau, pairs fine modern bistro cuisine with an antique French setting of hewn beams and stone walls (tables are quite close together). The food, which Pasteau buys fresh daily at the Rungis green market, runs to traditional rural French, with lighter, modern alternatives such as salmon carpaccio or endive *tatin* with goat cheese. Service, though friendly, can be seriously rushed as staff scramble to accommodate three seatings a night.

See map p. 140. 11 rue de Dupin (between rue de Sèvres and rue du Cherche Midi). ☎ *01-42-22-64-56. Reservations strongly recommended. Métro: Sèvres Babylone. Fixed-price menus: 25€ ($40) lunch, 35€ ($56) dinner. AE, MC, V. Open: Tues–Fri noon–2:30 p.m., Mon–Fri 7:30–10:30 p.m. Closed three weeks in Aug.*

Le Potager du Marais
$ Le Marais (3e)   VEGETARIAN

Privacy is out, and seating is at 13 tables pushed together at this vegetarian restaurant steps from Centre Pompidou that gets so packed that reservations are a must. The food, most of it organic, is generally very good. The dining room is small with exposed stone walls, plants, and apricot tones. Most of the offerings are organic and vegans can be accommodated. You may start with a bowl of vegetarian French onion soup or eggplant pâté and continue with a *crouistillant des légumes* (a cutlet made of vegetables) or shepherd's pie or a fondue made up of leeks and Comté cheese. A must for dessert is the *fondant au chocolat* with custard sauce. Browse the shops along Rambuteau as it meanders into the heart of the Marais.

22 rue Rambuteau. ☎ *01-42-74-24-66. Métro: Rambuteau. Three-course prix fixe: 22€ ($35); main courses: 15€–23€ ($24–$37). AE, MC, V. Open: Mon–Sat noon–2:30 p.m. and 7–10:30 p.m.*

Keep it fresh: Eating veggie

Being a vegetarian can be challenging for those who also like dining out. Paris is no exception: Everyone's primary food group seems to be ham. Luckily for the vegans and vegetarians among us, there are several places where one can eat fantastic French food without involving any butchers. Below is a list of places to get vegetarian grub during your time in Paris.

✔ **Au Grain de Folies** (24 rue de la Vieuville, 18e; ☎ **01-42-58-15-57**; Métro: Abbesses) is a five-table restaurant that feels like you're eating in someone's kitchen. Soups, veggie tarts, and homemade desserts leave nothing to be desired.

✔ **Le Grenier de Notre-Dame** (see earlier).

✔ **Le Potager du Marais** (see later).

✔ Though meat is on the menu here, you can get a veggie take out from **Chez H'anna** (54 rue des Rosiers, 4e; ☎ **01-42-74-74-99**; Métro: St-Paul) that may include a massive falafel with a big cucumber and tomato salad on the side.

✔ **Le Boutegrill Chez Hamadi** (12 rue Boutebrie, 5e; ☎ **01-43-54-03-30**; Métro: St-Michel) is a Tunisian restaurant that also prepares excellent couscous meals, one of which is only stewed vegetables. Sip along with your meal a glass of *Mascara*, a well regarded Algerian wine.

✔ **Lemoni Café** (5 rue Herold, 1er; ☎ **01-45-08-49-84**; Métro: Palais Royal or Bourse or Les Halles) is a Greek-influenced organic (bio) lunch counter with a lot of vegetarian options and good value specials from 8.10€ to 14€ ($13–$22).

✔ **Les Puits des Légumes** (18 rue Cardinal Lemoine, 5e; ☎ **01-43-25-50-95**; Métro: Cardinal Lemoine) is a tiny restaurant that looks like a brightly lit friend's kitchen. Simple vegetarian fare is served here, and every Friday is couscous night.

Maison Chardenoux
$$ Bastille (11e)   CLASSIC BISTRO

This restaurant's turn-of-the-20th-century décor is the very essence of old Paris (it has been appointed a Monument Historique), and though out of the way, a meal here is worth the trek to an uninteresting neighborhood. A variety of French regional dishes are served in a dining room filled with swirling stucco decorations and brightened by etched windows with lacy curtains. The specialty of the house is *tête de veau traditionelle* (yes, that's calf's head; the meat is served in a broth of vegetables, peppercorns, and parsley); appetizers may include *terine de canard maison avec pain grille* (duck pâté with toast), or *escargots de bourgogne* (snails prepared with garlic, butter, and parsley). Main courses may include *bar grille entire au fenouil, haricots verts* (whole fish grilled with fennel and served with green beans) or *foie de veau à échalote, écrasée de pommes de terre* (veal liver with shallots and mashed potatoes). Desserts are classically Gallic. Try the layered pastry topped with powdered sugar and raspberries or a crème brûlée infused with jasmine.

See map p. 138. 1 rue Jules-Valles. ☎ *01-43-71-49-52. Métro: Charonne. (Exit the station on rue Charonne and walk one block to rue Jules-Valles. Turn left and walk to the end of the street. The restaurant is on the corner of rue Jules-Valles and rue Chanzy.) Main courses: 19€–24€ ($30–$38). AE, MC, V. Open: Daily noon–2:30 p.m. and 7–10:30 p.m.*

Restaurant du Palais-Royal
$$–$$$ Louvre (1er) CLASSIC FRENCH

The elegant arcade that encircles the gardens inside the Palais-Royal also surrounds this restaurant, making it one of the most romantic locations in Paris. Service is lacking during midday, as it is a favorite lunch spot for professionals working in the area; better to eat dinner here and avoid over-worked waiters and waitresses. Sit at the terrace on warm, sun-filled days and begin your meal with starters such as a beet and leek terrine or sardines from the Midi Marinées accompanied by quinoa tabbouleh. Main dishes vary with the season but may include veal à la Milanese with fresh homemade pasta or *Homard Breton de Notre Vivier Rôti et Beurre Coraillé* (whole roasted Breton lobster with coral butter). Risottos are also a specialty here. Try the good house red wine, served Lyonnaise-style in thick-bottomed bottles. The desserts are delicious; the pistachio and chocolate *mille-feuille* (puff pastry) and the *petits beignets* (little doughnuts) are divine. When dining outside just isn't an option, you can enjoy the dining room that shines in tones of gold, silver, and garnet.

See map p. 138. 43 rue Valois or 110 gallerie Valois (on the northeast side of the Palais-Royal arcade). ☎ *01-40-20-00-27. Métro: Palais-Royal-Musée du Louvre. Main courses: 18€–46€ ($29–$74). AE, DC, MC, V. Open: Mon–Fri noon–2:30 p.m. and 7–10 p.m. Closed late Dec to late Jan.*

Restaurant Perraudin
$$ Latin Quarter (5e) CLASSIC BISTRO

At this historic bistro, with its red-checked tablecloths and lace lampshades, jolly atmosphere, and staff that welcomes kids, you can get a bargain three-course lunch that may start with a goat cheese profiterole with tomato coulis or marinated raw salmon slices with dill, followed by the house specialty, *chateaubriand* (porterhouse steak) served in a variety of ways, including with foie gras, or try the beef filet with green pepper. Classic dishes such as duck confit and *gigot d'agneau* (leg of lamb) with *gratin Dauphinois* (cheese-topped potatoes) are on the à la carte menu. Desserts include nougat flavored ice cream with raspberry sauce and a hot apple tart with vanilla ice cream. Arrive early for a table because reservations aren't accepted here.

See map p. 140. 157 rue St-Jacques (on the west side of the Panthéon, take rue Soufflot to rue St-Jacques and turn left). ☎ *01-46-33-15-75. Reservations not accepted. RER: Luxembourg. Main courses: around 14€–23€ ($17–$29); three-course lunch menu: 19€ ($35); three-course dinner menu: 29€ ($46). No credit cards. Open: Mon–Sat noon–2 p.m. and 8–11 p.m.*

Restaurant Plaza Athénée (Alain Ducasse)
$$$$ Champs-Elysées (8e) HAUTE CUISINE

Multi-starred Michelin chef Alain Ducasse divides his time between his restaurants in Paris, New York, and Monaco. His "modern and authentic" dishes reflect the room created by celebrated designer Patrick Jouin (the chandeliers have 10,000 crystal pendants) and contain produce from every corner of France — rare local vegetables, fish from the coasts, and dishes incorporating turnips, celery, turbot, cuttlefish, and Bresse fowl. Specialties may include duck foie gras from the Landes region served with frozen black tea, or thick, oozing slabs of pork grilled to a crisp.

See map p. 138. In the Hotel Plaza Athénée, 25 av. Montaigne. ☎ 01-53-67-65-00. www.alain-ducasse.com. *Reservations required. Métro: FDR or Alma-Marceau. Main courses: 85€–175€ ($136–$280); fixed-price menus: 240€–360€ ($384–$576). AE, DC, MC, V. Open: Thurs–Fri 12:45–2:15 p.m., Mon–Fri 7:45–10:15 p.m. Closed mid-July to mid-Aug.*

Un Jour à Peyrassol
$$ Bourse (2e) PROVENÇAL

The order of the Knights of Malta once owned the Commanderie of Peyrassol, and this petite restaurant serves and sells the wines that have been made there, along with delicious Provençal dishes. Located on a street where those who aren't in the know flock to Le Grand Colbert, this well-kept secret also serves regional truffles in most of its dishes in a rustic atmosphere made up of exposed stone and brick, wood, and wine barrels. You may start with a salad with two duck breasts on a bed of green beans or a homemade truffled foie gras. Main courses include grilled *tartines* with 8 grams of black or *brumale* truffles or gnocchi served in a cream sauce of *brumale* truffle. This is worth the visit, and you can buy many of the products sold here in their next-door shop.

See map p. 138. 13 rue Vivienne. ☎ 01-42-60-12-92. www.zekitchengalerie.fr. *Métro: Bourse. main courses: 14€–35€ ($22–$56). AE, DC, MC, V. Open: Mon–Fri 12:30 to 2 p.m., Mon–Sat 7:30–10 p.m. Closed weekends.*

Ze Kitchen Galerie
$$ St-Germain-des-Prés (6e) MODERN BISTRO

William Ledeuil opened this hip and sophisticated place in 2002 near the trendy Les Bookinistes, where he worked as chef. It is indeed an art gallery and kitchen: The walls of the spacious and spare dining room feature as their only decoration artwork that changes every three months. The innovative, Asian-inspired menu, created from a tiny windowed kitchen at the far side of the room, changes every five weeks. The menu is broken down into soup and pasta starters and grilled main courses (*à la plancha*). Starters may include a soup of snail and conchigli pasta flavored with a horseradish-parsley emulsion or duck ravioli with Thai herbs. Mains may be grilled milk-fed lamb shoulder served with a spicy tamarind and miso condiment or grilled squid and octopus with green apple and curcuma.

Since portions are small, you'll more than likely have room for dessert, which may include tasty ginger-orange cake served with a blood-orange sorbet. Reservations are recommended because this restaurant fills up fast.

See map p. 140. 4 rue des Grands Augustins. ☎ *01-44-32-00-32.* www.zekitchen galerie.fr. *Reservations recommended. Métro: St-Michel. Main courses: 22€–30€ ($35–$51). AE, DC, MC, V. Open: Mon–Fri noon–2:30 p.m., Mon–Sat 7–11 p.m.*

Dining and Snacking on the Go

Face it: Who can sit down to multiple-course meals every day — even if they are cooked by legendary chefs? Fortunately, many alternatives to a full meal are available. Choose from street carts, sandwich places, and tea salons. And of course, there's that Parisian institution, the cafe. Listed here are some of Paris's best cafes and their more sophisticated sisters, the wine bars where you, too, can join in the great French art of people-watching!

See the "Light Meals in the Heart of the Right Bank" and "Light Meals in the Heart of the Left Bank" maps for locations of establishments in this section.

Partaking of Paris street food

Some street vendors sell Belgian waffles, called *gaufres,* served warm with powdered sugar or chocolate sauce, but the Parisian street food you see the most is the *crêpe* — a thin wheat pancake stuffed with a filling that's either salty or sweet. When served with savory fillings, such as cheese or mushrooms, a street vendor may either call it a *crêpe salé* (salted or savory), or a *galette.* A true *galette,* a specialty from Normandy, is made with buckwheat and is only cooked on one side, unlike a tradi-tional crêpe cooked on both sides. However it is cooked, both are deli-cious and constitute a meal. Sweet crêpe fillings include plain powdered sugar, chocolate-hazelnut spread, ice cream, or jam (called *compote*). Talk about a sugar rush!

You can find stalls or carts selling crêpes near most of the major attrac-tions, in the parks and bigger gardens, and along the rue de Rivoli between the Marais and the place de la Concorde. When you buy a crêpe from a street vendor, you won't have much of a choice of sweet fillings; for a more extensive menu visit a crêperie.

 Make a meal of crêpes at one of the many good establishments on rue du Montparnasse, where you can settle down in a peaceful atmosphere with a bowl of cider (a Breton specialty), a *galette* for a main course, and a crêpe for dessert — usually under 12€ ($19) a person (Métro: Edgar Quinet or Montparnasse-Bienvenüe).

The other typical Parisian street food, *panini,* is also sold just about any-where. Named for the Italian-style bread with which they're made, panini can be almost any filling stuck between two slices of bread, then flattened and grilled between two hot plates. The most common fillings are mozzarella, basil, and sun-dried tomatoes (a pizza sandwich, if you will). Panini are cheap, tasty, and easy to eat on the run.

Snacking on sandwiches

Even sandwiches are delicious in France. Sandwich (and more) shops Lina's, Cosi, and Le Pain Quotidien, open until the early evening, make their own breads. Following is a list of sandwich shops you may want to try:

- ✔ **Cosi,** 54 rue de Seine, 6e (☎ 01-46-33-35-36; Métro: St-Germain-des-Prés; see map p. 162), has branched out across the ocean and now has locations around the U.S. and U.K. It serves its sandwiches on delicious homemade flatbread, and fillings are plentiful and delicious. You can even build your own salads if you want — this place is a bit of New York–style service in the heart of Paris.

- ✔ **Le Pain Quotidien,** 18 place du Marché-St-Honoré, 1er (☎ **01-42-96-31-70;** Métro: Tuileries; see map p. 160), like Cosi, now has stores in other countries. It's part of a Belgian chain serving mouthwatering *tartines* (open-faced sandwiches) made with combinations such as country ham and Gruyère, a goat-cheese-and-honey duo; or a combination of tuna, hummus, and fresh vegetables. The fresh salads here are also a good choice. There are five locations all around Paris; one is in the Marais at 18 rue des Archives, 4e (☎ **01-44-54-03-07**) and another is in the Latin Quarter, not far from the Panthéon at 138 rue Mouffetard, 5e (☎ **01-55-43-91-99**).

- ✔ **Lina's,** 22 rue St-Pères, 6e (☎ **01-40-20-42-78;** Métro: St-Germain-des-Prés; see map p. 160), packs an assortment of fillings onto whole-grain breads and rolls, American deli–style. Other locations are at 15 rue du Louvre, 1er (☎ **01-40-41-15-00**), and 1 bd. de Courcelles, 8e (☎ **01-40-08-01-00**), not far from the designer boutiques.

- ✔ **Pomme de Pain,** 76 rue de Rivoli, 4e (☎ **01-42-78-57-29;** Métro: Hôtel de Ville; see map p. 160), boasts a fast-food-style counter where staff slice baguettes in half and layer on the toppings of your choice. The menu specials (a sandwich, potato or dessert, and one drink) are usually a fair deal. Branches are located all across the city, including one at 2 bd. Haussmann, 9e (☎ **01-48-24-20-60**), and another at 1-7 rue Pierre Lescot, Basement level 3, Forum des Halles, 1er (☎ **01-40-39-94-63**).

Assembling a picnic, Parisian style

Grab a crusty baguette or two, some dried sausage, a wedge of cheese, and a few pieces of fruit and head to the nearest park or to a garden that strikes your fancy. Picnicking in Paris can be as fun and as unforgettable as a meal in a three-star restaurant at just a fraction of the cost. In this

Light Meals in the Heart of the Right Bank

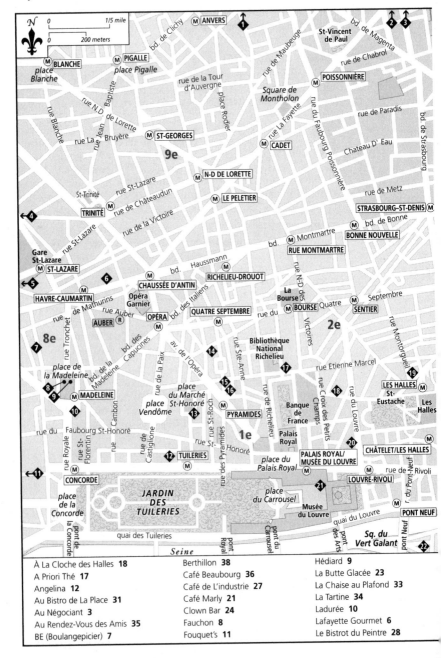

À La Cloche des Halles **18**	Berthillon **38**	Hédiard **9**
A Priori Thé **17**	Café Beaubourg **36**	La Butte Glacée **23**
Angelina **12**	Café de L'industrie **27**	La Chaise au Plafond **33**
Au Bistro de La Place **31**	Café Marly **21**	La Tartine **34**
Au Négociant **3**	Clown Bar **24**	Ladurée **10**
Au Rendez-Vous des Amis **35**	Fauchon **8**	Lafayette Gourmet **6**
BE (Boulangepicier) **7**	Fouquet's **11**	Le Bistrot du Peintre **28**

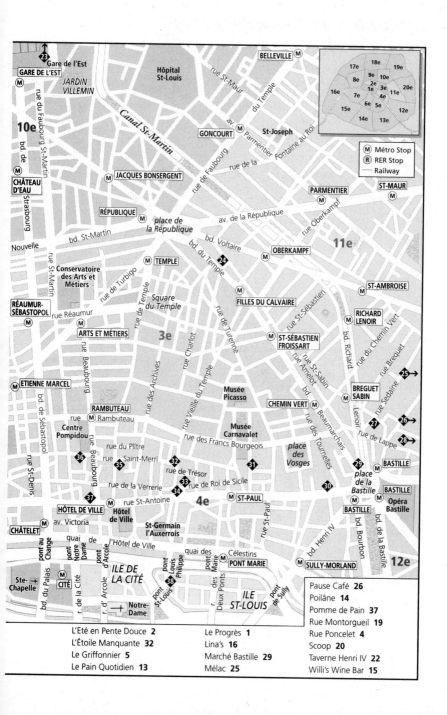

Pause Café **26**
Poilâne **14**
Pomme de Pain **37**
Rue Montorgueil **19**
Rue Poncelet **4**
Scoop **20**
Taverne Henri IV **22**
Willi's Wine Bar **15**

L'Eté en Pente Douce **2**
L'Étoile Manquante **32**
Le Griffonnier **5**
Le Pain Quotidien **13**

Le Progrès **1**
Lina's **16**
Marché Bastille **29**
Mélac **25**

Light Meals in the Heart of the Left Bank

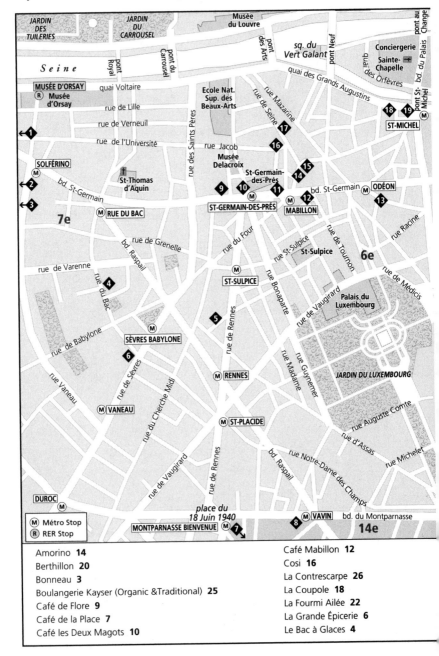

Amorino **14**
Berthillon **20**
Bonneau **3**
Boulangerie Kayser (Organic &Traditional) **25**
Café de Flore **9**
Café de la Place **7**
Café les Deux Magots **10**

Café Mabillon **12**
Cosi **16**
La Contrescarpe **26**
La Coupole **18**
La Fourmi Ailée **22**
La Grande Épicerie **6**
Le Bac à Glaces **4**

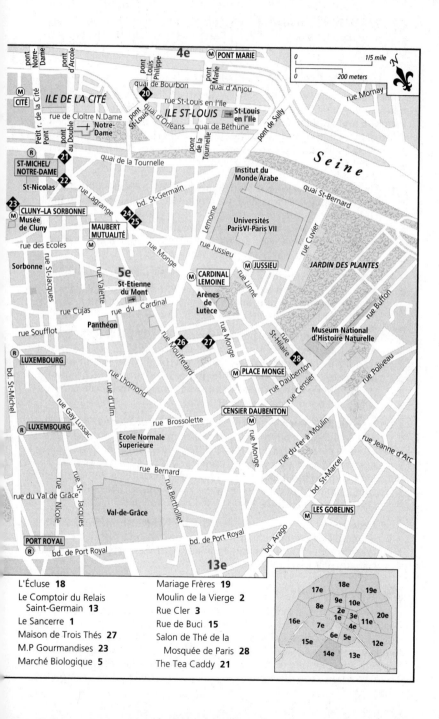

L'Écluse **18**

Le Comptoir du Relais
  Saint-Germain **13**

Le Sancerre **1**

Maison de Trois Thés **27**

M.P Gourmandises **23**

Marché Biologique **5**

Mariage Frères **19**

Moulin de la Vierge **2**

Rue Cler **3**

Rue de Buci **15**

Salon de Thé de la
  Mosquée de Paris **28**

The Tea Caddy **21**

section, discover where to stock up on provisions. (Note: You can also assemble picnic fixings cheaply at Parisian supermarkets all across the city.)

The traiteurs (gourmet food shops)

Look for the word *traiteur,* which designates a food shop that sells ready-made meat, pasta, and salad dishes. The two most famous, **Fauchon** and **Hédiard,** have main stores at place de la Madeleine, 8e (Métro: Madeleine), and branches all across Paris. Every neighborhood has several good *traiteurs* so be on the lookout, and don't hesitate to ask your hotel staff for recommendations.

- ✔ **Fauchon,** 30 place de la Madeleine, 8e (☎ **01-70-39-38-00;** Métro: Madeleine; see map p. 160), was founded in 1886. This is *the* high-end food shop with everything from foie gras and Norwegian smoked salmon to caviar to fancy breads and cheeses. Their *épicerie* and cave together will entirely stock your picnic basket. Open Monday to Saturday 9 a.m. to 8 p.m.

- ✔ **Hédiard,** 21 place de la Madeleine, 8e (☎ **01-43-12-88-88;** Métro: Madeleine; see map p. 160), is a gourmet food shop that sells upscale products, wine, and ready-made food to go. Open Monday to Saturday from 9 a.m. to 10 p.m.

- ✔ **Lafayette Gourmet,** 48 bd. Haussmann, 9e (☎ **01-42-82-34-56,** or 01-42-81-25-61; Métro: Havre-Caumartin; see map p. 160), is another wonderful grocery store that has everything you need for a picnic. It's located smack in the middle of the Galeries Lafayette complex (in the men's store). Open Monday to Saturday from 9:30 a.m. to 7:30 p.m.; open Thursday until 9 p.m.

- ✔ **La Grande Épicerie,** Le Bon Marché, 38 rue de Sèvres, 7e (☎ **01-44-39-81-00;** Métro: Sèvres-Babylone; see map p. 162), may be the best grocery store on the Left Bank. It has large *traiteur* and wine departments and sells everything from cleaning supplies to gourmet chocolate to fresh fish. Picnics just aren't complete without fresh salad expertly measured and mixed from this foodie wonderland. Open Monday to Saturday from 8:30 a.m. to 9 p.m.

- ✔ **Lenoire,** 10 rue St-Antoine, 4e (☎ **01-53-01-91-91;** Métro: Bastille), is an up-and-coming chain with locations around the city. Especially good are its chocolates and exquisite little desserts. Open Monday to Saturday 10 a.m. to 8 p.m.

The street markets

Every neighborhood in Paris has its street market, and it's probably the best place to find the freshest produce, cheeses of excellent quality, and other picnic supplies. Even when you don't buy anything, visiting one or two is worth the authentic reflection of Parisian society you encounter. Markets are generally open from Tuesday through Saturday, from around 7 a.m. to 1 p.m., and of course, the pickings are better the earlier you go.

The ones open on Sunday are indicated. Some of the more well known include:

- ✔ **Marché Bastille,** 11e (Métro: Bastille; see map p. 160): This huge market sells everything from game, cheese, and vegetables to fish and condiments. Open Thursday from 7 a.m. to 2:30 p.m. and Sunday 7 a.m. to 3 p.m.

- ✔ **Marché Biologique,** boulevard Raspail between rue du Cherche-Midi and rue de Rennes, 6e (Métro: Rennes; see map p. 162): This all-organic market features greengrocers, winemakers, butchers, and bakers. Open Sunday 9 a.m. to 2 p.m. An "inorganic" market takes place here Tuesday and Friday from 7 a.m. to 2:30 p.m.

- ✔ **Place Monge,** 5e (Métro: Monge): One of the oldest markets in Paris on one of the city's more interesting streets. Sing along with accordion players on Sunday mornings. Open Wednesday and Friday between 7:30 a.m. and 2:30 p.m., 7 a.m. to 3 p.m. on Sundays.

- ✔ **Rue Cler,** 7e (Métro: Ecole-Militaire; see map p. 162): See how diplomats shop for their dinner in this chic market. Open Tuesday through Saturday mornings between 8:30 a.m. and 1 p.m. and again from 5 to 7 p.m. Sundays open only in the morning up to noon.

- ✔ **Rue de Buci,** 6e (Métro: Odéon; see map p. 162): This lively market is close to all the Latin Quarter action. Open Tuesday to Sunday mornings between 8 a.m. and noon.

- ✔ **Rue Montorgueil,** 1er (Métro: Les Halles/Châtelet; see map p. 160): Have breakfast at one of the many sidewalk cafes before choosing your produce. Open Tuesday through Saturday from 8 a.m. to 1 p.m. and 4 to 7 p.m.

- ✔ **Rue Poncelet,** 17e (Métro: Ternes; see map p. 160): The Poncelet market is especially renowned for its fresh fruit stalls. Open Tuesday through Saturday mornings between 8:30 a.m. and noon and again from 2:30 until 6 p.m.

The best bakeries

You want a fresh baguette for your picnic, and you can find bakeries *(boulangeries)* on nearly every corner in residential neighborhoods. Keep in mind that quality of the breads varies considerably.

Long lines of locals on weekend mornings or evenings before dinner give away the best bakeries. You can get a sandwich or a quiche to go, but be warned that bakeries here offer what seem to be very plain sandwiches — often just a slice of bread or cheese on a baguette with no condiment or other accoutrement. If you want a sandwich with more filling, look for the name of an ingredient plus *"crudités,"* which means that it comes with raw vegetables, usually lettuce, cucumbers, or even tomatoes, and mayonnaise). For a chicken sandwich with raw veggies, for example, ask for *poulet crudités* (poo-*lay* crew-dee-tay). Below are some of Paris's best bakeries.

✔ **BE (Boulangepicier),** 73 bd. de Courcelles, 8e; ☎ **01-46-22-20-20.** Open Monday to Saturday from 7 a.m. to 8 p.m. Métro: Courcelles or Ternes; see map p. 160.

✔ **Bonneau,** 75 rue d'Auteuil, 16e; ☎ **01-46-51-12-25.** Open Tuesday through Sunday from 6:30 a.m. to 8:30 p.m. Métro: Michel-Ange-Auteuil; see map p. 162.

✔ **Boulangerie Kayser** (organic), 14 rue Monge, 5e; ☎ **01-44-07-17-81.** Open Tuesday through Sunday 8 a.m. to 8 p.m. Métro: Maubert Mutualité; see map p. 162.

✔ **Boulangerie Kayser** (traditional), 8 rue Monge, 5e; ☎ **01-44-07-01-42.** Open Wednesday through Monday from 6:30 a.m. to 8:30 p.m. Métro: Maubert Mutualité; see map p. 162.

✔ **Caumont,** 33 rue Coquillière, 1e; ☎ **01-45-08-57-60.** Open Monday through Friday from 7 a.m. to 8 p.m.

✔ **Le Grenier au Pain,** 38 rue des Abbesses, 18e; ☎ **01-46-06-41-81.** Open Friday through Tuesday, from 7:30 a.m. to 8 p.m. Métro: Abbesses.

✔ **Moulin de la Vierge,** 166 av. de Suffren, 15e; ☎ **01-47-83-45-55.** Open Friday to Wednesday from 7 a.m. to 8 p.m. Métro: Sèvres-Lecourbe; see map p. 162.

✔ **Poilâne,** 8 rue du Cherche-midi, 6e; ☎ **01-45-48-42-59.** Open Monday to Saturday from 7:15 a.m. to 8:15 p.m. Métro: St-Sulpice or Sèvres Babylone; see map p. 160.

There are so many different types of bread available in these bakeries that a complete list would probably be impossible to compile accurately. However, the most common is the *baguette* — long, fat, and crispy. If you're feeling a little adventurous, spend a euro and change, instead of the requisite 85 centimes, on a *baguette de campagne, à l'ancienne,* or *de tradition.* These names mean that the baguette dough, which is prepared by hand, is left overnight in order to let the yeast develop. The result is a much more flavorful and chewier interior with an off-white, more rustic look than the simple white-interior baguettes. The extra 20 to 40 centimes will go a long way. Look for *boulangeries* that say ARTISINAL, which means that they prepare all of their goods on the spot: These places sell pastries and bread with a mouthwatering taste that cannot be described in any language!

Watching the world go by at a cafe

Compiled here are some of my favorite cafes — places where you'll be comfortable reading the paper, writing postcards, people-watching, and soaking up the city's atmosphere while relaxing with a cup of coffee, a glass of wine or beer, or a sandwich, salad, or traditional French specialty like *pot-au-feu* (beef boiled with vegetables). Cafes are generally open from about 8 a.m. until 1 a.m., and most take MasterCard and Visa.

Au Bistro de La Place

This square on the place du Marché Sainte-Catherine is a pedestrian zone on the site of an 18th-century market, and this cafe's plant-covered terrace is the prettiest of all the bistros here. The food is terrific; you may find fresh vegetable soup served hot or cold or an artichoke pâté with salad, topped off with butter-browned salmon served with a saffron sauce. Even if you don't come here for a meal, visit during the afternoon to enjoy a leisurely drink or pastry on the terrace.

See map p. 160. 2 place du Marché Sainte-Catherine (between rue de Turenne and rue de Sevigné), 4e. ☎ *01-42-78-21-32. Métro: St-Paul. Closed Fri.*

Au Rendez-Vous des Amis

The ultramodern décor of so many Marais establishments has been left behind in favor of wood counters and well-worn chairs, with simple sketches and old photos on the walls. A hot goat cheese salad with some red wine is mouthwatering, and the people-watching on the chic rue Saint-Croix de la Bretonnerie is never boring. There are good wines by the glass starting at 4€ ($6.40).

See map p. 160. 10 rue Sainte-Croix de la Bretonnerie, 4e. ☎ *01-42-72-05-99. Métro: Hôtel de Ville.*

Café Beaubourg

This cafe overlooking the Centre Pompidou used to be the first word in hip, but now it's more of a hangout for the tourists visiting the site, about 60m (200 ft.) away. The backs of its white terrace chairs still resemble the lips in the Stravinsky Fountain just around the corner. The dark bi-level interior has large circular columns that soar to an illuminated ceiling and the walls are filled with books. A small wooden bridge spans the upper part of the cafe and leads to quieter, artistically designed tables. Tourist-filled or not, it's still a good place to recover with a beverage and a quick bite after perusing the attractions of the modern art museum next door.

See map p. 160. 43 rue St-Merri, 4e. ☎ *01-48-87-63-96. Métro: Rambuteau or Hôtel-de-Ville.*

Café de Flore

In the heart of St-Germain-des-Prés, this cafe will always be popular, even though the famous writers have moved on and its prices are high. Sartre is said to have written *Les Chemins de la Liberté (The Roads to Freedom)* at his table here, and he and Simone de Beauvoir saw people by appointment here. Other regulars included André Malraux and Guillaume Apollinaire. Paris's leading intellectual bookstore, La Hune, is right next door.

See map p. 162. 172 bd. St-Germain, 6e. ☎ *01-45-48-55-26. Métro: St-Germain-des-Prés.*

Café de la Place

If you're headed out of Paris via the Gare Montparnasse and you have a bit of extra time, skip the train station food stalls and come to this old-fashioned cafe overlooking small, tree-lined place Edgar Quinet, just around the corner and down the street. It's a calm and popular spot for young neighborhood residents. Browse the menu of inexpensive bistro specialties, or opt for a simple sandwich and a glass of wine. If you're lucky, there will be a *brocante* (flea market) or art fair in the square across the street.

See map p. 162. 23 rue d'Odessa, 14e. ☎ *01-42-18-01-55. Métro: Edgar-Quinet.*

Café de l'Industrie

This cafe is young, friendly, casual, and extremely popular; so much so that at night the crowd constantly overflows to the sidewalks next door and even across the street. To capitalize on its popularity, Café de l'Industrie bought its next-door neighbor and the former Moroccan restaurant across the street. Mod meets retro meets country in the spacious rooms that also have a vaguely colonial flavor. Hip Bastille denizens drift in and out all day. Bartenders like to mix "specialties," and if you ask for one with a winning smile, you may get a reduced price.

See map p. 160. 15-17 rue St-Sabin (the corner of rue Sedaine and rue St-Sabin), 11e. ☎ *01-47-00-13-53. Métro: Breguet-Sabin or Bastille.*

Café les Deux Magots

Like its neighbor, Café de Flore, Café les Deux Magots was a hangout for Sartre and Simone de Beauvoir. The intellectuals met here in the 1950s, and Sartre wrote at his table every morning. Hemingway also haunted this place (when he had the money to do so, at least). With prices that start at 4.40€ ($7.05) for coffee, the cafe is an expensive place for literary-intellectual pilgrims, but a great spot to watch the nightly promenade on the boulevard St-Germain.

See map p. 162. 6 place St-Germain-des-Prés, 6e. ☎ *01-45-48-55-25. Métro: St-Germain-des-Prés.*

Café Mabillon

If you only have one night in Paris, make the most of it and welcome the dawn at Café Mabillon, which stays open all night. During the day, pleasant lounge music draws the young and hip as well as older BCBG locals, who dine in fantastic outfits that you'd be afraid to spill food on. If you're hungry, try the ravioli with foie gras; it's to die for. Or just have a *café* or glass of wine and relax on the outdoor terrace or in the ultramodern interior. At night the music changes to techno and electro, and the bordello-red banquettes fill with a wide assortment of night owls. As dawn approaches, the sound drops to a level just loud enough to keep you from dozing off in your seat.

See map p. 162. 164 bd. St-Germain, 6e. ☎ *01-43-26-62-93. Métro: Mabillon.*

Café Marly

This is one of the prettiest cafes in Paris and its location can't be beat. Sinking into one of the plush red chairs here amid high ceilings, warmly painted pastel walls, and luxurious sofa chairs with a drink or cup of tea is the best antidote to Louvre fatigue! This stunning cafe has a gorgeous view of the glass pyramid that is the museum's main entrance. You almost forget food is served here, but that would be a mistake — it's very good, if not abundant. It's on the expensive side, but that is normal considering your location. Enjoy the exquisite lighting on the pyramid and surrounding 18th-century facades from the outdoor balcony. After 8 p.m., seating is for dinner only.

See map p. 160. 93 rue de Rivoli, cour Napoléon du Louvre, 1er. ☎ *01-49-26-06-60. Métro: Palais-Royal-Musée du Louvre.*

Fouquet's

This 20th-century Parisian institution is the place with the red umbrellas on the Champs-Elysées, not far from the Arc de Triomphe, and counts such patrons as James Joyce, Charlie Chaplin, Marlene Dietrich, Winston Churchill, Franklin D. Roosevelt, François Truffaut, Claude Chabrol, and Jean-Luc Godard. Opened in 1899, it is now registered as a historic monument.

See map p. 160. 99 av. des Champs-Elysées, 8e. ☎ *01-47-23-50-00. Métro: George V.*

La Chaise au Plafond

This friendly, stylish place tucked away on a pedestrian-only side street in the heart of the Marais is always packed. Maybe that's because it's the perfect spot to refuel after visiting the Musée Picasso. It serves enormous salads, imaginative sandwiches, and thick *tartes* to a local crowd sprinkled with tourists in the know. The menu and kitchen here are the same as another well known cafe just around the corner, les Philosophes, but la Chaise au Plafond has more personality and more twinkly-eyed waiters.

See map p. 160. 10 rue Trésor, 4e. ☎ *01-42-76-03-22. Métro: Hôtel-de-Ville.*

La Contrescarpe

The dimly lit book-filled interior here is perfect for an intimate tête-à-tête, while the tables outside, which overlook four lilac trees and a fountain, seem to seat a more boisterous clientele. This is a good place to take a break after marketing on rue Mouffetard or visiting the nearby Panthéon. The 15€ ($24) menu is a good deal.

See map p. 162. 57 rue Lacépède, 5e. ☎ *01-43-36-82-88. Métro: Cardinal Lemoine.*

La Coupole

The more things change, the more they stay the same at this Lost Generation cafe that has been packing them in for nearly a century. Henry Miller came here for his morning porridge, and now Japanese business people, French yuppies, models, tourists, and neighborhood regulars keep the frenzied waiters running until 2 a.m. The food is good, too, though prices are high. There's dancing downstairs on the weekends.

See map p. 162. 102 bd. Montparnasse, 14e. ☎ *01-43-20-14-20. Métro: Vavin.*

Le Comptoir du Relais St-Germain

This tiny cafe on a narrow sidewalk right off boulevard St-Germain serves restaurant-class meals and quick pick-me-ups: You can get cheese or charcuterie with a traditionally made baguette while you sip some house red wine, but also try their chicken cream soup with spices — mmm. Le Comptoir is perfectly situated in the carrefour de l'Odéon where you can watch Left Bank habitués and students walk by, or wave to the people in the Horse's Tavern and Café les Éditeurs across the street.

See map p. 162. 9 carrefour de l'Odéon, 6e. ☎ *01-46-33-45-30. Métro: Odéon.*

Le Progrès

Situated near the footsteps of Sacre Coeur, le Progrès is quirky and simple and almost always packed. The benches and closely arranged tables put funky and bohemian locals next to tourists, all served by a youthful staff who yell jokes back and forth over the midday din. A *croque jeune homme* (their tongue-in-cheek name for a croque-monsieur) is only 8€ ($13), or you can just sip wine while watching the denizens of Montmartre pass you by. During the winter, their *vin chaud* (hot wine, with spices) will chase away the Parisian chill.

See map p. 160. 7 rue des Trois Frères, 18e. ☎ *01-42-64-07-37. Métro: Abbesses or Anvers.*

L'Eté en Pente Douce

To find this cute cafe away from Montmartre's tourist hordes, turn right after exiting the *funiculaire,* and take the first set of steps leading down to a leafy square facing a small park. The terrace here looks out on stairs and iron lamps once painted by Montmartre artist Utrillo, and someone almost always performs here for the captive audience. The interior is brightly decorated with painted borders of leaves and plants, mosaics, unusual objets d'art, and a painted ceiling. Between lunch and dinner, the restaurant serves tea, pastries, and sandwiches.

See map p. 160. 23 rue Muller, 18e. ☎ *01-42-64-02-67. Métro: Chateau-Rouge.*

L'Étoile Manquante

Located on a street known for funky cafes like Café des Philosophes and its neighbor, Au Pétit Fer à Cheval, this is a modern, tasteful, and fun place that hosts all kinds of locals, artists, and writers who enjoy reasonably priced, somewhat inventive and tasty food in an atmosphere that whispers rather than shouts "cool." Little stars in the floor tiles twinkle in the dim light from recessed round ceiling lights outlined in brown circles and from baguette-shaped sconces with artfully placed tiny holes to let the light through. The vibrant scene is reflected in the wall of rectangular mirrors in the back of the restaurant. A visit to the very dark bathrooms lit from above by "starlight" is a must.

See map p. 160. 34 rue e Vieille du Temple, 4e. ☎ *01-42-72-48-34. Métro: Hôtel de Ville or St-Paul.*

Le Sancerre

This is one of Montmartre's cheaper cafes located on rue des Abbesses where you can sit and watch the passing citizens of Montmartre in their hipster gear. They have great croque-monsieurs if you're hungry, or order a *café* and contemplate your next artistic endeavor like the other people sitting at neighboring tables. This lively place can get packed, so you may want to stop by late afternoon when things are calm.

See map p. 162. 35 rue des Abbesses, 18e. ☎ *01-42-58-0-20.*

Pause Café

This *cantine du quartier* (neighborhood canteen) with lemon-colored outdoor tables is almost always full, and if it's nighttime, the patrons are most likely stopping in for drinks on their way to a night of dancing. A bright-colored, modern interior with hanging light fixtures also features found art, while outdoors is made tropical with cloth and bamboo umbrellas and potted palms. The food is fresh and tasty.

See map p. 160. 41 rue de Charonne, 11e. ☎ *01-48-06-80-33. Métro: Lédru-Rollin.*

Steeping and sipping at a tea salon (Salons de thé)

Sitting down to tea in Paris can be an elegant and refined undertaking, or a relaxing break between bouts of shopping and *musée*-hopping. The tea salons have a wide range of blends, steeped to perfection, and the pastry selections are usually excellent (Ladurée's macaroons are world-famous). Save your full meals, however, for a restaurant because tea salons tend to be expensive.

- ✔ **Angelina,** 226 rue de Rivoli, 1er; ☎ **01-42-60-82-00.** Open daily from 9 a.m. to 7 p.m. Breakfast is served from 9 to 11:30 a.m. Métro: Concorde or Tuileries; see map p. 160.

- ✔ **A Priori Thé,** 35-37 Galerie Vivienne (enter at 6 rue Vivienne, 4 rue des Petits-Champs, or 5 rue de la Banque), 2e; ☎ **01-42-97-48-75.** Open Monday to Friday 9 a.m. to 6 p.m.; Saturday from 12:30 to 6:30 p.m., and Sunday from noon to 6:30 p.m. Métro: Bourse, Palais-Royal-Musée du Louvre, or Pyramides; see map p. 160.

- ✔ **Ladurée,** 16 rue Royale, 8e; ☎ **01-42-60-21-79.** Open Monday through Saturday from 8:30 a.m. to 7p.m. Métro: Concorde; see map p. 160. Also at 75 Champs-Elysées, ☎ **01-40-75-08-75,** Métro: Franklin-D-Roosevelt; and in Sainte Germain, 21 rue Bonaparte, ☎ **01-44-97-64-87.**

- **La Fourmi Ailée**, 8 rue du Fouarre, 5e; ☎ 01-43-29-40-99. Open daily from noon to midnight. Métro: Maubert-Mutualité; see map p. 162.

- **Maison des Trois Thés**, 1 rue St-Médard, 5e; ☎ 01-43-36-93-84. Open Tuesday to Friday 1 to 6:30 p.m. Métro: Place Monge.

- **Mariage Frères**, 13 rue Grands Augustins, 6e; ☎ 01-40-51-82-50. This location is open daily from noon to 7 p.m. Métro: St-Michel; see map p. 162. Another location is at 30 rue du Bourg-Tibourg, 4e; ☎ 01-42-72-28-11. Métro: Hôtel de Ville.

- **Salon de Thé de la Mosquée de Paris**, 39 rue Geoffroy-St-Hilaire, 5e; ☎ 01-43-31-18-14. Open daily from 10 a.m. to midnight. Métro: Place Monge; see map p. 162.

- **The Tea Caddy**, 14 rue St-Julien-le-Pauvre, 5e; ☎ 01-43-54-15-56. Open daily from noon to 7 p.m. Métro: St-Michel; see map p. 162.

A heady mix of wine bars

Paris's wine bars have a good selection of wines by the glass, and tasty light meals served all day in pleasant surroundings. These places are often a cozy and sophisticated alternative to the cafe.

À La Cloche des Halles

Look closely at the exterior for the bell that once tolled the opening and closing of the vast food market for which this neighborhood was named. This tiny bar and cafe is packed at lunchtime so you might want to go late afternoon. Patrons dine on plates of *jambon* (ham) or homemade quiche accompanied by a carafe of wine, and maybe the tarte tatin for dessert. It's convivial and fun, but very noisy and crowded, just like the rest of the quarter during the day. If you can't find a seat, you can usually stand at the bar and eat.

See map p. 160. 28 rue Coquillière, 1er. ☎ *01-42-36-93-89. Métro: Les Halles or Palais-Royal-Musée du Louvre. Mon–Fri 8 a.m.–10 p.m., Sat 10 a.m.–5 p.m.*

Au Négociant

You may walk right past this tiny wine bar the first time, so make sure to retrace your steps. Wine by the glass is reasonable, and the excellent pâtés and terrines are homemade and served with fresh, chewy bread. Photographer Robert Doisneau *(Le Baiser de l'Hôtel de Ville)* was a regular.

See map p. 160. 27 rue Lambert, 18e. ☎ *01-46-06-15-11. Métro: Château-Rouge or Lamarck-Caulincourt. Mon–Fri noon–2:30 p.m., Tues–Thurs 6:30–10:30 p.m.*

Clown Bar

Founded in 1904, this place became a second home three years later to circus people working at the Cirque de l'Hiver next door who would congregate here and drop off letters to be mailed. There's a zinc bar decorated with a mélange of circus posters and circus-themed ceramic tiles and statues. (One bust eerily resembles Jack Nicholson.) The wine list features an extensive selection of French offerings from the Rhone and Languedoc.

See map p. 160. 114 rue Amelot, 11e. ☎ *01-43-55-87-35. Métro: Filles du Calvaire. Mon–Sat noon–2:30 p.m. and 7 p.m.–1 a.m.*

La Tartine

It underwent a renovation in the early 2000s that took away its gritty character (new toilets and a fresh coat of paint made this a new place), and now La Tartine is simply another wine bar, albeit in a good location on rue de Rivoli. It's relaxed and comfortable and a mix of working class and well heeled frequent it. You can get a light lunch of goat cheese salad, or a pick-me-up of *tartine* (open-faced sandwich), cheese, or *charcuterie* (assorted sliced meats) plate along with one of many wines by the glass.

See map p. 160. 24 rue de Rivoli, 4e. ☎ *01-42-72-76-85. Métro: St-Paul. Wed–Mon noon–10 p.m.*

Le Bistrot du Peintre

The doors are Art Nouveau and the bar is zinc at this cozy place where painters, actors, and night crawlers hang out. The delicious and reasonably priced food, wood paneling, large terrace, and superb *belle époque* atmosphere make this wine bar a highlight. The wine selection is affordable — an added bonus.

See map p. 160. 116 av. Ledru-Rollin, 11e. ☎ *01-47-00-34-39. Métro: Ledru-Rollin. Daily 9 a.m.–2 a.m. (the kitchen closes at midnight).*

L'Écluse

L'Écluse is casually chic, authentic, and conveniently located smack in the middle of St-Germain. Have one of its 20 wines by the glass and a light bite such as *carpaccio,* salad, or soup.

See map p. 162. 15 quai des Grands-Augustins, 6e. ☎ *01-46-33-58-74. Métro: St-Michel. Daily 11:30 a.m.–1 a.m.*

Le Griffonnier

The kitchen staff at Le Griffonnier deliver first-rate cuisine, and the wine cellar is superb. Sample the entree du jour such as their *boeuf bourguignon* (beef stewed with red wine, onions, mushrooms, and bacon), or try a hearty plate of *charcuterie* (regional sliced meats), terrines, and cheese, usually from the Auvergne region of central France, and ask your waiter to recommend the wine. Hot meals are served at lunchtime Monday to Friday (until 3:30 p.m.) and Monday nights.

See map p. 160. 8 rue des Saussaies, 8e. ☎ *01-42-65-17-17. Métro: Champs-Elysées-Clemenceau. Mon–Fri 8 a.m.–9 p.m.*

Le Sancerre

Don't be put off by the unstylish interior which consists of a wooden bar with stools losing some of their caning. Le Sancerre is a wonderful place to unwind for a light meal or glass of wine after visiting the Eiffel Tower. Loire wines are the specialty here, including, of course, Sancerre. The friendly manager and bartender will discuss the best accompaniments for his wines. Typically French items are on the menu here, such as omelets of all varieties with a side of fried potatoes. Specials change all the time, so ask as well: The last sitting included a tasty house salad of Auvergne bleu cheese, tomatoes, and walnuts. The more adventurous can sample the ubiquitous *andouillette*, the sausage that is decidedly an acquired taste.

See map p. 162. 22 av. Rapp, 7e. ☎ *01-45-51-75-91. Métro: Alma Marceau. Mon–Fri 8 a.m.–10 p.m., Sat 8 a.m.–4 p.m.*

Mélac

If only this wine bar wasn't so out of the way in a neighborhood with not much to recommend it. But owner Jacques Mélac has an excellent selection of wine from nearly all the regions of France, which he dispenses to a lively crowd of regulars. He's happy to give you recommendations. Usually a hot *plat du jour* is available for lunch, but you can feast on a selection of first-rate pâtés, terrines, *charcuterie* (regional sliced meats), and cheeses all day.

See map p. 160. 42 rue Léon Frot, 11e. ☎ *01-43-70-59-27. Métro: Charonne. Mon 9 a.m.–2 p.m., Tues–Sat 9 a.m.–10:30 p.m.*

Taverne Henri IV

You can visit this authentic, old-fashioned bar for a quick pick-me-up after a Seine boat cruise. Although on the expensive side, the wine and food are excellent. The variety of wines by the glass can accompany open-faced sandwiches, pâtés, and such cheeses as Cantal and Auvergne blue.

See map p. 160. 13 place du Pont Neuf, 1er. ☎ *01-43-54-27-90. Métro: Pont-Neuf. Mon–Fri 11:30 a.m.–10 p.m., Sat noon–6 p.m. Closed Aug.*

Willi's Wine Bar

This has been a favorite of tourists and locals since its opening in 1980. An upscale crowd have sampled more than 250 different varieties of wine while seated at the polished oak bar or have dined in the high-ceilinged oak-beamed dining room from a prix-fixe menu starting at 20€ ($31). Each year the owners commission an image relating to wine from an artist, and the colorful paintings are available for sale as prints.

See map p. 160. 13 rue des Petits-Champs, 1er. ☎ *01-42-61-05-09. Métro: Bourse, Pyramide, or Palais Royale. Mon–Sat noon–2:30 p.m. and 7–11 p.m.; bar open Mon–Sat noon–midnight.*

Getting the scoop on Paris ice cream

If Paris doesn't have the best ice cream flavors in the world, it must run a close second. Such flavors (rhubarb, plum, cassis, honey nut . . .)! Ask for a *cornet seule* (kor-*nay* sul; single-scoop cone) or *cornet double* (kor-*nay* doobl; double scoop) — even the cone is yummy. Parisians cite **Berthillon,** 31 rue St-Louis-en-l'Ile, 4e (☎ 01-43-54-31-61; Métro: Cité; see map p. 160) as the best in the city, but the following establishments also put soft-serve to shame. Although Berthillon closes from July 15 through the first week in September, a note on the door directs customers to other nearby shops that sell its ice cream. **Le Flore en l'Ile,** 42 quai d'Orléans, 4e (☎ 01-43-29-88-27; Métro: Cité), a restaurant and *salon de thé,* always has an outside station to buy Berthillon ice cream. A chain of ice cream parlors called **Amorino** (locations listed below) also boasts excellent ice cream in numerous flavors (for pure ingenuity try the grapefruit).

- ✔ **Amorino,** 4 rue de Buci, 6e; ☎ 01-43-26-57-46; Métro: Odéon; see map p. 162. Other locations around the city.

- ✔ **Gelati d'Alberto,** 45 rue Mouffetard, 5e; ☎ 01-43-37-88-07; Métro: Monge.

- ✔ **La Butte Glacée,** 14 rue Norvins, 18e; ☎ 01-42-23-91-58; Métro: Abbesses; see map p. 160.

- ✔ **Le Bac à Glaces,** 109 rue du Bac, 7e; ☎ 01-45-48-87-65; Métro: Rue du Bac; see map p. 162.

- ✔ **M.P. Gourmandises,** 39 rue Harpe, 5e; ☎ 01-43-25-63-56; Métro: Cluny-La Sorbonne; see map p. 162.

- ✔ **Scoop,** 154 rue St-Honoré, 1er (behind the Louvre des Antiquaires); ☎ 01-42-60-31-84; Métro: Louvre-Rivoli; see map p. 160.

Index of Establishments by Neighborhood

Louvre, Les Halles (1er)
À La Cloche des Halles (Wine Bar, $)
Angelina (Tea Salon, $)
Au Pied de Cochon (Classic French, $$)
Café Marly (Cafes, $)
Fauchon (Traiteurs, $)
Georges (Modern Bistro, $$–$$$)
La Poule au Pot (Classic Bistro, $$)
La Tour de Montlhéry Chez Denise
(Classic French, $$–$$$)
Lemoni Café (Vegetarian, $)
Restaurant du Palais-Royal (Classic French, $$–$$$)
Scoop (Ice Cream, $)

Taverne Henri IV (Wine Bar, $)
Willi's Wine Bar (Wine Bar, $)

Sentier (2e)
A Priori Thé (Tea Salon, $)
Un Jour à Peyrassol (Provençal, $$)

**Le Marais, Ile St-Louis/
Ile de la Cité (3e, 4e)**
Au Bascou (Basque/Southwest, $$)
Auberge de Jarente
(Basque/Southwest, $$)
Au Bistro de la Place (Cafes, $)

Au Rendez-Vous des Amis (Cafes, $)
Brasserie de l'Ile St-Louis
(Alsatian/Brasserie, $$)
Café Beaubourg (Cafes, $)
Caveau du Palais (Classic French, $$)
Chez H'anna (Vegetarian, $)
La Chaise au Plafond (Cafes, $)
L'Ambroisie (Haute Cuisine, $$$$)
L'Aréa (Middle Eastern/Brazilian, $$)
La Tartine (Wine Bar, $)
Le 404 (Moroccan, $$)
Le Potager du Marais (Vegetarian, $)
L'Étoile Manquante (Cafes, $)
Pomme de Pain (Sandwiches, $)

Latin Quarter (5e)

Auberge Le Pot de Terre (Classic
French, $)
Boulangerie Kayser (Boulangeries, $)
Brasserie Balzar (Alsatian/
Brasserie, $$)
Breakfast in America (American, $)
ChantAirelle (Auvergne, $$)
Gelati d'Alberto (Ice Cream, $)
Hédiard (Traiteurs, $)
La Contrescarpe (Cafes, $)
La Fourmi Ailée (Tea Salon, $)
Le Grenier de Notre-Dame
(Vegetarian, $–$$)
Le Pain Quotidien (Sandwiches, $)
Les Puits des Légumes (Vegetarian, $)
Maison des Trois Thés (Tea Salon, $)
M.P. Gourmandises (Ice Cream, $)
Restaurant Perraudin (Classic
Bistro, $$)
Salon de Thé de la Mosquée de Paris
(Tea Salon, $)
The Tea Caddy (Tea Salon, $)

St-Germain-des-Prés (6e)

A La Petite Chaise (Classic French, $$)
Amorino (Ice Cream, $)
Café de Flore (Cafes, $)
Café les Deux Magots (Cafes, $)
Café Mabillon (Cafes, $)
Cosi (Sandwiches, $)
La Bastide Odéon (Provençal, $$)
La Grande Épicerie (Traiteurs, $)
L'Écluse (Wine Bar, $)

Le Comptoir du Relais St-Germain
(Cafes, $$)
L'Epi Dupin (French, $$)
Lina's (Sandwiches, $)
Poilâne (Boulangeries, $)
Ze Kitchen Galerie (Modern
Bistro, $$)

Eiffel Tower and Invalides (7e, 15e)

Au Bon Accueil (Modern Bistro, $$)
La Cigale Récamier (Classic Bistro, $$)
L'Atelier de Joël Robuchon (Modern
Bistro, $$–$$$)
Le Bac à Glaces (Ice Cream, $)
Le Père Claude (Classic Bistro, $$)
Le Sancerre (Wine Bar, $$)
Moulin de la Vierge (Boulangeries, $)

Champs-Elysées and Ternes (8e and 17e)

BE (Boulangepicier; Boulangeries, $)
Fouquet's (Cafes, $)
Ladurée (Tea Salon, $)
Le Cinq (Haute Cuisine, $$$$)
Le Griffonnier (Wine Bar, $)
Mariage Frères (Tea Salon, $)
Restaurant Plaza Athénée (Alain
Ducasse; Haute Cuisine, $$$$)

Opéra/Gare du Nord (9e, 10e)

Chez Casimir (Classic French, $$)
Chez Michel (Breton, $$)
Lafayette Gourmet (Traiteurs, $)

Bastille/Oberkampf (4e, 11e, 12e)

Bofinger (Alsatian/Brasserie, $$)
Café de l'Industrie (Cafes, $)
Clown Bar (Wine Bar, $)
Le Bistrot du Peintre (Wine Bar, $)
Maison Chardenoux (Classic
Bistro, $$)
Mélac (Wine Bar, $)
Pause Café (Cafes, $)

Montparnasse (14e)

Café de la Place (Cafes, $)
La Coupole (Cafes, $)

Trocadèro (16e)
Bonneau (Boulangeries, $)

Montmartre (18e)
Au Grain de Folies (Vegetarian, $)
Au Négociant (Wine Bar, $)
Au Poulbot Gourmet (Classic French, $–$$)

Chez Marie (Classic French, $$)
La Butte Glacée (Ice Cream, $)
Le Grenier au Pain (Boulangeries, $)
Le Kokolion (Classic French, $–$$)
Le Progrès (Cafes, $)
L'Eté en Pente Douce (Cafes, $)
Le Sancerre (Cafes, $)

Index of Establishments by Cuisine

Alsatian/Brasserie
Bofinger ($$, Bastille)
Brasserie Balzar ($$, Latin Quarter)
Brasserie de l'Ile St-Louis ($$, Ile St-Louis)

American
Breakfast in America ($, Latin Quarter)

Auvergne
ChantAirelle ($$, Latin Quarter)

Basque/Southwest
Au Bascou ($$, Le Marais)
Auberge de Jarente ($$, Le Marais)

Boulangeries
BE (Boulangepicier; $, Champs-Elysées)
Bonneau ($, Trocadèro)
Boulangerie Kayser ($, Latin Quarter)
Caumont ($, Latin Quarter)
Le Grenier au Pain ($, Montmartre)
Moulin de la Vierge ($, Eiffel Tower)
Poilâne ($, St-Germain-des-Prés)

Breton
Chez Michel ($$, Gare du Nord)

Cafes
Au Bistro de la Place ($, Le Marais)
Au Rendez-Vous des Amis ($, Le Marais)

Café Beaubourg ($, Le Marais)
Café de Flore ($, St-Germain-des-Prés)
Café de la Place ($, Montparnasse)
Café de l'Industrie ($, Bastille-Oberkampf)
Café les Deux Magots ($, St-Germain-des-Prés)
Café Mabillon ($, St-Germain-des-Prés)
Café Marly ($, Louvre)
Fouquet's ($, Champs-Elysées)
La Chaise au Plafond ($, Le Marais)
La Contrescarpe ($, Latin Quarter)
La Coupole ($, Montparnasse)
Le Comptoir du Relais St-Germain ($$, St-Germain-des-Prés, Odéon)
Le Progrès ($, Montmartre)
Le Sancerre ($, Montmartre)
L'Eté en Pente Douce ($, Montmartre)
L'Étoile Manquante ($, Le Marais)
Pause Café ($, Bastille)

Classic Bistro
La Cigale Récamier ($$, Invalides)
La Poule au Pot ($$, Les Halles)
Le Père Claude ($$, Eiffel Tower)
Maison Chardenoux ($$, Bastille)
Restaurant Perraudin ($$, Latin Quarter)

Classic French
A La Petite Chaise ($$, St-Germain-des-Prés)
Auberge Le Pot de Terre ($, Latin Quarter)
Au Pied de Cochon ($$, Les Halles)

Au Poulbot Gourmet ($–$$, Montmartre)
Caveau du Palais ($$, Ile de la Cité)
Chez Casimir ($$, Gare du Nord)
Chez Marie ($$, Montmartre)
La Tour de Montlhéry Chez Denise ($$–$$$, Les Halles)
Le Kokolion ($–$$, Montmartre)
L'Epi Dupin ($$, St-Germain-des-Prés)
Restaurant du Palais-Royal ($$–$$$, Louvre)

Haute Cuisine

L'Ambroisie ($$$$, Le Marais)
Le Cinq ($$$$, Champs-Elysées)
Restaurant Plaza Athénée (Alain Ducasse; $$$$, Champs-Elysées)

Ice Cream

Amorino ($, St-Germain-des-Prés)
Berthillon ($, Ile de la Cité)
Gelati d'Alberto ($, Latin Quarter)
La Butte Glacée ($, Montmartre)
Le Bac à Glaces ($, Eiffel Tower)
M.P. Gourmandises ($, Latin Quarter)
Scoop ($, Louvre)

Middle Eastern

L'Aréa ($$, Le Marais/Bastille)

Modern Bistro

Au Bon Accueil ($$, Eiffel Tower)
Georges ($$–$$$, Les Halles)
L'Atelier de Joël Robuchon ($$–$$$, Eiffel Tower)
Ze Kitchen Galerie ($$, St-Germain-des-Prés)

Moroccan

Le 404 ($$, Le Marais)

Provençal

La Bastide Odéon ($$, St-Germain-des-Prés)
Un Jour à Peyrassol ($$, Bourse)

Sandwiches

Cosi ($, St-Germain-des-Prés)
Le Pain Quotidien ($, Latin Quarter)
Lina's ($, St-Germain-des-Prés)
Pomme de Pain ($, Le Marais)

Tea Salons

Angelina ($, Louvre)
A Priori Thé ($, Sentier)
Ladurée ($, Champs-Elysées)
La Fourmi Ailée ($, Latin Quarter)
Maison des Trois Thés ($, Le Marais)
Mariage Frères ($, Champs-Elysées)
Salon de Thé de la Mosquée de Paris ($, Latin Quarter)
The Tea Caddy ($, Latin Quarter)

Traiteurs

Fauchon ($, various)
Hédiard ($, various)
Lafayette Gourmet ($, Opèra)
La Grande Épicerie ($, St-Germain-des-Prés)
Lenoire ($, various)

Vegetarian

Au Grain de Folies ($, Montmartre)
Chez H'anna ($, Le Marais)
Le Grenier de Notre-Dame ($–$$, Latin Quarter)
Lemoni Café ($, Louvre)
Le Potager du Marais ($, Le Marais)
Les Puits des Légumes ($, Latin Quarter)

Wine Bars

À La Cloche des Halles ($, Louvre/Les Halles)
Au Négociant ($, Montmartre)
Clown Bar ($, Bastille)
La Tartine ($, Le Marais)
Le Bistrot du Peintre ($, Bastille)
L'Écluse ($, St-Germain-des-Prés)
Le Griffonnier ($, Champs-Elysées)
Le Sancerre ($$, Eiffel Tower)
Mélac ($, Bastille)
Taverne Henri IV ($, Louvre)
Willi's Wine Bar ($, Louvre)

Index of Establishments by Price

$

À La Cloche des Halles (Wine Bar, Louvre/Les Halles)

Amorino (Ice Cream, St-Germain-des-Prés)

Angelina (Tea Salon, Louvre)

A Priori Thé (Tea Salon, Sentier)

Auberge Le Pot de Terre (Classic French, Latin Quarter)

Au Bistro de la Place (Cafes, Le Marais)

Au Grain de Folies (Vegetarian, Montmartre)

Au Négociant (Wine Bar, Montmartre)

Au Poulbot Gourmet (Classic French, Montmartre)

Au Rendez-Vous des Amis (Cafes, Le Marais)

BE (Boulangepicier; Boulangeries, Champs-Elysées)

Berthillon (Ice Cream, Ile de la Cité)

Bonneau (Boulangeries, Trocadèro)

Boulangerie Kayser (Boulangereis, Latin Quarter)

Breakfast in America (American, Latin Quarter)

Café Beaubourg (Cafes, Le Marais)

Café de Flore (Cafes, St-Germain-des-Prés)

Café de la Place (Cafes, Montparnasse)

Café de l'Industrie (Cafes, Bastille-Oberkampf)

Café les Deux Magots (Cafes, St-Germain-des-Prés)

Café Mabillon (Cafes, St-Germain-des-Prés)

Café Marly (Cafes, Louvre)

Caumont (Boulangeries, Latin Quarter)

Chez H'anna (Vegetarian, Le Marais)

Clown Bar (Wine Bar, Bastille/Oberkampf)

Cosi (Sandwiches, St-Germain-des-Prés)

Fauchon (Traiteurs, Louvre)

Fouquet's (Cafes, Champs-Elysées)

Gelati d'Alberto (Ice Cream, Latin Quarter)

Hédiard (Traiteurs, Latin Quarter)

La Butte Glacée (Ice Cream, Montmartre)

La Chaise au Plafond (Cafes, Le Marais)

La Contrescarpe (Cafes, Latin Quarter)

La Coupole (Cafes, Montparnasse)

Ladurée (Tea Salon, Champs-Elysées)

Lafayette Gourmet (Traiteurs, Opèra)

La Fourmi Ailée (Tea Salon, Latin Quarter)

La Grande Épicerie (Traiteurs, St-Germain-des-Prés)

La Tartine (Wine Bar, Le Marais)

Le Bac à Glaces (Ice Cream, Eiffel Tower)

Le Bistrot du Peintre (Wine Bar, Bastille/Oberkampf)

L'Écluse (Wine Bar, St-Germain-des-Prés)

Le Grenier au Pain (Boulangeries, Montmartre)

Le Grenier de Notre-Dame (Vegetarian, Latin Quarter)

Le Griffonnier (Wine Bar, Champs-Elysées)

Le Kokolion (Classic French, Montmartre)

Lemoni Café (Vegetarian, Louvre)

Lenoire (Traiteurs, various)

Le Pain Quotidien (Sandwiches, Latin Quarter)

Le Potager du Marais (Vegetarian, Le Marais)

Le Progrès (Cafes, Montmartre)

Le Sancerre (Cafes, Montmartre)

Les Puits des Légumes (Vegetarian, Latin Quarter)

L'Eté en Pente Douce (Cafes, Montmartre)

L'Étoile Manquante (Cafes, Le Marais)

Lina's (Sandwiches, St-Germain-des-Prés)

Maison des Trois Thés (Tea Salon, Latin Quarter)

Mariage Frères (Tea Salon, Champs-Elysées)

Mélac (Wine Bar, Bastille/Oberkampf)

Moulin de la Vierge (Boulangeries, Eiffel Tower)

M.P. Gourmandises (Ice Cream, Latin Quarter)

Pause Café (Cafes, Bastille-Oberkampf)

Poilâne (Boulangeries, St-Germain-des-Prés)

Pomme de Pain (Sandwiches, Le Marais)

Salon de thé de la Mosquée de Paris (Tea Salon, Latin Quarter)

Scoop (Ice Cream, Louvre)

Taverne Henri IV (Wine Bar, Louvre)

The Tea Caddy (Tea Salon, Latin Quarter)

Willi's Wine Bar (Wine Bar, Louvre)

$$

A La Petite Chaise (Classic French, St-Germain-des-Prés)

Au Bascou (Basque/Southwest, Le Marais)

Auberge de Jarente (Basque/Southwest, Le Marais)

Au Bon Accueil (Modern Bistro, Eiffel Tower)

Au Pied de Cochon (Classic French, Les Halles)

Au Poulbot Gourmet (Classic French, Montmartre)

Bofinger (Alsatian, Bastille)

Brasserie Balzar (Alsatian/Brasserie, Latin Quarter)

Brasserie de l'Ile St-Louis (Alsatian/Brasserie, Ile St-Louis)

Caveau du Palais (Classic French, Ile de la Cité)

ChantAirelle (Auvergne, Latin Quarter)

Chez Casimir (Classic French, Gare du Nord)

Chez Marie (Classic French, Montmartre)

Chez Michel (Breton, Gare du Nord)

Georges (Modern Bistro, Les Halles)

La Bastide Odéon (Provençal, St-Germain-des-Prés)

La Cigale Récamier (Classic Bistro, Invalides)

La Poule au Pot (Classic Bistro, Les Halles)

L'Aréa (Middle Eastern/Brazilian, Le Marais/Bastille)

L'Atelier de Joël Robuchon (Modern Bistro, Eiffel Tower)

La Tour de Montlhéry Chez Denise (Classic French, Les Halles)

Le Comptoir du Relais St-Germain (Cafes, St-Germain-des-Prés)

Le 404 (Moroccan, Le Marais)

Le Grenier de Notre-Dame (Vegetarian, Latin Quarter)

Le Kokolion (Classic French, Montmartre)

Le Père Claude (Classic Bistro, Eiffel Tower)

L'Epi Dupin (Classic French, St-Germain-des-Prés)

Le Sancerre (Wine Bar, Eiffel Tower)

Maison Chardenoux (Classic Bistro, Bastille)

Restaurant du Palais-Royal (Classic French, Louvre)

Restaurant Perraudin (Classic Bistro, Latin Quarter)

Un Jour à Peyrassol (Provençal, Bourse)

Ze Kitchen Galerie (Modern Bistro, St-Germain-des-Prés)

$$$

L'Atelier de Joël Robuchon (Modern Bistro, Eiffel Tower)

La Tour de Montlhéry Chez Denise (Classic French, Les Halles)

Georges (Modern Bistro, Les Halles)

Restaurant du Palais-Royal (Classic French, Louvre)

$$$$

L'Ambroisie (Haute Cuisine, Le Marais)

Le Cinq (Haute Cuisine, Champs-Elysées)

Restaurant Plaza Athénée (Alain Ducasse; Haute Cuisine, Champs-Elysées)

Part IV
Exploring Paris

The 5th Wave
By Rich Tennant

"Now THAT was a great meal! Beautiful presentation, an imaginative use of ingredients, and a sauce with nuance and depth. The French really know how to make a 'Happy Meal.'"

In this part . . .

So many things to see in Paris . . . what do you do first . . . and how long will it take? Chapter 11 tells you a bit about what's worth seeing; lists some more cool things to see and do for kids, teens, history buffs, and art and literature lovers; and suggests gardens and parks to relax in after visiting all those museums. You also find here guided-tour options, from buses to bicycles! Chapter 12 describes today's shopping scene in Paris, previews four great shopping neighborhoods, covers the outdoor markets, and provides reviews of local shops of interest. In Chapter 13, you have the chance to discover Paris in four itineraries and a walking tour. And just when you're getting used to Paris, Chapter 14 sends you away on one of five popular day trips in the Ile-de-France region.

Chapter 11

Discovering Paris's Best Attractions

*I*n Paris, you are never at a loss for something to see, and this chapter starts you off with a succinct review of 20 of the city's top attractions, giving you the lowdown on when to go, how to get there, and why to visit it in the first place.

 Before you leave, log onto www.weather.com and look at the extended forecast for Paris. Or when you arrive, pick up a copy of the *International Herald Tribune* or *USA TODAY*'s international edition for extended weather forecasts and save museum visits for rainy days. (Keep in mind that most museums close on Mon or Tues and admission is free the first Sun of the month at national museums. On free days, be prepared to wait in long lines.) For a list of suggestions of what else to do on rainy days in Paris, see Chapter 17 in the Part of Tens.

Paris's Top Sights

Paris is synonymous with the Eiffel Tower, the Louvre, the Arc de Triomphe, and you're probably planning to see at least one of them. A word of advice: Figure out which sights you would be heartbroken to miss, and plan to do those first. After that, if you have the flexibility, improvise! There's so much to see that you'll reorder your itinerary daily. This chapter gives you an idea of what's out there.

Paris's Top Attractions

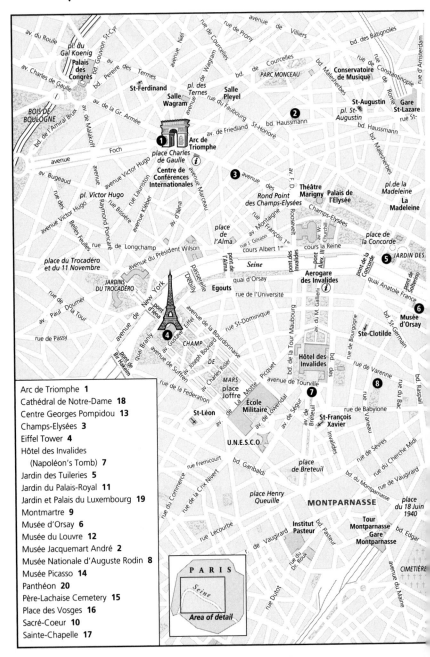

Arc de Triomphe **1**
Cathédral de Notre-Dame **18**
Centre Georges Pompidou **13**
Champs-Elysées **3**
Eiffel Tower **4**
Hôtel des Invalides
   (Napoléon's Tomb) **7**
Jardin des Tuileries **5**
Jardin du Palais-Royal **11**
Jardin et Palais du Luxembourg **19**
Montmartre **9**
Musée d'Orsay **6**
Musée du Louvre **12**
Musée Jacquemart André **2**
Musée Nationale d'Auguste Rodin **8**
Musée Picasso **14**
Panthéon **20**
Père-Lachaise Cemetery **15**
Place des Vosges **16**
Sacré-Coeur **10**
Sainte-Chapelle **17**

Saving on seeing the sights

One of the best bargains for tourists visiting Paris is the *Paris Museum Pass,* which offers free and unlimited admission to over 60 of the top sights of Paris and the Ile-de-France. The card also promises no waiting in admission lines, but you still have to stand in line for security checkpoints at the museums that have them. *Note:* The pass is *not* accepted at the Eiffel Tower. It's offered in three versions: a two-consecutive-day pass (30€/$48), a four-consecutive-day pass (45€/$72), and a six-consecutive-day pass (60€/$96). The biggest benefit is that you don't have to wait in line at most museums and monuments! You just saunter up to a separate window, and they wave you through. You can buy the pass at Charles de Gaulle airport in the tourist information areas in terminal 1 and in 2F, 2C, and 2D, any branch of the tourist office, at most museums and monuments, and at any Fnac store (a French chain store selling electronics and music), one of which is located conveniently at 74, Champs-Elysées.

Arc de Triomphe
Champs-Elysées (8e)

The Arc de Triomphe represents victory to the French, although it has also witnessed the agony of defeat, as in 1871 when Paris was seized by the Prussians during the Franco-Prussian War, and in 1940 when Nazi armies marched victoriously through the arch and down the Champs-Elysées. Napoléon commissioned the Arc to honor his army and its 128 victorious battles. Today it houses the Tomb of the Unknown Soldier, which was dedicated in 1921 to honor the 1,500,000 French soldiers who died during World War I. The panoramic view is the real attraction for visitors to the Arc de Triomphe, where joyous French citizens have celebrated everything from the end of World War II and their liberation to winning the World (soccer) Cup in 1998. From the top, 49m (162 ft.) up, you can see in a straight line the Champs-Elysées, the obelisk in the place de la Concorde, and the Louvre. Twelve streets and avenues, named for Napoleonic battles and war heroes, radiate out from the Arc. That big cube at the far end is the Grande Arche de la Défense in St-Denis, built to be the modern equivalent to this arch. Every year, the last day of the Tour de France sees the racers riding up the Champs and around the Arc in a series of laps before the victor is declared. An eternal flame beneath the Arc pays tribute to the lost soldiers and is symbolically relit every evening at 6:30 p.m. Allow an hour to visit, an hour and a half in high summer.

Don't try to cross to the Arc de Triomphe on surface streets! Attempting to dodge the warp-speed traffic zooming around the Arc will likely get you seriously hurt. Instead, use one of the clearly marked entrances to the underpass beneath the Arc, which you find on surrounding streets.

Buy your ticket at the end of the underpass from a clerk in a small booth, and then climb the stairs to find yourself standing at the base of the Arc near the Tomb of the Unknown Soldier. You have two choices to reach the top: by a set of more than 250 winding steps or by an elevator. The line for the stairs is always shorter. Both stairs and elevator lead to the small interior museum and store on the Arc's top floor. To get to the outdoor viewing platform you need to climb another flight of narrow steps; the viewing platform is *not* wheelchair accessible.

Keep in mind that on busy days, there will be a line of people in the underpass waiting to buy tickets. Go early if you're visiting during the height of tourist season.

See map p. 184. Place Charles-de-Gaulle. ☎ 01-55-37-73-77. Métro: Charles-de-Gaulle-Étoile. Bus: 22, 30, 31, 52, 73, 92. Admission: 9€ ($14) adults, 5.50€ ($8.80) students and seniors, free for children 17 and under. Open: Apr–Sept 10 a.m.–11 p.m.; Oct–Mar 10 a.m.–10:30 p.m. Closed major holidays.

Cathédral de Notre-Dame
Ile de la Cité (4e)

"Our Lady of Paris" is the heart and soul of the city, the Gothic church constructed between the 12th and 14th centuries that dominates the Seine and the Ile de la Cité, as well as the history of Paris. Notre-Dame is a study in Gothic beauty and gargoyles, at once solid with squat, square facade towers and graceful with flying buttresses around the sides. It's been remodeled, embellished, ransacked, and restored so often that it's a wonder it still has any architectural integrity at all (during the Revolution, it was even stripped of its religion and rechristened the Temple of Reason).

Construction of Notre-Dame (see the nearby "Notre-Dame de Paris" map) started in 1163 when Pope Alexander III laid the cornerstone and was completed in 1330. Built in an age of illiteracy, the cathedral windows tell the stories of the Bible in its portals, paintings, and stained glass. Angry citizens pillaged Notre-Dame during the French Revolution, mistaking religious statues above the portals on the west front for representations of kings and beheading them. (To see the statues removed by revolutionaries visit the Cluny Museum. See the write-up later in this chapter.)

Nearly 100 years later, after Notre-Dame had been turned into a barn, writer Victor Hugo and other artists called attention to its dangerous state of disrepair and architect Viollet-le-Duc began the much-needed restoration. He designed Notre-Dame's spire, a new feature, and Baron Haussmann (Napoléon III's urban planner) tore down the houses cluttering the views of the cathedral.

Visiting Notre-Dame takes a good hour to 90 minutes. The highlight for kids will undoubtedly be climbing the 387 narrow and winding steps to the top of one of the towers for a fabulous view of the gargoyles and of Paris (set aside at least 45 min. for this, more during high tourist season). And note that the entrance to the towers is outside the cathedral on the left side of the facade on rue du Cloître-Notre Dame. If you plan to visit the tower, go early in the morning! Lines stretch down the square in front of the cathedral and outside the towers' entrance during the summer. Before entering, walk around to the east end of the church to appreciate the spectacular flying

Notre-Dame de Paris

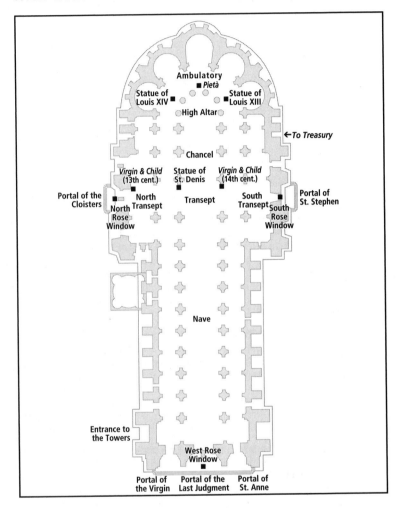

buttresses. Visit on a sunny morning to catch the giant rose windows — which retain some of their 13th-century stained glass — in all their glory. Of interest to history buffs will be the Cathedral's Treasury (on the Seine side of the building), which houses such valuable items as gold and jeweled chalices and other items from Notre-Dame's long history.

See map p. 184. 6 Parvis Notre-Dame. ☎ *01-42-34-56-10.* www.notredamede paris.fr. *Métro: Cité or St-Michel. RER: St-Michel. Bus: 21, 24, 38, 47, 85, 96. Admission (you must have exact change for the towers and undergo a bag search): Cathedral is free; towers are 7.50€ ($12) adults, 4.80€ ($7.70) students 18–25, free for children 17 and under. Open: Cathedral, daily 8 a.m.–6:45p.m., weekends until 7:15 p.m.;*

treasury, Mon–Fri 9:30 a.m.–6 p.m., Sat 9:30 a.m.–6:30 p.m., Sun 1:30 p.m.–6:30 p.m.; towers, daily Jan–March and Oct–Dec 10 a.m.–5:30 p.m., Apr–Sept 10 a.m.–6:30 p.m. (until 11 p.m. Sat–Sun in June–Aug); crypt, daily 10 a.m.–6 p.m.; free museum tours in English, Wed, Thurs, Sat 2:30 p.m., visits start inside at the great organ.

Centre Georges Pompidou
Le Marais (4e)

British architect Richard Rogers and Italian architect Renzo Piano designed this futuristic "guts-on-the-outside" building in the late 1960s as part of a redevelopment plan for the neighborhood, and since its opening in 1966, the Centre National d'Art et de Culture Georges Pompidou has been a surprisingly popular attraction — so popular that the wear and tear of about 160 million visitors caused the building to begin crumbling and it closed for a three-year renovation in 1997. It is a wonderfully spacious haven in which to view, touch, or listen to modern art and artists. The newer of Paris's two modern art museums, the Centre Georges Pompidou includes two floors of work from the Musée National d'Art Moderne, France's national collection of modern art. The Centre Pompidou also houses a cinema, a huge public library, spaces for modern dance and music, temporary exhibits that often include video and computer works, and nearly 150 drawings, paintings, and other works by Romanian sculptor Constantin Brancusi in the Brancusi Atelier, a small building near the Pompidou's entrance. Plan on spending at least two hours to do the works and a half-hour buying souvenirs here.

Sadly, taking a free escalator ride to the top for the breathtaking panoramic view of Paris is no more; you must purchase admission to the museum. However, if all you're interested in is the view, consider stopping at the Pompidou's ultrahip top-floor restaurant Georges. For the same price as an adult's full-package admission to the museum (10€/$16), you can relax with a glass of wine and enjoy the 360-degree view from indoors.

As a bonus, visit the nearby Igor Stravinsky fountain (informally *la Fontaine des automats*), which is free. Its animated sculptures by Jean Tinguely and Niki de Saint Phalle include red lips spitting water, a multicolored treble clef symbol, a mermaid squirting water from strategic body parts, and a twirling grinning skull, all representations of Stravinsky's compositions.

See map p. 184. Place Georges Pompidou. ☎ *01-44-78-12-33.* www.centre pompidou.fr. *Métro: Rambuteau. Admission: 10€ ($16) (12€/$19 May1–Aug 8,) adults, 8€ ($13) (9€/$14 May 1–Aug 8) students ages 18–25, free for ages 17 and under. Open: Wed–Mon 11 a.m.–9 p.m. Last admission 8 p.m.*

Champs-Elysées
Champs-Elysées (8e)

This is the avenue where the military march on Bastille Day, where cinephiles line up for French and American movies playing in the many theaters, where tourists wander the broad sidewalks and browse some of the same stores that can be found back home, where the Tour de France crowns the winner. But this isn't just a boulevard; if you were in Paris when the French won the World and Euro Cup soccer championships (1998 and 2000, respectively), you understand what the Champs-Elysées means to the French. They come here to celebrate victory and freedom. When close to a million singing, flag-waving Parisians spilled into the avenue, it was said that the country hadn't experienced such group euphoria since the days following the Liberation of Paris by the Allies in 1944. The scene on France's most famous street is liveliest at night, with people lining up for the numerous cinemas (see English-language films here by looking for *v.o.* for *version originale* on schedules and movie posters) and floodlights illuminating the Arc de Triomphe and place de la Concorde. Restaurants consist mainly of standard chain cafes (Chez Clément, Hippo) and American-style fast-food (McDonald's, Planet Hollywood), although good restaurants abound on the streets surrounding the avenue (see Chapter 10). You can shop at reasonably priced stores, such as Zara, get good deals on T-shirts at Petit Bateau, pick up what all of Europe is listening to at Fnac or Virgin, search for chic souvenirs at Le Drugstore, wander the very luxe (Louis Vuitton, whose flagship "cultural space" and store opened in 2006), and pass chain stores that you'd see in any American mall (the Disney Store, Quiksilver). Some of the stores are open on Sunday. Allow an hour to walk from top to bottom, longer if you want to shop, eat, or dawdle.

See map p. 184. Métro: Concorde, Champs-Elysées Clémenceau, Franklin-D-Roosevelt, George V, Charles-de-Gaulle-Étoile. Bus: Many lines cross it, but only the 73 travels its entire length.

Eiffel Tower (La Tour Eiffel)
Eiffel Tower/Les Invalides (7e)

Paris's most famous symbol weighs 7,000 tons, soars 317m (1,056 ft.), is held together with 2.5 million rivets and was due for destruction 20 years after the World's Fair of 1889 for which it was built. (Its usefulness as a communications tower saved it.) Praised by some and criticized by others, the tower created as much controversy in its time as did I.M. Pei's pyramid at the Louvre 100 years later. Upon completion, the Eiffel Tower was the tallest human-built structure in the world. People have climbed it, bungee-jumped from it, and cycled down the tower's steps. Since 2003, 20,000 lights sparkle for ten minutes an hour each evening until 2 a.m. in summer and 1 a.m. in winter. Parisians often comment that the final lighting hour is the best one, because the yellow ambient lighting on the tower's structure is turned off, and only the sparkling white lights can be seen.

But what you really want to know are the practicalities: *Do I have to climb stairs? Do elevators go to the top? Are there bathrooms? Do they have snacks? Can I ascend in a wheelchair?* The answers: The Tower has three levels that are accessible by elevator. No elevator goes directly from ground level to the top; you must change elevators at the second level. Although you can take stairs from the ground to the first and second levels, you can't take stairs from the second level to the top. Most likely you'll wait for elevators on the first and second levels in specially roped-off lines. In high season, the wait sometimes is as long an hour for each line. Restrooms are located on each level, and snack bars and souvenir stands are on the first and second levels. The tower is wheelchair accessible to the second level but not to the top.

Some advice: Six million people visit the Eiffel Tower each year. To avoid *loonnnggg* lines, go early in the morning or in the off season and take the stairs to Level 2 to avoid waiting in line for the elevators there (you can only get to the top by elevator, however, and will have to wait in line for it). If this isn't possible, allow about three hours for your visit: one hour to line up for tickets and another two to access the elevators on levels one and two.

Food is available at the Altitude 95 restaurant on the first floor, which is simply gorgeous, but overpriced for the quality of its meals. A first-floor snack bar and second-floor cafeteria are open, but again, they're not the best values (you'll pay about 7.50€/$12 for a slice of pizza or a sandwich and a drink). The best food at the Eiffel Tower is also its most expensive, without a doubt: The Michelin-starred Jules Verne, one of Paris's most celebrated restaurants, is on the Eiffel Tower's second level. (One of the pluses of dining here is that you get your own private elevator to the restaurant.)

If you have the patience to wait until sunset, the Eiffel Tower at night is recommended! Its lights frame the lacy steelwork beneath you in a way that daylight doesn't, and the Seine reflects it all.

See map p. 184. Champs-de-Mars. ☎ *01-44-11-23-23.* www.tour-eiffel.fr. *Métro: Trocadéro, Ecole-Militaire, Bir-Hakeim. RER: Champ-de-Mars-Tour Eiffel. Admission: First level by elevator 4.80€ ($7.70) adults, 2.50€ ($4) children under 12; second level by elevator 7.80€ ($12) adults, 4.30€ ($6.90) children under 12; second level by steps 4€ ($6.40) adults, 3.10€ ($4.95) children aged 3–11. Open: Daily Jan to mid-June and Sept–Dec 9:30–11 p.m., mid-June to Aug 9 a.m.–midnight.*

Hôtel des Invalides (Napoléon's Tomb)
Eiffel Tower/Les Invalides (7e)

Louis XIV, who liked war and waged many, built Invalides, one of Europe's architectural masterpieces, as a hospital and home for all veteran officers and soldiers "whether maimed or old or frail." It still has offices for departments of the French armed forces, and part of it is still a hospital. The best way to get the sense of the awe that the Hôtel des Invalides inspires is to walk to it by crossing the Alexander III bridge. The dome of the **Église du Dôme** (gilded with 12 kilograms of real gold), is one of the high points of classical art, with a skylight rising 107m (351 ft.) from the ground. Sixteen green copper cannons point outward in a powerful display.

Enemy flags captured during the military campaigns of the 19th and 20th centuries hang from the rafters in two impressive rows at the **Église de St-Louis,** known as the Church of the Soldiers, but most visitors come to see the **Tomb of Napoléon** where the emperor is buried in six coffins, one inside the other, under the great dome. The first coffin is iron, the second mahogany, the third and fourth lead, the fifth ebony, and the outermost oak. The emperor's remains were transferred here 20 years after his death in 1820 on the island of St. Helena, where he was exiled following his defeat at Waterloo. Buried along with Napoléon in smaller tombs are the emperor's two brothers, his son Napoléon II of France, Claude Rouget de Lisle (author of *La Marseillaise,* the French national anthem), and Henri de la Tour d'Auvergne, Viscount de Turenne — one of France's greatest military leaders. Napoléon was so respected that even the 1793 extremist revolutionaries, who scattered the remains of the other deceased French leaders interred at St. Denis, preserved his bones until their final resting place in les Invalides. A must-see is the **Musée de l'Armée,** one of the world's greatest military museums; admission is included when you buy your ticket for Napoléon's tomb. It features thousands of weapons from prehistory to World War II including spearheads, arrowheads, maces, cannons, and guns in addition to battle flags, booty, suits of armor, and uniforms from around the world. The Charles de Gaulle wing tells the story of World War II on video touch screens, a decoding machine, and other artifacts. Admission here allows access to Napoléon's Tomb, the Musée de l'Armée, a scale models museum, and the Order of the Liberation museum. Set aside two hours for a complete visit or a half-hour to see only the tomb.

See map p. 184. Place des Invalides. ☎ *01-44-42-38-77. Métro: La Tour Maubourg, Invalides, or Varenne. Bus: 28, 49, 63, 69, 92, 83, 87, 92. Admission: 8€ ($13) adults, 6€ ($9.60) seniors and students 18–26, free for children younger than 18 and to all on July 14. Open: Oct–Mar Wed–Mon 10 a.m.–5 p.m.; July and Aug Wed–Mon 10 a.m.– 6 p.m. Every Tues 10 a.m.–9 p.m. with reduced admission: 6€ ($9.60) adults, free for students and seniors after 5:30 p.m. Tomb of Napoléon open until 6:45 p.m. July and Aug. Closed the first Mon of every month, Christmas day, and Jan 1, May, and Nov.*

Jardin des Tuileries
Louvre (1er)

Come for a stroll here either before or after visiting the Louvre. Once a fashionable carriageway, today the Tuileries is Paris's most visited park and a great place to rest your feet and catch some rays on conveniently placed wrought-iron chairs surrounding the garden's fountains. In keeping with the French style of parks, trees are planted according to an orderly design and the sandy paths are arrow straight. Spread out across 25 hectares (63 acres), the gardens were originally laid out in the 1560s for Queen Mother Catherine de Medici in front of the Tuileries Palace, which was burned down during the 1871 Paris Commune. The Orangerie (which has finally reopened! — see later in this chapter) and the Jeu de Paume are at the garden's western edge, and to the east you'll find 40 beautiful Maillol bronzes scattered among the trees, as well as four sculptures by Rodin, and works by Jean Dubuffet, Alberto Giacometti, David Smith, Max Ernst, Henry Moore, and Henri Laurens. You can sit down for a light snack at one of the outdoor cafes. During the summer, a carnival features an enormous Ferris wheel (with great views of the city), a log flume, fun house, arcade-style games, snacks, and machine-made soft ice cream (but I find the best ice cream in the Tuileries is the homemade ice cream sold from a stand right beyond the Arc de Triomphe du Carrousel at the entrance to the Tuileries).

See map p. 184. Quai des Tuileries. Entrances on rue de Rivoli and place de la Concorde, 1er. ☎ *01-30-20-90-43. Métro: Concorde or Tuileries. Bus: 24, 42, 69, 72, 73, 84, 94. Admission: Free. Open: Daily 7:30 a.m.–7:30 p.m. in the winter, till 9 p.m. in the summer.*

Keeping an eye on your wallet while eyeing the goods

You won't be able to avoid pesky (and illegal) vendors trying to cajole you into buying everything from Eiffel Tower key chains to postcards to mechanical butterflies; they constantly approach tourists standing in line for Eiffel Tower admission tickets. Be attentive — some of these vendors work in tandem with pickpockets who will rip you off while you're busy looking at the displays. As for the quality of the merchandise — it's pretty bad. Buy your souvenirs from shops and licensed vendors. (See Chapter 4 for advice on what to do if you get pickpocketed.)

Jardin du Palais-Royal
Louvre (1er)

In past centuries, gamblers and those seeking more lascivious pleasures flocked to this garden where Cardinal Richelieu ordered the Royal Palace built in 1630 as his personal residence, complete with grounds landscaped by the royal gardener. Today the palace is no longer open to the public, but its statue-filled gardens, including Daniel Buren's wonderful prison-striped columns of staggered heights built in 1986 (which make for a great photo op), remain one of the most restful places in the city. The square is also ringed by restaurants, art galleries, and specialty boutiques, and it's home to the Comédie-Française.

See map p. 184. Entrances on rue de Rivoli and place de la Concorde. ☎ *01-47-03-92-16. Métro: Concorde or Tuileries. Bus: 21, 49, 42, 48, 67, 68, 69, 72, 81, 95. Admission: Free. Open: Daily 7:30 a.m.–8:30 p.m.*

Jardin et Palais du Luxembourg
St-Germain-des-Prés (6e)

No matter which entrance you walk through, you will fall in love with this beloved park not far from the Sorbonne and just south of the Latin Quarter. It's the 6e arrondissement's **Jardin du Luxembourg,** one of Paris's most beloved parks. Children love it for its playground, pony rides, puppet theater, and the Fontaine de Médicis (the central Médici Fountain) where they can sail toy boats and watch the ducks. Besides pools, fountains, and statues of queens and poets, there are tennis and *boules* courts (*boule* means ball; in this game, players compete to see who can roll their small steel ball closest to a larger steel ball that lies farther down the court). In recent years, art has been exhibited on the wrought-iron fence at the garden's northwestern entrance near boulevard St-Michel and rue de Médicis.

The park was commissioned by King Henri IV's queen, Marie de Medici, who also had the **Palais du Luxembourg** built at the northern edge of the park. The Palais resembles the Palazzo Pitti in Florence, where Marie spent her childhood and for which she was homesick. When the queen was banished in 1630, the palace was abandoned until the Revolution in 1789, when it was used as a prison. Now the seat of the French Senate, it is not open to the public.

Orchards in the park's southwest corner contain 360 varieties of apples, 270 kinds of pears, and various grapevines. Members of the French Senate get to eat the fruit, but leftovers go to a soup kitchen. Walk north and you come across a bevy of beehives behind a low fence. A beekeeping course is taught here on weekends. See whether you can find the Statue of Liberty tucked away nearby.

See map p. 184. Main entrance at the corner of bd. St-Michel and rue des Médicis. ☎ *01-43-29-12-78. Métro: Odéon. RER: Luxembourg, Port-Royal. Bus: 38, 82, 84, 85, 89. Admission: Free. Open: Daily dawn–dusk.*

Montmartre
On the Right Bank

This neighborhood/village is for anyone who admires the work of Toulouse-Lautrec, is interested in one of Picasso's earliest studios, or loved the films *Le Destin Fabuleux d'Amélie Poulain* or *Moulin Rouge.* You can get to Montmartre by taking the métro to the Anvers or Abbesses stop, the entrance of which is graced by a fabulous Art Nouveau métro sign. You can either walk to the top of the *butte* (hill) or take the *funiculaire* (outdoor small railway) up. (To take the *funiculaire,* walk from the Anvers Métro station the short distance from rue Steinkerque and turn left onto rue Tardieu, where, for a métro ticket, the *funiculaire* whisks you from the base of the Montmartre butte to the road right beneath Sacré-Coeur.) After visiting Sacré-Coeur and the touristy but fun place du Tertre, a square with overpriced restaurants and artists clamoring to sketch your portrait, wander down the hill where you eventually stumble across Paris from another era — surprisingly unspoiled lanes, quiet squares, ivy-clad shuttered houses with gardens, and even Paris's only vineyard. Altogether, it creates a sense of the rustic village it once was. (*Note:* See Chapter 13 for a detailed walking itinerary through Montmartre.)

Musée d'Orsay
Eiffel Tower/Les Invalides (7e)

This stone and iron former train station is one of the world's greatest museums of 19th century art, with an unsurpassed collection of Impressionist masterpieces. Opened in 1900 by the Campagnie des Chemins de Fer d'Orléans, it was virtually abandoned 39 years later. (You can see its sorry state in Orson Welles's film *The Trial.*) In 1979, it was classified as a historical monument to prevent its demolition and its transformation into a museum began in 1983. Paris's collections of 19th-century art, which had been scattered among many museums, now had a single home, and the Musée d'Orsay opened to the public in 1986.

Paris's top attraction:
The Seine river cruise

Is there anything more romantic than slipping down the current of one of the world's great rivers past famous cathedrals, museums, palaces — and the prison where Marie Antoinette spent her last days? Well, perhaps killing the canned PA sightseeing commentary and getting rid of all the other camera-clicking tourists would help the romantic mood, but if it's mood you're after you can always take a more refined, though wildly expensive, dinner cruise.

Three companies offer similar tours in the same price range with recorded commentaries. Perhaps the most well known are the **Bateaux-Mouches** that sail from the Right Bank and have huge floodlit boats. **Bateaux-Parisiens** sail from the Left Bank, while **Vedettes Pont Neuf** sail from the Ile de la Cité. Vedettes boats are smaller, more intimate, and not all of them are covered.

Bateaux les Vedettes du Pont Neuf, square du Vert-Galant, 1er. ☎ 01-46-33-98-38. Métro: Pont-Neuf, sail from the riverside where the Pont Neuf crosses the Ile de la Cité. Departures: March 15 to October 31 at 10:30, 11:15 a.m., noon and then every half-hour from 1:30 to 10:30 p.m.; November 1 to March 14 every 45 minutes Monday through Thursday from 10:30 a.m. to noon and 2 to 6:30 p.m., and at 8 and 10 p.m. Saturday and Sunday tours leave every 45 minutes from 10:30 a.m. to noon, every half-hour from 2 to 6:30 p.m., and at 8 p.m., and every half-hour from 9 to 10:30 p.m. Rates: 11€ ($18) adults, 6€ ($9.60) children under 12.

Tickets purchased on the Internet are 7€ ($11) for adults, 4€ ($6.40) children.

Bateaux-Mouches, pont de l'Alma, Right Bank, 8e. ☎ 01-42-25-96-10. www. bateaux-mouches.fr. Métro: Alma Marceau. Departures: In summer high season (approximately Apr–Sept) every 30 minutes from 11 a.m. to 10:30 p.m.; in winter (Oct–Mar) boats leave anywhere from 45 minutes to an hour between departures from 10:15 a.m. to 9 p.m. Rates: 10€ ($16) for adults, 5€ ($8) for children 4 to 12 and adults older than 65; children younger than 4 ride free.

Bateaux-Parisiens, port de la Bourdonnais, Left Bank, 7e. ☎ 01-44-11-33-44. Métro: Bir-Hakeim. Departures: From April through September every half-hour from 10 a.m. to 10:30 p.m.; from October through March every hour, some half-hourly from 10 a.m. to 10 p.m. Rates: 11€ ($18) adults; 5€ ($8) children under 12. Free under age 3.

A cheaper alternative to the daytime tour (without commentary) is the **Batobus** (☎ 08-25-01-01 [.15€/25¢ per min. for the call]; www.batobus.com), a water taxi with no piped-in commentary that stops every 25 minutes at eight major points of interest: the **Eiffel Tower,** the **Musée d'Orsay, St-Germain-des-Prés, Notre-Dame,** the **Jardin des Plantes, Hôtel de Ville, Louvre,** and the **Champs-Elysées.** A day ticket costs 12€ ($19) per adult or 6€ ($9.60) for children under 16; Batobus runs every 25 to 30 minutes mid-March to May and from September through the beginning of November from 10 a.m. to 7 p.m. and until 9:30 p.m. June through August. From November through January 8 and from February 3 through mid-March, Batobus runs every half-hour from 10:30 a.m. to 4:30 p.m.

There are three floors of exhibits. On the ground floor are Ingres's *La Source,* Millet's *L'Angelus,* the Barbizon school, Manet's *Olympia,* and other works of early Impressionism. Impressionism continues on the top level, with Renoir's *Le Moulin de la Galette,* Manet's *Déjeuner sur l'Herbe,* Degas's *Racing at Longchamps,* Monet's cathedrals, van Gogh's *Self-Portrait,* and Whistler's *Portrait of the Artist's Mother.* Works by Gauguin and the Pont-Aven school, Toulouse-Lautrec, Pissarro, Cézanne, and Seurat also are exhibited. Symbolism, naturalism, and Art Nouveau are represented on the middle level; the international Art Nouveau exhibit is worth a look for its wonderful furniture and objets d'art as well as Koloman Moser's *Paradise,* a beautiful design for stained glass. Give yourself three hours, including a lunch break in the museum's gorgeous, turn-of-the-20th-century Musée d'Orsay restaurant on the middle level. For less expensive and quicker light bites, the Café des Hauteurs is on the fifth floor (it has a great view of the Seine through its clock window) and a snack bar is on the mezzanine. In 2008, admission to both the Musée d'Orsay and the Musée Rodin was sold in a "passport" for 14€ ($22), a savings of 2€ ($3.20).

See map p. 184. 1 rue Bellechasse or 62 rue de Lille. ☎ *01-40-49-48-14.* www.musee-orsay.fr. *Métro: Solférino. RER: Musée-d'Orsay. Admission: 8€ ($13) adults, 5.50€ ($8.80) ages 18–25 and for everyone after 4:15 p.m. (except Thurs), free for ages 17 and under and for everyone on the first Sun of each month. Open: Tues–Wed and Fri–Sun 9:30 a.m.–6 p.m., Thurs 9:30a.m.–9:45 p.m. Last admission is 30 min. before close.*

Musée du Louvre
Louvre (1er)

The three steps to an enjoyable Louvre experience are to:

1. Buy your tickets in advance. Visitors from the United States and Canada can purchase tickets online from www.ticketweb.com (don't be put off by the Paris, CA location denoted on the website; this is the Louvre in Paris France) and have them delivered to their homes before departure. Visitors from other countries can use www.fnac.com or www.ticketnet.com. If you are already in France upon reading this, some métro stations have tickets for sale at the window or you can buy tickets from the distributors on the second floor of the Carrousel du Louvre. Take the escalator near the Nature et Découverte store to the second floor; distributors are on the left.

2. Grab a free map of the Louvre at the Information Desk under the Pyramid or get a free guide. The Louvre bookstore in the Carrousel du Louvre sells many comprehensive guides and maps in English; you can also grab brochures for "Visitors in a Hurry," or a guidebook, *The Louvre, First Visit.*

3. Take a guided tour. You can try a 90-minute tour by a museum guide (☎ **01-40-20-52-63**) that covers the most popular works and gives you a quick orientation to the museum's layout. Times and prices vary; generally, a tour of the most celebrated works is about

The Louvre

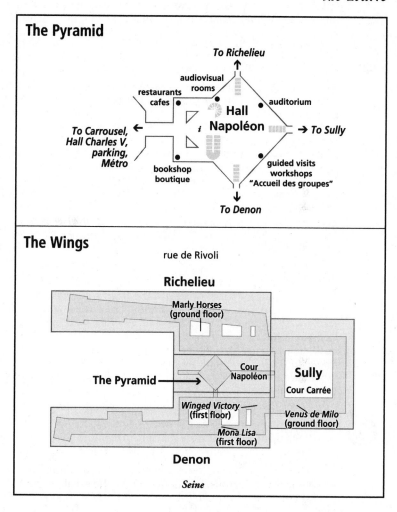

8€ for adults and 5€ for students under 26 years of age ($13 and $8, respectively). If you prefer to set your own pace, an audio tour (6€/$9.60) can be rented at the entrance to any of the wings.

I.M. Pei's glass pyramid is the main entrance to the museum; pregnant women, visitors with children in strollers, and those with disabilities have priority. Avoid this entrance and its long lines by using the **99 rue de Rivoli/Carrousel du Louvre** entrance, or take the stairs at the **Porte des Lions** near the Arc de Triomphe du Carrousel (the arch resembling a smaller Arc de Triomphe). Those who already have tickets or have the Carte Musées et Monuments can use the special entrance to the Louvre at the **passage Richelieu** between rue de Rivoli and the courtyard.

Tickets are valid all day so you can enter and exit the museum as many times as you prefer. Admission is reduced after 6 p.m. on Wednesday and Friday, and free the first Sunday of each month.

The Louvre palace (see "The Louvre" map nearby) evolved during several centuries, first built as the Château du Louvre in 1190 by Philip Augustus. It first opened as a museum in 1793, and it would take you a month of visits to see the more than 30,000 treasures it now houses. But a visit to the Louvre doesn't have to be overwhelming. The Louvre is organized in three wings — Sully, Denon, and Richelieu — over four floors exhibiting art and antiquities from Oriental, Islamic, Egyptian, Greek, Etruscan, Roman, Oceanic, European, and North and South American civilizations, and sculpture, objets d'art, paintings, prints, drawings, and the moats and dungeon of the medieval Louvre fortress.

When you're in a hurry, but want to do the Louvre on your own, do a quick, "best of the Louvre" tour on either Wednesday or Friday when the museum is open until 9:45 p.m. Start with Leonardo da Vinci's *Mona Lisa* (Denon wing, first floor); on the same floor nearby are two of the Louvre's most famous French paintings, Géricault's *The Raft of Medusa* and Delacroix's *Liberty Guiding the People*. Next, visit the *Winged Victory* and Michelangelo's *Slaves* (both Denon wing, ground floor) before seeing the *Venus de Milo* (Sully wing, ground floor). After that, let your own interests guide you. Consider that only Florence's Uffizi Gallery rivals the Denon wing for its Italian Renaissance collection, which includes Raphael's *Portrait of Balthazar Castiglione* and Titian's *Man with a Glove*. And the revamped Egyptian antiquities department is the largest exhibition of Egyptian antiquities outside Cairo.

If you want to purchase tickets in advance while in Paris, you can order tickets by phone from Fnac (☎ **08-92-68-46-94**; .35€/55¢ per minute), and pick them up at any Fnac store (except Fnac photo shops). A 1.50€ ($2.40) commission is charged by Fnac. A nearby branch is at Forum des Halles, 1 rue Pierre Lescot.

See map p. 184. ☎ *01-40-20-53-17 for the information desk, or 08-92-68-46-94 to order tickets.* www.louvre.fr. *Métro: Palais-Royal-Musée du Louvre. Admission: 9€ ($14), 6€ ($9.60) after 6 p.m. on Wed and Fri, free for ages 17 and under and for everyone (but crowded) the first Sun each month. Open: Wed–Mon 9 a.m.–6 p.m. (until 10 p.m. Wed and Fri). The entrance or entresol, with its information desks, medieval Louvre exhibit, cafes, post office, and shops, stays open daily until 9:45 p.m.*

Musée Jacquemart André
Champs-Elysées (8e)

This kid-friendly museum is very much worth a visit, not only for the Italian and Flemish masterpieces by Bellini, Botticelli, Carpaccio, Uccello, Rubens, Rembrandt, and van Eyck, but to see how very rich Parisians lived in the 19th century. Edouard André, the heir of a prominent banking family, and his wife, Nélie Jacquemart, a well-known portraitist, commissioned architect Henri Parent to build their "house," then traveled the world to find French, Flemish, and Italian paintings, furniture, and tapestries to fill it. They had no children, so Nélie willed the house and its treasures to the French government, giving the city of Paris one of its best museums. Highlights of the collection include Rembrandt's *Docteur Tholinx*, Van Dyck's *Time Cutting the Wings of Love*, a fresco by Jean Baptiste Tiepolo, Domenico Ghirlandaio's naturalistic *Portrait d'un Vieillard*, and a portrait of *Catherine Skavronskaia* by Elisabeth Vigée-Lebrun, one of Marie Antoinette's favorite artists, and a fascinating person in her own right. As you wander the ornate gilt-ridden rooms, pause in the "winter garden," a tour de force of marble and mirrors flanking an unusual double staircase. For kids, the museum has organized a special activity: At the beginning of the visit kids receive a free booklet with word mysteries. The kids use the contents of the museum to solve the puzzles, aided by clues spread throughout the museum, and find out the "secret letters." It is all worthwhile, especially for the surprise! Take advantage of the free interactive audio that guides you through the mansion with fascinating narrative. Visit at 11 a.m., allow at least an hour, then take a break in what was Madame Jacquemart's lofty-ceilinged dining room, now a pretty tearoom serving light lunches (the salads are all named for artists) and snacks.

See map p. 184. 158 bd. Haussmann. ☎ *01-45-62-11-59. Métro: Miromesnil. Bus: 22, 28, 43, 52, 54, 80, 83, 84, 93. Admission: 10€ ($16) adults, 7:30€ ($12) students and children from 7–17, free for ages 6 and younger. For families, one child is admitted free for every three paid admissions. Open: Daily (including Dec 25) 10 a.m.–6 p.m.; the cafe is open 11:45 a.m.–5:30 p.m.*

Musée Nationale d'Auguste Rodin
Eiffel Tower/Les Invalides (7e)

This may just be the "perfect" museum. It's a large house with just 16 rooms surrounded by bucolic gardens. Auguste Rodin, often regarded as the greatest sculptor of all time, lived and worked here from 1908 until his death in 1917, an era when his legendary sculptures were labeled obscene. This collection includes all of his greatest works. In the courtyard, *Burghers of Calais* is a harrowing commemoration of the siege of Calais in 1347, after which the triumphant Edward III of England kept the town's six richest burghers as servants. Also in the courtyard is *The Thinker*. The *Gates of Hell* is a portrayal of Dante's *Inferno*. Intended for the Musée des Arts Decoratifs, the massive bronze doors were not completed until seven years after Rodin's death. Inside the most popular attraction is *Le Baiser (The Kiss)*, which immortalizes in white marble the passion of doomed 13th-century lovers Paolo Malatesta and Francesca da Rimini. Studies done by Rodin before he executed his sculptures take up some of the 16 rooms. Particularly interesting is the evolution of his controversial nude of Balzac rising from a tree trunk. Don't miss the works of Camille Claudel, a top-rated artist and Rodin's student and lover for many years. The museum is in the 18th-century Hôtel Biron, which was a convent before it became a residence for such writers and artists as Matisse, Isadora Duncan, Jean Cocteau, and the poet, Rainer Maria Rilke. Count on spending at least an hour and a half here.

Mange with Mona Lisa

Refuel at the Louvre from the gastronomic Le Grand Louvre to a cafeteria serving plenty of ethnic eats. Note: The museum and its restaurants are closed Tuesdays.

Beneath the Pyramid:

- ✔ **Café du Louvre:** Open 9 a.m. to 7 p.m. Thursday to Sunday, until 9:30 p.m. Friday and Wednesday.

- ✔ **Café Napoléon:** Open Wednesday to Monday 10 a.m. to 6 p.m.

- ✔ **Café Universal (food court):** Open Wednesday to Monday 11:30 a.m. to 3 p.m.

- ✔ **Le Grand Louvre** (☎ 01-40-20-53-41): Open Wednesday to Monday noon to 3 p.m. and Friday and Wednesday 7 to 10 p.m.

In the Denon Wing:

- ✔ **Café Denon** (mezzanine): Open Thursday to Sunday 9 a.m. to 5 p.m.; open until 7:30 p.m. Friday and Wednesday.

- ✔ **Café Mollien** (first floor): Open Thursday to Sunday 10:30 a.m. to 5 p.m.; open until 9 p.m. Friday and Wednesday.

In the Richelieu Wing:

- ✔ **Café Richelieu** (first floor): Open Thursday to Monday 10:30 a.m. to 5 p.m.; open until 9:30 p.m. Wednesday.

In the Cour de Napoléon (facing the Pyramid):

- ✔ **Café Marly** (☎ 01-49-26-06-60): Open daily 8 a.m. to 2 a.m.

See Chapter 10 for restaurant reviews.

If you don't have much time or money, pay the 1€ ($1.60) admission to visit just the gardens, where Rodin's works stand among 2,000 rosebushes, bubbling springs, and other plants. A playground is also hidden within the grounds. Allow at least an hour to visit the garden, longer if you want to break for coffee in the garden cafe.

See map p. 184. 77 rue de Varenne (in the Hôtel Biron). ☎ *01-44-18-61-10.* www. musee-rodin.fr. *Métro: Varenne or St François Xavier. Admission: 6€ ($9.60) adults, 4€ ($6.40) ages 18–25, free for ages 17 and under. Open: Apr–Sept Tues–Sun 9:30 a.m.–5:45 p.m., Oct–Mar Tues–Sun 9:30 a.m.–4:45 p.m. Last admission 30 min. before close.*

Musée Picasso
Le Marais (3e)

This mansion in the Marais houses the world's largest collection of Spanish master Pablo Picasso's art, and you can pay a visit here on each trip to Paris and see something different each time because the works are constantly rotated. Located in the renovated Hôtel Salé, which was built in the mid–17th century for a salt tax collector (hence the name which translates as the salted mansion). The museum was created in 1973 by Picasso's heirs, who donated his personal art collection to the state in lieu of paying outrageous inheritance taxes after his death. The spectacular collection includes more than 200 paintings, nearly 160 sculptures, 88 ceramics, and more than 3,000 prints and drawings. Every phase of Picasso's prolific 75-year career is represented. Works can be viewed chronologically; particularly interesting is seeing how his paintings were influenced by the women he loved at the time: his first wife, Olga; Marie-Thérèse Walter, mother of his daughter, Maya; Françoise Gilot, mother of Paloma and Paul; and Dora Maar, among others. Budget at least two hours here, if not more. It is best to go early in the morning, as the narrow corridors in parts of the museum get particularly crowded during the afternoon (they need the wall space to exhibit this enormous collection). The museum also displays works by other artists collected by Picasso, including Corot, Cézanne, Braque, Rousseau, Matisse, and Renoir. A visit here is well worth the trip; make sure to walk around the neighborhood afterward to shop the trendy boutiques and fill up on falafel from one of the numerous stands on and around rue des Rosiers.

See map p. 184. 5 rue de Thorigny (in the Hôtel Salé). ☎ 01-42-71-25-21. www. musee-picasso.fr. Métro: Chemin-Vert, St-Paul, or Filles du Calvaire. Admission: 6.50€ ($10) adults, 4.50€ ($7.20) ages 18–25, free for ages 17 and under. Admission during special exhibitions may be slightly higher. Open: Apr–Sept Wed–Mon 9:30 a.m.–6 p.m., Oct–Mar Wed–Mon 9:30 a.m.–5:30 p.m.

Panthéon
Latin Quarter (5e)

Is it a church? Is it a museum? Is it a tomb? Perhaps the best description would be: The Panthéon is to France what Westminster Abbey is to England — a final resting place for many of the nation's greatest men and one woman, Marie Curie. Few other monuments in Paris have had as versatile a career as the neoclassical Panthéon, whose huge dome is one of the landmarks of the Left Bank. Inside the domed church's barrel-vaulted crypt are the tombs of Voltaire, Rousseau, Hugo, Braille, and Zola. French writer, politician, and adventurer André Malraux was the last to be entombed here in 1996. Louis XV originally built the Panthéon as a church in thanksgiving to St-Geneviève after his recovery from gout. Construction started in 1755, but after the French Revolution, the church was renamed the Panthéon, in remembrance of ancient Rome's Pantheon, and rededicated as a burying ground for France's heroes. All Christian elements were removed and windows were blocked. From 1806 to 1884, officials turned the Panthéon back into a church two more times before finally declaring it what it is today. Along with historical information of the great figures buried here, a small wing is devoted to explanation of the scientific theories and experiments discovered by Pierre and Marie Curie. A pendulum suspended from the central dome re-creates Jean-Bernard Foucault's 1851 demonstration proving the rotation of the earth. A plaque here is dedicated to 2,600 "righteous" people who helped save French Jews from deportation during World War II. The views from the top here are some of the best in Paris.

See map p. 184. Place du Panthéon. ☎ *01-44-32-18-00. Métro: Cardinal-Lemoine or Maubert-Mutualité. Bus: 21, 27, 83, 84, 85, 89. Admission: 7.50€ ($12) adults, 4.80€ ($7.70) ages 18–25, free for children younger than 18. Open: Apr–Sept daily 10 a.m.–6:30 p.m., Oct–Mar until 6 p.m.*

Père-Lachaise Cemetery
Montmartre and beyond (20e)

On a high hill overlooking Paris, this "city" is the final resting ground for some of the world's most illustrious composers, artists, writers, poets, singers, and philosophers. Chopin, Bizet, Proust, Balzac, Corot, Delacroix, Pissarro, Modigliani, Molière, Oscar Wilde, Isadora Duncan, Simone Signoret, Yves Montand, and of course, Jim Morrison (framed pictures of him grace the walls of neighboring brasseries, but his bust has been removed due to vandalism) have been laid to rest in this, the world's most visited cemetery. No wonder Parisians have always come here to stroll and reflect; with its winding, cobbled streets, park benches, and street signs, the 44-hectare (110-acre) Père-Lachaise is a minicity unto itself. Many visitors leave flowers or notes scrawled on métro tickets for their favorite celebrity residents. The tombs are artistic works, decorated with exquisite marble and stone statuettes or chiseled around diminutive stained-glass windows.

Legends abound. The 18th-century bronze tomb of murdered journalist Victor Noir is reputed to make women fertile when rubbed (the polished sheen of certain parts of his statue is testament to its lore!). Oscar Wilde's impressive tomb here, carved by Sir Jacob Epstein, is covered with lipstick spots from the kisses of his admirers. The tragic love story of Abélard and Héloïse (she was his student and her uncle castrated him when he found out about their affair) has faded, but in the 19th century, their tombs were magnets for disappointed lovers. You can obtain a free map from the gatekeeper at the main entrance, but the better map is one sold outside the entrance for 3€ ($4.80). Or you can just use the "Père-Lachaise Cemetery" map provided in this chapter. Allow at the very least two hours to visit.

See map p. 184. 16 rue du Repos. Main entrance on bd. du Ménilmontant. Métro: Père-Lachaise. Bus: 61, 69, 102. Admission: Free. Open: Mar 16–Nov 5 Mon–Fri 8 a.m.–6 p.m., Sat 8:30 a.m.–6 p.m., Sun and holidays 9 a.m.–6 p.m.; Nov 6–Mar 15 Mon–Fri 8 a.m.–5:30 p.m., Sat 8:30 a.m.–5:30 p.m., Sun and holidays 9 a.m.–6 p.m. Last entry to the cemetery is allowed 15 min. before closing time.

Place des Vosges
Le Marais (3e)

The place des Vosges sits right in the middle of the Marais — a symmetrical block of 36 rose-colored town houses, nine on each side, with handsome slate roofs and dormer windows. At ground level is a lovely arcaded walkway that's now home to galleries, cafes, antiques dealers, and smart boutiques. In the early 17th century, Henri IV transformed this area into the most prestigious neighborhood in France, putting his royal palace here, and the square quickly became the center of courtly parades and festivities. After the Revolution, it became place de l'Indivisibilité. Victor Hugo lived at No. 6 for 16 years (see "More Fun Things to See and Do," later in this chapter). This is one of the places in Paris where you can enjoy a sandwich in front of the fountain, and catch some rays alongside local students and older residents. Allow 30 minutes to walk all the way around the square under the arcades and a brief stroll in the park.

See map p. 184. Métro: St-Paul. Bus: 20, 29, 69, 76, 96.

Sacré-Coeur
Montmartre (18e)

The white Byzantine-Romanesque basilica dominating Paris's highest hill — the one that you can see from all around the city — is Basilique du Sacré-Coeur. Built from 1876 (after France's defeat in the Franco-Prussian War) to 1919, the church's interior is not as striking as its exterior and is, in fact, vaguely depressing. The best reason to come here is for the city-spanning views from its Dome — visibility is 48km (30 miles) across the rooftops of Paris on a clear day. Conserve your pre-Dome climbing energy by using the *funiculaire* to take you to Sacré-Coeur. Simply take the métro to the Anvers station, and then ride the elevator to exit the station. Walk the short distance from rue Steinkerque and turn left onto rue Tardieu, where, for the price of a métro ticket, the *funiculaire* whisks you from the base of the Montmartre butte to an area right below the church.

To reach the dome and crypt, face the church and walk around to its left side, following signs for the Dome and Crypte. You walk down a set of stairs and follow a walkway about 15m (50 ft.) to an iron gate. The entrance and ticket machine are on your right.

The climb from church floor to dome is up a flight of nail-bitingly steep corkscrew steps.

On the other side of Sacré-Coeur is the **place du Tertre,** where Vincent van Gogh once lived; he used it as a scene for one of his paintings. The place is usually swamped by tourists and quick-sketch artists in the spring and summer. Don't let the artists push you around too much: Their sketched likenesses of you or your companions may leave something to be desired, especially at their prices. Following any street downhill from the place du Tertre leads you to the quiet side of Montmartre. The steps in front of the church come alive around dusk, when street musicians entertain the crowd that gathers to watch the city's lights come on. Be alert: Pickpockets love Montmartre. Young men often hang around Sacré-Coeur and try to sell made-on-the-spot bracelets to tourists, tied directly on to your wrist — this is a classic way of partially incapacitating you while they rifle through the pockets of you or your fellow travelers. Don't stop for them; just give them a polite "non merci."

Père-Lachaise Cemetery

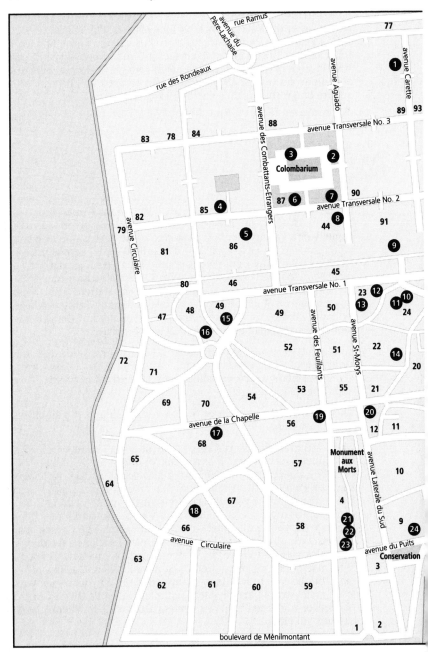

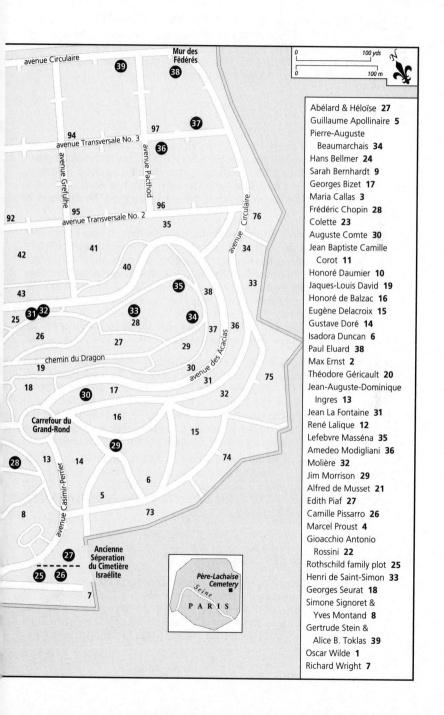

avenue Circulaire

Mur des Fédérés

avenue Transversale No. 3

avenue Grefulhe

avenue Pacthod

avenue Transversale No. 2

avenue Circulaire

avenue des Acacias

chemin du Dragon

Carrefour du Grand-Rond

avenue Casimir-Perrier

Ancienne Séperation du Cimetière Israélite

Père-Lachaise Cemetery

Seine

PARIS

0 — 100 yds
0 — 100 m

Abélard & Héloïse **27**
Guillaume Apollinaire **5**
Pierre-Auguste
 Beaumarchais **34**
Hans Bellmer **24**
Sarah Bernhardt **9**
Georges Bizet **17**
Maria Callas **3**
Frédéric Chopin **28**
Colette **23**
Auguste Comte **30**
Jean Baptiste Camille
 Corot **11**
Honoré Daumier **10**
Jaques-Louis David **19**
Honoré de Balzac **16**
Eugène Delacroix **15**
Gustave Doré **14**
Isadora Duncan **6**
Paul Eluard **38**
Max Ernst **2**
Théodore Géricault **20**
Jean-Auguste-Dominique
 Ingres **13**
Jean La Fontaine **31**
René Lalique **12**
Lefebvre Masséna **35**
Amedeo Modigliani **36**
Molière **32**
Jim Morrison **29**
Alfred de Musset **21**
Edith Piaf **27**
Camille Pissarro **26**
Marcel Proust **4**
Gioacchio Antonio
 Rossini **22**
Rothschild family plot **25**
Henri de Saint-Simon **33**
Georges Seurat **18**
Simone Signoret &
 Yves Montand **8**
Gertrude Stein &
 Alice B. Toklas **39**
Oscar Wilde **1**
Richard Wright **7**

See map p. 184. Place du Parvis du Sacré Coeur. ☎ 01-53-41-89-00. Métro: Anvers. Take elevator to surface and follow signs to funiculaire, which runs to the church (fare: one métro ticket). Bus: The only bus that goes to the top of the hill is the local Montmartrobus. Admission: Basilica free; dome and crypt 5€ ($8). Open: Basilica daily 6:45 a.m.–10:30 p.m.; dome and crypt daily 9 a.m.–5:45 p.m.

Sainte-Chapelle
Ile de la Cité (4e)

There are two ways to appreciate Sainte-Chappelle. Save it for the early afternoon on a sunny day, because the effect of its 15 perfect stained-glass windows soaring 15m (50 ft.) high to a star-studded vaulted ceiling is purely kaleidoscopic. Or, if you have the time, catch a classical music concert here, when light from the chandeliers dancing off the windows is magical.

Built between 1246 and 1248 by Louis IX, the only French king to become a saint, Sainte-Chapelle, the "Holy Chapel," was a shrine to house relics of the crucifixion, including the Crown of Thorns that Louis bought from the Emperor of Constantinople. Building Sainte-Chapelle certainly cost less than the outrageously expensive Crown of Thorns, which was said to have been acquired at the crucifixion. (Louis purchased the Crown from his cousin, Emperor Baldwin II of Constantinople, at a sum of 135,000 *livres tournois* — meanwhile Sainte-Chapelle cost only 40,000 to construct.) The Crown now resides in the vault at Notre-Dame.

Sainte-Chapelle actually consists of two chapels, one on top of the other. Palace servants used the *chapelle basse* ("lower chapel"), ornamented with fleur-de-lis designs. The *chapelle haute* ("upper chapel," accessed by 30 winding steps) is one of the highest achievements of Gothic art. If you spend the time (which can take hours or even a day!), you can see that the 1,134 scenes in the stained-glass windows trace the Biblical story from the Garden of Eden to the Apocalypse. St. Louis is shown several times.

See map p. 184. 4 bd. du Palais (in the Palais de Justice on the Ile de la Cité). ☎ 01-53-40-60-97. http://saintechapelle.monuments-nationaux.fr. *Métro: Cité, Châtelet-Les-Halles, or St-Michel. RER: St-Michel. Admission: 750€ ($12) adults, 4.80€ ($7.60) ages 18–25; free for children 17 and under. Open: Daily Mar–Oct 9:30 a.m.–6 p.m., Nov–Feb 9 a.m.–5 p.m.*

More Fun Things to See and Do

After you hit all of the city's top attractions, you may want to search out some of its lesser known sights that are worth visiting. This section introduces you to some of those spots. Organized with specific interests in mind, it gives you ideas about how to make Paris truly your own. The "More Fun Things to Do in Paris" map can help you locate the fun zones.

Especially for kids

If you're a kid visiting Paris, there are so many things to do and see, from zoos and boat rides to a city of science and magic museums! There's the fun Parisian tradition of *les guignols* (puppet shows) that, even though conducted in French, are pretty easy to figure out. You can find the shows in the Jardin du Luxembourg, the Champ de Mars, and the Jardin des Tuileries. All Parisian parks, in fact, are wonderful for children, even without the puppet shows; one of the best is the **Bois de Vincennes,** located at the most eastern edge of the city. You can rent a boat for a leisurely row on the lake, or a bike to ride on the park's miles of bike paths, or visit the great zoo with 1,200 animals (sadly, due to renovation it closed for four years at the end of 2008). Wander the wonderful maze at the more centrally located **Jardin des Enfants des Halles,** 105 rue Rambuteau (☎ **01-45-08-07-18;** access is free, generally open from 10 a.m.–4 or 6 p.m.; Métro: Châtelet). The French love well-behaved children and are happy to welcome them, especially in the following locations which have been designed with kids in mind.

Aquarium Tropical de la Porte Dorée

It's a little off the beaten path, but it's still a fascinating place to visit either before or after a visit to the nearby parc Zoologique de Paris. Aquatic life is grouped by theme and by oceanographic region in 80 aquariums. Your kids will love the circular aquarium where the Nile crocodiles live, and be excited to view sharks in natural looking environments. On display until May 2009 is an exhibit devoted to New Caledonia's coral reef. Allow at least an hour and a half.

See map p. 208. 293 av. Dausmenil, 12e. ☎ 01-44-74-84-80. Métro: Porte Dorée. Admission during special exhibits: 6.50€ ($9.10) adult, 5€ ($7) ages 4–25; no special exhibits 4.50€ ($7.20) adults, 3€ ($4.80) ages 4–25, free for children younger than 4. Open: Wed–Mon 9 a.m.–5:15 p.m.

Cité des Sciences et de l'Industrie/Parc de la Villette

This is basically a theme park about science. It's simply enormous, with interactive exhibits on everything from outer space to genetically manipulated plants, all in an incredibly cool setting. There's a planetarium, movie cinemas, ten themed gardens, and an aquarium, as well as an adventure playground designed specifically for 3- to 12-year-olds. On the complex's east side is **Explora,** which features exhibits, models, robots, and interactive games, demonstrates scientific techniques, and presents subjects that include the universe, the earth, the environment, space, computer science, and health (in one experiment, you can test your sense of smell). The **Cité des Enfants (Children's City)** was just remodeled and expanded and is divided into exhibits for 2- to 3-year-olds, 3- to 5-year-olds and 6- to 12-year-olds. Kids will learn how their bodies work in a variety of ways by seeing themselves from every angle, exploring mazes, discovering the properties

More Fun Things to Do in Paris

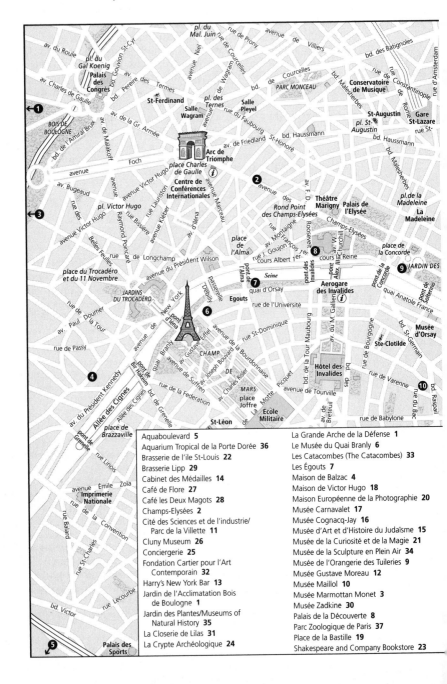

Aquaboulevard **5**

Aquarium Tropical de la Porte Dorée **36**

Brasserie de l'île St-Louis **22**

Brasserie Lipp **29**

Cabinet des Médailles **14**

Café de Flore **27**

Café les Deux Magots **28**

Champs-Elysées **2**

Cité des Sciences et de l'industrie/
Parc de la Villette **11**

Cluny Museum **26**

Conciergerie **25**

Fondation Cartier pour l'Art
Contemporain **32**

Harry's New York Bar **13**

Jardin de l'Acclimatation Bois
de Boulogne **1**

Jardin des Plantes/Museums of
Natural History **35**

La Closerie de Lilas **31**

La Crypte Archéologique **24**

La Grande Arche de la Défense **1**

Le Musée du Quai Branly **6**

Les Catacombes (The Catacombes) **33**

Les Égouts **7**

Maison de Balzac **4**

Maison de Victor Hugo **18**

Maison Européenne de la Photographie **20**

Musée Carnavalet **17**

Musée Cognacq-Jay **16**

Musée d'Art et d'Histoire du Judaïsme **15**

Musée de la Curiosité et de la Magie **21**

Musée de la Sculpture en Plein Air **34**

Musée de l'Orangerie des Tuileries **9**

Musée Gustave Moreau **12**

Musée Maillol **10**

Musée Marmottan Monet **3**

Musée Zadkine **30**

Palais de la Découverte **8**

Parc Zoologique de Paris **37**

Place de la Bastille **19**

Shakespeare and Company Bookstore **23**

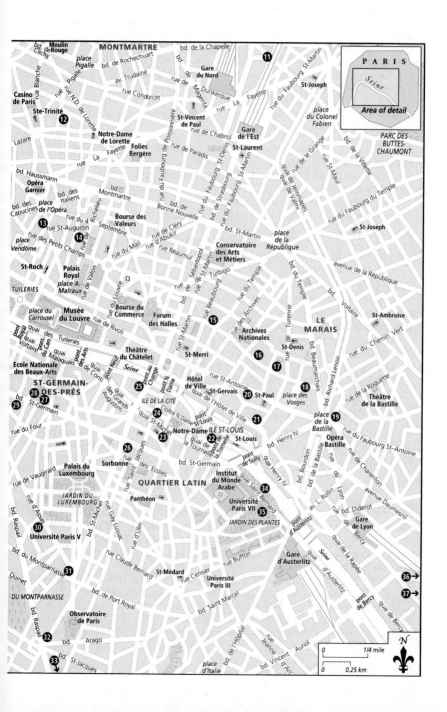

of water through experiments — the list of activities for children is simply endless here. The gigantic **Géode** sphere, on the complex's south side, is a wonder, with a huge hemispheric IMAX screen on which six or so films are shown daily. Another theater, the **Cinaxe,** is a simulator that projects movies on a screen while accelerating and moving the audience in different directions (children younger than three, pregnant women, and those with disabilities are not allowed). Kids can climb aboard an actual submarine in the **l'Argonaute** exhibit (on the complex's south side next to Géode) and participate in technology demonstrations at the **Science Actualités (Science Today).**

After the visit, let your kids run wild in the expansive, green **parc de la Villette,** where they can play in one of the ten gardens — especially neat are the **Garden of Childhood Terrors,** a blue spruce and silver birch "forest" where eerie music plays, and the **Dragon Garden** where kids and adults can cruise down the tongue of a dragon, an enormous slide. There are restaurants in the complex and food stands in the park. This could easily be an all-day visit. The Cité des Sciences et l'Industrie is bordered by the La Villette canal basin. Directly across is another smaller complex, the **Cité de la Musique,** accessible by a bridge. Its exhibits, museums, and concerts are also worth a stop.

See map p. 208. 30 av. Corentin-Cariou, 19e. ☎ 01-40-05-80-00. www.cite-sciences.fr. *Métro: Porte-de-la-Villette. Admission: Explora exhibitions 8€ ($13) adults, 6€ ($9.60) seniors and students under 25, free for children younger than 7. Admission to Cité des Enfants 6€ ($9.60); to Géode 11€ ($17) adults, 9€ ($14) 25 and under and per person in large families or groups; to Cinaxe Theater 4.80€ ($7.70) (children must be older than 3 to enter Cinaxe); the Argonaute submarine is 3€ ($4.80) for all. Check Web site for special combination tickets and seasonal deals. Open: Tues–Sat 10 a.m.–6 p.m., Sun 10 a.m.–7 p.m.*

Jardin de l'Acclimatation Bois de Boulogne

This is like an amusement park from another era, small enough to be manageable with such low-tech attractions as a petting zoo and a house of mirrors, a big chair swing, and mechanized boats. And after a half-day at this 10-hectare (25-acre) park, your children will sleep well! The park's layout is simple: Just follow its circular road in either direction, and it eventually gets you back to where you started. Attractions also include bumper cars, an archery range, a miniature golf course, individual mechanical horses that take "riders" on a little circuit, a farm, a quick little roller coaster, an American-style bowling alley, a playground, pony rides, and a "City of Merry-Go-Rounds," where young "citizens" can drive cars, firetrucks, and planes, try their hand at carnival games, and ride the carousel. Kids and their parents can also take in a puppet show. The park has an "enchanted river," a lake bordered by a bright blue-topped Korean pavilion, a restaurant, and snack and ice cream stands. The most fun way to get here is to take the Pétit Train from the métro's Porte Maillot exit (2.70€/$4.30 round-trip). Pay for rides by buying a carnet of 15 tickets for 32€ ($51).

See map p. 208. 16e. ☎ 01-40-67-90-82. Métro: Les Sablons, exit on rue d'Orléans, entrance is about 150m (500 ft.) away. Bus: 43, 73, 82, or 174. Or take the open-air Pétit Train from the Bois de Boulogne's Porte Maillot exit; 2.70€ ($4.30) round-trip. Admission: 2.70€ ($4.30) adults and children ages 3 and older, free for children younger than 3. Open: May–Sept daily 10 a.m.–7 p.m., Oct–Apr daily 10 a.m.–6 p.m.

Jardin des Plantes/Museums of Natural History

Children have visited this wonderful place for centuries to gape at bugs, bones, minerals, meteorites, dinosaurs, fossils, and endangered species in the galleries of the Jardin's Musée National d'Histoire Naturelle on the site of the former royal medicine garden. Here, the cavernous Grand Gallery of Evolution traces life and humankind's relationship to nature. A giant squid, Wheke, (19.7 ft. long and donated by the National Institute of Water & Atmospheric Research Limited), was exhibited here in March 2008. The endangered and extinct-species room displays (stuffed versions of) Gabonese monkeys, Sumatran tigers, lemurs of Madagascar, and a mock-up of the dodo bird. English explanations of some exhibits are available. Also part of the natural history museum in separate buildings are the Mineralogy and Geology Gallery (1,800 minerals, meteorites, and precious stones), the Entomological Gallery (1,500 insect specimens for bug-loving kids), and the Paleontology and Anatomy Gallery (the relationship between humans and animals shown with lots of skeletons). Walk outside amid 2,000 mountain plants from the Alps and the Himalayas in the Alpine garden, see the cacti in the Mexican garden, the greenhouse with tropical plants and rows of trees, beds of herbs and flowers, a 17th-century maze, and a carousel. Save for last the medium-sized *ménagerie* (zoo), one of the oldest in the world (it opened in 1794 with animals from the zoo at Versailles), containing live bears, buffalo, big cats, apes, antelope, reptiles (including an alligator found in a room at the Hôtel de Paris), tortoises, small Przewalski horses (which no longer exist in the wild), and birds. Don't overlook the super cool Vivarium — the spiders and insects are remarkable, especially the bugs that look like living tree branches! — or the Microzoo, where kids use microscopes to get a look at the life of the tiniest animals. A small restaurant on the zoo's premises offers pick-me-ups for the tired and cranky. Allow at least two hours.

See map p. 208. 57 rue Cuvier, 5e. ☎ 01-40-79-30-00. Métro: Gare d'Austerlitz (exit from the rue Buffon side; you're right next to the Gallery of Anatomy and Paleontology) or Jussieu (walk up rue Geoffroy St-Hilaire to the Grande Galerie de l'Evolution). Admission: Grande Galerie 8€ ($13) adults, 6€ ($9.60) students, seniors, and children 5 and under; other galleries 6€ ($9.60) adults, 4€ ($6.40) students, seniors, and children; ménagerie (zoo) 7€ ($11) adults, 5€ ($8) students, seniors, and children. Admission to gardens is free. Open: Park dawn–dusk; Grand Gallery weekdays 10 a.m.–6 p.m., Sat until 8 p.m.; other galleries weekdays 10 a.m.–5 p.m., 6 p.m. on weekends; Ménagerie mid-Mar to Sept 30 10 a.m.–6:30 p.m., Oct 1 to mid-Mar 10 a.m.–5:30 p.m.

La Grande Arche de la Défense

The Grand Arche de la Défense is the centerpiece of a very futuristic Paris suburb rife with glass and chrome skyscrapers lending their height to surreal sculptures. Built in 1989 to commemorate France's bicentennial, the arch completes a continuous line of perspective running from the Arc de Triomphe du Carrousel in the courtyard of the Louvre, down the Champs-Elysées, and through the Arc de Triomphe to the suburb of La Défense. As well, there's a full overview of the Bois de Bologne. The netting you see here is for catching any pieces of the facade that may fall down — several chunks have already. This is a popular destination with about 500,000 visitors a year, and kids will love the cool outdoor elevator to the top. There is a restaurant on the premises, but I suggest bringing snacks to stave off any hunger pangs and enjoying a better meal back in Paris. Allow about two hours for the round-trip journey from central Paris, including the climb to the top.

See map p. 208. 1 parvis de la Défense, 92040 Paris-La Défense. ☎ *01-49-07-27-27. Métro and RER: Grande Arche de la Défense. Admission: 9€ ($12) adults, 7.50€ ($12) students and seniors, free for children younger than 6. Open: Daily Apr–Sept 10 a.m.–8 p.m., Oct–Mar 10 a.m.–7 p.m.*

Musée de la Curiosité et de la Magie

It's a bit dusty at this easy-to-miss museum in an old building next to the Village St-Paul, but kids won't care. Bona fide magicians escort you through vaulted rooms containing a collection of trick mirrors, animated paintings, talking genies, and the history of illusion in general. Who amongst you is brave enough to risk sticking a hand in the mouth of a lion to see if it's really an illusion? While they won't disclose any secrets, you and your kids will have your senses tickled through many interactive displays. Live magic shows performed throughout the afternoon are also highly entertaining. The museum shop sells all the tools your kids need to cast (benevolent) spells back home.

11 rue St-Paul, 4e. ☎ *01-42-72-13-26. Métro: St-Paul. Admission: 9€ ($12) adults, 7€ ($11) children younger than 13. Open: Wed and Sat–Sun 2–7 p.m. and daily during national school breaks in winter, over Easter, Christmas, and Toussaint/All Saints Day (Nov).*

Palais de la Découverte

This museum is a full funhouse of science brought to life for kids. Here, you can explore a planetarium, a room devoted to the earth's geology from its beginnings to the future, a mathematics atelier that promises a fun experience, and lots of live experiments on weekends. Your hair will stand on end in the electrostatics room; kids can light up displays, test their muscle reactions on special machines, see experiments about electromagnetism in an annex off the Electricity Room, and learn about DNA in the Life Sciences wing. A very popular exposition in 2008 simulated volcanoes, earthquakes, and tsunamis. Count on spending at least two hours here.

See map p. 208. Grand Palais Av. Franklin-D-Roosevelt, 8e. ☎ 01-56-43-20-21.
`www.palais-decouverte.fr.` *Métro: Franklin-D-Roosevelt. Admission: 7€ ($11)*
adults, 4.50€ ($7.20) students and children 5–17. Planetarium supplement 3.50€
($5.60). Some workshops may cost an additional 1.50€ ($2.15) per person. Open:
Tues–Sat 9:30 a.m.–6 p.m., Sun 10 a.m.–7 p.m. Closed major holidays.

Especially for teens

The kid-friendly sights in the previous section are appropriate for
teenagers, as well. But here are a few more suggestions for kids who are
a bit older.

Aquaboulevard

If your teens are bored in Paris (and you're not visiting during July and Aug
when the banks of the Seine become a beach) go to Aquaboulevard, which
claims to be the biggest water park in Europe. Its seven water slides, wave
pool, against-the-current river, indoor and outdoor pools, spas and Jacuzzis,
whirlpool, geysers, water cannons, walls of water, waterbed with bubbles,
and waterfall make it a fun substitute, and it's safer than swimming in the
Seine. A McDonald's, an Oh! Poivrier!, a pizza place, a Hippopotamus, and a
first-run movie theater are located on the premises as well.

See map p. 208. 4 rue Louis-Armand, 15e. ☎ 01-40-60-10-00. Métro: Balard (head
down av. de la Porte de Sèvres; just after you walk under the overpass, you will see
Aquaboulevard straight ahead). Admission: 25€ ($40) ages 12 and older, 10€ ($16)
children 3–11, who must be accompanied by an adult. Open year -round: Mon–Thurs
9 a.m.–11 p.m., Fri 8 a.m.–midnight, Sat 9 a.m.–midnight, Sun 8 a.m.–11 p.m. Children
under 3 are not admitted.

Champs-Elysées

Teens can shop to their hearts' content on Paris's most famous street in
such clothing stores as O'Neill, Quiksilver, Zara, Naf Naf, and Kookaï, and
music stores Virgin and Fnac. They can catch movies in French or English
(look for "v.o.," for *version originale,* on the marquee or in newspaper listings for U.S. releases that aren't dubbed into French) in one of the many
movie theaters and eat familiar fast food at McDonald's or KFC. Many of
the stores on this street are open Sunday, and plenty of teens — both residents and tourists — hang out here.

See map p. 208. Métro: Concorde, Champs-Elysées, Clémenceau, Franklin-D-
Roosevelt, George V, Charles-de-Gaulle-Étoile. Many bus lines cross the Champs,
but only the 73 travels its entire length.

Les Catacombes (The Catacombs)

This is the coolest, creepiest, most macabre attraction in Paris. *"Arrête,*
c'est ici l'Empire de la Mort" ("Stop, here is the Empire of Death") reads the
inscription over the door of the Catacombs, and if they're open when you

visit (Les Catacombes seem to undergo repairs at the most inopportune times), you are in for a spooky visit like no other. This attraction is truly not for the faint-hearted, and thus perfect for hardy kids older than ten, because the tunnels are dark, damp, and frankly, a bit scary. A former quarry, Les Catacombes began housing bones in 1785 from the Cimetière des Innocents and an assortment of other overstocked Parisian cemeteries. Now Les Catacombes are the final resting place for about six million skulls and skeletons stacked in thousands of yards of tunnels.

You will need a flashlight (lampe de poche, lahmp duh puhsh) to navigate the tunnels. Your best bet is to bring one from home, but if you haven't, you can buy one in one of the stores on boulevard Raspail or the pedestrian rue Daguerre off avenue Général LeClerc. Before you buy, however, first check to see if the Catacombs are closed for repairs.

Those prone to claustrophobia should think twice about entering. The deep, dark tunnels close in rapidly and tightly. A flashlight will help navigate the poorly lit corridors and allow you to see the inscriptions. Wear non-slip shoes (such as hiking boots) to avoid a misstep on the rocky, often damp passageways and a hood to protect yourself from the water dripping overhead. Les Catacombes earned the nickname *place d'Enfer* ("Hell Square"), which later became *place Denfert-Rochereau,* and you can take Métro line 4 or 6, or RER B to the stop of the same name.

See map p. 208. 1 place Denfert-Rochereau, 14e. ☎ *01-43-22-47-63. Métro: Denfert-Rochereau. The entrance is an unassuming small door where a plate reads* ENTRÉE DES CATACOMBES. *Admission: 7€ ($11) adults, 3.50€ ($5.60) ages 14–26 and seniors, free for children younger than 14. Open: Tues–Sun 10 a.m.–5 p.m. (last entry at 4 p.m.).*

Les Égouts

One of Paris's most popular tours is that of its sewers — you sometimes have to wait as long as a half-hour in line. The tour starts with a short film about the history of sewers: Though the tunnels here were laid out in the 1850s during the reign of Napoléon III, at the same time that Haussmann was designing the grands boulevards, Paris's sewers date all the way back to Roman times. The film is followed by a visit to a small museum, and finally the short trip through the maze. Paris's sewers are laid out like an underground city, with streets clearly labeled and each branch pipe bearing the name of the building to which it's connected. Don't worry; you won't trudge through anything *dégoutant* (disgusting), but the visit may leave your clothes smelling a bit ripe. Make this the last of the day's attractions, and wear something you don't plan to wear again until after the next wash day. The ceiling occasionally drips water, but the tour guides insist that it is only condensation, and thus, clean. Guided tours are free, and most are in French, but English and also Spanish are available in summer. Toward the end, a long montage of the evolution of the city's drainage system also gives a beautiful timeline of the entire city's development as a whole, from the pre-Roman period until present day. Plan on spending an hour and a half to two hours.

See map p. 208. 7e. ☎ 01-53-68-27-81. Métro: Alma-Marceau, then walk across the bridge to the Left Bank. RER: Pont de l'Alma. The entrance is a stairway on the Seine side of the Quai d'Orsay, facing no. 93; look for a free-standing ticket booth. Admission: 3.80€ ($6.10) adults, 3.05€ ($4.90) for ages 5–16, free for children younger than 5. Open: May–Sept Sat–Wed 11 a.m.–5 p.m., Oct–May 11 a.m.–4 p.m. Closed two weeks in Jan.

Especially for history buffs

The city is filled with wonderful museums to satisfy even the pickiest buff's thirst for knowledge. Blue plaques on buildings tell you the names of famous people and the dates that they lived there. Brown-and-orange signs in French give you an overview of an area's particular story. (For those who have learned some French for the voyage, don't despair if you don't recognize some of the verb endings in these signs! Any historical writing makes use of a nonspoken literary past tense, the *passé simple*. It is used to make people think of the described events as truly historical, although personally it seems a bit pretentious!). This section gives a rundown on places worth a visit.

Cabinet des Médailles

People who stumble by mistake into this free museum (once France's original national library, still referred to as the Bibliothèque Nationale de France) love this place, and if you're a treasure hunter — or pirate — this is the place for you. Displayed here are archaeological objects, cameos, bronzes, medals, and money originally amassed by French kings. Among the more exceptional finds are the Treasure of Berthouville, a collection of Gallo-Roman money; the Cameo of Sainte-Chapelle, a huge multicolored cameo dating from the first century; and the Treasure of Childéric, one of the oldest remnants of the French monarchy. Take a peek into the Salle Labrouste, a lovely reading room built in 1868, which now echoes sadly without its book collection (ten million books were removed in 1998 to the Bibliothèque Nationale de France in the 13e). The garden, a virtual mini-Versailles, also merits a stop. Security is tight here. Plan to spend at least an hour.

See map p. 208. Bibliothèque Nationale de France, 58 rue de Richelieu, 2e (between rue des Filles St-Thomas and rue Colbert). ☎ 01-53-79-83-30. Métro: Palais-Royal-Musée du Louvre or Bourse. Bus: 20, 29, 39, 48, 67, 74, 85, 95. Admission: Free. Open: Mon–Fri 1–5:45 p.m., Sat 1–4:45 p.m., Sun noon–6 p.m.

Cluny Museum

This is one of the jewels of Paris museums, and a tranquil place to visit in the heart of the Latin Quarter. It's home to the famous tapestry series *The Lady and the Unicorn*. Officially called the Musée National du Moyen Age/Thermes de Cluny, this is no dull Dark Ages museum. It houses ancient Roman hot and cold baths, the original statues that furious revolutionaries tore from Notre-Dame in 1790 (thinking they represented royalty), one of the most beautiful tapestry series in the world, and a peaceful garden that makes reference to it. You also find remnants of clothing that royalty wore in the Middle Ages, coins, leatherwork, and gothic furniture, as well as church art — jeweled crosses, statues, sculptures, clothing, tapestries, and paintings of saints.

In the 19th century, the Hôtel de Cluny belonged to a collector of medieval art; upon his death in the 1840s, the government acquired the house and its contents. You enter through a medieval cobblestone courtyard, the *Cour d'Honneur* (Courtyard of Honor) — be sure to take in the turreted building and its gargoyles; this is one of the only medieval residences left in Paris. After paying for admission in the tiny lobby, turn left past the gift shop (save it until last) and try to take it all in. The fascinating Roman baths and the Notre-Dame statues are one floor down; one floor up is *The Lady and the Unicorn*. The tapestries hang in a dimly lit room by themselves. You can sit in one of the cushioned seats and try to figure out the meaning of the sixth tapestry. (The first five are an allegory representing the five senses; the meaning of the sixth tapestry remains a mystery.) In one of the medieval-period chambers being renovated, one can find a detailed miniature model of the Cluny hotel, which anyone can touch — it was placed there to give blind visitors the opportunity to feel the shapes and construction used in the medieval architecture. The gift shop is a wonderful place for souvenirs, and the renovated gardens are an oasis of calm off one of the Latin Quarter's busiest streets. Every plant (except two) in *The Lady and the Unicorn* tapestries was extensively researched and tracked down to be planted here.

See map p. 208. 6 place Paul-Painlevé, 5e (between rue du Sommerard and rue des Écoles). ☎ *01-53-73-78-00. Métro: Cluny-Sorbonne. Admission: 7.50€ ($12) adults, 5.50€ ($8.80) ages 18–26 and seniors, free for children younger than 18 and for all first Sun of month. Open: Wed–Mon 9:15 a.m.–5:45 p.m. Closed Christmas, New Year's Day, and May 1.*

Conciergerie

This was once one of the most elegant palaces in Europe, commissioned by Phillippe le Bel in the 14th century. But the kings moved to the Louvre and the building was left to be administrative offices of the crown. It was turned into a prison in the 15th century, and it is probably most famous for its days during the terror years of the French Revolution, when 4,164 "enemies of the people," including Marie Antoinette and her husband, Louis VXI, resided here before meeting their fate. Visitors pass through the Tour d'Argent (the Silver Tower), where the crown jewels were once stored, and the Tour César to the Salle des Gardes (Guard Room) entrance. Probably the most popular exhibit is Marie Antoinette's 1-sq.-m (11-sq.-ft.) cell. More than 4,000 of those imprisoned here headed for the guillotine on the place de la Révolution (now the place de la Concorde), including revolutionary ringleaders Danton and Robespierre, assassin Charlotte Corday, and the poet André Chenier. The far western tower, the Tour Bonbec, came to be known facetiously as the Tower of Babel because of the frequent screams from the many prisoners tortured there. Marie Antoinette's cell is now a chapel, and the other cells have been transformed with exhibits and mementos designed to convey a sense of prison life in a brutal era. Of welcome relief after the prison walls is the Women's Courtyard, with a small central garden and a fountain that was originally a bathhouse. Plan on spending two hours both here and in Sainte-Chapelle, the high-Gothic chapel and one of Paris's top sights (mentioned earlier in this chapter) with 15 spectacular stained-glass windows that are simply awe-inspiring.

See map p. 208. Palais de Justice, Ile de la Cité, 1er. ☎ 01-53-73-78-50. Métro: Cité, Châtelet-Les Halles, or St-Michel. (Exit the Métro at Cité, which is between rue de la Cité and bd. du Palais; the Palais is directly across bd. du Palais.) RER: St-Michel. Admission: 6.50€ ($10) adults, 4.50€ ($7.20) ages 18–25, free for children under 18. Open: Mar–Oct daily 9:30 a.m.–6 p.m., Nov–Feb daily 9 a.m.–5 p.m. Closed Christmas, New Year's Day, and May 1.

La Crypte Archéologique

This may be one of the best reasons to stop construction on a parking lot — ever. In 1965, excavations for a new parking lot under the parvis (a portico in front of the church) of Notre-Dame revealed Gallo-Roman ramparts, third-century Gallo-Roman rooms heated by an underground furnace system called a *hypocaust,* and cellars of houses dating back to medieval times. The parking lot project was abandoned, and the excavations were turned into this neat archaeological museum. Over the centuries, builders erected new structures over the ruins of previous settlements, raising the island about 7m (23 ft.). To help you visualize the buildings that once stood here, scale models show how Paris grew from a small settlement to a Roman city, and photographs show the pre-Haussmann parvis. Allow about 45 minutes, longer if you're a history buff.

See map p. 208. Place du parvis Notre-Dame, 4e (about 60m/200 ft. directly in front of Notre-Dame, accessed by downward-leading stairs). ☎ 01-55-42-50-10. Métro: Cité. RER: St-Michel-Notre-Dame. Admission: 8€ ($13) adults, 6€ ($9.60) ages 26 and younger. Open: Thurs–Tues 10 a.m.–6 p.m.

Musée Carnavalet

Housed inside two beautiful Renaissance mansions, Paris history comes alive here through an incredible selection of paintings, reassembled rooms in all their period glory, and other items from daily life long ago. The blue-and-yellow rooms of Louis XV and Louis XVI are here in all their ornately furnished glory. The chess pieces that Louis XVI played with while awaiting his beheading are here, as are Napoléon's cradle, Marie Antoinette's personal items, and a replica of Marcel Proust's cork-lined bedroom. The *Cabinet Doré de l'hotel La Rivière* room has a spectacular gilded, ceiling painting of Apollo and Aurora by Charles Le Brun; his other ceiling painting is of Psyche with the Muses. Many salons depict events related to the Revolution, and the paintings of what Paris used to look like are fascinating. Numerous models of the Bastille prison are represented, including one depicting the peasant revolt itself. There is a wing devoted to the archaeology of Paris's earliest settlements (some artifacts, such as the fishing boats used by settlers, date back to between 2200 and 4400 B.C.). Visitors can even touch some of the exhibits here. A beautiful garden with access only from the museum is a nice place to revive afterward. The courtyard houses bas-reliefs of the season by celebrated architect François Mansart (who enlarged the buildings) and next to it are zodiac signs carved in the 16th century by Jean Goujon. The statue in the center is Louis XIV, by Coysevox. You may want to buy an English-language guidebook in the museum's gift shop, because audio guides are in French.

See map p. 208. 23 rue de Sévigné, 3e. ☎ 01-44-59-58-58. Métro: St-Paul. (Turn left on rue de Sévigné.) Admission: Free for permanent collections; temporary exhibits vary in price. Open: Tues–Sun 10 a.m.–6 p.m.

Musée d'Art et d'Histoire du Judaïsme

The beautiful 17th-century mansion Hôtel de St-Aignan houses this enormous collection tracing the development of 2,000 years of Jewish culture in France and also in Europe, from life in the Middle Ages to the 20th century. In addition to beautifully crafted religious objects, including several copies of the Torah, with breastplates, crowns, and cloth coverings from different Jewish communities throughout the world, there are shofars, menorahs, ark curtains, and spectacular velvet cloaks reflecting both the Sephardic and Ashkenazi traditions throughout Europe and North Africa. The museum has medieval gravestones and 20th-century paintings and sculptures. The museum also presents very thoroughly the newly available documents relating to the Dreyfus affair, the notorious scandal that falsely accused a Jewish army captain of providing secret military information to the German government in 1894. The free audio tour is very informative. The exhibits end with a collection of works by Jewish artists, including paintings by Modigliani, Soutine, Zadkine, and Chagall. A fascinating 2008 exhibit, "Looking for Owners," traced the fate of art returned by Germany after World War II. Allow at least two hours. Security is tight here; you will have to pass through metal detectors.

See map p. 208. 71 rue du Temple, 3e (between rue Rambuteau and rue de Braque). ☎ 01-53-01-86-60. www.mahj.org. Métro: Rambuteau, Hôtel de Ville. Bus: 29, 38, 47, 75. Admission: 6.80€ ($11) adults, 4.50€ ($8.65) ages 18–26 and seniors, free for children younger than 18. Open: Mon–Fri 11 a.m.–6 p.m., Sun 10 a.m.–6 p.m.

Place de la Bastille

Ignore the traffic and try to imagine the place de la Bastille just more than 200 years ago, when it contained eight towers rising 30m (100 ft.). It was here, on July 14, 1789 (now commemorated in France as Bastille Day), that a mob attacked the old prison, launching the French Revolution. Although the Bastille had long since fallen into disuse, it symbolized the arbitrary power of a king who could imprison anyone for any reason, while the citizenry paid high taxes for his follies, his biggest being the maintenance of the court at Versailles. Prisoners of means could buy a spacious cell and even host dinner parties, but the poor disappeared within the prison's recesses and sometimes drowned when the Seine overflowed its banks. The attack on the prison was therefore a direct assault on royal power. The Bastille was razed in 1792. In its place stands the Colonne de Juillet, a

51m (171-ft.) bronze column built between 1830 and 1849 to commemorate Parisians killed in civil uprisings in 1830 and 1848.

11e. Métro: Bastille. (The Colonne de Juillet is across from the métro.)

Especially for art lovers

From galleries in the Marais, Bastille, St-Germain-des-Prés, and near the Champs-Elysées, through Egyptian, Assyrian, and Greco-Roman art at the Louvre, realism, Impressionism, and Art Nouveau at the Musée d'Orsay, to the modern international masters at the Centre Pompidou, it is an understatement to say that Paris offers a vast wealth of art.

But art in Paris is not merely French art. Though French movements began or developed here, generations of artists from all parts of the world have thrived in Paris, and the city's museums and galleries hold enough art for several lifetimes of daily viewing. If you're an art lover and happen to be in town in October, Paris presents the enormous *Foire Internationale d'Art Contemporain* (www.fiac.com), one of the largest contemporary art fairs in the world with stands from more than 150 galleries, half of them foreign. The following museums are often less crowded than their larger and more famous counterparts, but each has plenty of wonders in store.

Fondation Cartier pour l'Art Contemporain

This trendy museum has displayed contemporary art since its opening in 1984. Supported by Cartier, the luxury jeweler and watchmaker, even the building where the art is displayed itself is a gorgeous and flashy work. Designed by architect Jean Nouvel it is too striking to miss: A glass-and-metal screen stands between the street and the glass-and-metal building, creating an optical illusion that makes the courtyard greenery appear as if it is growing indoors. Most of the first-rate contemporary art exhibits that the Cartier jewelry empire hosts are in the basement. Exhibitions at the time of writing included moving image and sound works of video-artist and poet Gary Hill; also the moving-image works of Japanese artist Tabaimo. The permanent collection is built around large groups of works by living artists and includes paintings by artists such as Vija Celmins, Sam Francis, and Matthew Barney, as well as photography by Nan Goldin, William Eggleston, Raymond Depardon, and others; sculpture; huge installations; and video works. Reservations are necessary for the *très* cool performance art and music of Les Soirees Nomades (Nomadic Evenings) from July to October on some Sundays, Wednesdays, and every Thursday night, from 5 to 9 p.m. There are also workshops for children; in 2008, kids imagined themselves as giants and sculpted artwork accordingly. Check the Web site for details about these events. Plan to spend at least an hour and a half here.

See map p. 208. 261 bd. Raspail, 14e (200m/650 ft. from the Raspail Métro stop, past Passage d'Enfer and rue Boissonade). ☎ *01-42-18-56-50, or 01-42-18-56-72 for Nomadic Evenings reservations.* www.fondation.cartier.fr. *Métro: Raspail. Admission to exhibits and Nomadic Nights: 6.50€ ($10) adults, 4.50€ ($7.20) students younger than 25, free for children younger than 10. Open: Tues–Sun 11 a.m.–8 p.m., until 10 p.m. Tues.*

Maison Européenne de la Photographie

Two renovated 18th-century town houses contain this sleek museum which has the goal of making the three fundamental mediums of photography — exhibition prints, the printed page, and film — accessible to all. It succeeds on all fronts. A first-floor gallery exhibits original period prints like Irving Penn's photo of Colette, the vaulted 18th-century basement displays cutting-edge photography, film projections, and installations. There is a space for young photographers to show their work, and the Roméo Martinez library displays some 12,000 titles spanning the last 50 years of photography. Martinez was editor-in-chief of *Camera* magazine for 20 years. There are permanent collections of Polaroid art and an excellent video library that allows you to look up thousands of photographs. Highlights of 2008 included an Annie Leibovitz exhibition, celebrating 15 years of her work. Allow at least an hour and a half including a pick-me-up in the cozy vaulted 18th-century basement cafe. (*Note:* This cafe closes at 5 p.m. on Wednesdays; all other opening days it is open until 7 p.m.)

See map p. 208. 5-7 rue de Fourcy, 4e. ☎ *01-44-78-75-00.* www.mep-fr.org. *Métro: St-Paul or Pont-Marie. Bus: 67, 69, 96, 76. Admission: 6€ ($9.60) adults, 3€ ($4.80) ages 8–26 and older than 60, free for children younger than 8, free for all Wed 5–8 p.m. Free guided tours are available on certain dates, which can be verified by calling or visiting the Web site; reservations necessary. Open: Wed–Sun 11 a.m.–8 p.m.*

Musée Cognacq-Jay

La Samaritaine department store founder Ernest Cognacq and his wife Marie-Louise Jay amassed at the turn of the 20th century this collection of 18th-century rococo art that features works by François Boucher, Jean-Honoré Fragonard, Peter Paul Rubens, Louis-Michel van Loo, Jean-Antoine Watteau, Elisabeth Vigée-LeBrun, and Giambattista Tiepolo displayed in elegant Louis XV and Louis XVI paneled rooms. There is a collection of everyday objects, such as dance cards, and snuff and candy boxes, shelves of porcelain and porcelain figures, rich wood cabinets, and furniture. The building housing it all is the beautifully preserved Hôtel Donon, built in the 16th century. You can walk through a little manicured garden, open May to September, to enjoy sunny days. Temporary exhibits are presented two to three times a year. In 2006 one of the exhibitions included the history of the big department stores *(grands magasins),* and the artwork associated with them, and how their invention elevated the couple for whom the museum is named.

See map p. 208. 8 rue Elzévir, 3e (between rue des Francs Bourgeois and rue Barbette). ☎ *01-40-27-07-21. Métro: St-Paul. Admission: Permanent collections are free. Open: Tues–Sun 10 a.m.–6 p.m.*

Musée de la Sculpture en Plein Air

You may wander through this open air sculpture garden on the Left Bank of the Seine between the Institut du Monde Arabe and the Jardin des Plantes and not realize that this is an actual museum. Works are from 29 artists, including César, Ossip Zadkine, and Stagio Stahly.

Quai St-Bernard, 5e (on the quay of the Seine between the Institut du Monde Arabe and the Jardin des Plantes). Métro: Sully-Morland or Gare d'Austerlitz. Admission: Free. If you go on a summer Thurs evening around 8 p.m., you can see outdoor dancing nearby.

Musée de l'Orangerie des Tuileries

Since spring, 2006, visitors have been delighting in the at-last renovated *Musée de l'Orangerie* which had been undergoing repairs for close to a decade. The highlight of the Orangerie is most definitely its two oval rooms wrapped nearly 360 degrees with Monet's *Nymphéas,* the water lily series he painted especially for the Orangerie, and these rooms were the primary focus of the renovations. The immense and awe-inspiring murals simply pop from their spotless cream-white walls, lit brightly enough to accentuate all of the beautifully emotional colors. But don't make the water lily paintings your sole reason to visit. Since 1984, the museum has also housed the remarkable John Walter and Paul Guillaume art collection, comprising works by Cézanne, Renoir, Rousseau, Matisse, Modigliani, Dérain, Picasso, and Soutine, among other artists.

See map p. 208. Jardin des Tuileries, 1er. ☎ 01-44-77-80-07. Métro: Concorde. Admission: 7.50€ ($12) for adults, 5.50€ ($8.80) for students under 26 years of age, free for all first Sun of month. Open: Wed–Mon 12:30–7 p.m., until 9 p.m. on Fri. Closed on May 1 and Christmas.

Musée du Quai Branly

This stunning museum, just a block from the Eiffel Tower, was designed by premiere French architect Jean Nouvel, who is also responsible for the Fondation Cartier and the Institut du Monde Arabe, and like these two centers, there is plenty of glass to let in light. Housed in four spectacular buildings (one has a wall of living plants) with a garden off from the quai Branly, are the art, sculpture, and cultural materials of a vast range of non-Western civilizations, separated into different sections that represent the traditional cultures of Africa, East and Southeast Asia, Oceania, Australia, the Americas, and New Zealand. The pieces here come from the now defunct Musée des Arts Africains et Océaniens, from the Louvre and the Musée de l'Homme. Temporary exhibits are shown off in boxes all along the 180m (600-ft.) exhibition hall. Incredible masterpieces are on display made by some very advanced traditional civilizations: Some of the most impressive exhibits present tribal masks of different cultures, some of which are so lifelike and emotional in their creation that you can feel the fear and elation involved in their use, which is well documented in descriptions in French and English. Allow two hours for a full visit; also take a stroll in their carefully manicured garden, or have a *café* in their small cafeteria across from the main building. There are numerous entrances to the museum grounds from the area near the Eiffel tower; the main entrance is on quai Branly. **Note:** You cannot buy your tickets at the museum. You also must reserve the time of your visit at the same time you buy tickets. Order online at www.ticketnet.com (the site is available in English; look for EN at the top of the home page) or at a Fnac store (there is one at 74 av. du Champs-Elysées open Mon–Sat 10 a.m.–midnight, Sun 11 a.m.–midnight).

See map p. 208. 27 or 37 quai Branly and 206 or 218 rue de l'Université, 7e. ☎ 01-56-61-70-00. Métro: Alma-Marceau, cross le pont d'Alma, turn right, and follow along the Seine until you come across a large glass-paneled wall, which among other things, will say "Musée du Quai Branly." RER: Pont d'Alma. Admission: 15€ ($24) adults, 10€ ($16) for students 18–26 and seniors, free for children under 18. Open: Tues, Wed, and Sun 11 a.m.–7 p.m., Thurs, Fri, and Sat until 9 p.m.

Musée Gustave Moreau

Some of the paintings here are downright bizarre, which makes a visit here all the more interesting. Gustave Moreau was a symbolist painter influenced by the English pre-Raphaelites who may have been better known as Henri Matisse's teacher. He painted mythological fantasies in a sensuous, romantic style with work that looks as if it is encrusted with jewels. The artist himself established and designed this duplex museum studio so that his symbolist work could be displayed the way he wanted long after his death. More than 6,000 of Moreau's works can be found here. Among them are *The Pretenders, The Life of Humanity, The Apparition, Orpheus by the Tomb of Eurydice,* and *Jupiter and Semele.* Moreau taught at the École des Beaux-Arts; his museum's first curator, Georges Rouault, was his favorite student, among other famous artists such as Henri Matisse. The artist's apartment is also preserved here. An hour and a half should be plenty.

See map p. 208. 14 rue de la Rochefoucault, 9e (between rue la Bruyère and rue St-Lazare). ☎ 01-48-74-38-50. Métro: Trinité d'Estienne d'Orves. Bus: 32, 43, 49, 68, or 74. Admission: 5€ ($7.70) adults; 3€ ($4.50) students, ages 18–25, seniors older than 60, and for adults on Sun; free for children younger than 18. Open: Wed–Mon 10 a.m.–12:45 p.m. and 2–5:15 p.m.

Musée Maillol

Curvaceous, bold, and graceful bronze statues of Aristide Maillol's favorite model, Dina Vierny, are on vibrant display as well as the works of Impressionist and Postimpressionist artists in this renovated 18th-century convent. Outside is the sculpted fountain of the four seasons by Edme Bouchardon. But it is the important modern art collection inside that rightly draws the most notice. The elegant upper floors of the museum display crayon and pastel sketches of Vierny, who Maillol discovered when she was only 15 years old. He believed her voluptuous figure was the personification of femininity and she served as his exclusive model for ten years. Maillol's personal collection includes the work of his friends, Matisse and Bonnard, as well as two sculptures by Rodin, works by Gauguin, Dégas, Rousseau, Odilon Redon, Maurice Denis, Kandinsky, and Renoir. Vierny, who collected art most of her life, has an important collection of modern primitives that include Douanier, Rousseau, and Camille Bombois, as well as drawings by Suzanne Valadon, Dégas, Picasso, and Foujita. The museum features splendid temporary exhibits; a recent exhibit was an ensemble of 59 photographs taken by Bert Stern in 1962 of the striking and fragile Marilyn Monroe.

See map p. 208. 61 rue de Grenelle, 7e. ☎ *01-42-22-59-58.* www.museemaillol. com. *Métro: Rue du Bac. Admission: 8€ ($9.60) adults, 6€ ($7.20) students 16–26, free for children younger than 16. Open: Wed–Mon 11 a.m.–6 p.m. (last ticket sold at 5:15 p.m.).*

Musée Marmottan Monet

It's a little off the beaten path — out in the 16th in an area of beautiful buildings between the Ranelagh garden and the Bois de Boulogne — but if you have the time and the weather's on your side, this exquisite museum devoted to the works of Claude Monet is worth the trip. It contains the world's largest collection of Monet's work, including his water lily paintings as well as his more abstract representations of the Japanese Bridge at Giverny. The painting that coined the term describing the painting style and artistic movement, *Impression: Sunrise,* is located here. Monet's personal collection can also be found here, with paintings and sculpture by his contemporaries Pissarro, Manet, Morisot, and Renoir.

The museum is in a 19th-century mansion that belonged to the art historian Paul Marmottan. He donated his house and collection of Empire furniture and Napoleonic art to the Académie des Beaux-Arts upon his death in 1932.

Donations have expanded the collection to include more Impressionist paintings and the stunning Wildenstein collection of late medieval French, Italian, English, and Flemish illuminated manuscripts. Allow at least an hour and a half for a visit.

See map p. 208. 2 rue Louis-Boilly, 16e. ☎ *01-42-24-07-02.* www.marmottan.com. *Métro: La-Muette. Admission: 9€ ($9.60) adults, 5.50€ ($5.40) ages 8–25, free for children younger than 8. Open: Daily 11 a.m.–6 p.m., until 9 p.m. Tues. Closed Christmas, New Year's Day, and May 1.*

Musée Zadkine

Head to this tranquil small museum before or after a trip to the Jardin du Luxembourg; it's located across the street from the park on the rue d'Assas. It's the perfect spot to view the works — about 300 sculptures and more than 350 drawings — of Belarussian sculptor Ossip Zadkine. The small statue garden is sheltered within walls of Virginia creeper, and Japanese cherry, maple, and birch trees lend shade to the garden's changing artwork. The garden and museum are free, the temporary exhibits don't cost much, and it's worth a visit if you like contemporary sculpture or you are familiar with the artist's work. Zadkine moved to Paris around 1909 and lived and worked in this house and studio from 1928 until his death in 1967. His art, books, tools, and furniture are all on display, as well as many of his works in brass, wood, and stone. His bronze, *Destroyed City* (1953), is considered a masterpiece; the model is exhibited here (the original is in Rotterdam). The museum is accessed through an alleyway.

See map p. 208. 100 bis rue d'Assas, 6e. ☎ *01-55-42-77-20. Métro: Notre-Dame-des-Champs or Vavin. Bus: 38, 82, 83, 91. Admission: Free for permanent exhibits; temporary exhibits 4€ ($6.40) adults, 3€ ($4.80) children and students ages 7–26 and seniors. Open: Tues–Sun 10 a.m.–6 p.m.*

Especially for the literary

Paris's literary landmarks aren't all connected to Ernest Hemingway, F. Scott Fitzgerald, and the "Lost Generation," though it sure can seem that way sometimes.

Brasserie de l'Ile St-Louis

If you're a fan of *From Here to Eternity* or *The Thin Red Line,* pay a visit to this brasserie (see also Chapter 10 for a review of the food), where novelist and regular customer James Jones kept his own *chope* (mug) at the bar. Not only is the location excellent — the building is situated directly off the footbridge from Ile de la Cité to Ile St-Louis with a gorgeous view of the eastern tip of Ile de la Cité (including the back of Notre-Dame and the Panthéon in the distance) — but this eatery is one of the last remaining independent brasseries in Paris. Jones lived with his family around the corner on Ile de la Cité, and the film about their lives, *A Soldier's Daughter Never Cries,* was filmed in the neighborhood.

See map p. 208. 55 quai de Bourbon. ☎ *01-43-54-02-59. Métro: Pont Marie. Main courses: 15€–30€ ($29–$48) lunch and dinner. V. Open: Thurs–Tues noon–12 a.m.*

Brasserie Lipp and Café les Deux Magots

You can't talk about literary Paris without mentioning Ernest Hemingway, and two of his favorite hangouts are just across the street from each other on boulevard St-Germain-des-Prés. Brasserie Lipp is where Hemingway lovingly recalls eating potato salad in *A Moveable Feast,* and the Café les Deux Magots is where Jake Barnes meets Lady Brett in *The Sun Also Rises.* Tourism has driven up prices, so just go for a glass of wine or a coffee (and remember that it's cheaper standing up at the bar than sitting down at a table). The people-watching will undoubtedly be good. Refrain, if you can, from snapping flash photos; the regulars can get mighty annoyed!

See map p. 208. Brasserie Lipp: 151 bd. St-Germain, 6e. ☎ *01-45-48-53-91. Open: Daily 9 a.m.–1 a.m. Café les Deux Magots: 170 bd. St-Germain, 6e.* ☎ *01-45-48-55-25. Open: Daily 7:30 a.m.–1:30 a.m. Both are less than 46m (151 ft.) from the St-Germain-des-Prés Métro stop.*

Café de Flore

Next door to Les Deux Magots is this other infamous St-Germain-des-Prés cafe. Sartre is said to have written *Les Chemins de la Liberté (The Roads to Freedom)* at his table here, and he and Simone de Beauvoir saw people by appointment here. Other regulars included André Malraux and Guillaume Apollinaire. Since 1994, the cafe has each autumn awarded the approximately $8,000 Prix de Flore to a young writer of promising talent.

See map p. 208. 172 bd. St-Germain, 6e. ☎ 01-45-48-55-26. Métro: St-Germain-des-Prés.

Harry's New York Bar

This place is still going strong all these years after — guess who? — Ernest Hemingway and F. Scott Fitzgerald went on a few famous benders. It has a cabaret in the cellar, and the Bloody Mary was said to have been invented here, but Harry's high prices may dissuade you. If cost is no concern kick back and have what might just be the best martini in Paris.

See map p. 208. 5 rue Danou, 2e. ☎ 01-42-61-71-14. Métro: Opéra; head down the rue de la Paix and take the first left. Open: Daily 10:30 a.m.–4 a.m.

La Closerie de Lilas

Lilac bushes still bloom here (the name means the "courtyard of lilacs"), and the place is just as crowded as it was in the 1930s, although its high, high prices are geared toward a tourist crowd. Notable luminaries were author John Dos Passos, Picasso, and Leon Trotsky. The Cloiserie's true claim to fame, however, is that Hemingway completed *The Sun Also Rises* on the terrace here in just six weeks. Much of the novel also takes place here.

See map p. 208. 171 bd. du Montparnasse, 6e. ☎ 01-40-51-34-50. Métro: Vavin. RER: Line B to Port-Royal. Exit onto bd. du Port-Royal and walk west. Cross av. de l'Observatoire. Bd. du Port-Royal turns into bd. du Montparnasse. The restaurant is on the north corner of av. de l'Observatoire and bd. du Montparnasse. Open: Daily noon–1 a.m.

Maison de Balzac

Novelist Honoré de Balzac wrote some of his most famous novels while living in this rustic cabin in the very posh residential Passy neighborhood from 1840 to 1847. He lived under a false name (M. de Breugnol) to avoid creditors, and allowed entrance only to those who knew the password. He wrote some of his *La Comédie Humaine (The Human Comedy)* here. See his preserved study with portraits, leather-bound books, letters, and manuscripts on display. You can also see his jewel-encrusted cane (why spend on bills when you can have jewels?) and the Limoges coffeepot that bears his initials in mulberry pink. Expect to spend about 45 minutes here.

See map p. 208. 47 rue Raynouard, 16e. ☎ 01-55-74-41-80. Métro: Line 6 to Passy; walk 1 block away from the river and turn left into rue Raynouard. Bus: 32, 50, 70, 72. Admission: Permanent collections free; temporary exhibits 4€ ($6.40) adults, 3€ ($4.80) seniors, 2€ ($3.20) students to age 26, free for children 13 and younger. Open: Tues–Sun 10 a.m.–6 p.m. Closed holidays.

Maison de Victor Hugo

Here's your chance to explore one of those gorgeous place des Vosges apartments! Of course, if you or your kids have read *The Hunchback of Notre-Dame* or *Les Miserables,* you may want to visit here anyway. Victor Hugo lived on the second floor of this town house (built in 1610) from 1832 to 1848. The museum was designed to reflect the way Hugo structured his life: Before Exile, During Exile, and After Exile. (He fled the country after an unsuccessful revolt against President Louis Napoléon [who later became Napoléon III], and returned to Paris 16 years later after the collapse of the Second Empire.) You can see some of his furniture, samples of his handwriting, his inkwell, first editions of his works, and a painting of his 1885 funeral procession at the Arc de Triomphe. Portraits of his family adorn the walls, and the fantastic Chinese salon from Hugo's house on Guernsey where he was exiled is reassembled here. The highlight is more than 450 of Hugo's drawings, illustrating scenes from his own works. Plan to spend an hour here.

See map p. 208. 6 place des Vosges, 4e (between rue des Tournelles and rue de Turenne, nearer to rue de Turenne). ☎ *01-42-72-10-16. Métro: St-Paul. Bus: 20, 29, 65, 69, 96. Admission: Free. Open: Tues–Sun 10 a.m.–6 p.m. (ticket window closes at 5:15 p.m.).* **Note:** *Though admission is free, you still must stand in line for a ticket from the cashier in the gift shop (enter on the right).*

Shakespeare and Company Bookstore

The newest of the Shakespeares was opened by George Whitman in the mid-1960s and named in honor the original Shakespeare & Co (he also named his daughter, Sylvia Beach Whitman, after the original proprietor, and she now manages the place with her father). It serves as a haven for Americans and English speakers, playing the dual role of gathering place and bookstore. Poetry readings take place on Sunday nights, and Whitman will give lodging to a (debatably) lucky few writers or poets in exchange for work in the store. Note that this is *not* the original Shakespeare and Company. The original opened in 1919 at 6 rue Dupuytren (take the métro to Odéon, walk through the square there, and turn left) by Sylvia Beach. Two years later, Beach moved the shop to 12 rue de l'Odéon (the building is no longer there) and stayed until the United States entered into World War II (in German-occupied Paris, Beach was considered an enemy alien and was forced to abandon shop).

See map p. 208. 37 rue de la Bûcherie, 5e. ☎ *01-43-26-96-50. Métro or RER: St-Michel.*

Especially for nature lovers

Most parks are open until sunset, unless otherwise noted. Count on spending at least one hour (much of that relaxing in the beautiful surroundings).

Bois de Boulogne

This huge park on the west side of Paris was once a royal forest and hunting ground. Napoléon III donated it to the city and Baron Haussmann transformed it, using London's Hyde Park as his model. Today the Bois is a vast reserve of more than 880 hectares (2,200 acres) with jogging paths, bridle trails, bicycling (bike rental available Apr–Oct near the Les Sablons entrance to the park), and boating on its Lac Inférieur and Lac Supérieur (boat rental available at the northern edge of the Lac Inférieur). Also here are the **parc de la Bagatelle** (see the listing later in this section); the famous **Longchamp** and **Auteuil** racecourses; the **Stade Roland Garros,** where the French Open is held; the **Musée National de des Arts et Traditions Populaire** (documents French everyday life from the year 1000 to the present); and the beautiful **Pré Catalan,** a lovely park in which it is said the copper beech here has a span wider than any other tree in Paris. The Pré Catalan contains the **Jardin Shakespeare** in which you can find many of the plants and herbs mentioned in Shakespeare's plays and the Pré Catalan restaurant, one of Paris's prettiest and most expensive restaurants. The **Jardin de l'Acclimatation** (see "Especially for kids" earlier in this chapter) is one of Parisian children's favorite amusement parks. **Les Serres d'Auteuil,** at the southeastern edge of the Bois, are the municipal greenhouses and gardens that supply Paris with its flowers and plants. Open to the public, the greenhouses are especially nice to visit in winter; they provide a taste of the Caribbean with orchids, tropical plants, and palm trees. As the sun sets, prostitutes in parked cars and vans line the road on each side of the Porte Dauphine entrance, so the Bois is best enjoyed in daylight. This park is so big that you can spend an entire afternoon here.

See map p. 208. 16e. Métro: Porte Dauphine or Les Sablons.

Bois de Vincennes

Once a hunting ground for kings, this is the largest green space in Paris. Rent a boat at the two lakes here: **Lac Daumesnil,** on the west side of the park has two islands connected by a bridge; **Lac des Minimes** is located on the northwestern edge of the Bois. The Bois de Vincennes is home to the **parc Zoologique** (which will be closed until 2012 years for renovations); a **Buddhist center** right next to the bridge at Lac Daumesnil, complete with temple and Buddha effigy; and the **Château de Vincennes,** in which early monarchs Charles V and Henri III sought refuge from war and where Mata Hari was executed in 1917. The Bois de Vincennes houses the spectacular **parc Floral de Paris** (see the listing later in this section), the **Hippodrome de Vincennes** for harness racing, and the **Aquarium Tropical de la Porte Dorée** (see the "Especially for kids" section). This is also a big park where you can enjoy spending an entire afternoon.

12e. Métro: Porte Doree or Chateau de Vincennes.

The Center for Nature Discovery, Garden in Memory of Diana, Princess of Wales

Diana fans now bring their messages and bouquets here instead of to the flame at place de l'Alma (Métro: Alma-Marceau), near the entrance to the tunnel where the princess, her friend Dodi Fayed, and driver Henri Paul were killed in an automobile accident on August 31, 1997. In this small park that opened in 2002, children discover how to grow flowers, vegetables, and decorative plants and learn about nature. Plan on spending at least a half-hour here.

21 rue des Blancs-Manteaux, 3e. Métro: Rambuteau.

Parc de Belleville

If you visit the bustling neighborhood of Belleville, stop in this park for its beautiful views of western Paris. Topped by the Maison de l'Air, a museum with displays devoted to the air that we breathe, there are fountains, a children's play area, and an open-air theater with concerts during the summer. Rock formations and grottoes evoke the days when the hill was a strategic point for fighting enemies such as Attila the Hun. Access the park by taking the rue Piat off rue de Belleville and enter through an iron gate spelling out the words Villa Ottoz. A curved path leads you to tree-lined promenades (more than 500 trees are here), with the first of the magnificent Left Bank views peeping through the spaces between pretty houses. Beds of roses and other seasonal flowers line walks, and views of the city's Left Bank become more pronounced the higher up the terraced pathways you go.

20e. Métro: Pyrénées (walk down rue de Belleville and turn left onto rue Piat where you see arched iron gates leading into the park) or Courrones (cross bd. de Belleville and turn left onto rue Julien Lacroix to find another entrance).

Parc de la Bagatelle

Located in the Bois de Boulogne, the parc de la Bagatelle is known for its gardens, which reveal the art of gardening through the centuries. The rose garden was planted by Monet's friend, Jean-Claude-Nicolas Forestier, whose claim to fame was as designer of the Champs-de-Mars and other gardens. His 10,000 roses of 1,200 varieties, peak in June. You can enjoy bulbed plants (tulips, hyacinths, and so on) in March; peonies, clematis, and irises in May; water lilies in June; dahlias and autumn foliage in October; and winter-flowering trees, shrubs, and snowdrops during the cold months. A water lily pond pays homage to that certain famous painter of water lilies. Forestier was inspired by the Impressionists and their way of showing flowers by species and emphasizing the effects of mass planting. The Orangerie here is home to the Festival Chopin à Paris from mid-June to mid-July. The château, which you can view from the outside only, was built by the Comte d'Artois in 1775, after he made a bet with his sister-in-law, Marie Antoinette, that he could do it in less than 90 days. It took 66 days. Under Napoléon, it was used as a hunting lodge.

16e. Métro: Porte Maillot. Exit at av. Neuilly. Bus: 244 to the Bagatelle-Pré Catalan stop.

Parc de la Villette

This modern park is part of the grounds of the Cité des Sciences et de l'Industrie and has a series of themed gardens, including an exotic bamboo garden and one featuring steam and water jets. Scattered throughout the park are playgrounds and other attractions. (See "Especially for kids" earlier in this chapter.) In the summer, you can catch an outdoor movie or listen to a concert, and kids can play on a giant dragon slide. You can get to the parc de la Villette by métro, but a fun, alternative route worth trying is the guided canal trip to the park from Pont l'Arsenal or Musée d'Orsay with **Paris Canal** (☎ 01-42-40-96-97; Métro: Bastille) or with **Canauxrama** (☎ 01-42-39-15-00; Métro: Jaurés). See "Paris by Guided Tour" later in this chapter. *See map p. 208. 19e. Métro: Porte de la Villette.*

Parc des Buttes-Chaumont

This former gypsum quarry and centuries-old dump is one of four man-made parks Napoléon III commissioned to resemble the English gardens he grew to love during his exile in England. It features cliffs, a suspension bridge, waterfalls, a lake, and a cave topped by a temple. The waterfall cave is musty, but romantic — it is listed in *Où S'Embrasser à Paris (Where to Kiss in Paris)* as one of the top hidden make-out spots in the city (in the mornings you may even have it to yourselves). This is worth a stop if you're in the area.

19e. Métro: Buttes-Chaumont. (The station is located within the park.)

Parc Floral de Paris

The Bois de Vincennes houses the spectacular parc Floral de Paris, with a butterfly garden, library, and miniature golf course, as well as the parc Zoologique de Paris. You can rent bikes here and ride around the extensive grounds, or row a rented canoe around a winding pond. (You can even rent quadricycles — bicycles built for four — for around 10€/$12).

12e. ☎ 01-55-94-20-20. Métro: Château de Vincennes. Exit at cours des Maréchaux and walk south; the château is on the right. Cross av. des Minimes into the park. Open: 9:30 a.m.–dusk.

Parc Monceau

This was Marcel Proust's favorite park. A Dutch windmill, a Roman temple, a covered bridge, waterfall, farm, medieval ruins, and a pagoda, all designed by Carmontelle are some of the oddities in this park in Paris's ritzy 8th. It contains what is said to be Paris's largest tree, an Oriental plane tree with a circumference of almost 7m (23 ft.). Have a picnic on a bench here with supplies from the rue de Levis (open Tues–Sun; Métro: Villiers) and watch the English nannies from the nearby palatial apartment buildings stroll with their charges.

Boulevard de Coucelles, 8e. Métro: Monceau. (The métro station is at the edge of the park.)

Promenade Plantée

New York City's new High Line green space took as its example this old railroad bridge that was converted into a clever 5-km-long (3-mile) garden that begins behind the Opéra Bastille, runs along the length of avenue Daumesnil, the Reuilly Garden, and the Porte Dorée to the Bois de Vincennes (it makes a great jogging path). Beneath the promenade, artisans have built boutiques and studios into the bridge, collectively known as the Viaduc des Arts. Check them out for eclectic, unusual gifts.

12e. Métro: Bel Air or Dugommier. Walk from the métro to av. Daumesnil. The elevated railroad bridge above av. Daumesnil is the Promenade Plantée.

Houses of the holy

Paris has had a tradition of worship since the first settlers on the Isle of Parisii in the third century B.C. In fact, many of Paris's churches were built on the ruins of pagan temples. Today Paris's churches are treasure troves of fine art, stained glass, and architecture. Included here are some of those worth a visit.

Église St-Etienne du Mont

Standing directly behind place du Panthéon, this is one of Paris's most extraordinary churches. Completed and consecrated in the 17th century, on the site of a 13th-century abbey, the church is a unique blend of late Gothic and Renaissance styles. Preserved near the chancel and set in an ornate copper-trimmed shrine is the sarcophagus stone for Paris's patron saint Geneviève, who saved the city from the Huns in the fifth century. The most impressive attraction here, however, is the 16th-century rood screen, embraced by twin spiraling marble staircases — a stunning display of Renaissance design. The tombs of Pascal and Racine are also here.

1 place St-Geneviève, 5e. ☎ 01-43-54-11-79. Métro: Cardinal Lemoine. Open: Daily Sept–June Mon–Sat 8:30 a.m.–noon and 2–7 p.m., Sun 9 a.m.–noon and 3:30–7:30 p.m.; July–Aug Tues–Sun 10 a.m.–noon and 4–7:15 p.m.

Église St-Eustache

This massive church at the heart of Les Halles was built between 1532 and 1637, combining a Gothic structure with Renaissance decoration. Molière and Mme. de Pompadour were baptized here, and Molière's funeral was held here in 1673. This was the first church to contain the tombs of celebrated Parisians, most notably Louis XIV's finance minister, Colbert. The organ is one of the finest in Paris and has been entirely restored and modernized. Franz Liszt used to play the organ here, and there is a free concert every Sunday at 5:30 p.m. There are also free jazz and piano concerts from time to time.

2 Impasse St-Eustache, 1er. ☎ 01-42-36-31-05. www.saint-eustache.org. *Métro: Les Halles. Open: Mon–Fri 9:30 a.m.–7:30 p.m.*

Église St-Germain-des-Prés

This is the most famous church in the 6th and one of the most important Romanesque monuments in France. Built in the 11th century, St-Germain-des-Prés was an important abbey and center of learning during the Middle

Ages. At the time of the French Revolution, the monks were expelled and the church was vandalized. But much still remains, including the large tower, the oldest in Paris. King John Casimir of Poland is buried at the church, as is the heart of René Descartes. A small square at the corner of place St-Germain-des-Prés and rue de l'Abbaye contains Picasso's small sculpture of the head of poet Guillaume Apollinaire.

3 place St-Germain-des-Prés, 6e. ☎ *01-55-42-81-33. Métro: St-Germain-des-Prés. Open: Daily 8 a.m.–8 p.m.*

Église St-Julien le Pauvre

One of the oldest churches in Paris, this small example of Gothic splendor sits in the lovely square René Viviani. Originally constructed in the 12th century, it lies on the original pilgrimage route of St-Jacques de Compostelle to Spain. The oldest tree in Paris, an acacia reputedly planted in 1602, still stands in its garden. The church contains a stunning wooden screen, which encloses a beautiful chancel. Many classical concerts take place here throughout the year.

79 rue Galande, 5e. ☎ *01-43-54-52-16. Métro: St-Michel. Open Mon–Sun 9:30 a.m.–1 p.m.*

Église St-Roch

This 17th-century church has the richest trove of painting and sculpture in Paris outside a museum. Beginning on the right aisle, notice the bust of *Maréchal François de Créqui* by Geneviève, *Cardinal Dubois and Priests* by Coustou, and paintings by Louis Boulanger in the fourth chapel. The celebrated statue by Falconet, *Le Christ au Jardin des Oliviers* is at the entrance to the choir, and other highlights include *La Nativité* by Anguier (on the altar), the bust of Le Nôtre by Coysevox, and the monument to the painter Mignard by Girardon (both on the left side). Classical music concerts are played here on Tuesdays, often featuring compositions by Bach and Vivaldi, starting around 12:30 p.m.

296 rue St-Honoré, 1er. ☎ *01-42-44-13-20. Métro: Tuileries or Palais-Royal-Musée du Louvre. Open: Mon–Sat 8 a.m.–7:30 p.m., Sun 8:30 a.m.–7:30 p.m.*

Église St-Severin

A religious building has stood here since the sixth century. The current building, begun in the 13th century, is in flamboyant Gothic style. The west portal came from the church of St-Pierre-aux-Boeufs on the Ile de la Cité before it was demolished in 1837. The dramatic palm-tree-shaped vaulting only serves to enhance the brilliant stained-glass windows behind the altar depicting the seven sacraments. Also notable is the chapel to the right of the altar, which was designed by Mansart and contains an intensely moving series of etchings by Georges Rouault and an extraordinary rendering of the crucifixion by G. Schneider.

1 rue des Prêtres-St-Severin, 5e. ☎ *01-42-34-93-50. Métro: St-Michel. Open: Mon–Sat 11 a.m.–7:30 p.m., Sun 9 a.m.–8:30 p.m.*

Église St-Sulpice

This church, unfinished since the funds ran out in the mid–18th century, houses three of Eugène Delacroix's greatest masterpieces: *Jacob Wrestling with the Angel, Heliodorus Driven from the Temple,* and *St. Michael Vanquishing the Devil.* And that's not all: During both equinoxes and at the midday winter solstice, sunlight hits the bronze meridian line running along the north-south transept, climbs the obelisk to the globe on top, and lights the cross. The organ here is one of the grandest in Paris, built in 1781. More recently, and to the chagrin of the church caretakers, St-Sulpice has become a tourist hot spot due to its feature in Dan Brown's *The DaVinci Code.* Among other things, the book suggests that the church had been built on the site of a round pagan temple, with the meridian line as the original outline of its boundaries. This is all untrue; however, it does not make this beautiful and grand church any less interesting to visit.

Place St-Sulpice, 6e. ☎ *01-42-34-59-65. Métro: St-Sulpice. Open: Daily 7 a.m.– 7:30 p.m.*

La Madeleine

Resembling a Roman temple, the Madeleine is one of Paris's minor landmarks. Although construction started in 1806, the Madeleine wasn't consecrated as a church until 1842. The building was originally intended as a temple to the glory of the Grande Armée (Napoléon's idea, of course). Climb the 28 steps leading to the facade and look back: You'll be able to see rue Royale, place de la Concorde and the obelisk, and, across the Seine, the dome of Invalides. Inside, Rude's *Le Baptême du Christ* is on the left as you enter.

Place de la Madeleine, 8e. ☎ *01-44-51-69-00. Métro: Madeleine. Open: Daily 7 a.m.– 7 p.m., closed Sun from 1:30–3:30 p.m.*

La Mosquée de Paris

Built from 1922 to 1926 in the Hispano-Moorish style and overlooked by a green and white minaret, this is one of the newer religious establishments in Paris. The complex is divided into three sections for study, leisure, and worship. At the heart is a patio surrounded by finely carved arcades, modeled on the Alhambra in Granada, Spain. The Salon du Thé here is a lovely place for refreshment, as popular for its Arabian Nights décor as it is for its mint teas and baklava. Fountains, North African music, plush banquettes, and mosaics create an exotic but casual hangout for the local student population. The *hammam* (steam baths) are a popular place with trendy types who get massaged and exfoliated here (I hear it's pretty painful!).

39 rue Geoffroy-St-Hilaire, 5e. ☎ *01-43-31-18-14. Métro: Monge. Open: Daily 10 a.m.–10 p.m.*

Paris's Bridges

When you buy métro tickets, have a look at the logo. What looks like the profile of a woman in a circle is actually an artistic rendering of the Seine as it meanders through Paris. Here are just a few of the works of art spanning that river.

Petit Pont

A bridge has spanned the Seine from the Left Bank to the Ile de la Cité since the times of Julius Caesar, who wrote about one in his Commentaries. The current incarnation is the Petit Pont (Little Bridge) which was built in 1853.

Pont des Arts

The Pont des Arts is one of Paris's prettiest bridges. It's a seven-arched pedestrian-only footbridge connecting the Louvre and the Acadèmie Française that originally opened in 1804 and was the first iron bridge on the Seine. It suffered much bomb damage during World Wars I and II, and barges often ran into it. It finally collapsed in 1979 and was replaced with this steel version in 1984. You see plenty of artists painting the views of the northern tip of Ile de la Cité, the Louvre, and the Acadèmie Française, as well as pedestrians navigating the potted plants on their way to the Louvre. During the warm seasons it becomes a popular picnic spot. Art exhibits are occasionally displayed; this is one place perfect for photo ops.

Pont Neuf

The 12-arched Pont Neuf (New Bridge) is probably Paris's most famous bridge, and its design marks the end of the Middle Ages. Started in 1578, it was finally completed in 1603 and opened to the public by Henri IV in 1603. A statue of Henri IV astride a horse divides the bridge into its two spans, which are anchored on the tip of Ile de la Cité.
Métro: Pont Neuf.

Pont St-Michel

The Pont St-Michel has three arches and is decorated with a large letter N which causes some to mistake it for the Pont Neuf. The N refers to Napoléon III who had it built in 1857 to replace the crumbling bridge that preceded it. Up until 1808, people lived in houses on the bridge.
Métro: St-Michel.

Paris by Guided Tour

If you're a newcomer to the wonders of Paris, an orientation tour can help you understand the city's geography. But even if you've been coming to Paris for ten years or more, one of the various tours can introduce you to sides of the city you never knew existed. As you see in this chapter, you have many good reasons for taking a guided tour. In fact, being shown around by guides whose enthusiasm makes the city come to life can be the high point of your entire trip.

Embarking on a bus

Paris is the perfect city to explore on your own, but if time is a priority, or your energy is at low ebb, consider taking an introductory bus tour. The top tour-bus company in town is Grayline's **Cityrama** (☎ 01-44-55-60-00; www.cityrama.com), which has a one-and-a-half-hour, top-sights tour daily at 10 and 11:30 a.m. and 2:30 p.m.; the cost is 20€ ($32) adults, 10€ ($16) children 4 to 11, free for children under 3. Cityrama also offers various full-day tours of Paris from 78€ to 100€ ($125–$160), and three- and four-hour historic and major sights tours starting at 48€ ($77). The four-hour "Seinorama" tour (daily at 2:15 p.m.) includes a drive up the **Champs-Elysées,** a one-hour cruise on the Seine, and a stroll to the second-floor of the **Eiffel Tower.** It costs 48€ ($77) for adults and 24€ ($38) for children under 12.

Cityrama also offers a variety of "Paris by Night" tours with bus trips around the illuminated city and perhaps a dinner and Seine Cruise starting from 27€ ($43); more deluxe packages include a show at the **Moulin Rouge** or **Paradis Latin** or dinner in the **Eiffel Tower** (prices start at 98€/$157). Cityrama offers free pickup from some hotels, or you can meet at their office at 2 rue des Pyramides (Métro: Pyramides) between rue St-Honoré and rue de Rivoli (across from the **Louvre**).

Paris L'OpenTour, 13 rue Auber, 9e (☎ 01-42-66-56-56; www.parisopen tour.com; Métro: Havre-Caumartin), from Paris's public transportation system (the RATP), has quickly come to rival Cityrama. Its bright yellow and green convertible double-decker buses take you to four different areas, and you listen to recorded commentary in English through a set of headphones given to you when you board. The "Paris Grand Tour" covers Paris's most central sights, minus the Islands: the Madeleine, Opéra, the Louvre, Notre-Dame, St-Germain-des-Prés, Musée d'Orsay, place de la Concorde, Champs-Elysées, Arc de Triomphe, Trocadéro, Eiffel Tower, and Invalides. The "Montmartre-Grands Boulevards" tour goes to the Montmartre funiculaire (but not up the Montmartre hill), the Gare du Nord, Gare de l'Est, and the Grands Boulevards. The "Bastille-Bercy Tour" goes east to Notre-Dame, the Bibliothèque Nationale de François Mitterrand, Gare de Lyon, and parc Bercy. The "Montparnasse-St-Germain-des-Prés" tour goes to the Jardin du Luxembourg, the

Observatory, the Tour Montparnasse, the Catacombes, Invalides, and St-Germain-des-Prés.

L'OpenTour makes its stops at regular city bus stops marked with the L'OpenTour logo. You can board at any of these stops and buy a pass right on the bus. The pass is also on sale at any branch of the Paris Tourist Office, L'OpenTour kiosks near the Malesherbes (8e) and Anvers (9e) bus stops, the RATP office at place de la Madeleine (8e), the Montmartre tourist office (21 place du Tertre), the main Batobus docks on the Seine, and the offices of Paris L'Open Tour at 13 rue Auber (9e), and even the Cityrama office (address above). Your hotel may also have the passes for sale; ask at the reception desk.

A one-day pass costs 29€ ($46) for adults, 15€ ($24) for children aged 4 to 11; a two-day pass costs 32€ ($51) for adults, 15€ ($24) for children 4 to 11, and 22€ ($35) for holders of the Paris Visite pass. You can get on or off the bus as many times as you want, which, in my opinion, makes this the more worthwhile tour. The buses run daily every 15 to 30 minutes throughout the year from about 9:15 a.m. to 6:30 p.m.

The **RATP** also runs the **Balabus** (☎ **01-58-76-16-16**), a fleet of orange-and-white buses that runs only on Sundays and holidays, 12:30 to 8 p.m., from April to September. Routes run between the Gare de Lyon and the Grand Arche de La Défense, in both directions, and cost just one métro ticket. Look for the *Bb* symbol across the side of the bus and on signs posted along the route.

Touring by boat

One of the most beautiful ways to see Paris is by taking a sightseeing boat cruise up and down Paris's waterways. In addition to the Seine River cruises (see the "Paris's top attraction: The Seine river cruise" sidebar earlier this chapter), try a longer and more unusual tour with **Paris Canal** (☎ **01-42-40-96-97**; www.pariscanal.com; Métro: Bastille). Its two-and-a-half-hour cruises leave the Musée d'Orsay at 9:30 a.m. and end at parc de la Villette. The boat passes under the Bastille and enters the Canal St-Martin for a lazy journey along the tree-lined quai Jemmapes. You cruise under bridges and through many locks. The boat leaves the parc de la Villette at 2:30 p.m. for the same voyage in reverse, in front of the sign that says "Folie des Visites du Parc," and returns to quai d'Orsay at 5 p.m. Reservations are essential. The trip costs 17€ ($27) for adults, 14€ ($22) for ages 12 to 25 and older than 60, and 10€ ($16) for children 4 to 11.

If you have restless young children, the wait for the water to rise at each lock may prove too long. You may want to consider one of the shorter Seine boat trips mentioned in Chapter 17 or take the canal cruise one way and travel back by métro.

Canauxrama (☎ **01-42-39-15-00**; www.canauxrama.com; Métro: Jaurès) offers two-and-a-half-hour tours similar to Paris Canal's at 9:45 a.m. and 2:30 p.m., leaving from Port l'Arsenal in the 12e and ending at the parc de la Villette in the 19e. The cost is 15€ ($24) for adults, 11€ ($18) for ages 12 to 25, 8€ ($13) for children 6 to 11, and free for children younger than 6. Reservations are required.

Horsing around — a guided tour at two horsepower

Cruising around Paris in a tiny car with an open roof and a hilarious tour guide is a terrific way to see the city! The Citroën 2CV (meaning two *chevaux,* or two horsepower) was to France what the VW Beetle was to the United States, and it was France's most popular car from its debut before World War II up to 1990, when Citroën stopped production. Now you can tour Paris in its best-loved car with **4 Roues Sous 1 Parapluie** (Four Wheels Under an Umbrella; ☎ **08-00-80-06-31** inside France; outside France 06-67-32-26-68; www.4roues-sous-1parapluie.com). One to three people can choose from numerous tours that introduce essential monuments such as the Eiffel Tower, Notre-Dame, and the Place de la Concorde, or see plazas and sites not normally frequented by tourists, but that are still very much a part of the city's charm: a *DaVinci Code* tour, a tour of different gardens throughout the city, a shopping tour, a secret Paris insider tour, a romantic evening for two that throws in dinner and dessert, a cosmopolitan escapade four-hour tour. You can even custom design your own tour. Prices start at 19€ ($30) for a half-hour trip to 144€ ($230) per person in a group of three for the four-hour Versailles tour. There are a variety of tours lasting a half-hour up to four hours for trips outside the city. The chauffeur/tour guides are very funny and full of knowledge, and each speaks English and French. These are not big cars and a three-hour three-person (adult) tour could get uncomfortable. Reservations required by telephone or contact them online through their secure server.

Walking your way across Paris

Paris Walks (☎ **01-48-09-21-40**; www.paris-walks.com) is a popular English-language outfit offering fascinating two-hour guided walks with such themes as Paris During the Revolution, Hemingway's Paris, the Marais, the Village of Montmartre, Chocolate tour, the Latin Quarter, and the Two Islands. Call for tours being offered during your visit and for where and when to meet — usually at a métro station entrance at 10:30 a.m., and again at 2:30 p.m. Tours cost 10€ ($16) adults, 8€ ($13) students under 25, and 5€ ($8) children. They also offer weekend jaunts to places such as **Fontainebleau** or **Monet's Gardens** at Giverny or **Normandy landing beaches** by car.

French Links (☎ **01-45-77-01-63**; www.frenchlinks.com) is run by Rachel Kaplan, the author of numerous guidebooks about living in Paris, such as *Best Buys to French Chic in Paris,* as well as the continuously updated *Paris Insider Guides,* who lets you customize your tour from a two-hour walking tour, to a full-day cultural tour. Trained, experienced guides with degrees in art and history lead you on such walks as Paris in a Basket: Gourmet Market Tour, Gastronomical Paris Tour, Parisian Art Nouveau, The Liberation of Paris, Photographer's Walking Tour, and many others. And they're happy to help you design your own tour. The talks are entertaining and fun, geared to everyone from high-school and college-age students to retirees. Four-hour tours without transportation start at 438€ ($700) for one to four people. All tours must be prebooked and prepaid with a U.S. bank check or by credit card (MasterCard, Visa, or American Express) using their secure server.

Seeing Paris by bike

One of the best ways to see Paris — and burn off some of those rich dinners, too — is from the seat of a bike. Mayor Bertrand Delanöe, a huge proponent of improving the city's air quality, has introduced two initiatives. The first, **Paris Respire** (Paris Breathes), opens the roadways on the banks of the Seine in the 1er, 4e, and 7e, the banks of the Canal St-Martin in the 10e, roads in the 6e near Jardin du Luxembourg (Mar–Nov), in the 14e, near Montmartre in the 18th, and the two big parks flanking the city, the Bois de Vincennes (12e) and the Bois de Boulogne (16e) to bikers, inline skaters, runners, and walkers on Sundays between 10 a.m. and 5 p.m.

The second is the wildly popular bike rental program, **Velib'**. Since 2007, some 20,000 bikes and their corresponding parking stations have popped up all over the city. You can rent a bike near the Louvre and return it anywhere a bike parking station is located in the city (per the Paris Tourist Office, these stations are located 300m/984 ft. apart). You must first buy a special card from a machine at any of the parking stations: Residents can buy a one-year "subscription" card, and visitors can buy cards for shorter durations (Abonnement Courte Durée) of one day for 1€ ($1.60) or one week for 5€ ($8). (Note: 150€ [$240] is automatically debited from your bank account as a security deposit and credited back into the account after you safely return the bike.) With bike parking stations located everywhere, many near métro stations, there is really no reason *not* to ride, and the number of cyclists in Paris these days is making the city resemble its neighbor to the north, Amsterdam. In fact, the program is so popular, that sometimes, namely after 1 a.m. when the métro shuts down and public transportation is hard to come by, there aren't enough bikes to go around. The disadvantage for Americans is the payment system which takes only *cartes à puces* (European credit cards or other cards with a microchip). Some American credit cards have these, but if you aren't sure, call your credit card company.

Not only can you rent bikes from **Fat Tire Bike Tours** (24 rue Edgar Faure, 15e; ☎ **01-56-58-10-54**; www.fattirebiketoursparis.com), but you can also take one very funny guided tour of the city on bikes or on the Segway scooter. Look for someone holding a large white meeting-point sign in front of the Pilier Sud (South Pillar) of the Eiffel Tower (Pilier Sud is spelled out above the ticket booth) for the bike tour; look for the guide on the Segway in the same place for the Segway tour. Friendly guides take you on day or night bike tours of the city (24€/$38 day for adults; 22€/$35 day for students; night tours are $45 adults; 26€/$42 students; 48€/$77 and 44€/$70, respectively, for both tours).

The tours last four to four and a half hours. Day tours are at 11 a.m. year-round, and also at 3 p.m. April 1 through October 31. Night tours, which are beautiful (especially the ride past the Grand Pyramid through the courtyard at the Louvre), take place at 7 p.m. nightly April 1 through October 31, and at 6 p.m. nightly the month of March. Night tours take place the month of November and February 15-30 on Saturday, Sunday, Tuesday, and Thursday at 6 p.m. Reservations are required for Segway tours (http://citysegwaytours.com).

Chapter 12

Shopping the Local Stores

· ·

In This Chapter

▶ Getting an overview of Paris's shopping scene
▶ Understanding Customs and the VAT
▶ Finding the best department stores, street markets, and bargain shops
▶ Searching the prime shopping neighborhoods

· ·

*W*ith the way the economy is in many English-speaking parts of the world, shopping in Paris may not be high on one's list of things to do when visiting the city. Fortunately (or maybe not) even the window-shopping is exquisite: Enticing goods are arranged just so in windows — and the prices are listed. Believe it or not, bargains *do* exist here. From the toniest haute couture shop to the hidden *dépot-vente* (resale shop) selling last year's Yves Saint Laurent at fabulously reduced prices, even non-shoppers can find something. This chapter gives you an overview of the Parisian shopping scene, providing hints about where to find the bargains, how to get it all home, and even how to get some of your money back.

Surveying the Scene

The cost of shopping in Paris isn't always astronomical. If you plan only to buy haute couture clothing, then yes, you'll pay top prices. However, Paris has many stores that sell clothing and goods at prices comparable to what you'd pay in the United States. And some items in Paris are cheaper even than they are in your hometown, including some French and European brands of perfume and cosmetics, shoes, clothing from French-based companies such as Petit Bateau and Lacoste, and French-made porcelain, cookware, and glassware. You'll obviously pay more for any name brand imported from the United States, such as Donna Karan and Calvin Klein, and for any souvenirs in areas heavily frequented by tourists.

 Keep in mind that a 19.6 percent value-added tax (VAT) is tacked on to the price of most products, which means that most things cost less at home. (For details on getting a VAT refund, see the next section "Getting the VAT back.") Appliances, paper products, housewares, computer supplies, electronics, and CDs are notoriously expensive in France, but checking out prices of French products before your trip can help you recognize a bargain.

Paris Shopping

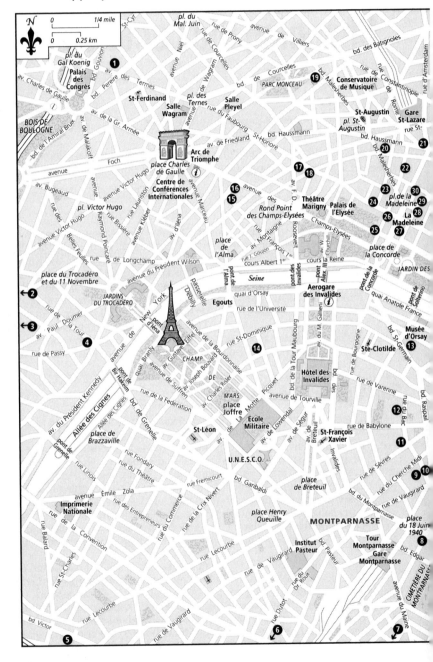

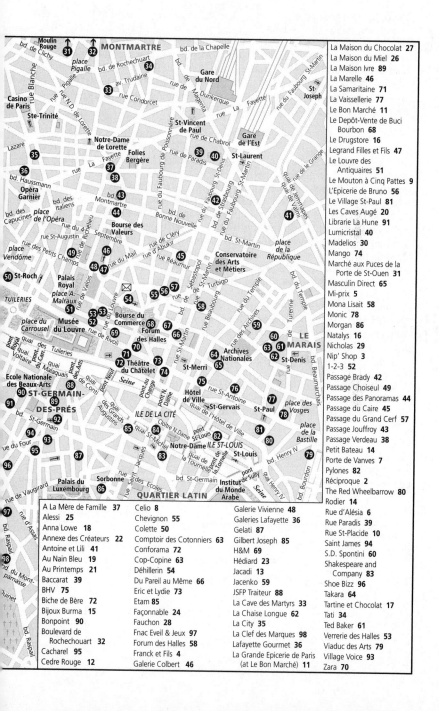

La Maison du Chocolat **27**
La Maison du Miel **26**
La Maison Ivre **89**
La Marelle **46**
La Samaritaine **71**
La Vaissellerie **77**
Le Bon Marché **11**
Le Depôt-Vente de Buci
   Bourbon **68**
Le Drugstore **16**
Legrand Filles et Fils **47**
Le Louvre des
   Antiquaires **51**
Le Mouton à Cinq Pattes **9**
L'Epicerie de Bruno **56**
Le Village St-Paul **81**
Les Caves Augé **20**
Librarie La Hune **91**
Lumicristal **40**
Madelios **30**
Mango **74**
Marché aux Puces de la
   Porte de St-Ouen **31**
Masculin Direct **65**
Mi-prix **5**
Mona Lisait **58**
Monic **78**
Morgan **86**
Natalys **16**
Nicholas **29**
Nip' Shop **3**
1-2-3 **52**
Passage Brady **42**
Passage Choiseul **49**
Passage des Panoramas **44**
Passage du Caire **45**
Passage du Grand Cerf **57**
Passage Jouffroy **43**
Passage Verdeau **38**
Petit Bateau **14**
Porte de Vanves **7**
Pylones **82**
Réciproque **2**
The Red Wheelbarrow **80**
Rodier **14**
Rue d'Alésia **6**
Rue Paradis **39**
Rue St-Placide **10**
Saint James **94**
S.D. Spontini **60**
Shakespeare and
   Company **83**
Shoe Bizz **96**
Takara **64**
Tartine et Chocolat **17**
Tati **34**
Ted Baker **61**
Verrerie des Halles **53**
Viaduc des Arts **79**
Village Voice **93**
Zara **70**

A La Mère de Famille **37**
Alessi **25**
Anna Lowe **18**
Annexe des Créateurs **22**
Antoine et Lili **41**
Au Nain Bleu **19**
Au Printemps **21**
Baccarat **39**
BHV **75**
Biche de Bère **72**
Bijoux Burma **15**
Bonpoint **90**
Boulevard de
   Rochechouart **32**
Cacharel **95**
Cedre Rouge **12**

Celio **8**
Chevignon **55**
Colette **50**
Comptoir des Cotonniers **63**
Conforama **72**
Cop-Copine **63**
Déhillerin **54**
Du Pareil au Même **66**
Eric et Lydie **73**
Etam **85**
Façonnable **24**
Fauchon **28**
Fnac Eveil & Jeux **97**
Forum des Halles **58**
Franck et Fils **4**
Galerie Colbert **46**

Galerie Vivienne **48**
Galeries Lafayette **36**
Gelati **87**
Gilbert Joseph **85**
H&M **69**
Hédiard **23**
Jacadi **13**
Jacenko **59**
JSFP Traiteur **88**
La Cave des Martyrs **33**
La Chaise Longue **62**
La City **35**
La Clef des Marques **98**
Lafayette Gourmet **36**
La Grande Epicerie de Paris
   (at Le Bon Marché) **11**

Probably the best time to find a bargain in Paris is during the government-mandated twice-annual sales *(soldes)* in January and July when merchandise gets marked down 30 percent to 50 percent or more. You will often see lines of Parisians outside their favorite stores the first days of the sales. If you can brave the crowds, you just may find the perfect designer outfit at a fraction of its retail price. *Note:* Though the sales are supposed to last two weeks, they often run on much longer, often into the next month, according to the amount of merchandise left.

Generally, store hours are Monday through Saturday from 9:30 a.m. (sometimes 10 a.m.) to 7 p.m., and later on Thursday evenings, without a break for lunch. Some smaller stores are closed Monday or Monday mornings, and break for lunch for one to three hours, beginning at around 1 p.m., but this schedule is becoming increasingly rare. Small stores also may be closed for all or part of August and on some days around Christmas and Easter. Sunday shopping is gradually making inroads in Paris but is limited mostly to tourist areas; try the Carrousel du Louvre at the Louvre, rue de Rivoli across from the Louvre, rue des Francs-Bourgeois in the Marais, and the Champs-Elysées. The department stores are open the five Sundays before Christmas, and occasionally one or two Sundays during the annual sales.

Politeness is imperative when you shop in Paris. Always greet sales-people at smaller stores with *"Bonjour, madame"* or *"Bonjour, monsieur"* when you arrive (the Glossary in Appendix B can help with pronunciation). And regardless of whether you buy anything, say, *"Merci, au revoir"* ("Thank you, goodbye") when you leave.

Clothing sizes are different around the world. In French men's trousers, for example, add 10 to the waist size you wear in U.S. clothing to get the French size. To determine what size you need to look for, check out Table 12-1, which lists conversions for U.S. and Continental sizes.

Table 12-1	The Right Fit: Size Conversions		
U.S.	*Continental*	*U.S.*	*Continental*
Women's Clothes		*Women's Shoes*	
4	36	5	36
6	38	6	37
8	40	7	38
10	42	8	39
12	44	9	40
14	46	10	41

U.S.	Continental	U.S.	Continental
Men's Shirts		**Men's Shoes**	
14½	37	7	39½
15	38	8	41
15½	39	9	42
16	41	10	43
16½	42	11	44½
17	43	12	46

Getting the VAT back

Whenever you spend more than 175€ to 182€ ($280–$291) in a single store, you're entitled to a partial refund on the value-added tax (VAT), also referred to in France as TVA. The refund, however, isn't automatic. Food, wine, and tobacco don't count, and the refund is granted only on purchases that you take out of the country — not on merchandise that you ship home. The amount of the refund varies; it's 12 percent in Galeries Lafayette and Printemps, and it may be anywhere from 15 percent to 18 percent at smaller boutiques.

When applying for a refund, you must show the store clerk your passport to prove your eligibility. You're then given an export sales document (in triplicate — two pink sheets and a green one), which you must sign, and usually an envelope addressed to the store.

Two private tax refund companies operate in Paris, the bigger **Global Refund** (www.globalrefund.com) and **Premier Tax Free** (www. premiertaxfree.com).

When you spend more than 175€ ($280) in a store that participates in Global Refund's Europe Tax-Free shopping program (indicated by the *Tax-Free* sticker in the store's windows), you're given a Tax-Free Shopping Cheque that shows the amount of refund owed to you when you leave the country. Have this check stamped by a Customs officer in the airport, and then take it to the special Global Refund counter for an instant refund. Global Refund offices are located within department store Galeries Lafayette and in the men's boutique, Madelios, at 23 bd. de la Madeleine, 1er (Métro: Madeleine), in Charles de Gaulle airport at Terminal 1 departures level, Gate 26; Terminal 2A, Gate 5; Terminal 2B, Gate 7; Terminal 2C, Gate 5; Terminal 2F, Gate 11; and in Terminal 3 on the Departures level. In Orly Airport, there is only one Global Refund office in Orly South near the international baggage claim on the departures level.

It works the same way with Premier Tax Free. Look for Premier Tax Free stickers in the windows of stores participating in this program, and spend more than 175€ ($280) to get your refund. Premier Tax Free offices are located at American Express, 11 rue Scribe, 9e (Métro: Opéra); Travelex Opéra, 45 av. de l'Opéra (Métro: Opéra); at two Travelex Champs-Elysées locations: 73 and 125 (Métro: Franklin D. Roosevelt and Charles de Gaulle-Étoile, respectively), in Charles de Gaulle Airport Terminal 1, Gate 26; and in Orly South on the departures level.

Department stores that cater to foreign visitors, such as Au Printemps and Galeries Lafayette, have special *détaxe* areas where clerks prepare your invoices for you. You must present your passport. Otherwise, when you leave the country, bring all documents to the airport's *détaxe* booth and have a Customs official stamp them. Enclose the appropriate document (the pink one) in the store envelope the clerk provided when you bought your merchandise and mail it from the airport from which you are leaving the European Union. The wait for a refund is anywhere from one to six months. Travelers leaving from Charles de Gaulle Airport can visit the *détaxe* refund point in Terminal 1 on the departure level between Gate 14 and 16; in Terminal 2, Hall B between Doors 6 and 7 near the baggage claim area; or in Hall A between Doors 5 and 6; and in Terminal T9, near the departure gates. At Orly, the *détaxe* booth is in Orly West between Halls 3 and 4 on the departure level.

Whenever you're claiming a tax refund, try to arrive at the airport as early as possible because you must show everything you're declaring to a Customs official, and you may have to wait in line. Plus, after you finish with *détaxe,* you must stand in line again to check your luggage.

If you're traveling by train, go to the *détaxe* area in the station before boarding because you can't have your refund documents processed on the train. Give the three sheets to the Customs official, who stamps them and returns a pink and a green copy to you. Keep the green copy and mail the pink copy to the store.

Your reimbursement is either mailed as a check (in euro) or credited to your credit card account, which is better, as you may find it difficult to cash a check for euro in your own country. If you don't receive your tax refund within six months, write to the store, giving the date of purchase, and the location where the forms were given to Customs officials. Include a photocopy of your green refund sheet.

Getting your goodies through Customs

Returning **U.S. citizens,** who've been away for 48 hours or more, are allowed to bring back, once every 30 days, $800 worth of merchandise duty-free (a *duty* is a tax). You're charged a flat duty of 3 percent on the next $1,000 worth of purchases; on gifts, the duty-free limit is $100 (any item that costs more than $100 is subject to the full tax). U.S. citizens have the right to bring back up to 200 cigarettes, 100 cigars, and one liter of alcohol duty free; any larger amount will be taxed regardless of whether or not you have reached the $800 limit. You can't bring fresh food into the United States (ignore what the people in the Paris duty-free stores tell you; fresh meats and cheeses are *not* allowed); canned foods, however, are allowed.

Citizens of the United Kingdom and **Ireland** who are returning from a European Union (E.U.) country have no limit on what they can bring back from an E.U. country, as long as the items are for personal use (including gifts), and the necessary duty and taxes have been paid. Limits are set at: 3,200 cigarettes, 200 cigars, 3kg (6.6 lbs.) smoking tobacco, 10 liters of spirits, 90 liters of wine, and 110 liters of beer.

Canada allows its citizens a once-a-year C$750 exemption after spending seven days out of the country, and you're allowed to bring back duty free: 200 cigarettes, 50 cigars, 200 grams smoking tobacco, 1.5 liters of wine or 1.14 liters of liquor, and 50 cigars. In addition, you can mail gifts to Canada from abroad at the value of up to C$60 a day, provided they're unsolicited and don't contain alcohol, tobacco, or advertising matter. Write on the package *Unsolicited gift, under $60 value.* All valuables need to be declared on the Y-38 form before your departure from Canada, including serial numbers of valuables you already own, such as expensive foreign cameras.

The duty-free allowance in **Australia** is A$900 or A$450 for those younger than 18 and does not include tobacco or alcohol. Upon returning to Australia, citizens can bring in 250 cigarettes or 250 grams of loose tobacco, and 2.25 liters of alcohol. If you're returning with valuable goods that you already own, such as foreign-made cameras, you need to file form B263.

The duty-free allowance for **New Zealand** is NZ$700. Citizens older than 17 can bring in 200 cigarettes or 50 cigars, or 250 grams total of tobacco products, plus 4.5 liters of wine or beer, or up to three bottles of liquor products that don't exceed 1.125 liters.

Checking Out the Big Names

Two of Paris's major department stores, Au Printemps and Galeries Lafayette, offer visitors a 10 percent discount coupon, good in most departments. If your hotel or travel agent doesn't give you one of these coupons (they're sometimes attached to a city map), you can ask for them at the stores' welcome desks; the clerks speak English.

Check out the "Paris Shopping" map for the locations of the stores listed here.

BHV

This store near the Marais and next door to l'Hôtel de Ville finally underwent a much-needed renovation which removed its cute basement bricolage cafe in favor of more room for its hardwares. BHV (Bazar de l'Hôtel de Ville) sells the usual clothing, cosmetics, luggage, and leather ware at decent prices, but it's really worth a visit because of its giant basement-level hardware store with everything you need to fix up your home. Check out its very cute pet store, BHV La Niche, at 42 rue de la Verriere (it has some of the best small dog and cat carriers I've ever seen!).

52 rue de Rivoli, 1er. ☎ *01-42-74-90-00. Métro: Hôtel de Ville.*

Forum des Halles

This was the site of the original wholesale market of Paris, where merchants would come from kilometers away to set up tables of fruits, vegetables, dairy products, and so forth. In 1971 the market was formally moved to a suburb outside the city limits, and a major RER and métro stop — "les Halles" — and a mall complex were built. The forum is the closest thing to a "mall" shopping center that one can find in Paris. In the place where once stood fish-mongers and butchers of Emile Zola's *Le Ventre de Paris* (les Halles market is a centerpiece of the story) one can go clothes shopping in the Gap, Celio, and H&M, buy CDs and DVDs at Fnac, buy furniture at Habitat, get lunch, and even see a movie at the UGC theaters on the lowest underground level. In 2007 architects Patrick Berger and Jacques Anziutti won the bid for the total redesign of the Forum des Halles. Parisians have regarded this central area of the shopping mall as an eyesore since its redesign in 1975. Beware that the area can be seedy later on at night.

101 Porte Berger, 1er. ☎ *01-44-76-96-56. Access from numerous doors surrounding the complex, on rue Rambateau, rue Berger, and rue de Pierre Lescot; or enter directly from métro station. Métro: Les Halles. Open: Sun.*

Galeries Lafayette

Of the three major Paris department stores, Galeries Lafayette is probably the most-visited by a hair due to its prolific advertising campaigns, such as its billboards featuring supermodel Laetitia Casta. Merchandise here ranges from good to excellent with lots of deals during the sales. Look for women's clothing from Sonia Rykiel, Comptoir des Cotonniers, and agnès b. And check out the gourmet grocery store, Lafayette Gourmet, in the men's store. Main store restaurants include: Häagen-Dazs, Lina's gourmet sandwiches, Fauchon tearoom and restaurant, McDonald's, Café Sushi, and Lafayette Café on the sixth floor, which has great views of Paris (it's a self-serve cafeteria and my personal favorite). If you don't already have one, ask at the front desk for the 10 percent discount coupon, good in most departments. All the advertising has only benefited Galeries Lafayette: This store gets downright crowded, and if you visit during the sales, pace yourself or you can become thoroughly fatigued. Détaxe is 12 percent here.

40 bd. Haussmann, 9e. ☎ *01-42-82-34-56. Métro: Opéra or Chaussée-d'Antin. Open: Mon–Sat 9:30 a.m.–7:30 p.m.*

La Samaritaine

Alas! Parisians bemoan the temporary closing of their beloved shopping destination and 1920s architectural monument. La Samaritaine closed in June 2005 after its president announced that the building had become, in its advanced age, a serious fire risk. It will remain closed for around five more years (estimates and official announcements dance around four to six years); all of the electrical systems, plumbing, and fire systems will be completely renovated. The owner of La Samaritaine (LVMH, the Möet-Hennessy Louis Vuitton luxury group) has plans to relaunch the store as an outlet for luxury brand clothing and other items, not unlike Harrods of London fame. Located between the Louvre and the Pont Neuf, the department store is housed in four buildings with Art Nouveau touches and an Art Deco facade on quai du Louvre. Possessing the arguably perfect rooftop view of Paris, it was named after a hydraulic pump originally installed near the Pont Neuf in 1609. La Samaritaine will return, but for now enjoy the view of Paris from the top of the Pompidou center, and its chic restaurant, Georges (see Chapter 10).

19 rue de la Monnaie, 1er. ☎ *0800-010-015 for a free phone call for any questions or updated information (Mon–Fri 10 a.m.–6 p.m.). Métro: Pont-Neuf or Châtelet–Les Halles.*

Le Bon Marché

This is the Left Bank's only department store, and it's a wonderful respite from the multibuilding, crowded shopping experience of Au Printemps and Galeries Lafayette. Elegant, but small enough to be manageable, much of the store's merchandise is exquisite and includes designers such as Sonia Rykiel, Bensimon, Vivienne Westwood, Burberry, and Yohji Yamamoto. The main store's third floor is particularly renowned for its large shoe selection and grand lingerie department (where dressing rooms have phones to summon your salesperson). The basement features a beautiful bookstore and upscale toys as well; in fact, many bourgeois Parisians head to Le Bon Marché for their every shopping need. Thus, nothing here is cheap. Make sure to visit Le Grand Épicerie next door (is there anything you can't get at Le Bon Marché?), where you can buy everything from toilet paper to truffles. A cafe, Delicabar, above Le Grand Épicerie, has a menu divided into tasty sweet and salty offerings, while the Café de la Grand Épicerie on the second floor in the Home Décor section, features selections chosen by the gourmet grocery store's food, wine, and pastry professionals.

24 rue de Sèvres, 7e. ☎ *01-44-39-80-00. Métro: Sèvres-Babylone.*

Le Drugstore

Though not a department store (it's more a mini-mall), Le Drugstore is included here because it was once an important part of Parisian culture in the 1960s, and its owner, ad giant Publicis, is hoping to regain that status with a stunningly modern glass renovation that cost millions of euros. Inside is a brasserie run by a disciple of multistarred French chef Alain Ducasse (waitstaff is clothed by French designer Jean-Charles Castelbajac), an invitation-only restaurant, Privé Marcel, an international newsstand, a gift shop, a drug store (naturally), gourmet food, wine, and cigar stores, and a Shu Uemura beauty products shop. Also here are movie theaters and a cool bar with a terrace overlooking the Champs and the Arc de Triomphe. Owned by Publicis since the late '50s, Le Drugstore was the height of cool in the 1960s when it was one of the few places in Paris you could pick up a pack of cigarettes or a magazine at 2 a.m. (and in a sense, it still is since most *tabacs* are closed by 11 p.m. at the latest, not to mention newsstands). Has its new revamping made it the hip place it once was while helping to push the Champs-Elysées into the 21st century? The jury is still out.

131 av. du Champs-Elysées, 8e. ☎ *01-44-43-79-00. Métro: Georges V, Charles de Gaulle-Étoile. Open: Daily 10 a.m.–2 a.m.*

Monoprix

These Target-like stores are Paris's best-kept secret, where you can find wonderful clothing, much of it fashion-forward, at reasonable prices along with accessories, low-priced cosmetics, lingerie, and housewares. Many locations also have large grocery stores, although the food is a bit pricey (see below for cheaper supermarkets). The Champs-Elysées branch at no. 52 is open until midnight Monday to Saturday.

Various locations. ☎ *08-10-08-40-00.*

For those looking for grocery stores that are a little more reasonable than Monoprix, **Le Marché Franprix** is the most inexpensive grocer that still sells good quality vegetables, fruits, cheeses, mustards, and all the normal French sundries. Their stores are on practically every other street throughout the city. Another supermarket that's a little bigger and a bit more polished is **Champion** (☎ **08-10-05-50-00**). They have a wider selection than Franprix but still won't break the bank.

Printemps

Printemps (formally and formerly known as *Au Printemps*) is one of Paris's largest department stores. Merchandise is sold in three different buildings: Printemps de l'Homme (menswear), Printemps de la Maison (furniture and accessories), and Printemps de la Mode (women and children's fashion). Well-known designers represented here include (but are certainly not limited to) Dolce & Gabbana, Armani, and Burberry. Fashion shows take place under the 1920s glass cupola (seventh floor) at 10 a.m. every Tuesday year-round, and every Friday from March to October. You can easily spend a day here, and there are eight restaurants scattered throughout the three buildings. The beauty department in the main building is, according to Printemps, the largest in the world. There is a fabulous selection of lingerie in the basement level of the main building, as well. Détaxe is offered at 12 percent here.

64 bd. Haussmann, 9e. ☎ *01-42-82-50-00. Métro: Havre-Caumartin. Open: Mon–Sat 9:35 a.m.–7 p.m., until 10 p.m. Thurs.*

Tati

For the most part, Tati is frankly tacky, but where else can you find the occasional funky top for 2€ ($3.20)? Or wear-for-one-season shoes at 10€ ($16)?

In fact, you never know what you may find here if you dig; the occasional gem rewards those who are persistent. Tati also has a jewelry branch called Tati Or, an eyewear store known as Tati Optic, and a travel agency called Tati Vacances. Despite rumors of closing and the near-buyout of its Barbès-Rochechouart location, business has bounced back and cheap clothing and accessory items abound! Expect crowds.

4 bd. Rochechouart, 18e. ☎ *01-55-29-52-20. Métro: Barbès-Rochechouart. Other branches are located at 68 av. du Maine (*☎ *01-56-89-06-80; Métro: Gaîté), 30 av. d'Italie (*☎ *01-53-80-97-70; Métro: Place d'Italie), and 76 av. Clichy, 17e (*☎ *01-58-22-28-90; Métro: La Fourche).*

Taking It to the Street (Markets)

The huge **Marché aux Puces de la Porte de St-Ouen**, 18e, purportedly the largest flea market in the world, is a real shopping adventure and although you probably won't snag a bargain, it's still well worth the visit. Open Saturday, Sunday, and Monday, it features several thousand stalls, carts, shops, and vendors selling everything from vintage clothing (see if you can find the vendor whose specialty is wearing her merchandise from the mid-1800s) to antique chandeliers, paintings, furniture, and toys. You need to arrive early to snag the deals — if you can find any. The best times for bargains are right at opening time and just before closing time. To reach the market, take the métro to the Porte de Clignancourt stop; exit onto avenue de la Porte de Clignancourt. (You can also exit onto bd. Omano, which turns into avenue de la Porte de Clignancourt.) Head north a block and cross beneath an underpass; the markets begin on your left. Open Saturday through Monday 9 a.m. to 8 p.m.

 Starting at the underpass just past the Clignancourt Métro stop, you'll see stalls selling cheap junk, but don't stop here! Turn left onto rue des Rosiers, the market's main street. Be alert; pickpockets roam the markets, especially the stalls on the periphery.

 Don't pay the ticketed price or the price the vendor first quotes you; always haggle. You can usually get at least 10 percent off.

Visitors to Paris usually choose the Clignancourt market over the convivial market at **Porte de Vanves**, 14e, a gem still waiting to be discovered. Probably the smallest of the fleas, it's nevertheless a good place to browse among friendly dealers. To reach the market, take the métro to the Porte de Vanves stop; exit at boulevard Brune; follow it east to avenue Georges Lafenestre, and turn right. Open Saturday and Sunday 8:30 a.m. to 1:00 p.m. A cheap clothing market takes its place after 1 p.m. Other flea markets include one at **Porte Montreuil** (Métro: Porte de Montreuil) and another at **place d'Aligre**, 14e (Métro: Ledru-Rollin, open 9 a.m.–noon). Much more downscale, these markets give the term "junk" a whole new meaning.

Scoring Bargains in Paris

The savvy Parisian waits for sales, knows the addresses of discounters, and knows that some of the best fashion deals are found in resale shops that deal directly with designer showrooms for half-price designer clothing that has been worn on a runway or used in a fashion shoot. And four words are the key to her world: *soldes* (sales), *dégriffés* (designerwear with the labels cut out), *stock* (overstock), and *dêpot-vente* (resale). Most *depôts-vente* are on the Right Bank in the 8e, 16e, and 17e arrondissements. If you're itching for a bargain after shopping for full-price items, visit one of the streets where discount stores abound:

✔ **Rue d'Alésia,** 14e (Métro: Alésia), is filled with French designer discount outlets selling last year's overstock at up to 70 percent below retail. These stock boutiques are more downscale than their sister shops; be prepared to rifle through the racks to find the gems. Outlets include **Chevignon** at no. 122, **Darjeeling** (a French lingerie brand) at no. 68, **Cacharel** at no. 114, **Georges Rech** at no. 100, **Tout Compte Fait** at no. 101bis, **Via Veneto** at no. 72 (for Dior, Armani, and other designer menswear), and **Jacadi** at no. 116.

✔ **Rue Paradis,** 10e (Métro: Poissonnière), is filled with wholesale china and porcelain stores such as **Artoria** at no. 32 and **Editios Paradis** at no. 29.

✔ **Rue St-Placide,** 6e (Métro: Sèvres-Babylone), is also a street of dreams with many discount stores, including **Le Mouton à Cinq Pattes** (8 rue St-Placide) and **La Générale de Pharmacie** (no. 58), which sells French cosmetics and skincare products at up to half the normal prices. Discounted no-name shoes and housewares are also sold on this street. Perpendicular to Le Bon Marché, St-Placide is quite a relief on the pocketbook after perusing the wares at the luxury department store.

✔ **Boulevard de Rochechouart,** 18e (Métro: Anvers or Barbès-Rochechouart), is certainly not the prettiest of Paris's boulevards and can get awfully crowded. But for those who care about bargains, is a street of deep discounts with multiple branches of **Tati** (at 4 and 18), and a **Celio Club (formerly Celio Stock)** at no. 15, among others. If you have time to spare after visiting Sacré-Coeur, head south from the cathedral down rue Steinkerque or rue Seveste and make a left onto boulevard de Rochechouart.

You can also try these discount stores spread throughout the city.

Anna Lowe

The sales pitch here is "big brands at small prices," and if you consider only the very best designers, this store is for you. It carries Yves Saint Laurent, Chanel, and Giorgio Armani at a steep discount — at least 50 percent. The clothes may be overstock or last year's models with samples from the runway. Most of the staff speaks English.

104 rue du Faubourg-St-Honoré, 8e. ☎ *01-42-66-11-32 or 01-40-06-02-42. Métro: Miromesnil or St-Phillippe-de-Roule.*

Annexe des Créateurs

This is made up of two stores — one devoted to selling gently worn designer daywear, the other to barely worn evening wear. If you don't mind wearing resale togs, you could save yourself between 40 percent and 75 percent off the retail price of the items. The store has been described as an Ali Baba's cave entirely devoted to luxury, and the description is apt. You find names like Chanel, Dior, Thierry Mugler, Louis Vuitton, Hermès, Vivienne Westwood, and Jean-Paul Gaultier.

19 rue Godot de Mauroy, 9e. ☎ *01-42-65-46-40. Métro: Hauvre-Caumartin or Madeleine.*

Bonpoint

These exquisite children's clothes with such touches as hand-smocking, lace collars, and velvet usually come with a steep price. However, this Bonpoint branch, called boutique *fin de série* (end of series) sells end-of-season clothes at reduced prices; it's particularly good during the yearly sales in January and July.

42 rue de l'Université, 7e. ☎ *01-40-20-10-55. Métro: Rue-du-Bac.*

La Clef des Marques

This large, somewhat drab store sells baby clothes, shoes, lingerie, sports clothes, and end-of-series couture items. Racks are overfull so you have to hunt a bit for a bargain.

124 bd. Raspail, 6e. ☎ *01-45-49-31-00. Métro: Notre-Dame des Champs.*

La Marelle

Located in the wonderful Galerie Vivienne, this store resells clothing from some of the top designers in very good condition.

21 Galerie Vivienne, 2e. ☎ *01-42-60-08-19. Métro: Palais Royal.*

Le Depôt-Vente de Buci Bourbon

This resale store is actually two shops right next to each other with vintage and not-so-old clothing and accessories for men and women along with gently used furniture.

4 and 6 rue Bourbon Le Chateau, 6e. ☎ *01-46-34-45-05 and 01-46-34-28-28. Métro: St-Germain-des Prés or Mabillon.*

Le Mouton à Cinq Pattes

Visit "the sheep with five legs" when you're feeling energetic — racks at this *dégriffé* store are simply packed and the store is often crowded. It carries extremely well-known designer names (most of the tags are ripped out) on women's, men's, and children's clothing, shoes, and accessories. The stock changes constantly, so if you see something you like, grab it; it won't be there the next time.

8 and 18 rue St-Placide, 6e. ☎ 01-45-48-86-26 for all stores. Métro: Sèvres-Babylone. Another branch is located at 138 bd. St-Germain (☎ 01-43-26-49-25).

Masculin Direct

This sizable men's store, located directly behind the BHV, carries sports and evening wear by Pierre Cardin, Bayard, and Guy Laroche, all at discounted prices. During the sales you can go mad here, but the rest of the time the store is yours, with shopkeepers that only make you feel comfortable as you browse for that perfect-color shirt.

18 rue des Archives, 4e. ☎ 01-42-77-16-56. Métro: Hôtel de Ville.

Mi-prix

This store, though at the edge of the city in the 15e, is worth the long trip: Karl Lagerfeld, Missoni, and Gianfranco Ferré are just some of the labels that are steeply discounted in this men's discount store.

27 bd. Victor, 15e. ☎ 01-48-28-42-48. Métro: Balard or Porte de Versailles.

Nip' Shop

Yves Saint Laurent, Sonia Rykiel, and Guy Laroche are big labels here, but lesser-known designers are also represented. It's in the same neighborhood as Réciproque (see the next listing), but much more intimate. Ask the smiling woman who runs this shop for suggestions and advice; she knows her wares and will find the item that has been waiting for you all along.

6 rue Edmond-About, 16e. ☎ 01-45-04-66-19. Métro: Rue de la Pompe.

Réciproque

This series of *depôt-ventes* (resale shops) on rue de la Pompe is the largest in Paris for men, women, and children. Exhaust yourself among the jewelry, furs, belts, antiques, scarves, and designer purses (Hermès, Dior, Gucci, and Louis Vuitton are just a few of the names I've seen). This store is for shoppers willing to spend upwards of $1,000 on a gently worn Chanel suit, less for other designers (a careful search can result in Hermès scarves and ties at a third of their normal price!). Midrange labels are also well represented.

88, 89, 92, 93, 95, and 101 rue de la Pompe, 16e. ☎ 01-47-04-30-28. No. 88 is a "gift shop" with small accessories and jewels, nos. 89–95 are the different categories of women's clothing and shoes, and the men's shop is exclusively at no. 101. Métro: Rue de la Pompe. Closed Mon.

Hitting the Great Shopping Neighborhoods

You don't need beaucoup bucks to afford to shop in Paris (except for certain stores in the 8e!). Great deals for every taste and dollar amount can be found. Read this section to get a significant head start in the hunt for that perfect item.

Haute Couture at Haute Costs: The 8e

Head for the 8e to see why people like Carrie Bradshaw and Saudi princes in need of a luxury shopping spree jet to Paris. Nearly every French designer is based on two streets — **avenue Montaigne** (Métro: Alma-Marceau, Franklin-D-Roosevelt) and **rue du Faubourg St-Honoré** (Métro: Concorde) — where sales bills of more than 1,000€ ($1,600) are expected, and snooty sales clerks are par for the course. You can still have a good time window-shopping here (and get an idea of what's in style), even if you don't have a platinum card.

Although avenue Montaigne and rue du Faubourg St-Honor boast some of the same big designer names, they are completely different in temperament. Avenue Montaigne is wide, graceful, lined with chestnut trees, and undeniably hip, attracting the likes of **Dolce & Gabbana** at no. 54 (☎ 01-42-25-68-78) and **Prada** at no. 10 (☎ 01-53-23-99-40). Other designers on this street include **Céline,** 36 av. Montaigne (☎ 01-56-89-07-92); **Chanel,** 42 av. Montaigne (☎ 01-47-23-74-12); **Christian Dior,** 30 av. Montaigne (☎ 01-40-73-73-73); **Ferragamo,** 45 av. Montaigne (☎ 01-47-23-36-37); **Giorgio Armani,** 18 av. Montaigne (☎ 01-42-61-55-09) **Gucci,** 60 av. Montaigne (☎ 01-56-69-80-80); **Nina Ricci,** 39 av. Montaigne (☎ 01-40-88-67-60); **Ungaro,** 2 av. Montaigne (☎ 01-53-57-00-00); and **Valentino,** 17 av. Montaigne (☎ 01-47-23-64-61).

Rue du Faubourg St-Honoré is jammed with shoppers walking along the small, narrow sidewalks. Begin at the rue Royale intersection and head west. **Prada** is located at no. 6 (☎ 01-58-18-63-30); **Yves St-Laurent** for women is at no. 38 (☎ 01-42-65-74-59), men at no. 32 (☎ 01-53-05-80-80). Other high quality or haute couture designers include **Gianni Versace** at 54 rue du Faubourg St-Honoré (☎ 01-47-42-55-31); **Givenchy,** 28 rue du Faubourg St-Honoré (☎ 01-42-68-31-00); **Dominique Sirop,** 14 rue Foubourge St-Honoré (☎ 01-42-66-60-57); **La Perla,** 20 rue du Faubourg St-Honoré (☎ 01-43-12-33-60); **Chloé,** 56 rue du Faubourg St-Honoré (☎ 01-44-94-33-00); **Sonia Rykiel,** 70 rue du Faubourg St-Honoré (☎ 01-42-65-20-81); **Pierre Cardin,** 59 rue du Faubourg St-Honoré (☎ 01-42-66-92-25); and **Missoni,** 1 rue du Faubourg-St-Honoré (☎ 01-44-51-96-96).

Funky and Unique: The 3e and 4e

There's something for everyone in the Marais: Divide your time between culture (15 different museums are right here) and commercialism in this beautiful neighborhood crammed with magnificent Renaissance mansions, artists' studios, secret courtyards, and some of the most original shops in the city. **Rue des Francs-Bourgeois** (Métro: St-Paul or

Rambuteau), the highlight of the area, is full of small shops selling everything from fashion to jewels. And its stores are open on Sunday! **Rue des Rosiers** (Métro: St-Paul) is a fashion destination in its own right, with hot designers flanking Jewish delis and falafel joints. Everything is really close in the Marais, so don't be afraid to ramble down the tiniest lane whenever whim dictates. Part of the fun of this neighborhood is that it's such a mixed (shopping) bag.

Marais highlights include **Paule Ka,** 20 rue Mahler (☎ 01-40-29-96-03), for the sort of 1960s clothing made famous by Grace Kelly, Jackie Onassis, and Audrey Hepburn; **Jacenko,** 38 rue de Poitou (☎ 01-42-71-80-38), for unique and immediately stylish menswear that is beautifully tailored and soft to the touch; **Autour du Monde,** 8 and 12 rue des Francs-Bourgeois (☎ 01-42-77-16-18), a clothing/housewares store devoted to the innovative style line Bensimon: find comfortable dresses, chic refurbished uniforms, delicate linen sheets, and inventive tableware; and **Antik Batik,** 8 rue Foin (☎ 01-48-87-95-95), a reasonably well-known French company featuring clothes inspired by numerous cultures. Browsing their racks is a transcontinental flight: Find African prints, wood beaded shirts and necklaces, as well as Chinese silk outfits and *salwar kameez* ensembles accompanied by Indian-pattern inspired scarves. Also check out **Zadig et Voltaire,** 16 rue Pavée (☎ 01-44-59-39-06), a subtle and charming favorite of the well-dressed yet casual Parisian. For the truly unusual, haute couture star **Issey Miyake,** 3 place des Vosges (☎ 01-48-87-01-86), features loose but structured clothing that screams "artist." Fashion victims of the emaciated and avant-garde (think black, white, and lots of sequins) should check out **Tsutsu** (70 rue Vieille du Temple, 3e; 01-42-71-16-02). Covering your feet, **Jean-Claude Monderer,** 22 rue des Francs Bourgeois (☎ 01-48-04-51-41), sells stylish men's and women's sneakers, loafers, and sleek and slender going-out shoes for both sexes, while more traditional men's shoes are at **Edouard de Seine,** 119 rue de Turenne (☎ 01-48-87-31-01), with another location at rue Meslay.

Chic and Sophisticated: The 6e

Stylish young professionals with old family (called *Bon Chic Bon Genre* or BCBG) call this, one of the prettiest areas in Paris, home. Here you can shop with the BCBG amid bookstores, art and antiques galleries, high-end designer clothing shops, decently priced shoe and accessories stores, and sophisticated and trendy boutiques. You won't go thirsty with famed literary hangouts such as **Café de Flore, Les Deux Magots,** and **Brasserie Lipp** nearby, and you may not even go broke — all price ranges are represented here.

Louis Vuitton has a huge luggage-specialized store behind Les Deux Magots on 6 place St-Germain (☎ 01-45-49-62-32), and **Christian Dior** is nearby at 16–18 rue de l'Abbaye (☎ 01-56-24-90-53). **Giorgio Armani** is at 149 bd. St-Germain (☎ 01-45-48-62-15); **Céline,** 58 rue de Rennes (☎ 01-45-48-58-55); and **Christian Lacroix,** 2-4 place St-Sulpice (☎ 01-46-33-48-95). Much more pleasing price-wise includes Italian designers

Stefanel, 54 rue de Rennes (☎ 01-45-44-06-07); **Comptoir des Cotonniers,** 59 Ter rue de Bonaparte (☎ 01-43-26-07-56); **Et Vous,** 69 rue de Rennes (☎ 01-40-49-05-10); and **Tara Jarmon,** 18 rue de Four (☎ 01-46-33-26-60). Also check out **Blanc et Bleu,** 28 rue Bonaparte (☎ 01-44-07-38-54); their yacht-appropriate clothing evokes sailing images; it is for anyone who loves boats. A similar store that sells the ubiquitous and authentic horizontal-striped sweaters of virile French sailors is **Saint James,** 66 rue de Rennes.

The Marché St-Germain at 14 rue Lobineau is a modern shopping mall that's a bit out of place in a neighborhood known for bookstores and upscale boutiques. Visit if you need to experience air-conditioning and use the restrooms; otherwise don't waste your time — why visit the Gap and Zara kids when the styles are the same at home but the prices higher?

Fierce and Youthful: The 2e

The 2nd arrondissement has a spread of different kinds of stores that cater to Paris's hip or *branché* (a synonym literally meaning "plugged in") and younger fashion crowd. The area sells a mix of high fashion, specialty niche stores, and discounted wares; you can find the Jean-Paul Gaultier boutique in the picturesque **Galerie Vivienne** on one end and Kookaï Le Stock on the other. The cheapest shopping is in the **Sentier area,** around the Sentier Métro stop, which is Paris's garment district, overlapping parts of the 3e and 1er. The best — but not the cheapest — shops are found within a square formed on the south by rue Rambuteau, on the west by rue du Louvre, on the north by rue Réamur, and on the east by rue St-Martin. This area is where you can find hip secondhand clothes, funky club wear, and *stock boutiques* selling last season's designs at a discount.

The neighborhood is considered to be chic and wealthy, but prostitutes still frequent the area later in the afternoon and evening, especially rue St-Denis.

For last year's unsold stock of women's and teen's clothing, visit **Kookaï Le Stock,** 82 rue Réamur, 2e (☎ 01-45-08-93-69). **Espace Kiliwatch,** 64 rue Tiquetonne, 2e (☎ 01-42-21-17-37), seems like a never-ending tour through decades of vintage clothing and styles, persistence may reward you with a bargain. Meanwhile the neighborhood mecca of club and design gurus is at **Kokon To Zai,** 48 rue Tiquetonne, 2e (☎ 01-42-36-92-41), selling well-known and emerging designer wear in a small store decorated in vibrant colors. **Anthony Peto,** 56 rue Tiquetonne, 2e (☎ 01-40-26-60-68), has sold hats of all styles and colors (from the chic and classy to the totally outrageous) in this location for 22 years. **Le Shop,** 3 rue d'Argout, 2e (☎ 01-40-28-18-38), sells two floors of club wear, skateboards, and CDs — often to new music spun by a live DJ. Those with a more sophisticated palate (and deeper pockets) can go to **Barbara Bui,** 23 rue Etienne-Marcel, 1er (☎ 01-40-26-43-65), for elegant, contemporary fashion. Youthful and fresh, but still respectably fashionable for men is **Chevignon,** 26 rue Etienne Marcel, 1er (☎ **01-42-33-60-20**). For haute couture sophistication with an edge, head to **Jean-Paul Gaultier,** 6 rue Vivienne (☎ **01-42-86-05-05**). Find men's, women's, and children's clothes at **agnès b** at 2, 3, 6, and 19, rue du Jour (☎ **01-40-39-96-88,** 01-42-33-04-13, 01-45-08-56-56, and 01-42-33-27-34, respectively). These carefully designed store sells timelessly chic and carefully detailed outfits, with plenty of choices for the whole family (the men's store is at no. 3, children's at no. 2, women's at no. 6, and accessories at no. 19).

Bohemia: The 18th
There is some kinship between the Marais and Montmartre fashion, but les Montmartrois (citizens of Montmartre), with their offbeat outfits and offbeat jobs (artists, musicians, writers), have a style that seems to come from other aesthetic eras. A lot of the stores around here feature chunky but organic jewelry or dangling Indian metal decoratives, and careful searching will provide boutiques selling soft leathers and carefully tailored tweed trousers, all next to flowing linens and funky, often impossibly shaped hats. There are many more bargain finds here than you would find in the Marais. The window shopping shouldn't be missed: Be sure to check out rue d'Orsel (one of the consignment shops features a snow-white cat, sleeping on the shoes you might buy), rue Lépic, and rue des Abbesses.

The arcades

You can't speak of shopping without mentioning Paris's quaint arcades. In the 19th century, people, horses, and carriages crowded unpaved, dirty, badly lit streets. When it rained, everything turned to mud. Imagine shopping in these conditions! But one 19th-century shopkeeper looking for innovative ways to draw crowds to his store proposed displaying wares in pretty covered passageways with other merchants. And thus, the first malls were born. These days, the charming iron and glass arcades are still shopping havens, and the 2e has Paris's greatest concentration, each with its own character.

✔ **Passage Choiseul,** 44 rue des Petits-Champs (Métro: Quatre-Septembre), dates from 1827 and is the longest and most colorful arcade, selling discount shoes and clothing and used books. French writer Céline grew up here and included it in the books *Journey to the End of Night* and *Death on the Installment Plan.*

✔ **Passage des Panoramas,** 11 bd. Montmartre and 10 rue St-Marc (Métro: Grands Boulevards), opened in 1800 and was enlarged with the addition of galleries Variétés, St-Marc, Montmartre, and Feydeau in 1834. Its stores sell stamps, clothes, and gifts, and it's the passage with the largest choice of dining options: Korean food, a cafeteria, tea salons, and bistros.

✔ **Passage Jouffroy,** across the street at 10 bd. Montmartre (Métro: Grands Boulevards), was built between 1845 and 1846. It became an instant hit as Paris's first heated gallery. After an extensive restoration of its tile floors, the gallery now houses a variety of arty boutiques, including a dollhouse store, and an Italian cafe that sells fancy kitchen gizmos such as espresso machines and vacuum-pump wine stoppers.

✔ **Passage Verdeau,** 31 bis rue du Faubourg-Montmartre (Métro: Le Peletier), was built at the same time as its neighbor, Passage Jouffroy. You can find old prints, movie stills, books, and postcards here.

✔ **Galerie Vivienne,** 4 place des Petits-Champs, 5 rue de la Banque, or 6 rue Vivienne (Métro: Bourse), is hands down the most gorgeous of all the arcades. Its classical friezes, mosaic floors, and graceful arches have been beautifully restored. Built in 1823, this neoclassical arcade is now a national monument that attracts upscale art galleries, hair salons, and boutiques, including Jean-Paul Gaultier.

✔ **Galerie Colbert** is linked to the adjoining Galerie Vivienne. It was built with a large rotunda and decorated in Pompeian style in 1826 to capitalize on the success of Galerie Vivienne.

✔ The pretty **Passage du Grand Cerf,** 10 rue Dussoubs (Métro: Etienne-Marcel), has more of a modern bent, with jewelry designers, trendy clothing stores, furniture stores with funky, "ethnic-inspired" pieces, decorative tchotchkes, and an ad agency.

For a complete change of pace, head over to the following arcades, but keep in mind that the neighborhoods aren't the nicest. The **Passage Brady,** 46 rue du Faubourg St-Denis (Métro: Strasbourg St-Denis), has become an exotic bazaar where Indian restaurants and spice shops scent the air. The passage opened in 1828. The **Passage du Caire,** 2 place du Caire (Métro: Sentier), is one of the oldest arcades built in 1798 to commemorate Napoléon's triumphant entry into Cairo. It reflects the Egyptomania of the time with fake columns and death masks of pharaohs on its exterior. In the heart of Paris's Sentier garment district, it's home to clothing wholesalers and manufacturers.

The walking tour in Chapter 13 passes practically all of the boutiques listed here!

Passé Devant, 62 rue d'Orsel (☎ 01-42-33-41-40), is a high-demand (its number is unlisted) *depot-vente* or consignment shop that sells women's attire from couture lines or talented but discontinued boutique designers. Bargains are hit or miss. Discover **Heaven,** 83 rue des Martyrs (☎ 01-44-92-92-92), where co-owner and designer Jean-Christopher Peyrieux is one of the few Parisian boutique owners who is present to help his clients pick out the perfectly divine outfits for men and women. **Jo.,** at 47 rue d'Orsel (☎ 01-55-79-99-16), has slim-cut menswear from Emile Lafaurie (the best slacks in the city with reasonable price tags); **Jérémie Barthod,** 7 rue des Trois Frères (☎ 01-42-62-54-50), features unique costume jewelry — if twisted metal and glass beads could grow naturally out of the ground, this is how they would look. **Spree,** 16 Rue La Vieuville (☎ 01-42-33-41-40), is much larger than it seems, inconspicuously tucked away on a twisty street. Find good deals on the latest fashions from Marc Jacobs and some smaller designers. **Le Diable et Moi,** 29 rue des Abbesses (☎ 01-42-55-40-43), has hip and somewhat expensive attire, including ironic T-shirts and short skirts primarily for hipster chicks; while **Colline,** 20 rue des Abbesses (☎ 01-42-58-54-63), is the place to get timeless cashmere sweaters, plush jackets, dresses, and blouses with beautifully detailed and colorful prints.

Shopping in Paris from A (ntiques) to W (ine)

Listed here are some of the best stores representing both economy and first-class shopping in the City of Light.

Antiques

Le Louvre des Antiquaires

This enormous mall is filled with all kinds of shops selling everything from silverware to sketches by famous artists to Louis XIV furniture. Items are pricey, but rumors have it that some good deals exist here. A cafe and toilets are located on the second floor.

2 place du Palais-Royal, 1er. ☎ *01-42-97-27-27. Métro: Palais-Royal-Musée du Louvre.*

Le Village St-Paul

This indoor-outdoor arts and antiques fair was once a 17th-century village. Its shops display paintings, antiques, and other items, both inside and in the courtyard. It's easy to walk past the entrances, so look for the signs just inside the narrow passageways between the houses on rue St-Paul, rue Jardins St-Paul, and rue Charlemagne. Keep in mind that this is a very popular destination on the weekend. Closed Tuesday and Wednesday.

23–27 rue St-Paul, 4e. No phone. Métro: St-Paul.

Bookstores

Gibert Joseph

Gibert Joseph is *the* Parisian students' bookstore, selling new and second-hand books, records, videos, and stationery on several floors and in several branches on boulevard St-Michel. If you're looking to learn some basic French vocabulary or grammar, there are small practice textbooks for English-speakers at rock-bottom prices. Late September, when students at some of the nearby colleges buy their textbooks, it can get very crowded.

26 and 30 bd. St-Michel, 6e. ☎ *01-44-41-88-88. Métro: Odéon or Cluny-Sorbonne.*

Librarie Eyrolles

This convenient and charming bookstore has an extensive selection of books on every topic imaginable, as well as stationery, fancy pens, and even books in English, Spanish, and a handful of other languages. Its selling point for voyagers is the useful visitor information, like maps and neighborhood guides, and a whole assortment of gifts to bring home, including Paris flip-books for the kids and coffee-table book souvenirs for the grown-ups.

55, 57, 61, and 63 bd. St-Germain, 6e. ☎ 01-44-41-11-74. www.eyrolles.com. *Métro: Maubert-Mutualité.*

Librarie La Hune

Sandwiched between cafes Les Deux Magots and de Flore, this bookstore has been a center for Left Bank intellectuals since 1945 when Sartre was among its clients. Most books are in French. It's open until midnight every night except Sunday.

170 bd. St-Germain, 6e. ☎ 01-45-48-35-85. Métro: St-Germain.

Mona Lisait

The French hold their independent lifestyle very dear, and chain bookstores don't play a big part of the culture. Mona Lisait (a play-on-words of the famous painting by Da Vinci, it translates as "Mona was reading") is one of the chains, but one I find acceptable because its stores always have a great number of used books available — and the new ones are often on sale. Some of the used books are barely touched and you're sure to find a bargain on some beautiful editions of famous works.

9 rue St-Martin, 4e. ☎ 01-42-74-03-02. Métro: Rambuteau. Other locations at 7 bd. Bonne Nouvelle, 2e, ☎ 01-42-33-69-27, Métro: Bonne Nouvelle; and 39 rue Jussieu, 5e, ☎ 01-40-51-81-22, Métro: Jussieu.

The Red Wheelbarrow

Founded by Canadian bookseller Penelope Fletcher Le Masson in 2001, this cozy English-language bookstore not far from Le Village St-Paul (see "Antiques" earlier) stocks primarily contemporary and classic literature, with novels translated from French, general nonfiction, including a wide range of Paris- and France-related titles, and an extensive children's section. They also carry some French-English bilingual books and stories set in France.

22 rue St. Paul, 4e. ☎ 01-48-04-75-08. Métro: St. Paul.

Shakespeare and Company

No, this *isn't* the original (that was on rue l'Odéon), but English-speaking residents of Paris and backpackers still gather in this wonderfully dark and cluttered store, named after Sylvia Beach's legendary literary lair and run more and more these days by owner George Whitman's daughter, Sylvia Beach Whitman. There is a selection of new books, but most books are used. Backpackers and willing travelers can sleep in beds among the stacks, while working during the day to pay for a good night's sleep. A fat black cat lives there as well and has been sleeping on the same desk on the second level each time I visited — you can pet him, he's friendly. Note: Poetry readings are held on Sundays.

37 rue de la Bûcherie, 5e. ☎ *01-43-25-40-93. Métro or RER: St-Michel.*

Village Voice

Quality fiction in English is the highlight of this small two-level store in St-Germain-des-Prés, along with an excellent selection of poetry, plays, non-fiction, and literary magazines. Owner Odile Hellier has been hosting free poetry and prose readings with celebrated authors and poets since 1982, and this is a wonderful place to attend an English-language reading. (Check *Paris Free Voice* for readings.)

6 rue Princesse, 6e. ☎ *01-46-33-36-47. Métro: Mabillon or St-Germain.*

Ceramics, china, and glass

Baccarat

This famous crystal production house and museum used to be located at a landmark building at 30 rue de Paradis. However the museum, boutique, restaurant, and general quarters have moved to place des Etats-Unis in the 16e, a much more chic location. Several other boutiques throughout Paris sell this famous brand of crystal, for which one will pay dearly.

11 place des Etats-Unis, 16e. ☎ *01-40-22-11-00, museum,* ☎ *01-40-22-11-22, boutique. Métro: Boissière.*

La Maison Ivre

The Left Bank between St-Germain-des-Prés and the Seine is the unofficial antiques and art gallery district, and this store sits right in the district's heart. It carries an excellent selection of handmade pottery from across France, emphasis on the Provence region, and ceramics from southern France. You can purchase beautiful, well-made pieces of ovenware, bowls, platters, plates, pitchers, mugs, and vases.

38 rue Jacob, 6e. ☎ *01-42-60-32-88. Métro: St-Germain-des-Prés.*

Lumicristal

For discounted crystal by Daum, Limoges, and Baccarat, Lumicristal is the place to shop.

22 bis rue de Paradis, 10e. ☎ *01-42-46-60-29.* www.lumicristal.com. *Métro: Château-d'Eau, Poissonnière, or Gare-de-l'Est.*

Clothing for children

Du Pareil au Même

Du Pareil au Même is *the* place to buy clothes for every child on your list —
clothes are practical, *très mignons* (very cute), and very reasonably priced.
1 rue St-Denis, 1er. ☎ *01-42-36-07-57.* www.dpam.com. *Métro: Châtelet. Many
branches are located throughout the city.*

Jacadi

When BCBG women (see the "Chic and Sophisticated: The 6e" section earlier in this chapter) have children, Jacadi is where they buy their very
proper children's clothes that feature rich fabrics and such gorgeous
touches as hand-done smocking and pretty fabrics.
256 bd. St-Germain, 7e. ☎ *01-42-84-30-40.* www.jacadi.com. *Métro: Suferino.
Many branches are located throughout the city.*

Natalys

Part of a French chain with a dozen stores in Paris, Natalys sells children's
wear, maternity wear, and related products.
74 rue de Rivoli, 1er. ☎ *01-40-29-46-35. Métro: Hôtel de Ville. Other branches include
69 rue de Clichy, 9e,* ☎ *01-48-74-07-44; and 47 rue de Sèvres, 6e,* ☎ *01-45-48-77-12.*

Petit Bateau

For years, women in the know have been stocking up on T-shirts from this
very cute (and somewhat expensive) brand of clothing that uses simple
patterns and color pairings to give a sense of delightful and well-made simplicity. The signature "little boat" icons grace the front of their tops or
attach via little side-labels — anyone can feel like a small French kid chas-
ing pigeons through the Jardins de Luxembourg. I say *anyone* because Petit
Bateau, originally designed with infants, toddlers, and young children in
mind, now carries the same fun little-kid styles sized for adults!
24 rue Cler, 7e. ☎ *01-47-05-18-51.* www.petit-bateau.com. *Métro: La Tour
Maubourg. Another branch can be found at 116 av. des Champs-Elysées, 8e.* ☎ *01-
40-74-02-03. Métro: George V.*

Tartine et Chocolat

This store features more typically French, precious, and pricey clothes.
105 rue du Faubourg-St-Honoré, 8e. ☎ *01-45-62-44-04. Métro: Concorde. Another
branch is located at 266 bd. St-Germain, 7e.* ☎ *01-45-56-10-45.*

Clothing for men

Celio

Dressing like a youthful Parisian man doesn't have to kill your wallet. I often call Celio "the French Gap," which refers to their prices and their menswear — shirts, polos, button-down pants, belts, jackets, and so forth — basically everything that Gap sells but with a specifically French twist of small details and a bit more flair than the Gap would sell. Celio has over 20 locations in Paris, but some carry limited lines of their wares. Listed below are some of the bigger ones.

66 bd. du Montparnasse, 14e. ☎ *01-45-38-90-03. Other boutiques are found at 65 rue de Rivoli, 1e,* ☎ *01-42-21-18-04; and 4 rue Halèvy, 9e,* ☎ *01-42-68-30-60.*

Chevignon

This fashionable men's store gives fashion-forward looks that have industrial detailing and nice colors that follow season trends *de la mode*. A chain that's sold in many countries, it's almost impossible to find in the United States, and when you do it's heavily marked up. Ironically, printed text on the clothing is often in English. Check out their scarves, sweaters, and zip-ups that are very slimming and very French-looking.

26 rue Etienne Marcel, 2e. ☎ *01-42-33-60-20. Métro: Etienne Marcel.*

Façonnable

For quality shirts in nearly every color and casual pants, in addition to jackets, suits, and other men's finery (all a bit on the conservative side), Façonnable is the place. In the United States, Nordstrom carries some of Façonnable's fashions, but this store has the entire line.

9 rue du Faubourg-St-Honoré, 8e. ☎ *01-47-42-72-60. Métro: Madeleine or Concorde. Another branch is located at 174 bd. St-Germain, 6e.* ☎ *01-40-49-02-47.*

Madelios

This huge store offers one-stop shopping for men, selling everything from overcoats to lighters to luggage. If companions get bored waiting, the store is part of a small mall that has some nice stores for browsing.

23 bd. de la Madeleine, 1er. ☎ *01-53-45-00-00. Métro: Madeleine.*

S.D. Spontini

Looking like the urbane, ultra-Parisian man doesn't have to be difficult: S.D. Spontini has several boutiques throughout the city and boasts reasonable prices for very fashionable menswear. These boutiques sport funky button-down shirts good for drinks in lounges or sitting around in a cafe. They also sell trendy shoes, belts, and those rib-textured sweaters French men wear at almost any time of the year.

29 rue des Francs Bourgeois, 4e. ☎ *01-44-78-70-71. Métro: St-Paul.*

Ted Baker

This is the Paris branch of the London designer and sells relaxed dressy and casual clothes with little details (like large French cuffs or a wild pattern lining the collar) that set this brand apart.

20 rue des Francs Bourgeois, 3e. ☎ *01-44-54-02-98. Métro: St-Paul.*

Clothing for teens and the young-at-heart

Antoine et Lili

If you're strolling the quays of the hip Canal St-Martin, have a peek into this magenta-themed store selling youngish bohemian clothes and accessories, and decorations that look great in dorm rooms or kitschy apartments. Some fun items include picture frames made from colorful scrap metal, or funky notebooks bound with hand-made paper. A garden and small canteen also are located here.

95 quai Valmy, 10e. ☎ *01-40-37-41-55. Métro: Gare de l'Est. Another branch can be found at 90 rue des Martyrs, 18e,* ☎ *01-42-58-10-22.*

Cop-Copine

Cutting-edge and flattering, Cop-Copine makes great youthful clothes that enhance your good parts and disguise your not-as-good ones.

80 rue Rambuteau, 2e. ☎ *01-40-28-49-72. Métro: Les Halles. RER: Châtelet-Les Halles.*

H&M

Hennes & Mauritz, the Swedish "IKEA of fashion," has a large selection of up-to-the-minute men's and women's fashion at very low prices. This is where you run to get the latest Prada copy — the store markets to the fashion conscious. Due to its huge popularity, big fashion names like Karl Lagerfeld and Stella McCartney have created lines for H&M, and in 2008 Japanese couture house Comme des Garçons took the lead at this "fashion for all" equalizer.

120 rue de Rivoli, 1er. ☎ *01-55-34-96-86. Métro: Hôtel-de-Ville or Louvre-Rivoli.*

Mango

With locations throughout the city, this store is popular with young Parisian women for its inexpensive, fashion-conscious, body-hugging (sometimes tacky) clothes.

82 rue de Rivoli,1er. ☎ *01-44-59-80-37. Métro: Hôtel-de-Ville or Louvre-Rivoli.*

Morgan

Form-fitting suits, dresses, and casual wear in synthetics and blends can be found at low prices for young women here.

92 av. Champs-Elysées, 6e. ☎ *01-43-59-83-72. Métro: George V.*

Zara

Zara offers well-made copies of today's hottest styles for women, men, and children at extremely low prices. Expect bargains galore during the January and July sales.

128 rue de Rivoli, 1er. ☎ *01-44-54-20-42. Métro: Hôtel-de-Ville or Louvre-Rivoli. Locations all over the place, including 44 av. Champs-Elysées, 8e,* ☎ *01-45-61-52-81; and 45 rue de Rennes, 6e,* ☎ *01-44-39-03-50.*

Clothing for women

Cacharel

Beautiful women's, children's, and men's clothes are featured at Cacharel, some in pretty Liberty-flower printed fabrics. A Cacharel overstock boutique is at 114 rue Alésia, 14e (☎ **01-45-42-53-04**).

64 rue Bonaparte, 6e. ☎ *01-40-46-00-45. Métro: Saint-Sulpice.*

Colette

This is Paris's most cutting-edge clothing store, and everything from designer clothes to cameras and beauty products is artistically arranged. You can also find artsy tchotchkes, art magazines, and avant-garde coffee-table books. Even if you don't buy (the prices are astronomical), just looking is fun and you can break for a snack or drink from one of the extensive selection of waters at the basement Water Bar.

213 rue St-Honoré, 1er. ☎ *01-55-35-33-95. Métro: Tuileries.*

Comptoir des Cotonniers

This well-known designer has branches in the major department stores as well as its own boutiques scattered around the city. Clothes are fashionable without being too cutting-edge and made well from cotton, wool, or silk. Their numerous boutiques market to women from young to middle aged. Styles, though not timeless, will last a few seasons at home.

33 rue des Francs-Bourgeois, 4e. ☎ *01-42-76-95-33.* www.comptoirdes cotonniers.com. *Métro: St-Paul. Over 20 additional locations throughout the city.*

Etam

Women's clothing at Etam is made mostly from synthetic or synthetic-blend fabrics, but the fashions are recent, and the stores are simply *everywhere*. Etam's lingerie, sold in regular Etam stores and separately at Etam Lingerie, has the best deals on pretty and affordable nightclothes and underwear.

17 rue de l'Arrivée, 1er. ☎ *01-43-27-03-04. Métro: Pont Neuf. There's an Etam Lingerie at 135 rue de Rennes, 6e.* ☎ *01-45-44-16-88.*

Franck et Fils

Franck et Fils is not a simple boutique: It is a mini department store of high-class fashion, located in the snobby-chic 16e arrondissement village of Passy. Catering to women only, one can pick up here such luxuries as Chanel suits, new couture creations, fur-lined gloves, and beautiful hair accessories, as well as elaborate hats, feather headbands, handbags, and more. A staple shopping destination for chic Parisians.

80 rue de Passy, 16e. ☎ *01-44-14-38-00. Métro: La Muette.*

Gelati

Paris is home to exquisite shoe designers such as Christian Louboutin, Robert Clergerie, and Maude Frizon, but if you can't afford their high, high prices, come to this fun shoe store that carries styles inspired by top designers but doesn't reflect their couture prices.

6 rue St-Sulpice, 6e. ☎ *01-43-25-67-44. Métro: Mabillon.*

La City

The clothes sold in numerous boutiques across Paris are perfect for work or for going out to dinner, and young women are the target audience. Although everything is synthetic, the prices are reasonable.

37 rue Chaussée d'Antin, 9e. ☎ *01-48-74-41-00. Métro: Chaussée d'Antin.*

1-2-3

Like La City, 1-2-3 targets young women looking for stylish suits, blouses, and sweaters to wear to work and *après* (after). Most clothes are synthetics or synthetic blends; clothing and accessories are sold at moderate prices.

146 rue de Rivoli, 1er. ☎ *01-40-20-97-01. Métro: Louvre-Rivoli. Other branches around the city.*

Rodier

For quality, stylish knitwear, Rodier is the upscale choice. Prices are high for ready-to-wear, but you can often find good bargains during the sales.

46 rue Notre-Dames des Champs, 6e. ☎ *01-42-84-40-37. Métro: Ternes. Other branches include 27 rue Tronchet, 8e.* ☎ *01-45-01-79-88.*

Shoe Bizz

Here you will find the latest well-made fashions for your feet at budget-friendly prices.

42 rue Dragon, 6e. ☎ *01-45-44-93-50. Métro: Ternes. Another branch is at 48 rue de Beaubourg, 3e.* ☎ *01-48-87-12-73.*

Crafts

Viaduc des Arts

When the elevated railroad cutting across the 12e was transformed into the Promenade Plantée, the space beneath was redesigned to accommodate a long stretch of artisan shops, galleries, furniture stores, and craft boutiques. Some of the glasswork artists here are absolutely superb. If you plan to visit the Bois de Vincennes via the Promenade Plantée, duck in for a look on any day except Sunday, when it's closed. The Viaduc Café here (43 av. Daumensil) is a pleasant place for a light bite or a glass of wine.

9–147 av. Daumensil, 12e. Métro: Bastille, Lédru-Rollin, Reuilly-Diderot, or Gare-de Lyon.

Food

A La Mère de Famille

What other city has a candy store with over 240 years of experience? Founded in 1861, this store sells the best chocolates, jams, herbal teas, sweet bonbons, candied fruits, and everything you know you shouldn't eat but will anyway. Still in its original location on a picturesque corner near Montmartre, try the rhubarb jam and pick up some candied chocolates that look exactly like olives. Of course, everything is fantastic, so a simple entry to inhale the perfume of a classic French candy store is the best way to begin.

35 rue du Faubourg Montmartre, 9e. ☎ 01-47-70-83-69. Métro: Cadet or Grands Boulevards.

Fauchon

Paris's original gourmet store is still going strong, opening small branches all over the city. This is its flagship store, and here the signature pink-labeled cans of coffee, caviar, foie gras, biscuits, wines, oils, candy, and pastries fight for beautifully organized shelf space. If you're in the area, take a peek inside if only for its long history. Split into two parts, one section carries the many prepackaged gourmet delights, clearly meant to be gifts; the other carries staples. But save your shopping for other, cheaper grocery stores that may stock, incidentally, some of Fauchon's products. Its tea salon is next door.

26 place Madeleine, 8e. ☎ 01-70-39-38-00. Métro: Madeleine.

Hédiard

Across the street from rival Fauchon is Hédiard, a gourmet food shop that sells most of the same products as Fauchon, but packaged in red and black stripes. Hédiard is slightly cheaper than Fauchon and has good prepared hot and cold food. If you must have foie gras with your baguette, then Hédiard is one of the places you can count on finding it. Branches are located throughout the city.

21 place de la Madeleine, 8e. ☎ 01-43-12-88-88. Métro: Madeleine.

JSFP Traiteur

If you're visiting the rue de Buci market, have a look inside this store (originally known as Jacques Papin) if only to salivate over some of the most exquisite foods you may ever see, including trout in aspic, fine pâtés and salads, lobsters, and smoked salmon. The name has changed, but the quality remains the same in this busy pedestrian street in the Latin Quarter.

8 rue de Buci, 6e. ☎ *01-43-26-86-09. Métro: Odéon.*

Lafayette Gourmet

They keep this large, well-stocked supermarket well hidden in the men's building at Galeries Lafayette. Once you find it, you'll discover it's a terrific spot to browse for gifts or for yourself. It has a good selection of wines, and the house-brand merchandise, often cheaper than other labels, is of very good quality. Eat at the prepared-food counters or sit at the small bar for a glass of wine.

40 bd. Haussmann, 9e. (Enter through the men's dept. of Galeries Lafayette. It's on the mezzanine level, accessed by an escalator.) ☎ *01-42-82-34-56. Métro: Chaussée-d'Antin.*

La Grande Epicerie de Paris (at Le Bon Marché)

This is one of the best luxury (meaning it's not cheap) supermarkets in Paris and a great place to look for gourmet gifts, such as olive oils, homemade chocolates, fresh pastas, and wine. Food is artfully arranged in glass cases, and the produce is some of the freshest around. It makes for wonderful one-stop picnic shopping, too, offering a wide array of prepared foods and cheeses and terrific snack food (some of it from the U.S.!).

38 rue de Sèvres, 7e. ☎ *01-44-39-81-00. Métro: Sèvres-Babylone.*

La Maison du Chocolat

Each candy here is made from a blend of as many as six kinds of South American and African chocolate, flavored with just about everything imaginable. The salespeople here know everything there is about mixing chocolates and their fillings; ask them to help you with an assortment if you think you can contain yourself from stuffing them in your mouth all at once! Possibly the classiest chocolate shop ever, the man selling ice cream at the exterior of the shop wears a full suit, even during mid-July.

225 rue du Faubourg-St-Honoré, 8e. ☎ *01-42-27-39-44. Métro: Ternes. Another branch is at 52 rue François Premier, 8e.* ☎ *01-47-23-38-25.*

La Maison du Miel

For an unusual but very welcome gift, try bringing back some French honey from this little shop. It has more than 40 varieties of honey you never dreamed possible (pine tree or lavender), identified according to the flower to which the bees were exposed. Honey being the favored refreshments of the Greek gods, Zeus would have approved of this fine shop!

24 rue Vignon, 9e. ☎ *01-47-42-26-70. Métro: Madeleine or Havre-Caumartin.*

L'Epicerie de Bruno

In his recently opened spice store and gourmet grocery, Bruno, the owner and creative director, hopes to broaden the palate of Parisians by introducing specially made curries, rare and particular spices, and impossible to find chilies from around the world. The spices are well organized and beautifully packaged; these would make a great gift for your gourmet friend who couldn't make it to Paris with you.

30 rue Tiquetonn, 2e. ☎ *01-53-40-87-33. Métro: Etienne Marcel.*

Gifts and jewelry

Biche de Bère

Chunky and unusual jewelry in sterling silver and gold plate can be found here.

15 rue des Innocents, 1er. ☎ *01-40-28-94-47. Métro: Châtelet.*

Bijoux Burma

To make others whisper "Are they real or aren't they?", visit Bijoux Burma for some of the best costume jewelry in the city. (You can always reply: "They're real and they're *fabulous!*")

50 rue François 1er, 8e. ☎ *01-47-23-70-93. Métro: Franklin-D-Roosevelt. Other branches are at 8 bd. des Capucines, 9e,* ☎ *01-42-66-27-09; and 249 rue St. Honoré, 1er,* ☎ *01-42-60-06-27.*

La Chaise Longue

This bi-level gift shop is open on Sunday (when it gets very crowded) and is simply bursting at the seams with cool gifts such as dinnerware, designer teapots, three-dimensional picture frames, patterned drinking glasses, bath towels with fun prints, among many, many other things. It's very reasonably priced and definitely worth a visit — this is one of those stores where you find something you didn't know existed but cannot live without.

20 rue des Francs Borgeois, 3e. ☎ *01-48-04-36-37. Métro: St-Paul. Another location is at 8 rue Princesse, 6e.* ☎ *01-43-29-62-39. Métro: St Michel.*

Monic

There's so much to look at in this store in the Marais — open Sunday afternoons — that it's overwhelming! Here awaits a wide range of affordable costume jewelry and designer creations, many at discount prices.

5 rue des Francs-Bourgeois, 4e. ☎ *01-42-72-39-15. Métro: St-Paul. Another location can be found at 14 rue de l'Ancienne-comédie, 6e.* ☎ *01-43-25-36-61. Métro: Odéon.*

Pylones

These boutiques sell Simpsons and Tintin collectibles, children's umbrellas that stand on their own, bicycle bells shaped like ladybugs, pastel-colored toasters, back massagers shaped like octopi, and a variety of other unusual and brightly colored gift items. It's a fun place to browse.

57 rue de St-Louis-en-l'Ile, 4e. ☎ *01-46-34-05-02. Métro: Cité. Branches at 7 rue Tardieu, 18e,* ☎ *01-46-06-37-00, and 13 rue Ste-Croix de la Bretonnerie, 4e,* ☎ *01-48-04-80-10.*

Takara

For the funky, big-earring-wearing, fashionable pseudo-hippie in your life, Takara (formerly Kazana) will undoubtedly provide a fun and colorful keepsake. This chain of stores carries fashion accessories including colorful scarves (handmade in Central America, West Africa, and Southeast Asia), a huge assortment of bracelets, necklaces, and dangly earrings made of materials such as wood and seashells; also look for decorated pocketbook mirrors, glasses cases, and other hand-luggage-sized tokens from across the globe. Gift-wrapped in happy fuchsia- and magenta-colored packaging, Takara is surprisingly inexpensive.

67 rue St-Martin, 5e. ☎ *01-48-87-49-65. Métro: Hôtel de Ville. Another boutique can be found at 4 rue Yvonne le tac, 18e.* ☎ *01-55-79-98-47. Métro: Abbesses.*

Home and housewares

Alessi

Alessi offers bright and affordable kitchen implements, such as magnetized salt and pepper shakers and dish scrubbers that look a bit *human*. You can find some cutlery, dishes, and linens, too. Check out the Mr. Suicide drain plug — a yellow man chained to a blue stopper that floats to the surface when you take a bath.

31 rue Boissy d'Anglas, 8e. ☎ *01-42-66-14-61. Métro: Madéleine or Concorde.*

BHV

I've already listed the BHV once in this chapter but it has some of the best selection and prices in the entire city for house and kitchenware. Head up to the fourth floor (niveau 3) to pick up any kind of kitchen item from marked down Le Creuset sauté pans to champagne flutes and the perfect garlic press. Stop in the basement level for the *cave* (wine cellar) section, which sells all sorts of fun toys for oenophiles, including pretty and functional wine stoppers.

52 rue de Rivoli, 1er. ☎ *01-42-74-90-00. Métro: Hôtel de Ville.*

Cedre Rouge

Cedre Rouge sells that urban rustic look made with natural materials for the garden or terrace, apartment, or country home. It isn't cheap, but you can find some unusual gifts (like cute, but tiny, snail candleholders for 20€/$32). Finds include Tuscan pottery, Irish linen tablecloths and napkins, Murano glass, teak and wicker furniture, beeswax candles, and surprisingly lifelike synthetic plants.

22 av. Victoria, 1e. ☎ *01-42-33-71-05. Métro: Châtelet.*

Conforama

This huge store sells everything for your home at reasonable prices: furniture, appliances, garden tools and accessories, and everyday china and glass. Check out their selection of kitchen tools: It always boggles my mind how many different gadgets the French have available for making delicious food.

2 rue de Pont-Neuf, 1er. ☎ *01-42-33-37-09. Métro: Pont Neuf.*

Déhillerin

Filled with high-quality copper cookware, glasses, dishes, china, gadgets, utensils, ramekins, pots, and kitchen appliances, this place makes cooks go wild — especially because the prices are discounted. With the current rate of exchange, don't be surprised when you find out how much a discounted price still turns out to be!

18 rue Coquillière, 1er. ☎ *01-42-36-53-13.* www.e-dehillerin.fr. *Métro: Les Halles.*

La Vaissellerie

These boutiques are always crammed full of very cute and inexpensive white porcelain tableware, as well as clever postcards, placemats, and tablecloths in check-patterns or simple Provençal designs (think yellow and blue borders with pictures of olives and jugs). Don't miss the unique spice containers, labeled jars for *farine* and *sucre* (flour and sugar) — essentially anything you could need for a cute French kitchen. I suggest as a gift a set of espresso cups because they are easily portable and have fun designs.

92 rue St-Antoine, 4e. ☎ *01-42-72-76-77. Métro: St-Paul. Another location is at 85 rue de Rennes, 6e.* ☎ *01-42-22-51-49. Métro: Rennes or Montparnasse Bienvenue.*

Verrerie des Halles

The restaurant industry buys its china, glassware, furniture, and other supplies here, and you can, too, at discount prices.

15 rue du Louvre, 1er. ☎ *01-42-36-80-60. Métro: Louvre-Rivoli.*

Toys

Au Nain Bleu

FAO Schwarz in Manhattan emulated this, the world's fanciest toy store. Translated as "at the blue dwarf's," for more than 150 years Au Nain Bleu has been selling toy soldiers, stuffed animals, games, and puppets in a gorgeous space. More modern toys are also on hand, including airplanes and model cars. After over a century in its location on rue Faubourg St-Honoré, in 2007 the store moved to its new location on boulevard Malesherbes, near le parc Monceau. Obviously, this would be a terrific place to bring your kids!

5 bd. Malesherbes, 8e. ☎ 01-42-65-20-00. Métro: Villiers or Monceau.

Fnac Eveil & Jeux

An outpost of the Fnac chain, Fnac Eveil & Jeux sells books, videos, and music for children, and has story hours and other activities for its young guests.

19 rue Vavin, 6e. ☎ 01-56-24-03-46. Métro: Vavin.

Galeries Lafayette

Floor 4 of the Galeries Lafayette main store is devoted to toys and children's clothing, and there's a play area kids love.

40 bd. Haussmann, 9e. ☎ 01-56-24-03-46. Métro: Havre-Caumartin, Chaussée-d'Antin-La Fayette, Opéra, or Trinité.

Wine

La Cave des Martyrs

Written on the window of this store is *Les Cavistes Pas Ordinaires,* which translated reads "not your ordinary wine store." The friendly staff members here have an extensive knowledge of wine and are not shy at all with customers. Definitely ask them for help because they will pick you out something fantastic in any price range. For extended trips, they offer quarterly wine-tasting courses. They also carry spirits, liquors, and champagne, of course.

39 rue des Martyrs, 9e. ☎ 01-40-16-80-27. Métro: Notre-Dame de Lorette.

Legrand Filles et Fils

In addition to fine wines, this store stocks brandies, chocolates, coffees, and oenophile (wine-lover) paraphernalia. It also conducts wine tastings one night a week.

1 rue de la Banque, 2e. ☎ 01-42-60-07-12. Métro: Bourse.

Les Caves Augé

This is the oldest wine shop in Paris with a sommelier (wine steward) on site who can advise you on the vintage French and international wines this store carries. If you're looking for something delightful, you'll be very pleased; if you're looking for delightfully inexpensive, you may have a bit of trouble.

116 bd. Haussmann, 8e. ☎ *01-45-22-16-97. Métro: St-Augustin.*

Nicolas

This Nicolas is the flagship store of the almost 125-year-old wine chain that has more than 110 branches in and around Paris. It offers good prices for bottles you may not be able to find in the United States. Look for the maroon or wine-colored facade with yellow lettering; if you're going on a picnic, you can always depend on Nicolas.

31 place de la Madeleine, 8e. ☎ *01-42-68-00-16. Métro: Madeleine.*

Chapter 13

Following an Itinerary

In This Chapter

▶ Visiting for three days
▶ Staying for five days
▶ Taking a tour of the Marais

*W*ith so much to see in Paris, where do you start first? The itineraries in this chapter help you figure it out. Branch out and explore Paris's interesting alleyways and pretty green spaces, which you'll encounter all around you. That is what is so much fun about Paris: It reveals itself in all kinds of ways.

Making the Most of Paris in Three Days

On **Day One,** start early by having coffee and croissants at a cafe or pick up a pastry at a *boulangerie* near your hotel to eat on the run, or if you just can't live a day without an American breakfast, take yourself to Breakfast in America in the Latin Quarter or Marais. Then begin at the true center of Paris: **Notre-Dame** on the **Ile de la Cité.** The cathedral is *the* starting point for any tour, and Paris's starting point, as well — you're at Kilomètre Zéro, from which all distances in France are measured. From there, take a short walk west to the island's other Gothic masterpiece — **Sainte-Chapelle** in the **Palais de Justice.** Afterward, cross the Seine to the **Louvre** on the Right Bank. Select just a few rooms in a particular collection for your first visit. The Louvre is one of the world's largest and finest museums, and it would take months to see everything. Take a well-deserved lunch break in the museum's comfortable **Café Marly** (see Chapter 10 for a description) overlooking I.M. Pei's pyramid, or if you want more, cheaper food choices, try the food court on the Louvre's second floor (escalators in the Carrousel de Louvre where you enter give access).

From the museum, stroll west through the beautiful **Jardin des Tuileries** looking out for the beautiful statues by Maillol, Rodin, and others to the **place de la Concorde,** with its Egyptian obelisk and fountains. Continue west up the **Champs-Elysées,** browsing some of the same stores you can find in your own hometown (though **Fnac** and **Virgin Megastore** are good places to buy music, and each has a cafe on the premises for a break; **Zara** is good for the latest fashion at low prices; and **Le Drugstore** has exquisite but pricey gifts and books), on either side of the avenue until you come to the **Arc de Triomphe**. Pay it a visit, then find avenue Marceau on the south side of the Arc and walk south or take bus 92 to Alma Marceau and board the **Bateaux-Mouches** for a **Seine boat ride** (see Chapter 11). After you disembark, have dinner at the friendly and reasonably priced **L'Assiette Lyonnaise**, 21 rue Marbeuf, 8e (from Pont L'Alma walk down av. George V to rue Marbeuf and make a right; L'Assiette Lyonnaise is on your right).

Explore the **Left Bank** on **Day Two**. Take the métro to LaMotte-Picquet-Grenelle and stop into **Monoprix** just across the street for cheap picnic food from its grocery store. Walk north up avenue de Suffren until you reach the **École-Militaire**. Facing it is the **Eiffel Tower** and its front lawn, the **Champs-de-Mars**, where you can spread out to have a picnic after visiting the tower. After your climb and subsequent lunch, head east on the quai Branly and pay a quick visit to the beautiful **Musée de quai Branly** to experience the art of traditional cultures of Africa, East and Southeast Asia, Oceania, Australia and New Zealand, and the American continents (note the live plants growing on the building's outside walls). Afterward head east on quai Branly (which turns into quai d'Orsay) until you reach the grounds of Invalides and visit the gold-topped **Église du Dôme** (which contains the **Tomb of Napoléon**). Admission also includes entrance to the **Musée de l'Armée**. Across boulevard des Invalides is the **Musée Rodin,** where you can enjoy a slow walk around the beautiful gardens before gazing at the artwork inside. Still have energy? Great! Hop on the métro at Varenne, at the corner of boulevard des Invalides and Varenne (you should be able to buy a pick-me-up soda from one of the machines on the platform), change to RER Line C, and arrive at **Musée d'Orsay**. Afterward, walk over to the métro's **Assemblée Nationale** station at the intersection of boulevard St-Germain and rue de Lille. Take the métro two stops to rue du Bac and exit onto boulevard St-Germain, making sure to walk in the direction traffic is heading, all the while browsing in upscale shops and art galleries. At place St-Germain-des-Prés, look for one of the famous cafes, **Café de Flore, Café Les Deux Magots** (see Chapter 10), or **Brasserie Lipp** and have a well-deserved drink. When you finish, take rue Bonaparte (which intersects St-Germain-des-Prés) south to Parisians' favorite park, the **Jardin du Luxembourg**. Stroll through the park (keeping an eye out for beehives and a mini Statue of Liberty) and exit at the boulevard St-Michel gates on the park's east side. Walk north on boulevard St-Michel toward the river. You'll be in the **Latin Quarter**. The **Panthéon** is at the top of the hill on rue Soufflot. You can enjoy a nice meal at one of the many inexpensive restaurants located behind the Panthéon on rue Mouffetard.

On **Day Three**, get up early and hop on the métro to St-Paul, in the heart of the **Marais**. Head east on rue St-Antoine, then turn north onto rue de Birague which will take you right to Paris's oldest square, the aristo-cratic **place des Vosges,** bordered by 17th-century town houses. Exit on rue des Francs-Bourgeois (for some great but a bit pricey shopping), then turn north onto rue Vieille du Temple until you see the **Musée Picasso.** Try to arrive when it opens at 9:30 a.m., and allow two hours for your visit. Afterward double back on rue du Vieille du Temple to rue des Rosiers and pick up a filling lunch from **one of the many falafel places.** Browse the stores here and head west on rue des Francs Bourgeois, which turns into rue Rambuteau. Follow rue Rambuteau west to rue Beaubourg, where you'll face the back of the wonderful **Centre Georges Pompidou.** Spend two hours exploring it. Afterward, jump on the métro at the Rambuteau station and head for Père-Lachaise. Spend the afternoon searching out **Cimitière Père-Lachaise's** famous residents with the 2€ ($3.20) map (it's the best one) sold outside the gates on boulevard de Ménilmontant. Afterward, take the métro's Line 2 to the Anvers station. Walk north on rue Tardieu to the base of **Sacré-Coeur.** Take the funicular (one métro ticket) to the top and then spend 15 to 20 minutes inside Sacré-Coeur before climbing to its dome. After climbing down, head behind the church to the **place du Tertre,** which still looks like an old-fashioned Parisian square, despite artists begging to paint your picture (some can be quite persuasive, but they're too expensive, and it's better to just politely tell them *"non, merci"*). Even though the cafes are picturesque — and more expensive — save your appetite for **Au Poulbot Gourmet,** 39 rue Lamarck (follow rue Lamarck down the hill to no. 39) for dinner.

Planning a Five-Day Visit

Spend the first three days as outlined in the "Making the Most of Paris in Three Days" itinerary. Add the **Conciergerie** to your tour of Ile de la Cité on Day One; the entrance is on the Seine side of the Palais de Justice.

On **Day Four,** visit **Versailles.** On **Day Five,** take the métro to Opéra to visit the stunning **Opéra Garnier** with its mural by Marc Chagall. Then head north to boulevard Haussmann to shop the rest of the afternoon away at department stores **Printemps** and **Galeries Lafayette.** The sixth-floor cafeteria at Galeries Lafayette offers plenty of lunch or dinner choices — from a salad bar to grilled steaks and dessert.

A Walking Tour through the Marais

The **Marais** (translation: "swamp," which it used to be), the old Jewish quarter of Paris, is also now one of its hippest, chicest neighborhoods with the new edging out a population that has called this area home since the Middle Ages. Jo Goldenberg, a kosher deli, restaurant, and Paris institution, closed its doors in 2006, and as rents skyrocket, the family-run kosher pizza places, delis, and religious shops are giving way to designer boutiques and restaurants. There is still a Jewish presence here; the rue Pavée Orthodox Synagogue is the heart of the community, but the beloved working class neighborhood is much changed. Some Jewish residents are adapting, and others are moving to Paris's farther reaches in the 19e and 20e arrondissements. The mix of old and new only enhances this quarter's attractions, however, making the Marais one of the best places to visit for tourists and locals alike.

Take the métro to the St-Paul station and after climbing the steps from the station, turn right (or east) along the rue St-Antoine. On your right will be the baroque church of **St-Paul-St-Louis** (badly in need of restoration) where Victor Hugo was a parishioner and donated the holy water fonts on each side of the entrance. Delacroix's *Christ in the Garden of Olives* is in the left transept, if you want to take a peek inside.

Turn right when leaving the church and walk across rue St-Antoine to the **Hôtel de Sully**, a 17th-century mansion commissioned by Henri IV, that houses the **Caisse Nationale des Monuments Historiques et des Sites** that features some great photography exhibits. Walk through the front courtyard into lovely formal gardens. This is a popular place for locals to catch some sun on warm days. Walk through the courtyard in the direction of the building's Orangerie, passing a bookstore on the left side (inside you can see the building's original painted wood beams) and exit on the right side of the Orangerie to **place des Vosges** (see Chapter 11).

Thirty-six brick and stone pavilions rise from graceful arcades surrounding a gorgeous central plant- and flower-filled square. This used to be the court of Henri IV, and the buildings were constructed according to strict plan: The height of the facades equals their widths, and triangular roofs are half as high as the facades. In the southeastern corner here is the **Maison de Victor Hugo** (see Chapter 11), the prolific author of *Les Misérables* and *The Hunchback of Notre-Dame*. After a quick (and free) visit to his house, leave the square at the end opposite the entrance and make a left onto **rue des Francs-Bourgeois** for some window shopping (don't miss the mouthwatering women's clothing at **BGN** at 21, **Zadig & Voltaire** at 42, and **Barbara Bui** at 43) before hitting the **Musée Carnavalet** (see Chapter 11) on the corner of rue de Sévigné. Facing the Musée Carnavalet, turn right and continue up rue de Sévigné. Turn left at rue du Parc-Royal, continue to place de Thorigny and make a right onto rue de Thorigny. At no. 5 is the **Musée Picasso.**

This is one of the must-see museums of Paris, one of the largest collections of the master's paintings (if not the largest) in the world. When finished, retrace your steps to the corner of rue du Parc-Royal and rue Payenne. Turn right onto rue Payenne and stop by the pretty Square Georges-Cain on the left, where you can see remnants from some of the city's demolished mansions. Follow rue des Francs-Bourgeois to no. 38, the **Allée des Arbalétriers**, a typical medieval street with large paving stones and overhanging floors. This was where Louis d'Orléans, King Charles V's brother, was hacked to death by goons for the duc de Bourgogne. Make a right onto rue Vieille-du-Temple. On the corner is the late Gothic turret that is the only remnant of a mansion (the **Hôtel Hérouet**), built around 1510. At no. 87 is the Hôtel de Rohan-Strasbourg, no. 60 is the **Hôtel de Guénegaud des Brosses** which houses the Musée de la Chase et Nature, no. 58 are the towers of the **Hôtel de Clisson,** a 14th-century mansion. No. 60 is the **Hôtel de Soubise,** where the **Musée de l'Histoire de France** is located. Cross rue des Francs-Bourgeois, continuing on rue Vieille-du-Temple for the **Hôtel Amelot-de-Bisseuil** at no. 47 where Beaumarchais wrote *The Marriage of Figaro* in 1784. This is also a terrific shopping street with **Mosavitra** (reasonably priced stained and painted glass tiles) at 23, Japanese-influenced clothing at **A la Bonne Renommée** at 26, award-winning lamp designer **Salih Mekhici** at 100, and sporty and chic women's clothing at **A.P.C.** at 112, among many others. At the Hôtel Amelot-de-Bisseuil take a right and then turn left onto the **rue des Rosiers,** the heart of the old Jewish quarter.

Much of the Jewish community here dates back to the 13th century and references to the "street of rosebushes" *(rosiers)* appeared as early as 1230. This is where you'll want to grab something filling, like a falafel from **L'As du Falafel** at no. 34. If you turn right onto rue Pavée at the end of rue des Rosiers, you will see the **synagogue** at no. 10, built by Hector Guimard, artisan of the Art Nouveau subway entrances. At the end of the street is the St-Paul Métro station across rue St-Antoine. If you still have energy, cross rue St-Antoine, take a right and walk to rue St-Paul. At no. 10 is the **Musée de la Curiosité et de la Magie** (see Chapter 11) and a bit farther down is the Village St-Paul, a secluded 17th-century village–cum–outdoor art and antiques fair. It's easy to walk past the entrances which are tucked between rue St-Paul, rue Jardins St-Paul, and rue Charlemagne (look for the signs just inside the narrow passageways between houses). You'll find yourself in a cluster of interlocking courtyards lined with shops selling antiques, paintings, and bric-a-brac. The haphazard arrangement of courtyards dates from the 14th century when they were the walled gardens of King Charles V. Also on rue St-Paul, for those travelers who miss the United States, is **Thanksgiving,** a store selling such items as Marshmallow Fluff and Fritos at no. 20. The English-language Little Red Wheelbarrow bookstore is next door at no. 22. Retrace your steps up rue St-Paul to rue St-Antoine to catch the métro to your next destination.

Take a Stroll through a Parisian Village

Montmartre has been revitalized by tourists, and the quarter itself is fashionable and hip again. Its twisted streets and ivied walls are still just as charming as the days before it was incorporated into the city, when it was a village known for its cheap wines and artistic inhabitants (many artists left Paris proper for Montmartre at night precisely because of the cheap drinks). The twisting streets here can sometimes mean very confused voyagers, but fear not! This half-day's tour of Montmartre will have you walking around like a local in no time.

Bring a map that has a good rendering of the 18th arrondissement. Though getting lost is part of the fun of Montmartre, it's getting out that can get a bit frustrating.

✔ **Scoping Abbesses, Part One:** Start out at Place Blanche, to see what might be the world's most famous nightclub, the **Moulin Rouge.** Take the requisite picture (lit up at night, it is most impressive!), and walk up **rue Lepic.** Open during the day are great cheese shops and small produce shops. At no. 12 is **Lux-Bar,** which opened a century ago and continues to give locals a place to soothe their palates. Across the street at no. 15 is **Café des Deux Moulins** of *Amélie* fame. The interior remains mostly the same, with the glass "toilettes" sign and the copper-topped bar (the cigarette counter was removed a while ago for more space). A big poster of Amélie graces the back wall. Turn right and walk down **rue des Abbesses.** Here is some great shopping (**Colline** at no. 20 and **Le Diable et Moi** at no. 29 bis). You will also pass fantastic *boulangerie* **Le Grenier du Pain,** at no. 38, and a good people-watching cafe, **Le Sancerre,** at no. 35, eventually ending up in place des Abbesses. Here you will see the **Eglise St-Jean-de-Montmartre,** which was built in 1904, and also the beautiful Art Deco entrance to the Abbesses stop, designed by Hector Guimard. It is one of the last two original métro entrances left in the city.

A good place to have a picnic lunch if you buy your sandwich from Le Grenier à Pain is next to the "I love you wall" located in the Square Jehan Rictus (just off of place des Abbesses, on the other side of the métro entrance and the merry-go-round). In this small green space is a wall with the words "I love you" (*Je t'aime* in French) written in over a hundred different languages. *Comme c'est romantique!*

✔ **Scoping Abbesses, Part Two:** The next part of the tour leads up to everyone's favorite Montmartre landmark: Sacre Coeur. However, the streets leading up to it are quite important — especially if you like shopping. Walk along rue des Abbesses until you cross **rue des Martyrs.** You'll see an **Antoine et Lili** at no. 90, a shop perfect for interesting little gifts for the college crowd. Then, take a quick left and right onto rue Yvonne le Tac. At no. 9 you pass the entrance to the chapel built on the supposed spot of the beheading of St. Denis, for whom all of Montmartre (the word Montmartre comes from mountain, or *mont,* of the martyr) is named. At no. 8 is a lovely ivied building, while around the corner you pass the local cafe **Au Progrès** at 7 rue des Trois Frères, perfectly situated in a four-way crossroads, with the ideal panoramic view of Parisian streets. Make another right and traverse rue d'Orsel. Here are art galleries, an antique bookstore, and some really ugly modern furniture shops. If it's later at night, a great restaurant on this street is **le Kokolion,** at no. 62. For menswear, go to **Jo.,** at no. 47, and **S.D. Spontinini,** just up the street at 1 rue de Trois Frères. A real circus supply store (fun gift ideas!) is at **Bonjour l'Artiste,** at no. 35.

✔ **Sacre Coeur and Place du Tertre:** Climb the lamppost-divided stairs famously depicted in the photograph by Brassaï, or for the price of a métro ticket, take the *funiculaire* (walk from the Anvers Métro station the short distance to rue Steinkerque and turn left onto rue Tardieu). Enjoy the fantastic, free view for which you don't have to wait in line. Work started on this basilica in the 1870s and the building is a pastiche of Romanesque and Byzantine styles. Renoir, Picasso, Seurat, Degas, Van Gogh, and Zola all hung out in Pigalle and Montmartre. And there was no keeping Toulouse-Lautrec away, of course. Follow around the western side of the basilica, passing the dwarfed Église St-Pierre du Montmartre, and wander around Place du Tertre without letting yourself get too abused by the painters dying to paint your picture. Here you can truly see how this place was once its own village, with adorable houses, old paned windows, and tiny cobblestone passageways (not to mention some of the highest rents in the city). Walk around the edges of the Place du Tertre area to the **Espace Dalí** at 11 rue Poulbot, a small museum dedicated to Dalí's work, of which there is a plethora to see (and hear — his voice plays over eerie ambient music). Then wander up rue des Saules, passing the famous cabaret **Au Lapin Agile** at no. 22, a famous haunt of artists Picasso, Modigliani, and Utrillo (they still have music shows here, but they are vastly overpriced). Around the corner is the **Musée de Montmartre,** at 12 rue Cortot, where you can learn all about the history and art associated with this beloved part of Paris.

✔ **There and back again:** Once you've had enough of the hilltop, make your way down through place Jean Baptiste Clément and down rue de la Mire to rue Ravignan, where you can see a beautiful house (built in 1911), located right across the street from 49 rue Gabrielle, where Picasso had his first studio in Paris. On this street are more art studios and funny narrow passages, as well as the very fairly priced **Chez Marie** (no. 27; see Chapter 10 for the review). Continue east to the upper portion of rue Lepic, where you can catch a glimpse of the oldest and only remaining windmill in Montmartre, **Le Moulin de la Galette** (unfortunately, you can't visit it). Descend farther past rue Berthe and onto rue Androuet, where you will find the little Collignon grocery store from *Amélie* — she really did live in Montmartre! You are again on rue des Trois Frères. Follow it along and you will shortly pick up rue Ravignan again. Here you can find the Bateau Lavoir, another studio haunted by the likes of Picasso and Modigliani, at 11 bis place Emile Godeau. In this spot, there are benches where you can rest before you end up back at Abbesses, enjoying another quick view of the Paris skyline.

Chapter 14

Going Beyond Paris: Five Day Trips

● ●

In This Chapter

▶ Enjoying the excesses of Versailles

▶ Reliving history at Fontainebleau

▶ Basking in the stained-glass light at Chartres's cool cathedral

▶ Hanging out with "Le Mickey" at Disneyland à la français

▶ Lingering at the lilies in Monet's gardens

● ●

*T*he day trips outlined in this chapter are well worth tearing yourself away from Paris, even though it may be difficult to tear yourself away from the City of Light. Don't worry; you'll be back in the city in time to enjoy a nightcap in a cafe. The "Day trips from Paris" map can help you plan your excursions.

The Château de Versailles

Sofia Coppola's movie version of the life of Marie Antoinette, "teen queen," generated renewed interest in the opulent Austrian import, but even if you haven't seen the film, you'll discover that there's more to Versailles (☎ 01-30-83-78-00; www.chateauversailles.fr) than its incredible château, of which the words "awe-inspiring" don't begin to do justice. This palace is a small city on more than 800 hectares (2,000 acres) that houses formal and fanciful gardens, meadows (with sheep), a mile-long Grand Canal modeled on the one in Venice, the Grand and Petit Trianon mansions, a hamlet (the Hameau) where Marie Antoinette played peasant, the restored royal stables, a coach museum, fountains, and woods. All this attests to the power royalty once had and to one king who truly believed he deserved it: Louis XIV. The king hired the best to build Versailles: Louis Le Vau and Jules Hardouin-Mansart, France's premier architects; André Le Nôtre, designer of the Tuileries gardens; and Charles Le Brun, head of the Royal Academy of Painting and Sculpture, who fashioned the interior. Construction got underway in 1661.

Day Trips from Paris

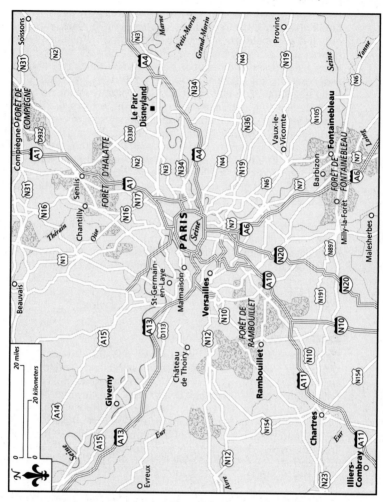

In 1682, Louis XIV transferred the court to Versailles to live with him and thus prevent plots against him. Historians estimate that anywhere from 3,000 to 10,000 people, including servants, lived at Versailles in the 100 years between the rules of Louis XIV and Louis XVI, and court etiquette grew to be absurd. (Sometimes attendants engaged in power struggles about who ranked high enough to dress Marie Antoinette while the young queen waited, shivering. And Versailles's female royalty gave birth before a live audience; the higher the rank, the better the seat.) When you see all this over-the-top magnificence and try to estimate the cost, you may have a better understanding of the anger of the revolutionaries a century later.

Louis XIV enjoyed an incredibly long reign of 72 years (though he was only five years old when he inherited the title). When he died in 1715, he was succeeded by his great-grandson, Louis XV, who continued the outrageous pomp and ceremony and made interior renovations and redecorations until lack of funds forced him to stop. Louis XV's son and daughter-in-law, Louis XVI and Marie Antoinette, made no major changes at Versailles, but by then it was too late. On October 6, 1789, a mob voicing the feelings of the average French citizen sick of bearing the brunt of the costs of royalty's foibles, marched on the palace and forced the royal couple to return to Paris. This was the beginning of the French Revolution. The royal family eventually lost their lives, save one daughter (though some report that the young *dauphin*, or heir to the throne, never really died in prison, but was spirited away from the country), and Versailles ceased to be a royal residence.

The monarchy was reinstated in 1830, and Louis-Philippe, who reigned from 1830 to 1848 and succeeded Louis XVIII, prevented Versailles's destruction by donating his own money to convert it into a museum dedicated to the glory of France. In the mid–20th century, John D. Rockefeller also contributed to the restoration of Versailles, and the work from that contribution continues to this day. The nearby "Versailles" map shows the current configuration.

Getting there

Catch the **RER line C** to Versailles from one of the stops at the Gare d'Austerlitz, St-Michel, Musée d'Orsay, Invalides, Ponte d'Alma, Champ de Mars, or Javel and take it to the Versailles Rive Gauche station (take "direction Versailles-rive-gauche-château"), from which there's a shuttle bus to the château. Or, you can take the 15-minute walk through the town, which is very pretty on its own. Round-trip tickets cost 5.80€ ($9.30) and the trip takes about 35 minutes. Eurailpass holders travel free on the RER but must show their Eurailpass at the kiosk near any RER entrance to receive a ticket that opens the turnstile leading to and from the RER platforms.

An alternative method of reaching Versailles from central Paris involves regular **SNCF Transilien trains,** which make frequent runs from two railway stations — Gare St-Lazare and Gare Montparnasse — to Versailles. Trains departing from Gare St-Lazare arrive at the Versailles Rive Droit railway station; trains departing from Gare Montparnasse arrive at Versailles Chantiers. The cost of the tickets is the same as the RER. Both stations lie within a ten-minute walk of the château, which is a wonderful way to orient yourself with the town, its geography, its scale, and its architecture. If you can't or don't want to walk, you can take bus H, X, or G, or (in midsummer) a shuttle bus marked either TRI or *Château* from any of the three stations directly to the château for a fee of 2.50€ ($4) each way per person. Because of the vagaries of the bus schedules, it

Versailles

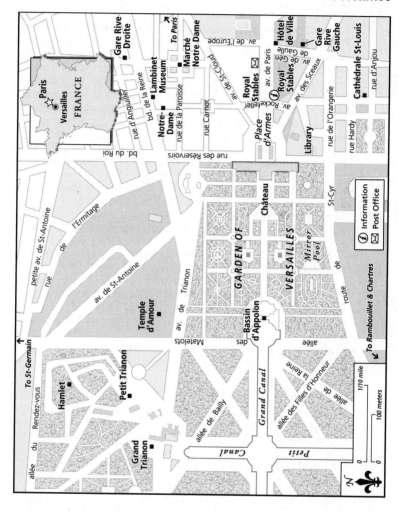

may be easier to walk. Directions to the château are clearly signposted from each railway station. Another method of arrival for the adventurous is to take the 171 bus toward Versailles-place d'Armes. The bus leaves from the Pont de Sèvres Métro station, at the southern end of line 9. The journey is roughly 25 minutes this way.

To reach Versailles by car, drive west on the A13 highway from Porte d'Auteuil toward Rouen. Take the Versailles-Château exit, about 23km (14 miles) from Paris. Park in the visitors' parking lot at place d'Armes for 4.50€ ($7.20) Monday through Friday, 5.50€ ($8.80) on weekends.

The drive takes about a half-hour, though in traffic it can take more than an hour.

You can also take advantage of the Versailles **Passeport** (☎ 01-30-83-78-00), a one-day pass to visit the entire Château de Versailles and all of the surrounding attractions within the city. This includes audio guided tours in the château, the chapel, the King and Queen's Grand Apartments, the Dauphin's (Crown Prince) Apartments, and the Appartements de Mesdames (ladies-in-waiting, open only on weekends during the low season). The opera house, normally opened to the public, was closed in June 2007 for renovations until further notice. After this massive opulent castle visit, you have free reign of the parks, gardens, and forest groves, the **Grand Trianon** (the nearby private retreat of Louis XIV), the **Domaine de Marie-Antoinette** (Marie-Antoinette's private fields, open from Apr 1 to the end of Oct), and all of the temporary exhibits. If you use the Passeport during the high season, the spectacle of **Les Grands Eaux Musicales** (see later in this section) is also included. The tickets cost 20€ ($32) during the week and 25€ ($40) during weekends and holidays; 16€ ($26) for visitors under 18. Keep in mind that seeing each attraction separately requires purchasing your ticket at an Fnac or SNCF ticket booth.

Don't want the hassle of getting to Versailles yourself? You can also take a tour bus there. **Cityrama,** 2 place des Pyramides, 1er (☎ 01-44-55-61-00; www.cityrama.fr), has different trips to Versailles ranging from 47€ to 137€ ($75–$219) for adults, 24€ to 96€ ($38–$153) children (the higher-priced tickets also include trips to Giverny, Fontaineblue, and Barbizon). **Paris Vision,** 214 rue de Rivoli, 1er (☎ 01-42-60-30-01; www.parisvision.com), offers bus excursions starting from 47€ to 159€ ($75–$254); it's half-price for ages 4 to 11.

Exploring Versailles

I cannot be more serious when I lay down two words of advice — arrive early! If you really want to beat the crowds, get there at 8 a.m. when it opens. More than three million tourists visit Versailles each year, and you'll want to have as much of a head start as possible. Plus, there's been additional influx since the Hall of Mirrors was reopened. The lines have been a nightmare since then. Also, don't be surprised by various renovations taking place in public areas that have not been announced: It seems that a lot of repair work is going on, which may affect your visit.

The first rooms you see in the palace are the six Louis XIV–style **Grand Appartements,** which kings used for ceremonial events, and the **Petit Appartements,** where they lived with their families. Louis XV stashed his mistresses, Madame du Barry and Madame de Pompadour, in his second-floor apartment, which you can visit only with a guide (the Petit Trianon was built as a retreat for the king's mistress, but Madame de Pompadour died before it was completed). Attempts have been made to restore the original décor of the Queen's bedchamber, which Marie Antoinette renovated with a huge four-poster bed and silks in patterns of lilacs, her favorite flower, and peacock feathers. Look for the secret door through which she attempted to escape.

Other magnificent rooms include the **Salons of War and Peace,** which flank the palace's most famous room, the 71m-long (236-ft.) **Hall of Mirrors.** Hardouin-Mansart began work on the hall in 1678, and Le Brun added 17 large windows and corresponding mirrors. The ceiling paintings represent the accomplishments of Louis XIV's government. Jacques-Ange Gabriel designed the **Library** with its delicately carved panels. The **Clock Room** contains Passement's astronomical clock, which took 20 years to make; it's encased in gilded bronze.

Gabriel also designed the **Royal Opéra** for Louis XV. Try to imagine it the way it used to be during a concert — bearskin rugs under foot and the light of 3,000 powerful candles. Hardouin-Mansart built the gold-and-white **Royal Chapel** between 1699 and 1710. After his father's death, Louis XVI and Marie Antoinette prayed for guidance here, fearing they were too young to run the country.

After you see the château, plan to spend at least an hour strolling through the **Formal Gardens,** spread across 100 hectares (250 acres). Here Le Nôtre created a Garden of Eden, using ornamental lakes and canals, geometrically designed flowerbeds, and avenues bordered with statuary. Louis XV, imagining he was in Venice, would take gondola rides with his lover of the moment on the mile-long Grand Canal. The restored vegetable gardens *(le Potager de Roi)* are here, as well. If you visit on a weekend in the summer, try to take in **Les Grands Eaux Musicales,** a show in which the fountains move in time to the classical music of Bach, Mozart, or Berlioz. Cost is 8€ ($13) adults, 6€ ($9.60) ages 10 to 26 and seniors, children younger than 10 are free. Another spectacle is **Les Fêtes de Nuit de Versailles,** a variety of breathtaking shows, combining sound-and-light displays with fireworks, but also featuring dance, puppetry, and high quality theatrics that the French do well. Held between June and September, the kids will definitely enjoy these as much as you. Prices range from 30€ ($48) for adults to 20€ ($32) under 18. Seniors, children younger than ten are free. (For reservations to either show, see www.chateauversaillesspectacles.fr or call ☎ **01-30-83-78-89** or ☎ 01-39-20-16-20.)

Because of the crowds and long lines, most guests are content to visit only the château and gardens, but you can see much more at Versailles if you have the stamina. The most important of the remaining sights are the **Grand Trianon** and the recently renovated **Petit Trianon.** *Trianon* was the name of the town that Louis bought and then razed in order to construct a mansion, le Grand Trianon, where he could eat light meals away from the palace. Designed in 1687, again by Hardouin-Mansart, the Grand Trianon has traditionally served as a residence for the country's important guests, although former President Charles de Gaulle wanted to turn it into a weekend retreat for himself. Napoléon I spent the night here, and U.S. President Richard Nixon slept in the room where Madame de Pompadour (Louis XV's mistress) died. Gabriel, the designer of the place de la Concorde, built the Petit Trianon in 1768 for Louis XV, who used it for trysts with Madame du Barry, his mistress after de Pompadour. Marie Antoinette adopted it as her favorite residence, where she could escape the constraints of palace life.

Behind the Petit Trianon is the **Hamlet,** a collection of small thatched farmhouses and a water mill, a setting where Marie Antoinette pretended she was back at her family's country retreat in Austria. Near the Hamlet is the **Temple of Love,** built in 1775 by Richard Mique, Marie Antoinette's favorite architect. In the center of its Corinthian colonnade is a reproduction of Bouchardon's Cupid shaping a bow from the club of Hercules.

Louis XIV's stables, **La Grande Ecurie,** are newly restored and open to the public. Also designed by Hardouin-Mansart, the stables held as many as 600 horses owned by the king. These days, you'll see 20 ivory-colored Lusitano horses from Portugal. A morning tour here includes a dressage demonstration with riders in costume on horses performing to music. Near the stables is the entrance to the **Le Musée des Carrosses,** which houses horse-drawn coaches from the 18th and 19th centuries, among them one used at the coronation of Charles X and another used at the wedding of Napoléon I and his second wife, Marie-Louise. One sleigh rests on tortoiseshell runners. A ticket to the Petit Trianon also admits you to this museum, and to the **Salle du Jeu de Paume.** Constructed by Louis XIV, this museum space was originally an indoor court intended for *le jeu de paume,* a sport that was the precursor to tennis. It has historical significance, as it is the place where, on June 20, 1789, the French revolution began: Representatives of the Third Estate, unsatisfied with the reforms of Louis XVI, met at the Jeu de Paume and swore they would not leave the chamber until they were given a Constitution.

Admission to La Grande Ecurie is 6€ ($9.60) adults, 3€ ($5) 17 and under. It is open on specific Tuesdays and Thursdays at 11 a.m. Admission to the coach museum is 2€ ($2.40), free for children younger than 18. It's open every weekend from April to October 9 a.m. to 6:30 p.m. and the first two weekends in November 12:30 to 5:30 p.m. The Musée des Carrosses and the Salle du Jeu de Paume are open only on certain weekends and holidays; you must call ahead to the Versailles info line to see if they are available for viewing.

Admission to the palace is 14€ ($8.60) for adults. It's free for those younger than 18 and for all on Sunday. Combined admission to the Grand and Petit Trianons is 9€ ($5.75) for adults; children younger than 18 are free. Audio guides are available in iPods for a 3€ ($5) fee. Admission to the gardens is free except for the days of Grands Eaux Musicales (see earlier for prices).

Lecturer-led one-hour tours of the palace are admission price plus 6€ ($9.60), 4€ ($6.40) ages 10 to 17 and seniors; one-and-a-half-hour tours are admission plus 6€ ($9.60), 4.50€ ($7.20) ages 11 to 17 and seniors;

two-hour tours are admission plus 8€ ($13) for adults, 6€ ($9.60) ages 10 to 17. Tours are free for children younger than ten.

From May to September, the palace is open Tuesday through Sunday from 9 a.m. to 6:30 p.m. The rest of the year, the palace is open Tuesday through Sunday from 9 a.m. to 5:30 p.m. From May through September the Grand Trianon and Petit Trianon are open daily noon to 6:30 p.m.; from October to April, the Grand Trianon and Petit Trianon are open daily noon to 5:30 p.m. The park and the gardens are open every day, except in bad weather, from 7 a.m. in summer and 8 a.m. in winter until sunset (between 5:30 and 9:30 p.m., depending on the season).

Dining options

The town of Versailles has no shortage of places where you can break for lunch, but after you're on palace grounds, you may find it infinitely more convenient just to stay put — otherwise you have to hike back into town and back out to the palace again. In the château, you can eat at Le Café, a snack bar just off the Cour de la Chapelle. In the Formal Gardens is an informal restaurant, **La Flotille,** on Petite Venise. (To get there from the château, walk directly back through the gardens to where the canal starts. Petite Venise and the restaurant are to your right.) There is La Petite Venise, a wood-beamed restaurant, brasserie, and tearoom with outdoor seating between the Grand Canal and the Apollo Fountain. Finally, several **snack bars** and fresh-squeezed orange juice stands are located in the gardens near the Quinconce du Midi and the Grand Trianon.

Note: For those with limited mobility, electric cars are available at the south entrance (☎ **01-30-83-75-05**).

The Palais de Fontainebleau

Fontainebleau is much less crowded than Versailles, and you can combine culture and outdoor activities. It's a terrific day trip from Paris. After you tour the castle, hike the trails, rock climb, or rent bikes to ride in the 16,800-hectare (42,000-acre) Forêt (forest) de Fontainebleau that 13 million guests visit each year. The palace (☎ **01-60-71-50-70**; check out the nearby "Fontainebleau" map) is probably most famous as the site of Napoléon's farewell to his imperial guard before he went into exile. It also contains more than 700 years of royal history from the enthronement of Louis VII in 1137 to the fall of the Second Empire in 1873. And artist Leonardo da Vinci played a small role in its history.

On the palace Web site is a link to purchase a *Forfait Loisirs* from the SNCF, in which you pay a single fee for the round-trip train ticket to the palace, an entry for a viewing of the Grandes Appartements, and a guidebook which you can collect at the Tourist Office next to the château (this may help avoid some lines). Per person the tickets are 23€ ($37) for adults, 17€ ($27) for minors aged 10 to 17, and 8.10€ ($13) for children four to nine years (children under four enter for free).

Fontainebleau

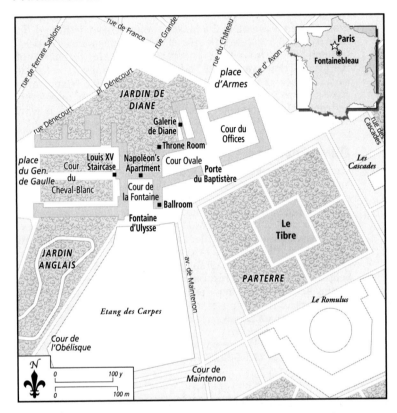

Getting there

To reach Fontainebleau by train, take the SNCF Montargie line to
Fontainebleau Avon station; it departs hourly from the Gare de Lyon
in Paris. The trip takes 35 to 60 minutes and costs 7.80€ ($13).
Fontainebleau Avon station is just outside the town in Avon, a suburb
of Paris. From the station, the town bus (direction Château) makes the
3km (2-mile) trip to the château every 10 to 15 minutes on weekdays
and every 30 minutes on Saturdays and Sundays.

You can also reach Fontainebleau on a tour bus. **Cityrama,** 4 place des
Pyramides, 1er (☎ 01-44-55-61-00; www.cityrama.fr), combines both
Fontainebleau and the nearby artist's village of Barbizon (see later in
this section) for 65€ ($104) adult, 33€ ($50) child. **Paris Vision,** 214 rue
de Rivoli, 1er (☎ 01-42-60-30-01; www.parisvision.com), offers a 154€
($246) extended minibus tour which includes Barbizon, Fontainebleau,
and Vaux le Vicomte, another château with beautiful gardens. Children
go for half-price.

Exploring Fontainebleau

Fontainebleau was built for love. François I transformed a run-down royal palace into Fontainebleau in 1528 for his mistress, and his successor, Henri II, left a beautiful memorial to the woman he loved — a **ballroom** decorated with the intertwined initials of his mistress, Diane de Poitiers, and himself.

The *Mona Lisa* once hung here, and it is said that its creator, Leonardo da Vinci, personally brought the painting to its buyer, his friend François I. The *Mona Lisa* remained in the royal family for years before it was gifted to the Louvre. Stucco-framed paintings now hanging in the **Gallery of François I** include *The Rape of Europa* and depict mythological and allegorical scenes related to the king's life. Make sure to see the racy ceiling paintings above the **Louis XV Staircase,** which was originally painted for the bedroom of a duchess. The stairway's architect simply ripped out the bedroom floor, using its ceiling to cover the stairway. One fresco depicts the Queen of the Amazons climbing into Alexander the Great's bed.

When Louis XIV ascended the throne, Fontainebleau was largely neglected because of his preoccupation with Versailles, but it found renewed glory under Napoléon I. You can walk around much of the palace on your own, but most of the Napoleonic rooms are accessible only on guided tours, which are in French. Napoléon had two bedchambers; mirrors adorn either side of his bed in the grander chamber (look for his symbol, a bee), while a small bed is housed in the aptly named **Small Bedchamber.** A red-and-gold throne with the initial "N" is displayed in the **Throne Room.** You can also see Napoléon's **offices,** where the emperor signed his abdication; however, the document on exhibit is only a copy. Minor apartments include those once occupied by Madame De Maintenon, the second wife of Louis XIV; those of Pope Pius VII, whom Napoléon kept a virtual prisoner; still another was Marie Antoinette's.

After a visit to the palace, wander through the gardens, paying special attention to the lovely, bucolic carp pond, and take caution while walking by some of the fearless swans. If you'd like to promenade in the forest, a detailed map of its paths is available from the **Office de Tourisme,** 4 rue Royale, near the palace (☎ 01-60-74-99-99; www.tourisme-fontaine bleau.com). You can also rent bikes nearby from **À la Petite Reine,** 32 rue des Sablons (☎ 01-60-74-57-57), for about 5€ ($8) an hour, 13€ ($21) a half-day, 16€ ($26) a full day, with a credit card deposit. The **Tour Denencourt,** about 5km (3 miles) north of the palace, makes a nice ride and has a pretty view. Other mapped-out walking and bike tours of the city and environs can be downloaded from the Tourist Office Web site or you can get a map once you're there.

The Palais de Fontainebleau (☎ 01-60-71-50-70) is open Wednesday through Monday, and is closed on New Year's Day, Christmas Day, and the first of May. The opening hours October through March are from 9:30 a.m. to 5 p.m.; from April to September the hours are 9 a.m. to 6 p.m. Admission to the Grand Appartements is 13€ ($20) for adults,

11€ ($18) for ages 18 to 26 and older than 60, free for those under age 18. Free for all on the first Sunday of the month.

Dining options

If you're arriving by train and plan to visit only Fontainebleau, consider bringing a picnic from Paris. In fine weather, the château's gardens and nearby forest beckon. If you have a car, however, save your appetite for Barbizon (see later).

On the western edge of France's finest forest lies the village of **Barbizon**, home to a number of noted landscape artists — Corot, Millet, Rousseau, and Daumier. The colorful town has a lively mix of good restaurants, boutiques, and antiques shops — the perfect place to while away an afternoon. For lunch, try the **Relais de Barbizon**, 2 av. Charles de Gaulle (☎ **01-60-66-40-28**). They have a prix-fixe menu at 27€ ($43) which features hearty home-style dishes such as *confit de canard* and *baba au rhum* for dessert. The restaurant is open Thursday through Monday noon to 2:30 p.m. and 8 to 10 p.m. (Only lunch is served on Tues.) Reservations required on weekends.

If you stay in Fontainebleau for lunch, try **Le Table des Maréchaux** in the Hôtel Napoléon, 9 rue Grande (☎ **01-60-39-50-50**). Its 40€ ($42) three-course *ménu* may include a mackerel and mozzarella spring roll, or a Parmesan-encrusted cod with eggplant purée. Finish up with a strawberry and grapefruit tart. In warm weather, diners can eat on the outdoor terrace.

The Cathedral at Chartres

The French sculptor Rodin dubbed this building "The Acropolis of France." Upon laying eyes on this greatest of High Gothic cathedrals, Napoléon declared, "Chartres is no place for an atheist." Perhaps the would-be emperor had been moved by the ethereal world of colored light that fills the cathedral (still the fourth-largest church in the world) on a sunny day, streaming through an awe-inspiring more than 2,500 sq. m (27,000 sq. ft.) of 12th- and 13th-century stained glass, turning the church walls into quasi-mystical portals to heaven.

It survived the French Revolution, even though it was scheduled for demolition. It withstood two world wars, when volunteers took down all of its 12th- and 13th-century stained glass piece by piece. But for a majority of its visitors, the Cathédrale de Notre-Dame de Chartres (☎ **02-37-21-59-08;** see the nearby "Notre-Dame de Chartres" map), one of the world's greatest Gothic cathedrals and one of the finest creations of the Middle Ages, comes second in importance to a small scrap of material housed inside. Known as the *Sancta Camisia,* it is said that it was worn by the Virgin Mary when she gave birth to Jesus. This sacred scarf was supposedly a gift from the Empress Irene of Byzantium to

Notre-Dame de Chartres

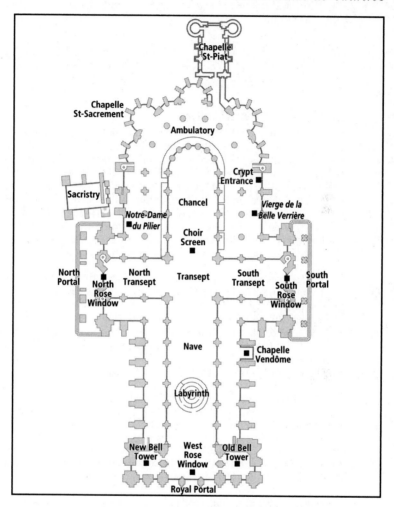

Charlemagne, and has been resting in the cathedral of Chartres since A.D. 876 (Note: This refers to a different or earlier construction than the Chartres cathedral that we know today).

Getting there

You can see all this for around a 26€ ($46) round-trip train ticket from Paris's Gare Montparnasse, less than an hour's ride away. The tourism office (☎ 02-37-18-26-26) is right on the place de la Cathédral.

If you'd like to drive to Chartres, take the A10/A11 highway from Porte d'Orléans and follow the signs to Le Mans and Chartres. The drive takes about 75 minutes.

Traveling to Chartres by tour bus is another option. **Cityrama,** 4 place des Pyramides, 1er (☎ **01-44-55-61-00;** www.cityrama.fr), offers five-hour excursions leaving from Paris every Tuesday, Thursday, and Saturday for 59€ ($94) adult, 30€ ($47) child.

Exploring the cathedral

Take one of Malcolm Miller's excellent 75-minute guided tours of Chartres Cathedral. Miller, an Englishman who has made the study of the cathedral his life's work, has published such books as *Chartres Cathedral* (Riverside Books Co.) and *Chartres Stained Glass* (Jarrold Publishing) and has been giving fascinating tours of the cathedral for 45 years. No need to reserve; meet inside the cathedral at the gift shop. Miller also gives private tours for groups up to 15 at 10€ to 15€ per person ($16–$24). Call ☎ **02-37-28-15-58** or e-mail millerchartres@aol.com for more information. Tours are Monday through Saturday at 11 a.m. and 2:45 p.m. from Easter to November (although he is sometimes available in winter, too).

If you can't get in touch with Malcolm Miller, call the cathedral Welcome Center at ☎ **02-37-21-75-02.** Guided Crypt visits are available, but in French only. They meet outside of the cathedral at the La Crypte store from April 1 to October 31 at 11 a.m., and June 22 to September21 at 3:30, 4:30, and 5:15 p.m. (excluding Sun and holidays). From November to March the tours leaves from the cafe gift shop in the North tower, at 11 a.m. and 4:15 p.m. Climb the tower for gargoyle close-ups Monday through Saturday from 7:30 a.m. to noon and from 2 to 7 p.m., and also on Sunday from 8:30 a.m. to noon and from 2 to 7 p.m.; admission is 6.20€ ($9.90) adults and 4.20€ ($6.70) ages 18 to 25; free for children under 18. Note that the stone stairs are steep and winding and the climb isn't for everyone.

Sunday afternoons are a terrific time to visit, when free organ concerts (4:45–5:45 p.m.) and the filtered light coming in from the western windows make the church come wonderfully alive.

The cathedral that you see today dates principally from the 13th century, when it was built with the combined efforts and contributions of kings, princes, church officials, and pilgrims from across Europe. This Notre-Dame was among the first to use flying buttresses.

On your tour, begin at the very beginning — with the **entryway.** People say that Rodin sat for hours on the edge of the sidewalk, contemplating the portal, spellbound by its sculptured bodies draped in long, flowing robes with amazingly lifelike faces. Before entering, walk around to both the north and south portals, which date from the 13th century. The bays depict such biblical scenes as the expulsion of Adam and Eve from the Garden of Eden, and episodes from the life of the Virgin.

Next, just inside, are the **Clocher Vieux** (Old Tower) with its 105m (350-ft.) steeple dating from the 12th century, and the **Clocher Neuf** (New Tower). Originally built in 1134, the new tower's elaborate ornamental tower was added between 1507 and 1513 following one of the many fires that swept through the cathedral.

You can climb to the top of the Clocher Neuf, but make sure your shoes aren't slippery — parts of the tower are without a railing and are quite steep and narrow.

The cathedral is also known for its celebrated **choir screen.** Don't let the simple term fool you; this is a carved wood structure that took nearly 200 years to complete. The niches, 40 in all, contain statues illustrating scenes from the life of Mary. The screen is in the middle of the cathedral toward the altar.

Few of the rushed visitors ever notice the screen; they're transfixed by the stained-glass windows. Bring a pair of binoculars to better focus on the panes, which cover more than 2,508 sq. m (26,996 sq. ft.). The glass is unequaled anywhere in the world and is truly mystical. It was spared in both world wars, because in both wars, the glass was removed piece by piece. Currently, the Association Chartres Sanctuaire du Monde has undertaken the considerable task of raising the millions of euro necessary for the restoration of the windows, which have suffered on both sides from smoke from the cathedral's candles and from pollution.

Most of the stained glass dates from the 12th and 13th centuries. Many visitors find it difficult to single out one panel or window of particular merit; however, the oldest is the 12th-century **Notre Dame de la belle verrière** (Our Lady of the beautiful window, sometimes called the Blue Virgin) on the south side. The colors from the glass are such a vibrant, startling blue that many find it hard to believe that the window is 1,000 years old. In the **nave** (the widest in France), have a look down at the 13th-century labyrinth. It was designed for pilgrims to navigate on their hands and knees as a form of penance, all 300m (1,000 ft.) of it. These days, much of it is covered with folding chairs for Mass. The wooden **Virgin of the Pillar,** to the left of the choir, dates from the 14th century. The **crypt** was built over a period of 200 years, beginning in the 9th century. Enshrined is **Our Lady of the Crypt,** a Madonna made in 1976 that replaced one destroyed during the Revolution. The **Sancta Camisia,** the holy relic that some people believe Mary wore during the birth of Jesus, is behind the choir screen in a chapel to the left of the church's treasury.

The cathedral is open daily April through September from 8 a.m. to 8 p.m., October through March from 7:30 a.m. to 7:00 p.m. Ask at the Chartres tourist office (☎ 02-37-18-26-26) outside the cathedral for information about tours in English and a schedule of masses open to the public.

Dining options

Restaurants, cafes, and snack bars abound around town, but just a stone's throw from the cathedral is **Le Café Serpente,** 2 Clôitre Notre-Dame (☎ 02-37-21-68-81). Facing the south side of the cathedral with outside tables, this restaurant serves traditional French fare at reasonable prices between 13€ and 20€ ($21–$32) for two courses that may start with a dish of leeks and asparagus with foie gras and include a main course of *filet de rouget* (red fish filet). House specialties are pigs' feet and veal kidneys. If you're just there for a snack or light meal, the *salade composée* (large meal-salads) and tasty omelets are available. The restaurant is open daily for lunch, and Monday through Saturday for dinner.

On the other side of the cathedral you can find **Le Cloître Gourmand,** 21 Cloître Notre-Dame (☎ 02-37-21-27-02), a charming and inexpensive restaurant that feels like you're eating in someone's kitchen. Here you can get simple entrees for 6€ ($9.60) such as a pea-mint soup or a spinach pastry, and for a main course they have a great pan-fried salmon with perfumed rice. The restaurant faces a shady side of the cathedral, allowing a view of medieval sculpture as you sip your *café*. The restaurant is open Monday through Saturday at noon through 2 p.m., opening again around 7 p.m. for dinner.

For more upscale dining, take the time to wander through town where you'll discover **Le Moulin de Ponceau,** 21-23 rue de la Tannerie (☎ 02-37-35-30-05). This chic restaurant can be on the expensive side, but it's worth it from the fresh market–menu to the gorgeous scenery. Beautifully situated on the banks of the Eure river, this restaurant's terrace overlooks a stunning panorama of ancient houses, stone bridges, and weeping willows leaning into to the gently flowing water of the Eure, which is more of a stream than a river at this juncture. A la carte you can order a duo of lobster and monkfish or veal sweetbreads in puff pastry with asparagus and wild mushrooms. Menus are at 39€ and 53€ ($62 and $85) for three courses. Relax, listen to the water flowing, and throw your bread crumbs to the ducks that paddle along the current. To find rue de la Tannerie, head through old town, on rue au Lait, for example, in the direction of the Eure. The streets are very twisted and there is no perfect route. Once you end up at the bank, cross the nearest bridge — rue de la Tannerie follows along its East bank. The restaurant is open Tuesday to Saturday noon to 2 p.m. and 7:30 to 9:30 p.m., and Sunday noon to 2 p.m. If you have extra time, spend it by exploring the medieval cobbled streets of the **Old Town.** At the foot of the cathedral are lanes with gabled and turreted houses and humped bridges spanning the Eure River. The turreted Norman house (it's the oldest-looking one there) on rue Chantault, dates back nine centuries.

Stop in at the **Musée de Beaux-Arts de Chartres,** 29 Cloître Notre-Dame (☎ 02-37-90-45-80), to see paintings by old masters such as Watteau, Brosamer, and Zurbarán, and admire the museum's architecture, some of which dates back to the 15th century. The museum is open Wednesday through Monday, 10 a.m. to noon and 2 to 5 p.m., Sundays 2 to 5 p.m. The museum is open until 6 p.m. May to November 30. It is closed on November 1 and 11 and Christmas Day. Admission is 2.90€ ($4.35) adults and 1.50€ ($2.40) for children under 12 and senior citizens (students get in free).

Disneyland Paris

Disneyland Paris, known locally as *Le Parc Disneyland* (☎ 407-934-7639 in the United States, 01-60-30-60-53 in Paris; www.disneylandparis. com), is France's number-one attraction, with more than 50 million visitors a year and celebrated its 15th anniversary in 2007. When it opened in 1992 the French were dead set against it; now 40 percent of its visitors are French, and half of those are Parisian. Set on a 2,000-hectare (5,000-acre) site (about one-fifth the size of Paris) in the suburb of Marne-la-Vallée, the park incorporates the elements of its Disney predecessors but gives them a European flair. Allow at least a full day to see Disneyland Paris.

Information about hotels and packages is constantly changing, so your best bet for staying up to date is to obtain the Disneyland Resort Paris brochure from the Web site a few months in advance.

Getting there

To get there, take the A line RER from such central Paris RER/métro stops as Châtelet-les-Halles or Nation or Gare de Lyon to Marne-la-Vallée/Chessy, within walking distance of the park. The RER station is in Zone 5 of the public-transport system, so the cheapest way there (and back again) is to buy a single-day Mobilis pass good through Zone 5, which costs 13€ ($20). Admission to the park from April to November is 57€ ($91) adults and 49€ ($78) children 3 to 11; children under three are admitted free.

Avoid lines at the resort by buying Disneyland passes at all RER A stations, except Marne-la-Vallée, and métro stations including Charles-de-Gaulle-Etoile, Franklin-D-Roosevelt, Gare de Lyon, Porte Maillot, Esplanade de la Défense, Anvers, Père-Lachaise, Place de Clichy, Gallieni, Havre-Caumartin, Villiers, Alésia, Barbès-Rochechouart, Châtelet, Denfert-Rochereau, and Gare de l'Est. The pass is good for either Disneyland Park or Walt Disney Studios but not both.

Within the park, a free shuttle bus connects the various hotels with the theme park, stopping every 6 to 15 minutes, depending on the time of year. Service begins an hour before the park opens and stops an hour after closing.

If you prefer to drive to Disneyland Paris, take the A4 highway east and exit at Park Euro Disney. Guest parking at any of the thousands of spaces costs 8€ ($13). A series of moving sidewalks speeds up pedestrian transit from the parking areas to the theme park entrance.

Exploring the park

The Disneyland Paris resort consists of two theme parks. The first, **Disneyland Park,** clusters together five "lands" of entertainment (Main Street, U.S.A.; Frontierland; Adventureland; Fantasyland; and Discoveryland) and is where most of the massive and well-designed hotels, a nightlife center (Le Festival Disney), swimming pools, tennis courts, dozens of restaurants, shows, an aquarium, and the Manchester United Soccer School are located. If your kids are younger than seven, they'd be best suited for Main Street, U.S.A., Fantasyland, Sleeping Beauty's Castle, and the afternoon parade. Children ages 7 through 12 will most likely enjoy Frontierland, the Phantom Manor ghost house, the Big Thunder Mountain roller coaster, Adventureland, Indiana Jones and the Temple of Doom roller coaster, and the Pirates of the Caribbean ride. Discoveryland, the Space Mountain roller coaster, and the Star Tours simulated spacecraft ride should please your teens.

Walt Disney Studios Park is the newer of the two parks and is set up as a movie studio come to life, where children participate in the movie-making process. The entrance is called the Front Lot and resembles the Hollywood Disney studios — water tower, gates, and all. En Coulisse restaurant is located here, serving the kind of food kids like and Americans are known for — hamburgers, pizza, salads, and ice cream. In a film studio resembling a street, kids can become a part of the filming of impromptu comedy sketches as they walk around the park; later in the day, they get to see themselves on screen. In the Animation Courtyard, cartoon characters come to life via black light and mirrors, and children can play at being animators at interactive displays. The French Disney Channel has its studios here, in the Production Courtyard; kids get to see how a TV studio really works and may be asked to serve as extras. An international buffet, Rendez-Vous des Stars, is located here. The Back Lot features the Backlot Express Restaurant, serving sandwiches and other quick fare, and the Rock-n-Roller Coaster, a very fast and very loud ride (120 speakers playing Aerosmith) that whips you through an Aerosmith rock video. Calm down afterward by watching the stunt show spectacular, which is highlighted by a high-speed car chase. Food kiosks sell popcorn, ice cream, hot dogs, and so on throughout the park.

A guide for visitors in wheelchairs gives important information about access to rides and other attractions all around the park. You can pick up a copy at City Hall in the Disneyland Park or call to have a copy sent to you (☎ 01-60-30-60-30).

Admission to the park from April to November is 57€ ($91) adults and 49€ ($78) children 3 to 11; children under three are admitted free. The hours of Disneyland Paris vary with the weather and season, so call before setting out. In general, however, the park is open from 9 a.m. to 8 p.m. daily. It sometimes opens an hour later in mid-May, mid-June, and September and October. From September to December, the scheduling hours become erratic during certain weekends due to various school holidays, and they also vary with the weather. Definitely call or check online before you go at the Web site and phone number listed in the first paragraph of this section.

Avoid waiting in long lines with the free **FASTPASS.** After presenting the pass at the ride you want, you're given a time frame for when to come back and board the ride first upon your return. Ask for it at the ticket booth or City Hall.

Staying at Disneyland

If you want to stay at Disneyland overnight or for a few days, you need to book well in advance. Plenty of hotels are available at different price levels, and you can explore the options and book accommodations on the park's Web site at www.disneylandparis.com.

Monet's Gardens at Giverny

Monet moved to Giverny (☎ **02-32-51-28-21;** www.fondation-monet. com for Fondation Claude Monet, which runs the museum) in 1883, and the water lilies beneath the Japanese bridge in the garden and the flower garden became his regular subjects until his death in 1926. In 1966, the Monet family donated Giverny to the Académie des Beaux-Arts in Paris, perhaps the most prestigious fine-arts school in France, which subsequently opened the site to the public. Giverny has since become one of the most popular attractions in France, inspiring millions with its landscape and Provençal-themed house, but even the crowds can't completely overwhelm the magic.

Getting there

Catch an SNCF train at the Gare St-Lazare in Paris approximately every hour for the 45-minute trip to Vernon, the town nearest the Monet gardens. The round-trip fare is about 24€ ($38). From the station, the 241 bus makes the 5km (3-mile) trip to the museum for 2€ ($3.20); a taxi ride will cost 7€ to 10€ ($11–$16); you can rent a bike in Vernon, or even go on foot — the route along the Seine makes for a nice walk.

If you're driving to Giverny, take the A13 highway from the Porte d'Auteuil to Bonnières, then D201 to Giverny. The whole trip takes about an hour.

Traveling to Giverny by tour bus is another option. **Cityrama,** 4 place des Pyramides, 1er (☎ 01-44-55-61-00; www.cityrama.com), has two trips to Giverny: a five-hour trip on Tuesday, Thursday, or Saturday for 67€ ($107) adults, 34€ ($54) children 4 to 11 (children under age four ride free); and an all-day Giverny-Auvers-sur-Oise trip on Sunday or Wednesday for 113€ ($181) for adults, 80€ ($128) for children, which includes lunch at the American Museum. Call for specific dates. **Paris Vision,** 214 rue de Rivoli, 1er (☎ 01-42-60-30-01; www.parisvision. com), offers several trips: a Versailles-Giverny all-day trip on Tuesday through Sunday that includes lunch at the **Moulin de Fourges** and a visit

A calendar of flowers

Check the month corresponding to that of your visit (if it falls between Apr and Oct when Monet's gardens are open), and see the blooms in store.

✔ **April:** Tulips, pansies, forget-me-nots, narcissi, daffodils, cherry, crabapple, lilacs

✔ **May:** Irises, peonies, rhododendrons, geraniums, wisteria

✔ **June:** Roses, poppies, clematis, tamaris

✔ **July:** Roses, rhododendrons, zinnias, dahlias, verbena, salvias, gladioli, beginning of water lilies, sunflowers, hollyhocks

✔ **August:** Dahlias, cosmos, hibiscus, end of water lilies

✔ **September:** Nasturtiums, asters, dahlias, cosmos

✔ **October:** Dahlias

to the American Art Museum for 159€ ($254) for adults, 111€ ($178) for children; and a trip to the house, gardens, and American Art museum on Tuesdays through Sunday for 85€ ($136) for adults and 43€ ($69) for children.

Exploring the gardens

Even before you arrive at Giverny, you probably have some idea of what you're going to see — but nothing prepares you for the spectacular beauty of seeing the gardens up close. The gardens are usually at their best in May, June, and July. Should you yearn to have them almost to yourself, plan to be at the gates when the gardens open, or go on a rainy day (June is probably the busiest month, although they will all be busy). You'll probably spend at least a half-day at Giverny, longer if you plan to eat lunch and visit the American Museum.

The gardens are open from April to November Tuesday through Sunday from 9:30 a.m. to 6 p.m., as well as Easter Monday and Whit Monday (51 days after Easter). Admission to the house and gardens is 5.50€ ($8.80) for adults, 4€ ($6.40) for students, and 3€ ($5.75) for ages 7 to 12 (children under age seven get in free); reservations are required.

Some say Monet's influence was responsible for the influx of American artists into the village of Giverny in the late 1880s. Others say that Monet had little contact with the Americans, and it was Giverny's beauty that captured the hearts of painters such as John Singer Sargent and William Metcalf, who began spending their summers there. In any case, at one point, more than 50 American artists lived in Giverny with their families. You can see much of their work at the **Musée d'Art Américain Giverny** (☎ **02-32-51-94-65**), just 91m (299 ft.) from Monet's house and gardens.

The museum is open April 1 through October 31, Tuesday through Sunday from 10 a.m. to 6 p.m., as well as Easter Monday and Whit Monday (51 days after Easter). Admission is 5.50€ ($8.80) for adults, 4€ ($6.40) for students and seniors, 3€ ($4.80) for ages 12 to 18, and free for children younger than 12. Admission is free for all on the first Sunday of every month.

Dining options

Your entry ticket is no longer valid once you leave Monet's home, so think ahead about whether you want to eat lunch before or after your visit. It may be smart to arrive in early afternoon to have a better chance of avoiding the crowds in the morning.

There are many little cafes and crêperies in the square directly across from Monet's house and on the adjacent street. But a short walk from the gardens is **Les Jardins de Giverny,** 1 rue du Milieu (☎ 02-32-21-60-80). This beautiful and tranquil restaurant opens its doors onto a rose garden in warm weather and serves delicious regional specialties. A *trou Normand* (cider and Calvados sorbet) aids digestion between courses that may include smoked breast of goose marinated in port wine or guinea fowl filleted with apples and potatoes. Main courses cost between 17€ and 32€ ($27–$51). The 33€ ($53) and 45€ ($72) menus are better deals. Another good restaurant in town is **Le Relais Normand** (☎ 02-32-21-16-12) in the Hôtel d'Evreux, an old Norman manor house with a fireplace and terrace. It serves such delicious dishes as roasted Normandy oysters with a nut and mushroom filling, beef filet with Livarot cream cheese, and duck filet with caramelized red fruit. The three prix-fixe menus cost 23€ and 29€ ($37 and $46). The restaurant is open for lunch Tuesday through Sunday from noon to 3 p.m.

Part V
Living It Up After Dark: Paris Nightlife

The 5th Wave   By Rich Tennant

WHILE IN PARIS, DAVE VISITS THE
MUSÉE d'ORSAY – FAMOUS FOR
ITS IMPRESSIONISTS

Now I do for you
the actor James
Cagney. You dirty
rat...

In this part . . .

Paris may not be a city that never sleeps, but it's just as fabulous after the sun sets as it is during the day. There is so much to do! Take your pick of French-language, English-language, or avant-garde theater, ballet, opera, symphony, and even cabaret spectacles like Moulin Rouge. But beware! Events can sell out quickly. Chapter 15 gives you the lowdown on Paris's vibrant theater scene and previews the symphony, opera, and ballet. Chapter 16 hits the bars and clubs, jumping jazz spots, live-music venues, classy cocktail joints, and those naughty cabarets.

Chapter 15

Applauding the Cultural Scene

*W*hatever your choice of the classic arts, you can be guaranteed to find it in excellent form in Paris. This is the city that gave the world playwrights Molière, Victor Hugo, Pierre Corneille, and Jean Racine; and produced actors Sarah Bernhardt and Antonin Artaud. Fortunately for visitors, you don't need to understand French to take in an evening of culture here. Paris has a world-class orchestra, opera, ballet companies — and brilliant venues that house them. There's a flourishing English-language theater scene, and cutting-edge theater productions with scope and visuals that make language secondary!

This chapter helps you find out what's going on and then gets you there.

Getting the Inside Scoop

Paris is one of *the* places in the world to see top-tier ballet and listen to world-renowned symphonies. Unlike New York City, where theaters are located in the area around Broadway and 42nd streets, and serious music and ballet happen at Carnegie Hall and Lincoln Center, in Paris cultural offerings are scattered around the city, from the **Opéra Bastille** in the 12th to **Théâtre National de la Colline** in the 20th.The 2008–2009 season will be the last for the Opéra Bastille's director, **Gérard Mortier,** who is leaving to take over the New York City Opera. Mortier, who made his mark on Europe by shaking up the Salzberg Festival, is known for being cutting edge. A 2008–09 highlight here is: Verdi's *Macbeth.* The **Palais Garnier** presents in 2009 the French national ballet company's premiere dancers in John Cranko's *Onéguine,* after the book Eugene Onegin by Pushkin, with music by Tchaikovsky. In other spectacles, the Opéra Nationale will perform Puccini's *Tosca,* conducted by the boyish Stefan Solyom.

Paris is home to an *early music* scene (music of the Middle Ages, Renaissance, baroque, rococo, and the early classical eras) led by the early music group **Les Arts Florissants** (www.arts-florissants.com), which was founded in 1979 and has performed baroque operas in Paris's biggest venues. Check out the Web site of the Paris Convention and Visitors' Bureau (www.parisinfo.com) for venues and pricing.

The musical is a hot ticket here: *West Side Story* celebrated its 50th anniversary in Paris to rave reviews and *The Lion King* and *Cabaret* also enjoyed huge success, with over 200,000 theatergoers seeing *Cabaret* alone. Songs from musicals are especially popular and mainstream in France, sometimes selling albums before the show even opens. If you see a show, don't be surprised to hear some of its music on the radio.

On any given day, close to 100 theatrical productions may be going on in Paris and the surrounding area. Because Paris is just a three-and-a-half-hour Eurostar ride from London, some of that city's finest actors have found their way across the Channel and into the city's English-language theater community, where they joined up with American, Australian, and even some bilingual French *confrères* (colleagues). Productions in English may not be plentiful, but quality is high, and a wide range of styles is offered.

Arrive early to performances. On the reverse side of some Paris theater tickets may be written: *Les spectateurs retardaires ne peuvent à être placés que lors d'une interruption du spectacle et en fonction de l'accessibilité.* In other words, late arrivals cannot be seated until there is an interruption (intermission) in the play, if they are seated at all. Others may say: *Pour bien garantir votre place, nous vous remercions en avance d'arriver un quart d'heure avant l'ouvrerture de la spectacle.* This means if you show up to the theater exactly at curtain-opening (instead of 15 min. in advance), your seat may have been already given away depending on the popularity of the show. Opera tickets say: *Les spectateurs retardaires ne peuvent à être placés qu'à la fin du premier tableau, du premier acte de l'ouvrage ou à l'entracte,* meaning that late arrivals cannot be seated until the end of the first scene, the first act, or between acts. Some theaters will not even seat those who arrive after the curtain rises, in many cases because the plays being performed are short with no intermission. You want to arrive at the theater or opera early anyway; the bars in these locations are generally very good and are relaxing places to unwind before the shows.

A *placeuse* (an usher, usually female) wearing a small purse around her neck will show you to your seats. Yes, that purse is for tips, which are expected; generally tip 1€ or 2€ ($1.60–$3.20) per person.

Paris audiences tend to dress up for performances, in nice jewelry and dressy pants or skirts for the women, jackets for the men. Generally, the nicer the venue, the dressier the look. Thus, for men a tie and jacket are recommended at the Palais Garnier, whereas an open collar under a stylish jacket would be the look for a performance at Bouffes du Nord.

Dinner and a show

Because performances tend to start around 8 p.m. and French restaurants tend to open at 7 p.m., with dining lasting anywhere from one and a half to three hours and more, what's a hungry show-goer to do? Have a snack before the show, and feast afterward at one of the many cafes or brasseries open late. The following are listed in Chapter 10, and plenty more can be found around the city.

✔ **Au Pied de Cochon,** in the 1er, is open 24 hours.

✔ **Bofinger,** in the 4e, is open until 1 a.m.

✔ The Latin Quarter's infamous **Brasserie Balzar,** 5e, stays open until midnight.

✔ **Brasserie Ile St-Louis,** on the tip of Ile St-Louis right across from Notre-Dame, is open until midnight.

✔ **Café Marly,** 1er, in the Louvre's courtyard, is open until 1 a.m.

✔ You can order food at showy **Fouquet's,** 8e, on the Champs-Elysées, until 2 a.m.

✔ **La Coupole** on boulevard du Montparnasse, 14e, is open until 1:30 a.m. on weekends.

Finding Out What's Playing and Getting Tickets

Several local publications provide up-to-the-minute listings of performances and other evening entertainment. *Pariscope: Une Semaine de Paris* (.40€/65¢) is a weekly guide with thorough listings of movies, plays, ballet, art exhibits, clubs, and more. It can be found at any newsstand. *L'Officiel des Spectacles* (.45€/70¢) is another weekly guide in French. You can pick up the free music monthly, *Cadences,* outside concert venues. The *Paris Free Voice* is a free monthly publication that spotlights events of interest to English speakers, including poetry readings, plays, and literary evenings at English-language bookstores and libraries. You can find it at cybercafes and English-language bookstores or at www. parisvoice.com.

 You can also get information on the Web from the **French Government Tourist Office** (www.francetourism.com), the **Paris Convention and Visitors' Bureau** (www.parisinfo.com), and the **Maison de la France** (www.franceguide.com). Likewise, try **Culture Kiosque** (www.culture kiosque.com) for excellent magazine-style sites about opera and dance in Europe, including schedules, reviews, and phone numbers for ordering tickets.

Saving money on tickets

For half-price theater tickets for national theaters and other venues, go to the **Kiosque-Théâtre** at the northwest corner of the Madeleine Church (directly across from no. 15 place de la Madeleine; Métro: Madeleine) to buy tickets for same-day performances. The panels all around the kiosk indicate sold-out shows with a little red man; a little green man tells you that tickets are still available. The Kiosque-Théâtre is open Tuesday through Saturday from 12:30 to 8 p.m., Sunday from 12:30 to 4 p.m. A second branch of the discount-ticket counter is located on the esplanade between the Tour Montparnasse and the Gare Montparnasse, and a third at Ternes in Montmartre in the center of the square near the métro. Try to arrive no later than noon, because lines are usually long.

Ticket prices in this chapter are approximate; costs vary, depending on who is performing what on which day of the week. Call the theaters for information, or consult *Pariscope* and other entertainment listings. Many concert, theater, and dance tickets are sold through **Fnac** department stores and at the box office. You can find a dozen or so Fnac outlets throughout Paris; the most prominent is 74 av. des Champs-Elysées (Métro: George V). You can also reserve online at Fnac (www.fnac spectacles.com, in French only). Easier is **TicketNet** (www.ticket net.fr), in French and English (look for the tiny EN to the right of the Contact tab at the top of the welcome page), which allows you to buy tickets to cultural events online.

Raising the Curtain on the Performing Arts

The theaters listed here are national theaters supported by the government, but many private ones also exist. For full listings, consult *Pariscope: Une Semaine de Paris* (.40€/65¢), a weekly guide with thorough listings of movies, plays, ballet, art exhibits, and clubs sold at all newsstands.

Attending the theater

A good mix of modern and classic tragedies and comedies comes alive in breathtaking performances in the **Salle Richelieu** of the **Comédie-Française,** 2 rue de Richelieu, 1er (☎ **01-44-58-15-15;** www.comedie-francaise.fr; Métro: Palais-Royal-Musée du Louvre). Performances are in French. Tickets cost 11€ to 44€ ($18–$70). Last-minute seats are on sale one hour before the start of the performance; for ages 28 and older, one can purchase a section C ticket for 50 percent off, sometimes costing as low as 5€ ($8); and for people 27 and younger, an empty seat in section C costs 8€ ($13). For those who want to buy tickets at the theater, the ticket window is open daily 11 a.m. to 6 p.m. Or, purchase full-priced tickets online; though the Web site is in French with some English, it is fairly easy. Those purchasing tickets at a reduced rate from abroad can call ☎ 33-(01)-44-58-15-15. (Remember to factor in the time difference.)

Also a part of the Comédie-Française, the **Théâtre du Vieux Colombier,** 21 rue Vieux Colombier, 6e (☎ **01-44-39-87-00/01;** Métro: St-Sulpice), is an intimate 300-seat venue where mostly modern works are performed. Tickets cost 8€ to 28€ ($13–$45) for adults, 6€ to 13€ ($9.60–$16) for people under 27, and 6€ to 22€ ($9.60–$35) for seniors. Buy non-discounted tickets online at www.comedie-francaise.fr. Those purchasing tickets at a reduced rate from abroad can call daily 11 a.m. to 6:30 p.m. ☎ 33-(01)-44-58-15-15. (Remember to factor in the time difference.)

The Comédie-Française also has a workshop in the **Carrousel du Louvre Studio-Théâtre,** where actors perform one-hour plays and readings. Video projections of plays and films are also shown here. Tickets are sold online at www.comedie-francaise.fr or at the ticket window one hour before the performance and cost 7€ to 17€ ($11–$27) for adults, 5€ to 13€ ($8–$21) for seniors, and 4€ to 8€ ($6.40–$13) for people 27 and younger.

Directly across the Seine from the Eiffel Tower in the Art Deco Palais de Chaillot, is the **Théâtre National de Chaillot,** 1 place du Trocadéro, 16e (☎ **01-53-65-30-00;** www.theatre-chaillot.fr; Métro: Trocadéro), your place for contemporary, popular plays. Highlights of the 2008–09 season are *Impressing the Czar* from the Royal Ballet of Flanders and Dostoyevsky's *The Idiot.* The bar has a good view of the Eiffel Tower. Tickets are 28€ to 33€ ($44–$53) for adults, 16€ to 27€ ($25–$43) for seniors, and 10€ to 17€ ($16–$27) for people 26 and younger. Purchase online. Box office hours are 11 a.m. to 7 p.m. and you can also visit Sundays from 1 to 5 p.m.

The **Théâtre National de la Colline,** 15 rue Malte-Brun, 20e (☎ **01-44-62-52-52;** www.colline.fr; Métro: Gambetta), has modern drama from around the world, and the **Petit Théâtre,** located upstairs, has short plays and offerings from international theater's less famous but up-and-coming playwrights. Arrive early to have a glass of wine and admire the view from the Café de la Colline in the lobby. Chekov's *The Cherry Orchard* is on the bill from March to June 2009. Tickets cost 27€ ($43) for adults, 22€ ($35) for seniors, and 13€ ($21) for people younger than 30. On Tuesdays, adults and seniors pay 19€ ($30). To purchase tickets visit the box office Monday to Saturday from 11 a.m. to 6:30 p.m. or buy online. This was the first theater in France where Shakespeare was performed in English. These days, spectacles at **Odéon Théâtre de l'Europe,** 6 place de l'Odéon (☎ **01-44-85-40-00;** www.theatre-odeon.fr; Métro: Odéon), are varied and eclectic (Lou Reed once read his poems at the Odéon). Tickets in the Berthier theaters are 26€ ($31) for adults, 13€ ($24) for seniors and people younger than 30. At Theatre de l'Odéon tickets range from 7.50€ to 30€ ($12–$48) for adults, 6€ to 20€ ($9.60–$32) for students and seniors. To purchase tickets by phone, call ☎ 01-44-85-40-40 Monday to Saturday 11 a.m. to 6:30 p.m. Tickets also go on sale at the box office at each of the theaters 90 minutes before the show or you can purchase online.

Seeking English-language theater

Summer is a good time to catch English-language theater in Paris. The **Théâtre de Nesle,** 8 rue de Nesle, 6e (☎ 01-44-07-35-49; Métro: St-Michel), and **Les Déchargeurs,** 3 rue des Déchargeurs, 1er (☎ 01-42-36-00-02; www.lesdechargeurs.fr; reservations at ☎ 08-92-70-12-28 [.45€/70¢ per minute]; Métro: Châtelet), sometimes stages English-language plays. Or, for comedy in English, try **Laughing & Music Matters,** in the salsa club La Java, 105 rue Faubourg du Temple, 10e (☎ 01-53-19-98-88; www.anything matters.com; Métro: Goncourt-Hôpital Saint-Louis). This company is thriving; the lineups are always terrific, featuring award-winning comics from the United States, the United Kingdom, Ireland, and Australia. Shows usually start at 8:30 p.m.; admission varies, but count on paying 20€ to 25€ ($32–$40) at the door.

Other English-language theaters include the **International Players** (www.internationalplayers.info), a nonprofessional but still high-quality Anglophone theater company that performs musicals and plays in its space just outside of the city limits in St-Germain en Laye (RER: St-Germain en Laye). Past productions include *The Boyfriend* (2008), *Oklahoma* (2007), and *Sleeping Beauty* (2006). Actors in the international drama company **Drama Ties** (☎ 01-75-50-16-91), started in 1901, put on their own original plays in English and use various theaters in and around Paris; last season included runs of *Snow White's Black Heart* and *Rapunzel*. The **Théâtre en Anglais** (☎ 01-55-02-37-87; http://theatre.anglais.free.fr), outside the city in Asnières-sur-Seine, performs classic plays in English with an excellent troupe. The 2008–09 season includes *Oliver Twist,* Pinter's *The Dumb Waiter,* and *Romeo and Juliet.*

Then again, some theater isn't meant to be understood. In fact, sometimes *not* understanding the language can actually be a bonus. Several well-known avant-garde theater companies are located in Paris, including **Les Bouffes du Nord,** at 37Bis bd. Chapelle, 10e (☎ 01-46-07-34-50; www.bouffesdunord.com), run by the legendary Peter Brook with Micheline Rozan, and **Le Théâtre du Soleil,** in the bois de Vincennes (☎ 01-43-74-24-08; www.theatre-du-soleil.fr), known for its stunning adaptations of both classics and original works. Up for 2009 is *Les Projets des Théâtre Aftaab,* a collaboration with a theater company from Kaboul. Even though these performances are usually in French, the scope of these productions is so large, and the visuals so profound, you may not even notice that you haven't understood a single word.

Listening to classical music and the symphony

Classical music concerts occur throughout the year, and many of them are quite affordable. Look for flyers at churches announcing schedule times, prices, and locations.

More than a dozen Parisian churches regularly schedule relatively inexpensive organ recitals and concerts. The most glorious, where the music is nearly outdone by the gorgeous stained-glass windows, is **Sainte-Chapelle,** 4 bd. du Palais, 1e (☎ 01-44-07-12-38; Métro: Cité). Concerts take place every day between March and November at 7 and 8:30 p.m. You can also hear music at **St-Eustache,** 1 rue Montmartre, 1er (☎ 01-42-36-31-05;** Métro: Les Halles); **St-Sulpice,** place St-Sulpice (☎ 01-42-34-59-60;** Métro: St-Sulpice), which has wonderfully resonant eight-columned pipe organ concerts on most Sundays at 4 p.m.; **St-Germain-des-Prés,** place St-Germain-des-Prés (☎ 01-55-42-81-33; Métro: St-Germain-des-Prés); the **Madeleine,** place de la Madeleine (☎ 01-44-51-69-00;** Métro: Madeleine); and **St-Louis en l'Ile,** 19 rue St-Louis-en-l'Ile (☎ 01-46-34-11-60; Métro: Pont-Marie). It may be a less magnificent setting, but the friendliness of the people attending Sunday concerts at the **American Church,** 65 quai d'Orsay (☎ 01-40-62-05-00; www.acp.org; Métro: Invalides or Alma-Marceau), makes up for the décor. Their Ateler Concert series take place at 5 p.m. Sundays. Check the Web site for other musical events.

Free concerts are staged occasionally in the parks and gardens. (See Chapter 3 for a calendar.) **Maison de la Radio,** 116 av. du President Kennedy, 16e (☎ 01-56-40-12-12; Métro: Kennedy-Radio France), offers free tickets to recordings of some concerts. Tickets are available on the spot an hour before the recording starts. The **Conservatoire National Superieur de Musique** at the Cité de la Musique, 209 av. Jean Jaurés, 19e (☎ 01-40-40-45-45; Métro: Porte de Pantin), stages free concerts and ballets performed by students at the conservatory, while the **Concert Hall** here (☎ 01-44-84-44-84) plays host to all types of performances, from jazz to world music.

The **Salle Pleyel,** 252 rue du Faubourg-St-Honoré, 8e (☎ 01-42-56-13-13), is home to the Orchestre de Paris, and gives 50 concerts a year. The Radio France Philharmonic also plays about 20 concerts a year here, and the lucky traveler may catch a performance of the London Symphony Orchestra, which often visits several times a season. This magnificent concert hall has been acoustically fine-tuned and refurnished with more comfortable seating and delivers some grand musical experiences. Reservations are best made by phone Monday to Saturday 12 a.m. to 7 p.m. Senior citizens and youths under 27, take note: An hour before the show any available, last-minute tickets are offered at just 10€ ($16). There's a 15 percent discount on tickets for those with disabilities.

Enjoying opera and ballet

Whatever your choice of the classic arts — opera, ballet, concerts, recitals — you'll find it performed in Paris by local and international performers of the highest caliber in some of the most wonderful venues imaginable. Inaugurated in 1874, the **Châtelet, Théâtre Musical de Paris,** 1 place du Châtelet, 1er (☎ **01-40-28-28-40;** www.chatelet-theatre. com; Métro: Châtelet), is one of the top places to take in culture in Paris (*Edward Scissorhands,* the ballet, made its debut here in fall 2008). Upcoming highlights include a recital from the Martha Graham Dance Company (Mar 2009), pianist Radu Lupu playing selections of Debussy and Schubert (May 2009), and the Orchestre Nationale de France offering a special concert in honor of the first day of summer (Fête de la Musique). Tickets range from 10€ to 120€ ($16–$230). The box office is open daily from 11 a.m. to 7 p.m. To make reservations by phone, call between 10 a.m. and 7 p.m. daily. There is a 2.50€ ($4) surcharge for Internet and phone reservations.

You can see dazzling performances by the national opera and ballet troupes at both the radiant **Palais Garnier,** place de l'Opéra, 9e (☎ **01-72-29-35-35** from abroad or 08-92-89-90-90 for reservations [.35€/55¢ per minute]; www.opera-de-paris.fr; Métro: Opéra; RER: Auber), and the ultramodern **Opéra National de la Bastille** (see the next paragraph). The Palais Garnier conducts more ballet performances, and the Opéra Bastille puts on more opera. Tickets are priced from 5€ ($8) for seats that have little or no visibility (you can buy these only at the box office an hour before the performance) to 172€ ($275) for the first row of the balcony. Reserve by phone up to four weeks in advance and buy at the ticket windows for performances up to 14 days in advance (including same-day tickets). Making reservations online or by phone adds a 3€ ($4.80) surcharge. The box office, located in the building between the rue Scribe and rue Auber, is open Monday through Friday from 9 a.m. to 6 p.m., Saturday 9 a.m. to 1 p.m.

The **Opéra National de la Bastille,** place de la Bastille, 12e (☎ **08-92-89-90-90** for reservations [.35€/55¢ per minute]; www.opera-de-paris. fr; Métro: Bastille), offers first-class comfort and magnificent acoustics at each level of the auditorium, although Parisians tend to think the building is a badly designed eyesore. The opera house is located at the place de la Bastille; at night, kids crowd the steps, showing off their skateboarding moves, talking on cellphones, and flirting. Tickets are priced between 5€ ($8) for reduced and no-visibility seats to 172€ ($275) for the front rows of orchestra and balcony seating. Reserve by phone up to four weeks in advance and buy at the ticket windows for performances up to 14 days in advance (including same-day tickets). The cheapest seats are on sale only at the box office. Making reservations online or by phone incurs a 3€ ($4.80) surcharge; call Monday to Friday 9 a.m. to 6 p.m. and Saturday 9 a.m. to 1 p.m. to make a reservation by phone. The box office, located at 130 rue de Lyon (the side of the opera house facing the Bastille monument), is open Monday through Friday 10:30 a.m. to 6:30 p.m.

The other major venue for opera is the stunning Belle Epoque **Opéra-Comique,** 5 rue Favart, 2e (☎ **08-25-01-01-23** for reservations; www.opera-comique.com; Métro: Richelieu-Drouot), which offers wonderful musical theater in the Salle Favart, a more intimate venue (the auditorium is so small you can hear people whispering onstage) than its opera hall counterparts. It's currently undergoing renovation which is not supposed to affect performances. A highlight for the 2008–09 season is *Carmen* (June 2009). Tickets are priced from 6€ to 115€ ($9.60–$184) depending on the performance. The box office at place Boieldieu (front of the theater, 2e) is open Monday through Saturday from 11 a.m. to 7 p.m. and Sunday from 11 a.m. to 1 p.m.

Chapter 16

Hitting the Clubs and Bars

* *

In This Chapter

▶ Getting the lowdown on the latest hot spots
▶ Searching out your kind of music and dancing
▶ Unwinding over cocktails

* *

*P*aris affords plenty of opportunities to paint the town *rouge* all night long. Bars usually close around 2 a.m., but most clubs don't open until 11 p.m., and the music doesn't stop pumping until dawn. Check the listings (in French) in *Night Life, Nova,* or *Pariscope* magazines.

Hot Spots for Cool Jazz

If there's one thing you can count on in Paris, it's that the stalwart **Caveau de la Hûchette,** 5 rue de la Hûchette, 5e (☎ **01-43-26-65-05;** Métro or RER: St-Michel), will still be around. It's a legendary club in a cozy, cavelike space that has been welcoming jazz bands for more than 60 years. Locals and tourists of all ages converge here for jitterbugging with a noisy, friendly crowd. Cover is 11€ ($18) Monday through Thursday; Friday through Sunday and the eve of a holiday it's 13€ ($21) between 9:30 p.m. and 2:30 a.m. Music starts at 10:15 p.m.

New Orleans jazz is on the menu at **Le Petit Journal Saint-Michel,** 71 bd. St-Michel, 5e (☎ **01-43-26-28-59;** Métro: Cluny-La-Sorbonne; RER: Luxembourg). You can hit the club for the 48€ ($60) dinner, which includes a two-course meal, a drink, and music, or pay a 17€ or 20€ ($27 or $32) cover for entry with a drink included (the cheaper price is for nonalcoholic drinks). Open Monday to Saturday at 7 p.m. with concerts starting around 9:15 p.m. Check out their sister club, **Le Petit Journal Montparnasse,** 13 rue du Commandant-Mouchotte, 14e (☎ **01-43-21-56-70;** Métro: Gaîté or Gare Montparnasse).

Near Les Halles pedestrian district, the rue des Lombards is a terrific place to hear some of France's most interesting jazz, and clubs on this street have formed the "Paris Jazz Club." For 30€ ($48), one can purchase a membership that offers such promotions as a monthly free entry, reduced prices to clubs, and special theme nights. Go to www.parisjazzclub.net and click on the English flag for more information in English. Clubs on this street include **Duc des Lombards,** 42 rue des Lombards, 1er (☎ **01-42-33-22-88;** www.ducdeslombards.com; Métro: Châtelet-Les Halles), which is often crowded with casually dressed enthusiasts. A ticket to a show starts at 19€ ($30; you can also reserve online). **Le Sunset** and **Le Sunside,** both at no. 60 (☎ **01-40-26-46-60** and ☎ **01-40-26-21-25,** respectively), are temples to eclectic (Le Sunset) and more traditional (Le Sunside) jazz which can be heard in the venue's basement and street level bars. Concerts are priced around 25€ ($40). World music fans go to **Le Baiser Salé** at 56 (☎ **01-42-33-37-71;** Métro: Châtelet), an intimate venue that gets crowded with fans who love fusion jazz, funk, Brazilian, Afro-Caribbean, funk, and meringue. The cover starts around 18€ ($29). The club is open daily from 7 p.m. to dawn with concerts usually starting around 10 p.m.

It's often standing room only at **New Morning,** 7-9 rue des Petites-Ecuries, 10e (☎ **01-45-23-51-41;** www.newmorning.com; Métro: Château-d'Eau), where the best jazz musicians from around the world perform to an audience that knows its jazz. It's one of Paris's best jazz clubs, and past performers include Stan Getz, Miles Davis, and Wynton Marsalis. The venue opens at 8 p.m. and concerts start at 9 p.m. Cover starts at 19€ ($30), depending on the act.

Classy **Le Bilboquet,** 13 rue St-Benoit, 6e (☎ **01-45-48-81-84;** Métro: St-Germain-dès-Pres), starred alongside Louis Armstrong in the 1961 film *Paris Blues.* Not much has changed since the film; the piano bar, where a copper-plated ceiling makes for some interesting acoustics, has hosted such legends as Charlie Parker and Duke. Concerts start at 8:30 p.m. from Sunday to Thursday and at 9 p.m. on Fridays and Saturdays. There is no cover, but drinks can be expensive at the bar (around 12€/$19).

Jazz lovers who visit Paris during June and July weekends can laze among the flowers of the Bois de Vincennes's beautiful Parc Floral and hear world-renowned acts during the Paris Jazz Festival. Métro: Château de Vincennes. For more information: www.parisinfo.com/shows-exhibitions-paris/5397-paris-jazz-festival.

Listening to Live Music

Though it's located in the Pigalle red light district that can be less than savory at night, **La Divan du Monde,** 75 rue des Martyrs, 18e (☎ **01-42-52-02-46;** www.divandumonde.com; Métro: Pigalle), is a terrific venue. Famous patrons (when it was a bar) included Toulouse-Lautrec and Baudelaire and its décor reflects a bygone era. Plus, the music is eclectic; you can hear anything from live rock to a band from the Balkans playing regional music to DJs spinning New Wave. Concerts start anytime from 7 to 10 p.m. Monday through Saturday and at 5 p.m. on Sunday. Cover changes according to the act but can start at 6€ ($26) for a DJ to 35€ ($56) for a concert.

La Flèche d'Or, 102 bis rue de Bagnolet, 20e (☎ **01-44-64-01-02;** www. flechedor.fr; Métro: Alexandre-Dumas), prides itself in developing live acts and features four acts a night nearly every night as well as a DJ spinning tunes. The site is the former Charonne train station, and you can still see the tracks beneath a glass atrium. The club's weeknight openings vary, but count on its being in full-swing Thursday through Saturday from 8 p.m. until at least 2 a.m. Cover ranges from free to 15€ ($24), depending on the act.

Concerts and live reggae, dance hall, rock, funk, and North African Arabic as well as hip-hop and classic French, can be heard at off-the-beaten-track **Abracadabar,** 123 av. Jean Jaurès, 19e (☎ **01-42-03-18-04;** www.abracadabar.fr; Métro: Laumière ou Ourcq). The venue is intimate and the cover is cheap, starting around 5€ ($8). Concerts start at 9 p.m., and you can dance until 2 a.m. from Sunday to Wednesday, and until 5 a.m. from Thursday to Saturday.

La Scène Bastille, 2 bis rue des Taillandiers, 11e (☎ **01-48-06-50-70;** www.la-scene.com; Métro: Ledru-Rollin), is a trendy and upscale joint that has a cozy lounge with caramel-colored padded walls and room to dance to whatever music is playing. Nights without live bands are clubbing nights, led by a DJ. Concerts usually start at 10 p.m. and cost 11€ or 12€ ($18 or $19), nights with a DJ (check the Web site for calendar) usually cost 12€ or 14€ ($19 or $22).

Shaking Your Groove Thing at the Best Dance Clubs

Paris clubs change their programming from night to night, with house music *de rigueur* at many places. Check *Pariscope* magazine for concert schedules. Salsa, the hottest trend a few years back, is still going strong as are techno, house, world, classic rock, and indie rock.

A word of advice: Some of these clubs have strict door policies and turn away those wearing sneakers, sweat suits, baseball caps, and shorts. Many nightclubs accept reservations, so if you're worried about getting past the bouncers, give your club of choice a call (or ask the concierge of your hotel to do it). To club on a budget, go out during the week when cover charges may be (officially or unofficially) waived. Yes, it's sexist, but women often get in free, especially if they're dressed in something slinky, low-cut, or short (or all three). Black clothes seem to be the rule for men and women, and the later you go — or earlier in the morning as the case may be — the more fashionable people get.

Owned by the group who owns Barfly and Buddha Bar, **Barrio Latino,** 46-48 rue du Faubourg-Saint-Antoine, 11e (☎ **01-55-78-84-75;** Métro: Bastille), is a restaurant/bar/club in a gorgeous building designed by Gustave Eiffel that delivers a terrific time — if you can get in. The lines here on weekends are enormous which means it is packed inside. It has three bars on four levels, private areas where you can see (but not be seen), a lounge, winter garden, a second-floor restaurant serving Latino food, and energetic salsa and bossa nova music that sets everyone to dancing (and sweating!). Food ranges from tapas and hamburgers to Central, South American, and Caribbean specialties, each dish listed with its respective country. Open during the week from 11 a.m. to 2 a.m.; weekend club nights run until 5 a.m.

It's a rock club and a club for dancing, and **le Triptyque,** 142 rue Montmartre, 2e (☎ **01-40-28-05-55;** Métro: Grands bd. or Bourse), is one of the hippest spots in town. It hosts clubbing nights and live music by music groups or hot and up-and-coming DJs in the American and European music scene. Unlike some snooty nightclubs in Paris, Triptyque is very much "do-your-own-thing" and no bouncers should give any trouble. Entry changes based on who is performing, but many nights are free, and paid nights are usually between 6€ and 12€ ($9.60–$19). Open Monday to Wednesday 9:30 p.m. to 4 a.m., Thursday to Saturday 9 p.m. to 6 a.m., Sunday 8 p.m. to 2 a.m.

Cithéa Nova, 112 rue Oberkampf, 11e (☎ **01-40-21-70-95;** Métro: Parmentier or Ménilmontant), was taken over by the bar across the street and serves lunch, dinner, and brunch as well as an eclectic mix of world, jazz, and funk music. You can catch concerts Wednesday through Saturday, and a DJ spins after midnight or whenever the bands aren't playing. Cover is free; drinks range from 4€ to 12€ ($6.40–$19). Open daily 9 p.m. to 5 a.m.

All kinds of electronic music plays on the lightship **Batofar,** across from 11 quai François Mauriac, 13e (☎ **01-53-60-17-30;** Métro: Bibliothèque François Mitterand or Quai de la Gare). It's a hot, sweaty, and ultimately fun time. Music can be anything from drum-and-bass to British pop, and the party can go on all night. La Cantine, its small snack bar, serves lunch and dinner between noon and 2 p.m. and 7:30 and 11:30 p.m. The clientele, in their 20s and early 30s, crowd the ship all night, but it's still worth it. Hours can change based on the night, but plan on getting there between 11 p.m. and 6 a.m. Monday to Saturday. Cover ranges from free to 15€ ($18) depending on the band or DJ for the night. During July and August, Batofar has Outdoor Summer Sessions where, for 5€ ($8) between 6 and 8 p.m., you can learn African dance or how to make old clothes hip.

Elysée Montmartre, 72 bd. De Rochechouart, 18e (☎ **01-42-92-45-36;** Métro: Anvers), a club that serves the dual function of disco and major concert hall, celebrated its bicentennial in 2007. The birthplace of the can-can, now it's home to club nights that pull in more than 1,000 dancers. Moby, Björk, U2, and the Red Hot Chili Peppers are just some big musical acts that have headlined here. Check *Pariscope* for events and prices. Dances are usually held 11 p.m. to 5 a.m. Cover charges vary from 15€ to more than 25€ ($24–$40), depending on the event.

Where else in Paris will you dance to the Hives and the Cure followed by some electro-pop spun by great DJs (and down some great beer, too)? It's at the unassuming **Le Truskel,** 12 rue Feydeau, 2e (☎ **01-40-26-59-27;** Métro: Bourse, Grands Boulevards), an Irish pub with a basement "microclub" that has been drawing in crowds of 20-somethings since it opened in 2002. Bands are rumored to relax here after sets at bigger clubs; the U.K.'s Pete Doherty played in June 2008. Open Tuesday 8 p.m. to 3 a.m., Wednesday to Saturday 8 p.m. to 5 a.m.

Josephine Baker, Jean-Paul Sartre, and Simone de Beauvoir loved dancing in the basement dance hall at **La Coupole,** 102 bd. du Montparnasse, 14e (☎ **01-43-20-14-20;** Métro: Vavin). It's still a retro venue with plush banquettes but its sounds are 21st century: salsa, house, and electro-soul. The cover is around 14€ ($22). During the week, the club shuts down between 2 to 3 a.m., and Fridays and Saturdays the party lasts from midnight to 5:30 a.m.

Also in Montparnasse are two enormously popular clubs; **Red Light,** 34 rue du Départ, 15e (reservations ☎ **01-42-79-94-53** from 2–8 p.m.; www.enfer.fr; Métro: Montparnasse Bienvenue), a large club that welcomes an even larger crowd. With some seating and multiple raised platforms above the floor for those who dare to dance, you can watch the trendiest kids in town wearing the oddest new fashions available. Cover can vary, usually it starts around 15€ ($24) with a two-drink minimum, but some nights are free: Check the Web site to see if reduced or free passes can be printed out (usually you have to show up before a certain hour). Just around the corner is **Club Mix,** 24 rue de l'Arrivée (☎ **01-56-80-37-37;** www.mixclub.fr; Métro: Montparnasse Bienvenue). Groove with the fashionistas on Fridays and Saturdays until 5 a.m. to house and "tek-house" beats. Le Mix boasts spinning provided by some of Paris's best DJs. Le Mix also has a varying cover — many nights are free admission before midnight; always check on the Web beforehand.

You'll have to get past some of the strictest bouncers in Paris to dance in a basement that is essentially under the Louvre at classy **Cab** (formerly Cabaret), 2 place du Palais Royal, 1er (☎ **01-58-62-56-25;** www.cabaret.fr; Métro: Palais Royal-Musée du Louvre). It's also a restaurant until 11 p.m. Here you can rub shoulders with models, businessmen and -women, and some BCBG children of rich and old-name families, though this place has more of an out-of-town crowd. Indigo lighting illuminates furniture that looks like it was grown and not assembled. There are two bars with shiny black or glass surfaces, and three different seating areas (not counting the VIP section). Music is house, '80s, and rhythm and blues, with American hits mixed in. Admission runs 28€ to 30€ ($45–$48). Open Wednesday and Friday through Sunday from midnight until 5 a.m.

Located next door to le Moulin Rouge, huge trilevel **La Loco,** 90 bd. de Clichy, 18e (☎ **01-53-41-88-89;** Métro: Blanche), is popular with American students and young people from Paris and the surrounding suburbs. Each level is devoted to a different sound: You may hear house, techno, hip-hop, *raï* (remixed traditional music, mostly from Algeria, but consisting of all the countries of the Maghreb), or metal, so all can find their niche. The *sous-sol* (basement) is the most chilled-out of the three levels, where you can see the remnants of an old railway line (hence the name). Cover Tuesday through Thursday is 12€ ($19) without a drink and 14€ ($22) with one drink; cover on Friday is 15€ ($24) without a drink and 18€ ($29) with one drink; on Saturday it's 15€ ($24) without a drink and 20€ ($32) with a drink. Open daily 11 p.m. to 6 a.m.

On the outskirts of the Marais is the small bar/club **Favela Chic,** 18 rue Faubourg du Temple, 11e (☎ 01-40-21-38-14; Métro: République). Now that a branch of the club has opened up in London, this Brazilian music venue is even more packed, if that's possible. A restaurant by day, at night the long tables in the front area fill up with laughing 20- to 30-year-olds of diverse backgrounds and ethnicities. The dance floor is also always packed, and big comfy couches and chairs line the best areas to dance, if you can snag one. The music is often remixed Brazilian clubbing fare, but there is also electro, hip-hop, and other eclectic selections made by the DJs. It can get very sweaty, but drinks are reasonably priced (6€/$7 cocktails). Entry is free during the week and 10€ ($16) on weekends. Open Tuesdays through Thursdays from 8 p.m. to 2 a.m., on Friday and Saturday it stays open until 4 a.m.

Literally facing the door at the same address as Favela Chic is **Le Gibus** (☎ 01-47-00-78-88), another popular dance club that is also less expensive and rocks all night. The DJs here play more popular dance music, reggae, hip-hop, and top forties hits from the '70s to the '90s. A little less eclectic than its neighbor, it is still very popular among the diverse crowd. Cover is 20€ ($32), which includes a drink. One of Paris's most important and popular tech clubs, **Rex,** 5 bd. Poissonière, 2e (☎ 01-42-36-83-98; Métro: Bonne Nouvelle), has arguably Paris's best sound system and most popular DJs. Open Wednesday to Saturday 11 p.m. to 6 a.m. Closed August. Admission is free to 15€ ($24).

Gay Paree: The Scene

Paris has been a destination for gay parties since before the Code Napoléon decriminalized homosexual relations back in the 19th century. Although some of these delightful dens are mainstays that maintain clientele for years (like le Queen), others appear and disappear as quickly as quirky clothing trends.

The local weekly or bi-weekly rags devoted to the nightlife, which include *Gai Pied Hebdo, Illico,* and *Paris Next,* do their best to keep up with the hottest destinations. You can pick them up in most gay bars or bookstores in and around le Marais. The pickings for lesbian locations are less profound, as usual; check out *Lesbia* magazine for club and bar listings. Other reading material includes *Têtu* and *PREF (Préférences) Mag,* which have special nightlife inserts and cover most of the country's gay bars and clubs.

Amnesia Café, 42 rue Vieille-du-Temple, 4e (☎ 01-42-72-16-94; Métro: Hôtel-de-Ville), is a relaxed cafe/bar/bistro/club with three bar areas, including the basement level Amni-Club. A specialty here is Café Amnesia, whiskey-infused coffee topped with whipped cream. Decorated in warm, coppery tones and furnished with comfortable leather chairs and banquettes, the cafe is open daily 11 a.m. to 2 a.m.; the club is open daily 8:30 p.m. to 2 a.m., later on the weekends.

Le Carré, 18 rue du Temple, 4e (☎ 01-44-59-38-57), is a currently ultrahip bar and restaurant with modern décor. Eat dinner here on banquettes against a backlit wall of painted glass or snack on tapas beneath the bar's suspended light bulbs. Open daily 10 a.m. to 4 a.m.

For those who enjoy thumping music and large crowds, **Raidd,** 23 rue du Temple, 4e (call the Open Café for details; see later in this section; www.raiddbar.com; Métro: Hôtel de Ville), is the place for you. Dance, top-forties, and house music abound, and Raidd's a must-visit for those taking in the gay scene in Paris. Some nights have go-go dancers taking showers behind a glass wall. Open daily until 5 a.m.

L'Oiseau Bariolé, 16 rue de la St-Croix de la Brétonnerie, 4e (Métro: Hôtel de Ville, Rambuteau), is a cozy place featuring mauve and purple leather and velvet seating, a convivial crowd of locals, and a buy-one-get-one-free happy hour.

Located in the pedestrian zone of Les Halles, the **Banana Café,** 13 rue de la Ferronerie, 1er (☎ 01-42-33-35-31; Métro: Châtelet-Les Halles), often has a mixed crowd. Open all night, it has a street-level bar and a dance floor in the basement with live piano music or a DJ. After 10 p.m., things get crazy, with go-go boys dancing on the bar (look for holiday-themed costumes) or on platforms in the basement.

One of Paris's oldest lesbian bars, **La Champmeslé,** 4 rue Chabanais, 2e (☎ 01-42-96-85-20; Métro: Pyramides), is a few blocks east of the avenue de l'Opéra, and features an older, sophisticated crowd. This comfortable bar for women has cabaret singing each Thursday night, and on Tuesdays there are tarot card readings. Also featured are art exhibitions, literary readings, and other themed nights. Open daily 4 p.m. to dawn.

Previously Les Scandaleuses, **le 3w Kafé,** 8 rue des Ecouffes, 4e (☎ 01-48-87-39-26; Métro: St-Paul), sets a relaxed tone for a diverse mix of women, with styles running from pink-haired punk to denim and flannel. It features speed dating some weeknights. This place is simply jammed on weekends and the crowd spills out onto the sidewalk. Open daily 5 p.m. to 2 a.m.

Fridays and Saturdays are known for Le Bal Gai at **Le Tango/Le Bôite à Frissons** (the Thrill Box), 13 rue au Maire, 4e (☎ 01-42-72-17-78; www.

Off the beaten path in Paris

LGBT Parisians often complain that their urban life is concentrated into one place: the Marais. Gay travelers may find it refreshing to leave behind the Chelsea/Castro-esque "ghetto," as it is often referred to, and be themselves outside the narrow confines of the former marshland.

Le Clauzel, 29 Rue Clauzel, 9e (☎ 01-45-26-08-96), a bar-resto in the 9e arrondissement, is ideal because it caters to nobody in particular. Owned by a gay couple, neighborhood folks stop by all day to say hello or wet their whistles, as do the transvestites from Pigalle, gay tourists, and regulars, and anyone else looking for a regular neighborhood bar that happens to sport a big rainbow flag.

In the mood for some cabaret with your dinner? **L'Artishow,** 3 cité Souzy (☎ 01-43-48-56-04; www.artishowlive.com), is the best cross-dressing performance art you can see on this side of the pond, found in the newly hip 11e. Clever, queer, and wildly entertaining, L'Artishow's performances have seen much praise by *le Figaro,* along with other national media outlets. They even have a 12:30 p.m. lunch show if you had evening picnic plans.

In the nearby 10e arrondissement is an establishment that defies definition, a reminder of why Paris remains a world cultural center. **Le Point Éphémère,** 200 quai de Valmy, 10e (☎ 01-40-34-02-48; www.pointephemere.org; Métro: Jaurès or Louis Blanc), is many things; a cafe and restaurant, but also a concert hall, art gallery, discussion forum, dance studio, and so on and so forth. An urban commune of art and culture, it should be no surprise that le Point Éphémère, while mixed, is a haven for queer folks of all ages and backgrounds looking to express themselves, or to meet new friends to discuss philosophy over a double-espresso.

boite-a-frissons.fr; Métro: Arts et Métiers), with music ranging from accordion (the thrill box) to disco and an emphasis on couples dancing. (No techno gets played here!) Singles dances are often held; consult the Web site for more information. Tea dances start late afternoon Sundays. Open at 11 p.m. and continuing until 5 a.m.

Oh Fada! at 35 rue Ste-Croix de la Bretonnerie, 4e (☎ 01-40-29-44-40), was started by the night club team Follivores (they organize gay parties throughout Paris), and is populated by a friendly and convivial crowd of a mixed age. Described as *"atypique,"* it is popular among those who are tired of the gay-ghetto snobbism (but still want cute bartenders). Open Monday to Wednesday and Sunday 5 p.m. to 2 a.m., Thursday to Saturday 5 p.m. to 4 a.m.

Eager patrons often wait in a line outside to gain entry to **Open Café,** 17 rue des Archives, 4e (☎ 01-42-72-26-18; Métro: Hôtel de Ville). It is

THE classic gay watering hole of Paris, in business for years and still a favorite among locals and tourists. Basic cafe fare is served all day. Open Sunday to Thursday 11 a.m. to 2 a.m. and Friday and Saturday until around 4 a.m.

Queen, 102 av. des Champs-Elysées, 8e (☎ **01-53-89-08-90;** Métro: George V), is still one of the hottest clubs in town, with nightly crowds so thick you may find it difficult to get a drink. A walk-up balcony lets you watch the crowd from up high, and across the way is a stage suspended 6m (20 ft.) in the air, from which dancers perch and sway to the music. Weekends may include drag shows or strippers. Cover (including one drink, with or without alcohol) is 15€ ($24) Sunday and Tuesday to Thursday; Friday, Saturday, and Monday cover (including one drink, with or without alcohol) is 20€ ($32). Open daily from midnight to 6 a.m.

For a fairly small dancing venue, **Folies Pigalle,** 11 place Pigalle, 9e (☎ **01-48-78-25-56**), is quite popular. The crowd is a genial mix of gays and straights (the gays say there are more straights, and vice versa) dancing and drinking in a former cabaret-like theater. Sundays are Afro-Latino-House nights; the club claims it's the only such party in Paris.

Kicking Back with Classy Cocktails

Whether you're looking for a bar to go before clubbing or a quiet, romantic place to unwind with a drink, these locations are highly recommended. Most bars and lounges in Paris open daily at 9 p.m., but no one arrives until after midnight. They generally close around 4 a.m.

Andy Whaloo, 69 rue des Gravilliers, 3e (☎ **01-42-71-20-38;** Métro: Arts-et-Métiers), is owned by the people who run the terrific restaurant Le 404 next door and serves as that restaurant's unofficial waiting room as well as a hip spot to sip pricey drinks. Looking something like your grandparents' Moroccan-themed basement with old bottles displayed in the windows and Moroccan grocery sundries making up the décor, hip Parisian denizens pretend not to check each other out from low seats around the small room.

At **Alcazar,** 62 rue Mazarine, 6e (☎ **01-53-10-19-99;** Métro: Odéon), elements of traditional brasserie style, such as banquettes and mirrors, are slicked up with modern flair and mixed with innovations such as a mezzanine with indigo walls and heavenly overstuffed chairs. This place is ultra-sophisticated and its patrons quite chic.

In the swanky neighborhood near the Champs-Elysées is **Nirvana Lounge,** 3 av. Matignon, 8e (☎ **01-53-89-18-91;** Métro: Franklin D. Roosevelt), sporting a bright pink entrance with flashy curves, and celebutante clientele. The lounge music playing is this place's own, released every year and sold at the bar. The food is excellent, from a former chef at the Ritz, and super expensive, just like everything else here. Cocktails are superior, the bar staff attentive, and you will spend more than 14€ ($22) a pop on most drinks. Open every day, from 8 a.m. to 2 a.m.

Harry's New York Bar, 5 rue Daunou, 2e (☎ 01-42-61-71-14; Métro: Opéra or Pyramides), has been one of Europe's most famous bars, as popular today as it was in the time of that notorious Lost Generation of writers who really knew how to ring up a bar tab. It is said that the bloody mary was invented here, and the selection of whiskey is amazing. The 1930s Piano Bar resembles the inside of a cozy yacht. Founded in 1911, aged 30+ French locals and tourists make up the crowd. Open every day from 10:30 a.m. to 4 a.m.

Thinking about *flammenkeuche* on an empty stomach is not recommended. These large, square, thin-crusted pizzas topped with cream, herbs, and goodies such as salmon, ham, and goat cheese are the draw at **La Fabrique,** 53 rue du Faubourg St-Antoine, 11e (☎ 01-43-07-67-07; Métro: Bastille). The restaurant is sleek, the bar is minimalist, and the color to wear appears to be black, if the trendy crowd that frequents the place has anything to say about it. Although the bar is open until around 4 a.m., depending on the crowds, food is served only until midnight. Be ready to stand in line on the weekends, and look out for private parties when the restaurant is closed to the public. Open every day from 9 a.m. to 4 a.m.

In a neighborhood juxtaposed with chic and grunge, **Café Etienne Marcel,** 34 rue Etienne Marcel, 2e (☎ 01-45-08-01-03; Métro: Etienne Marcel), is another funky Paris hangout from the Costes brothers, who really seem to be buying up Paris bars and restaurants. White plastic seats and walls with bold colors and graffiti art in an airy space make a fine place for ordering a complicated drink. The music playing is from the yearly release of the *Hôtel Costes* CDs. Open every day from 11 a.m. to 2 a.m.

Le Bar, in the Hotel Plaza-Athénée, 25 av. Montaigne, 8e (☎ 01-53-67-66-65; Métro: Alma-Marceau), is one of the in spots in Paris, where a crowd with champagne taste sips drinks that cost more than some bottles of wine. Unless you're somebody (or on the arm of somebody), there's no guarantee you'll get in, and when you do, be prepared to withstand the once-over you'll receive from the other fabulously dressed people. Service is reportedly slow at times. Drinks start at around 20€ ($32).

The **Lizard Lounge,** 18 rue du Bourg-Tibourg, 4e (☎ 01-42-72-81-34; Métro: Hôtel-de-Ville), is small and stylish, a pleasant place to hang out with an arty, international crowd — if you can hear them. The music is loud the later into the night you get, and the heavy-gauge steel balcony overlooking the main bar doesn't offer much of a chance for quieter conversation. Still, this is a great venue on three levels with a menu of good beers and drinks. Even the bathrooms have funky décor, with their lizard logo inlaid on some surfaces. Live bands play or a DJ spins dance music in the refurbished basement weeknights and all weekend.

Sit outside for fantastic people-watching, or choose from three floors of funky art-covered walls and sit in one of the antique chairs at **Les Etages,** 5 rue de Buci, 6e (☎ 01-46-34-26-26). Popular among young professionals, the cocktails list here is extensive and complete: Try all sorts of champagne-mixed fruit cocktails, or trust their bartenders to mix you something stronger but with just as much flavor. You can eat as many of their fantastic honey-roasted peanuts as you want, but after two refills, they will definitely give a judgmental glare. Open every day from 11 a.m. to 2 a.m.

Spending an Evening at a French Cabaret

Forget everything you think Parisian cabaret is like. Today's "can-can girls" are often overshadowed by light shows, special effects, and tinny recorded music, though if you're expecting to see lots of flesh in today's Parisian revues, you won't be disappointed. The shows are highly overrated and very expensive but continue to be a huge attraction for tourists. The infamous Folies Bergères no longer exists as a cabaret; it's now a concert hall.

When seeing a Parisian cabaret show, have dinner somewhere else and save yourself some cash. For the money you'd spend at the cabaret, you can have an absolutely fabulous meal at one of the pricier suggestions in Chapter 10. Some of the cabarets admit children, though not kids younger than four. Be aware that every other member of the audience may be from another country — these are some of the least Parisian experiences you can have while still being in Paris.

The **Crazy Horse, Paris,** 12 av. George V, 8e (☎ 01-47-23-32-32; www. lecrazyhorseparis.com; Métro: George V), looks like a strip club with the red silhouette of a naked woman on its glass doors. One can see *Taboo,* a striptease show that highlights each dancer (who have names like Vanity Starlight, Bee Bee Opaline, and Nooka Karamel). Depending on your seats, cover and two drinks cost 100€ ($160) at the bar to 120€ ($192) in the orchestra with a half-bottle of champagne. Special dinner-show packages with restaurants De Vez, Chez Francis, and Fouquet's start at 150€ ($240). There are two shows nightly at 8:30 and 11 p.m., with three on Saturday at 7:30, 9:45, and 11:50 p.m.

The **Lido,** 116 av. des Champs-Elysées, 8e (☎ 01-40-76-56-10; www.lido. fr; Métro: George V), features the revue *Bonheur,* which pays tribute to the sensuality of women. Spanning Paris and India and including movie and cabaret classics, it is supposedly the most expensive spectacle in Europe. The show with dinner and a half-bottle of champagne costs 140€ to 280€ ($224–$448); with just drinks, the show starts at 90€ ($144) for the later show at 11:30 p.m., and 100€ ($160) for the earlier show at 9:30 p.m. Check the Web site for such promotions as a combined evening at the Lido and Seine river cruise.

Frank Sinatra once performed here, at probably the most famous of the cabarets, the **Moulin Rouge,** place Blanche, Montmartre, 18e (☎ 01-53-09-82-82; www.moulinrouge.fr; Métro: place Blanche). It's been packing in crowds since 1889, and its signature can-can dancers, made famous in paintings by Toulouse-Lautrec, still bare breasts in the show's finale today. Edith Piaf, Yves Montand, and Charles Aznavour made their reputations at the Moulin Rouge, though its show *Féerie,* is nothing like an evening of French *chanson.* Instead, expect comedy, animal, and magic acts with scantily clad women bumping and grinding around the stage. Table seats have better views than seats at the bar. A bar seat and two drinks cost 99€ ($158) for the 9 p.m. show, 89€ ($142) for the 11 p.m. show. Dinner followed by the 9 p.m. show costs 145€ to 175€ ($232–$280); you must arrive for dinner by 7 p.m.

The **Paradis Latin,** 28 rue Cardinal-Lemoine, 5e (☎ 01-43-25-28-28; www.paradislatin.fr; Métro: Cardinal-Lemoine), bills itself as the most Parisian of the French cafes, and its building has quite the pedigree; it was designed by Gustave Eiffel. A genial master encourages audience participation during a show that's less gimmick-filled with more song and dance routines than the others. To save money, forgo dinner for the lower-priced Champagne Revue, which includes a half-bottle of bubbly and costs 82€ ($131); dinner (at 8 p.m.) plus show packages range from 117€ to 170€ ($187–$272). Performances are Wednesday through Monday, with a 9:30 p.m. showtime.

Part VI
The Part of Tens

The 5th Wave   By Rich Tennant

"It serves you right for requesting a
lap-dance from someone doing the can-can."

In this part . . .

Okay, these little extras won't make or break your trip, but they may just make it a little more fun. In Chapter 17, we give you the inside scoop on where to find spectacular views of the city — without the other tourists. In Chapter 18, we show you where to make like Manet and have *déjeuner sur l'herbe* — in other words, the best places to go for a fabulous picnic.

Chapter 17

Ten (Well, Nine) Places to See Paris — Without the Lines

● ●

In This Chapter

▶ Finding a fantastic panorama off the beaten path

▶ Discovering some special Paris vistas

● ●

*W*ith wait times at the Eiffel Tower guaranteed to exceed an hour and sometimes two in high season (and not a whole lot less at the Arc de Triomphe) you may wish you could spend the time differently. Fortunately, there are lots of other places to observe Paris vistas without long lines, if any. Some are even free!

Galeries Lafayette

The sixth floor cafeteria of Galeries Lafayette's main store, 40 bd. Haussmann, 9e (☎ 01-42-82-34-56; Métro: Opéra or Chaussée-d'Antin), is sleek and modern and sells fresh hot and cold food. But one of the best reasons to come here is for the views over the rooftops of Paris. If you're not hungry for a meal, at least try the delicious hand-scooped ice cream from the cart here, grab a table beside a window, and enjoy! See Chapter 12.

La Madeleine

See rue Royale, place de la Concorde and the obelisk, and, across the Seine, the dome of Invalides after climbing the 28 steps of La Madeleine church, place de la Madeleine, 8e (☎ 01-44-51-69-00; Métro: Madeleine). After taking in the view, pop inside to see Rude's *Le Baptême du Christ*, which is on the left as you enter. See Chapter 11.

Panthéon

A spectacular view of the Eiffel Tower and the surrounding neighborhoods is available from the Panthéon's dome, place du Panthéon, 5e (☎ 01-44-32-18-00; Métro: Cardinal-Lemoine or Maubert-Mutualité; Bus: 21, 27, 83, 84, 85, 89). This museum, once a mausoleum that was once a church built in honor of the patron saint of Paris now boasts Foucault's pendulum hanging from the domed ceiling. The hill on which the Panthéon is built is a terrific place to see fireworks on Bastille Day. See Chapter 11.

Parc de Belleville

It's off the beaten track, sure, but this park in the 20e offers tree-lined promenades (more than 500 trees are here) and magnificent Left Bank views peeping through the spaces between pretty houses. Beds of roses and other seasonal flowers line walks and views of the city's Left Bank become more pronounced the higher up the terraced pathways you go. (Located in the 20e; take the métro to Pyrénées, then walk down rue de Belleville and turn left onto rue Piat where you see arched iron gates leading into the park; you can also take the métro to Courrones, cross bd. de Belleville and turn left onto rue Julien Lacroix, where another entrance is located.) See Chapter 11.

Pont des Arts

This steel-and-wood, seven-arched, pedestrian-only footbridge connects the entrance to the Louvre on one end with the magnificent Acadèmie Français on the other. The walk across offers breathtaking views all across the river, but especially of the tree-lined tip of Ile de la Cité with the spires of Notre-Dame and Sainte-Chapelle, the turrets of the Conciergerie, and the fabulous curving, white apartment and judicial buildings. (Métro: Pont Neuf; walk west along quai de Louvre or quai de la Conti. It's the bridge directly to the west of Pont Neuf.)

Restaurant Georges at the Centre Georges Pompidou

It used to be that visitors to the Centre Georges Pompidou could skip the museum entirely and ride the escalators on the outside of the building (enclosed in a plastic tube like a giant gerbil habitat) to the top for breathtaking views of the city. That's no longer permitted; you need to buy a ticket for the museum first. Unless, of course, you have drinks, lunch, or dinner at the trendy Costes brothers restaurant Georges (you need a reservation to gain access to the floor). The entrance is to the left of the museum's main entrance, 19 rue Beaubourg, 4e (☎ 01-44-78-47-99; Métro: Rambuteau or Châtelet). See Chapter 10.

Sacré-Coeur

To see the view from Sacré-Coeur in the 18e, 25 rue du Chevalier-de-la-Barre, 18e (☎ 01-53-41-89-00; Métro: Anvers — take the elevator up and follow signs to the *funiculaire*, which runs to the church; Bus: the local Montmartrobus is the only bus that goes to the top of the hill), you have two choices: The first method is the free panorama from the wall just in front of the church (use the coin-operated viewing machines); or you can pay 5€ ($8) to visit Sacré-Coeur's dome. To reach the dome, face the church and walk around to its left side, following signs for the Dome and Crypte. Walk down a set of stairs and follow a walkway about 15m (50 ft.) to an iron gate. The entrance and ticket machine are on your right. The climb from church floor to dome is up a flight of nail-bitingly steep corkscrew steps, but the view is worth it. See Chapter 11.

Tour Montparnasse

At a height of 207m (689 ft.), the Tour Montparnasse, 33 av. du Maine, 15e (that looming black skyscraper on the Left Bank; ☎ 01-45-38-52-56; Métro: Montparnasse-Bienvenüe), towers above Paris, and from its panoramic roof terrace on the 56th floor, you can see as far as 40km (nearly 25 miles) in nice weather. Right next to the Gare du Montparnasse, it's a bit pricey (9€/$15 adults, 6.50€/$11 students 16–20 years, 4€/$6.40 ages 7–15), but the views are exceptional — you've never seen Paris like this!

The Towers at Notre-Dame

Climb 387 narrow and winding steps to the top of one of the towers here for Quasimodo's view of the gargoyles and of Paris below. My advice: If you plan to visit the tower, go early in the morning! Lines stretch down the square in front of the cathedral during the summer. It's at 6 Parvis Notre-Dame, Ile de la Cité, 4e (☎ 01-42-34-56-10; Métro: Cité or St-Michel; RER: St-Michel; Bus: 21, 38, 85, 96). See Chapter 11.

Chapter 18

Ten-Plus Great Places for a Picnic

In This Chapter

▶ Finding that special place to enjoy a meal in *plein air* (fresh air)

▶ Enjoying Paris like a Parisian

*P*ick up some delicious meats, sweets, and wine (see Chapter 12 for recommendations) from one of Paris's open-air markets, *traiteurs* (gourmet food shops), or grocery stores and enjoy an open-air feast without the worry of tipping or dressing to dine. Best of all, you can lay down for a snooze right after you eat.

A word of advice: Such parks as the Luxembourg Gardens or the Tuileries jealously guard their lawns; you may have to walk a bit before you find a spot where you can spread out on the grass. But chairs are everywhere — some even have reclining backs! — and you can pull a few right up to a fountain and eat amidst the spray from the water. If this seems too public, your best bet is to try the vast Bois de Vincennes or Bois de Boulogne where you can picnic nearly anywhere. Don't forget to clean up afterward.

Banks of the Seine near the Musée de Sculpture en Plein Air

Twenty-nine artists created abstract works that complement the meditative mood that the banks of the Seine inspire (kids climb all over them). Sculptures include those by French sculptor César Baldaccini and the Belarorussian Ossip Zadkine. Wander amid the sculptures before you spread out your meal in this waterside park that's really a museum (the name Musée de Sculpture en Plein Air translates to "Open-Air Sculpture Museum") (Métro: Sully-Morland or Gare d'Austerlitz).

Bois de Boulogne

A former royal forest and hunting ground, this vast reserve of more than 880 hectares (2,200 acres) has jogging paths, horseback riding paths, cycling (rentals are available), and boating on two lakes. Picnic areas are abundant here. The **Longchamp** and **Auteuil racecourses** are located here, as is the **Jardin Shakespeare** in the Pré Catelan, a garden containing many of the plants and herbs mentioned in Shakespeare's plays (Métro: Porte Maillot, Porte Dauphine, or Porte Auteuil).

Bois de Vincennes

Rent canoes or bikes or visit the **parc Zoologique** (zoo) and petting zoo after you picnic on the extensive grounds at the Bois de Vincennes, which also has a Buddhist center, complete with a temple. The Chateau de Vincennes, where early monarchs such as Charles V and Henri III sought refuge from wars, is also the place where Mata Hari met her demise. The **parc Floral de Paris** (☎ 01-43-43-92-95) is here with its spectacular amphitheater (and jazz concerts on summer Sat), a butterfly garden, library, and miniature golf (Métro: Porte Dorée or Chateau de Vincennes).

Jardin des Tuileries

The Tuileries is a restful space in the center of Paris that houses the Orangerie and the Jeu de Paume at its western edge and plays home to 40 beautiful Maillol bronzes scattered among the trees to its east. This spot is the city's most formal garden, with pathways and fountains that invite you to sit on the metal chairs provided and munch on picnic treats while cooling off in the breezes off the waters.

The name comes from *tuiles,* which means "tiles" — the clay here was once used to make roof tiles. The gardens were originally laid out in the 1560s for Catherine de Medici in front of the Tuileries Palace (which burned down in 1871). In the 17th century, landscape artist André Le Nôtre, creator of the gardens at Versailles, redesigned a large section (Métro: Tuileries or Concorde).

Jardin du Luxembourg

You can sit on metal chairs near the boat pond or spread out on grass open to picnickers directly across from the Palais de Luxembourg, on the park's south edge. Not far from the Sorbonne and just south of the Latin Quarter, the large park is popular with students and children, so it isn't the quietest of places. Besides pools, fountains, and statues of queens and poets, tennis and *boules* (lawn bowling) courts are available.

See whether you can find the miniature Statue of Liberty (Métro: Odéon; RER: Luxembourg).

Parc de Belleville

Though the parc de Belleville is out of the way, it's still a wonderful place to visit with children, watch the sun set across western Paris, or nosh on a baguette with *saucisson sec* (cured sliced sausage, a bit like French salami). The park has fountains, a children's play area, an open-air theater with concerts during the summer, rock formations, and grottoes that evoke the long-ago days when the hill was a strategic point to fight enemies like Attila the Hun. Beds of roses and other seasonal flowers line the walks, and views of the city's Left Bank become more pronounced the higher up the terraced pathways you go.

Take the métro to Pyrénées; then walk down rue de Belleville and turn left onto rue Piat, where you see arched iron gates leading into the park (spelling out the words *Villa Ottoz*). A curved path leads you to tree-lined promenades (more than 500 trees are here) with the first of the magnificent Left Bank views peeping through the spaces between pretty houses. You can also take the métro to Courrones, cross boulevard de Belleville, and turn left onto rue Julien Lacroix where another entrance is located.

Parc de la Villette

Picnic at Parc de la Villette in the summer while watching an outdoor movie or listening to a concert. Afterward, you and your kids can visit the enormous children's museum complex, the **Cité des Sciences et de l'Industrie** (Museum of Science and Industry), and the Musée de la Musique (Music Museum), located on the grounds. This modern park has a series of theme gardens and includes an exotic bamboo garden and a garden featuring steam and water jets. Scattered throughout the park are playgrounds and other attractions (see Chapter 11). The most fun way to get here is to take a canal trip from Pont l'Arsenal or the Musée d'Orsay (see Chapter 11). You can also take the métro to Porte de la Villette.

Parc des Buttes-Chaumont

Parc des Buttes-Chaumont is one of the four man-made parks that Napoléon III commissioned to resemble the English gardens he grew to love during his exile in England. Built on the site of a former gypsum (a mineral used to make plaster) quarry and a centuries-old dump, it features cliffs, waterfalls, a lake, and a cave topped by a temple. You have plenty of places to lay out your picnic spread here. For a pleasurable walk to further whet your appetite, exit at Métro Danube. Walk east along rue David d'Angers until you find villa du Danube, a sloping road. Follow this through to villa de la Renaissance, and you will discover rue de Mouzaïa: Along this walk and around here you can wander beautiful cobblestoned streets (all called "villa" something) with houses that look nothing like the rest of Paris, sporting ivied balconies and Provençal-style roofs (Métro: Buttes-Chaumont or Danube).

Parc du Champ de Mars

Once a parade ground for French troops, parc du Champ de Mars is the vast green lawn beneath the Eiffel Tower, extending to the École Militaire (Military Academy), at its southeast end, where Napoléon was once a student. You have plenty of places to relax and contemplate the tower. If you have an evening picnic (bring wine; it's okay; everyone else does it!), you can count the hours passing by watching the blinking lights go on and off on the Eiffel tower (up until 1 a.m.); listen for cheers and "awwwws" as people admire the Parisian symbol. After your picnic, take a boat tour of the Seine from the nearby Bateaux Mouches (Métro: Bir-Hakeim).

Parc Monceau

Marcel Proust's favorite park, Monceau allegedly contains Paris's largest tree — an Oriental plane tree with a circumference of almost 7m (23 ft.). The painter Carmontelle designed several structures for parc Monceau, including a Dutch windmill, a Roman temple, a covered bridge, a waterfall, a farm, medieval ruins, and a pagoda. Garnerin, the world's first parachutist, landed here. In the mid–19th century, the park was redesigned in the English style. There is a small shop near the entrance where one can buy sweets and drinks; however, I suggest visiting a local *boulangerie* instead. Very close by are the fantastic market streets rue Poncelet and rue des Levis (Métro: Ternes).

Square du Vert Galant

This spot is one of the most romantic in Paris (and may be crowded with others depending on the time of day and year you visit; I guarantee you'll have it all to yourself in Jan, however). Descend the stairs near the middle of Pont Neuf (near the Pont Neuf tour boats) to this beautiful spot commemorating Paris's favorite king, Henri IV. You're at the very tip of Ile de la Cité, in the middle of the Seine. You can spread out on a bench under the trees and enjoy the stunning views of both banks and the river stretching out ahead. The square is 7m (23 ft.) lower than the rest of the island; this was the original level of Paris during the Gallo-Roman period. At sunset, this is a popular spot for romantics (Métro: Cité).

Appendix A

Quick Concierge

*H*ow do you use the telephones? Where can you find your embassy or consulate? This Quick Concierge offers answers to a variety of "Where do I . . . ?" and "How do I . . . ?" questions.

Fast Facts

American Express

The full-service office at 11 rue Scribe (☎ 01-47-14-50-00) is open Monday through Friday from 9 a.m. to 6:30 p.m., October to April; from May to September, it's open until 7:30 p.m. The bank is also open Saturday from 9 a.m. to 5:30 p.m., but the mail-pickup window is closed.

ATM Locations

As in big cities everywhere, ATMs are easy to find in Paris. Most bank branches have at least one outdoor machine, and there are ATMs in major department stores and in train stations. If you want a list of ATMs that accept MasterCard or Visa cards before you leave home, ask your bank, or print out lists from www.visa.com or www.mastercard.com.

Baby Sitters

Visit the American Church's basement bulletin board where English-speaking (often American) students post notices offering baby-sitting services. The church is located at 65 quai d'Orsay, 7e (☎ 01-45-62-05-00; Métro: Invalides). Or try one of the following agencies that employ some English-speaking baby sitters: Allo Maman Dépannage (☎ 01-47-55-15-75), or Kid Services (☎ 08-20-00-02-30 [10€/20¢ per

minute]). Specify when calling that you need a sitter who speaks English.

Business Hours

The *grands magasins* (department stores) are generally open Monday through Saturday from 9:30 a.m. to 7 p.m.; smaller shops close for lunch and reopen around 2 p.m., but this practice is rarer than it used to be. Many stores stay open until 7 p.m. in summer; others are closed Monday, especially in the morning. Large offices remain open all day, but some close for lunch. Banks are normally open weekdays from 9 a.m. to noon and from 1 or 1:30 to 4:30 p.m. Some banks also open on Saturday morning. Some currency-exchange booths are open very long hours; see "Currency Exchange," later in this list.

Camera Repair

Photo Suffren, 45 av. Suffren, 7e (☎ 01-44-67-25-25; www.photosuffren.com), repairs camera equipment on-site at this location not far from the Eiffel Tower.

Climate

From May to September you can expect clear sunny days and temperatures in the 70s to high 80s Fahrenheit (21 to 31 degrees Celsius) at the height of summer. But be prepared for rainy or searingly hot summers, too. From late October to April the weather is often gray and misty with a dampness that gets into your bones. Always bring an umbrella. Temperatures average about 45 degrees Fahrenheit (7 °C) in winter, and the low 60s Fahrenheit (17°C) in spring and autumn. *Note:* Ignore the song "April in Paris," and pack layers for your early spring trip to the City of Light. It is often quite chilly.

Collect Calls

For an AT&T operator: ☎ 0800-99-00-11.

Credit Cards

Call ☎ 0-800-90-11-79 if you've lost or had your Visa card stolen. American Express card and traveler's check holders in France can call collect ☎ 336-393-1111 for money and lost card emergencies. For MasterCard, call ☎ 0800-90-13-87.

Currency Exchange

It is so much easier to use your ATM card to get cash in Paris — you usually get a better rate of exchange than you do at *bureaux de change* (exchange offices), hotels, restaurants, and shops. Most banks in Paris have stopped cashing traveler's checks and now steer tourists to *bureaux de change*. If you must use traveler's checks, for good rates, without fees or commissions, and quick service, try the Comptoir de Change Opéra, 9 rue Scribe, 9e (☎ 01-47-42-20-96; Métro: Opéra; RER: Auber). It is open weekdays from 9 a.m. to 5:30 p.m., Saturday from 9:30 a.m. to 4:00 p.m. The *bureaux de change* at all train stations (except Gare de Montparnasse) are open daily; those at 63 av. des Champs-Elysées, 8e (Métro: Franklin-D-Roosevelt), and 140 av. des Champs-Elysées, 8e (Métro: Charles-de-Gaulle-Étoile), keep long hours.

Despite disadvantageous exchange rates and long lines, many people prefer to exchange their money at American

Express (see the "American Express" listing earlier in this Appendix).

Customs

Non-E.U. nationals can bring into France duty-free 200 cigarettes or 100 cigarillos or 50 cigars or 250 grams of smoking tobacco; 2 liters of wine and 1 liter of alcohol over 38.8 proof; 50 grams of perfume, one-quarter liter of toilet water; 500 grams of coffee, and 100 grams of tea. Travelers can also bring in 175€ ($280) in other goods; E.U. citizens may bring any amount of goods into France as long as it is for their personal use and not for resale.

Returning U.S. citizens who have been away for 48 hours or more are allowed to bring back, once every 30 days, $800 worth of merchandise duty free. You'll be charged a flat rate of 10 percent duty on the next $1,000 worth of purchases; on gifts, the duty-free limit is $100. You can't bring fresh food into the United States; canned foods, however, are allowed.

Returning U.K. citizens have no limit on what can be brought back from an E.U. country as long as the items are for personal use (including gifts), and the necessary duty and tax have been paid. Guidance levels are set at: 3,200 cigarettes, 200 cigars, 3kg (2.2 lb.) smoking tobacco, 10 liters of spirits, 90 liters of wine, and 110 liters of beer.

Canada allows its citizens a once-a-year C$750 exemption after seven days, and you're allowed to bring back duty-free 200 cigarettes, 1.5 gallons of wine or 1.14 liters of liquor, and 50 cigars. In addition, you may mail gifts to Canada from abroad at the rate of C$60 a day, provided they're unsolicited and don't contain alcohol, tobacco, or advertising matter. Write on the package "Unsolicited gift, under $60 value." All valuables need to be declared on the Y-38 form before departure from Canada, including serial numbers of valuables you already own, such as expensive foreign cameras.

The duty-free allowance in Australia is A$900 or, for those younger than 18, A$450. Upon returning to Australia, citizens can bring in 250 cigarettes or 250 grams of loose tobacco, and 2.25 liters of alcohol. If you're returning with valuable goods you already own, such as foreign-made cameras, you need to file form B263.

The duty-free allowance for New Zealand is NZ$700. Citizens older than 17 can bring in 200 cigarettes or 50 cigars or 250 grams of tobacco (or a mixture of all three if their combined weight doesn't exceed 250 grams), plus 4.5 liters of wine or beer or up to three bottles containing 1.125 liters of liquor.

Dentists

You can call your consulate and ask the duty officer to recommend a dentist. For dental emergencies, call SOS Urgences Stomatologique Dentaire (☎ 01-43-37-51-00 or 01-42-61-12-00) daily from 9 a.m. to midnight.

Doctors

Call your consulate (see "Embassies and Consulates" later in this list for numbers) and ask the duty officer to recommend a doctor, or call SOS Médecins (☎ 01-43-07-77-77), a 24-hour service. Most doctors and dentists speak some English. You can also call for an appointment at the Centre Médicale Europe, 44 rue d'Amsterdam (☎ 01-42-81-93-33). Consultations cost about 20€ ($32), and specialists are available.

Drugstores

Pharmacies are marked with a green cross and are often upscale, selling toiletries and

cosmetics in addition to prescription drugs and over-the-counter remedies. If you're shopping for products other than drugs, buying them elsewhere, such as a *supermarché* (supermarket), is almost always cheaper.

A 24-hour pharmacy, Pharmacie Les Champs, is conveniently located on the Champs-Elysées at 84 av. des Champs-Elysées, 8e (☎ 01-45-62-02-41; Métro: George V).

Electricity

The French electrical system runs on 220 volts. You need adapters to convert the voltage and fit sockets. These are cheaper at home than they are in Paris. Many hotels have two-pin (in some cases, three-pin) sockets for electric razors. Asking your hotel whether you need an adapter is a good idea before plugging in any electrical appliance.

Embassies and Consulates

If you have a passport, immigration, legal, or other problem, contact your consulate. Call before you go: They often keep strange hours and observe both French and home-country holidays. Here's where to find them: Australia, 4 rue Jean-Rey, 15e (☎ 01-40-59-33-00; Métro: Bir-Hakeim); Canada, 35 av. Montaigne, 8e (☎ 01-44-43-29-00; Métro: Franklin-D-Roosevelt or Alma Marceau); New Zealand, 7 ter rue Léonard-de-Vinci, 16e (☎ 01-45-01-43-43; Métro: Victor-Hugo); Consulate of Great Britain, 18 bis rue d'Anjou, 8e (☎ 01-44-51-31-02; Métro: Madeleine); Embassy of Ireland, 4 rue Rude, 16e (☎ 01-44-17-67-00). The embassy of the United States, 2 av. Gabriel, 8e (☎ 01-43-12-22-22; http://france.usembassy.gov; Métro: Concorde), is open Monday through Friday from 9 a.m. to 6 p.m. Passports are issued at its consulate at 2 rue St-Florentin, 1er (☎ 01-43-12-22-22; Métro: Concorde), between 9 a.m. and noon Monday through Friday. The consulate is open Monday to Friday from 9 a.m. to 12:30 p.m. and 1 to 3 p.m. and closed on all French and U.S. holidays.

Emergencies

Dial ☎ 17 for the police (gendarmerie). To report a fire or if you need an ambulance, call ☎ 18 (Sapeurs-Pompiers) or ☎ 15 for SAMU (Service d'Aide Medicale d'Urgence), a private ambulance company.

Hospitals

Two hospitals with English-speaking staff are the American Hospital of Paris, 63 bd. Victor-Hugo, Neuilly-sur-Seine (☎ 01-46-41-25-25), just west of Paris proper (Métro: Les Sablons or Levallois-Perret), and the Hôpital Franco-Brittanique, 3 rue Barbes Levallois-Perret (☎ 01-46-39-22-22), just north of Neuilly, across the city line northwest of Paris (Métro: Anatole-France). Note that the American Hospital charges about $600 a day for a room, not including doctor's fees. The emergency department charges more than $60 for a visit, not including tests or X-rays.

Information

Before you go, contact the French Government Tourist Office, Maison de la France, 825 Third Ave., 29th floor, New York, NY 10022 (France-on-call Hotline: ☎ 514-288-1904; www.francetourism.com). The city's tourist information office, L'Office du Tourisme et des Congrès de Paris (www.parisinfo.com), maintains two full-service welcome centers. Both offer basic information about attractions in the city, help with last-minute hotel reservations, make booking for day trips, and sell transportation and museum passes — but for a small fee. The first, in Gare du Nord (Métro: Gare du Nord) beneath the glass roof, is open daily from 8 a.m. to 6 p.m. The second, the Opéra-Grands

Magasins Welcome Center at 11 rue Scribe (Métro: Opéra or Chaussée d'Antin), is open Monday to Saturday from 9 a.m. to 6:30 p.m.

Several auxiliary offices, or welcome centers, are scattered throughout the city. The office in Gare de Lyon (Métro: Gare de Lyon) is open Monday through Saturday from 8 a.m. to 6 p.m. The welcome center in Gare du Nord is open daily from 8 a.m. to 6 p.m. There are two offices in Montmartre, at 21 place du Tertre (Métro: Abbesses), open daily from 10 a.m. to 7 p.m., and on the median strip facing 72 bd. Rochechouart (Métro: Anvers), open daily from 10 a.m. to 6 p.m. The welcome center in the Louvre (Métro: Palais Royal or Musée du Louvre) is open daily from 10 a.m. to 6 p.m., while the nearby Pyramides office, 25 rue des Pyramides (Métro: Pyramides), is open daily from 9 a.m. to 7 p.m. from June 1 to October 31, 10 a.m. to 6 p.m. the rest of the year. Paris's convention center, Paris Expo (Métro: Porte de Versailles), has an information desk open 11 a.m. to 7 p.m. during trade fairs.

Internet Access

There is no single chain of Internet cafes in Paris, so the best way to find one is to wander around the streets in the Latin Quarter, home to the Sorbonne and other colleges, which is the best thing to do while in Paris anyway. Rates start at around 1.50€ ($2.40) for the first 10 minutes. Most hotels now have wireless Internet (Wi-Fi) or free or low-cost computer access in the salon or lobby area.

Language

In the tourist areas of Paris, English is widely understood. As you move into more residential sections of the city, however, you will probably meet people who don't speak English. I suggest carrying a pocket-sized phrasebook such as *Berlitz Phrase*

Book: French, available at all bookstores (or use the glossary in Appendix B).

Laundry and Dry Cleaning

The more expensive your hotel, the more it costs to have your laundry or dry cleaning done there. Instead, find a laundry near you by consulting the Yellow Pages under *Laveries pour particuliers.* Take as many coins as you can. Washing and drying 6kg (13 lb.) usually costs 8€ ($13). Dry cleaning is *nettoyage à sec;* look for shop signs with the word PRESSING, and don't expect to have your clothes back within an hour; you may be able to get them back the next day if you ask nicely. The dry cleaning chain 5 à Sec has stores across Paris.

Liquor Laws

Supermarkets, grocery stores, and cafes sell alcoholic beverages. The legal drinking age is 16. Persons younger than 16 can be served an alcoholic drink in a bar or restaurant when accompanied by a parent or legal guardian. Wine and liquor are sold every day of the year. *Be warned:* The authorities are very strict about drunk-driving laws. If convicted, you face a stiff fine and a possible prison term of two months to two years.

Lost Property

Paris's Prefecture of Police runs the central Lost and Found, Objets Trouvés, 36 rue des Morillons, 15e (☎ 08-21-00-25-25 [.10€/20¢ per minute]; Métro: Convention), at the corner of rue de Dantzig. The office is open Monday to Thursday 8:30 a.m. to 5 p.m. and Friday 8:30 a.m. to 4:30 p.m. (except in July and Aug). For Lost and Found on the métro, call:

Gare de Lyon: 01-53-33-67-22

Gare Montparnasse: 01-40-48-14-24

Gare Saint-Lazare: 01-53-42-05-57

Gare de l'Est: 01-40-18-88-73

Gare d'Austerlitz: 01-53-60-71-98

Gare du Nord: 01-55-31-58-40

Luggage Storage

Most hotels will store luggage for you for free, and that's your best bet, especially when you plan to return to Paris after a tour of the provinces.

Maps

Maps printed by the department stores are usually available free at hotels, and they're good for those visiting Paris for only a few days and hitting only the major attractions. But if you plan to really explore all the nooks and crannies of the city, the best maps are those of the *Plan de Paris par Arrondissement,* pocket-sized books with maps and a street index, available at most bookstores. They're extremely practical, and prices start at around 9€ ($14). You can find them in Paris bookstores, at the Target-like chain store, Monoprix (there is one in nearly every Paris arrondissement), bookstores, and *presse* stores (large versions of newsstands). Most Parisians carry a copy because they too get lost at times.

Newspapers and Magazines

Paris has a terrific events/nightlife/sightseeing weekly, called *Pariscope* (www.pariscope.fr), sold at every newsstand for .40€ (65¢). A competitor is *L'Officiel des Spectacles,* costing a mere .35€ (55¢). You may also want to pick up the free English-language *Paris Voice* (www.parisvoice.com), which is widely available at hotels and English-speaking venues.

Pharmacies

See "Drugstores."

Police

Dial ☎ **17** in emergencies; otherwise, call
☎ **01-53-71-53-71**.

Post Office

Large post offices are normally open
weekdays from 9 a.m. to 7 p.m., Saturday
from 9 a.m. to noon; small post offices may
have shorter hours. Many post offices
(look for the bright yellow signs) are scattered around the city; ask anybody for the
nearest one. Airmail letters and postcards
to the United States cost .85€ ($1.35);
within Europe .65€ ($1.05); and to Australia
or New Zealand, .85€ ($1.35).

The city's main post office is at 52 rue du
Louvre, 1er (☎ **01-40-28-76-00**; Métro:
Louvre-Rivoli). It's open 24 hours a day for
urgent mail, telegrams, and telephone
calls.

Restrooms

Public restrooms are plentiful, but you usually have to pay for them. Every cafe has a
restroom, but it's supposed to be for customers only. The best plan is to ask to use
the telephone; it's usually next to the *toilette.* Street-side toilets, which are automatically flushed out and cleaned after
every use, were converted to free in 2006.
Some métro stations have serviced restrooms; you're expected to tip the attendant
.50€ (80¢).

Safety

Paris is a relatively safe city; your biggest
risks are pickpockets and purse snatchers,
so be particularly attentive in museum
lines, popular shopping areas, around
tourist attractions, on the métro, and on
crowded buses (especially in the confu-
sion of getting on and off). Popular pick-
pocket tactics include someone asking you
for directions or bumping into you while an
accomplice takes your wallet, and bands
of children surrounding and distracting you

and then making off with purchases and/or
your wallet.

Women need to be on guard in crowded
tourist areas and on the métro against
overly friendly men who seem to have
made a specialty out of bothering unsuspecting female tourists. Tricks include
asking your name and nationality and then
taking advantage of your politeness by
sticking like a burr to you for the rest of the
day. They're usually more harassing than
harmful, but if you're too nice, you may be
stuck spending time with someone with
whom you prefer not to. A simple *laissez-
moi tranquille* (*lay*-say mwa tran-*keel;*
leave me alone) usually works.

Smoking

Paris restaurants and cafes are smoke-
free with smoking sections often set up
outside.

Taxes

Watch out: You can get burned. As a
member of the European Community,
France routinely imposes a standard 19.6
percent value-added tax (VAT) on many
goods and services. The tax on merchandise applies to clothing, appliances, liquor,
leather goods, shoes, furs, jewelry, perfume, cameras, and even caviar. You can
get a rebate — usually 12 percent — on
certain goods and merchandise, but not on
services. The minimum purchase, depending on the store, is 180€ ($288) in the same
store for nationals or residents of countries
outside the European Union. Chapter 12 has
more on VAT and how to deal with it.

Taxis

Because cabs in Paris are scarce picking
up one at a stand may be easier than hail-
ing one in the street. Be careful to check
the meter when you board to be sure
you're not also paying the previous passenger's fare, and if your taxi lacks a

meter, make sure to settle the cost of the trip before setting out. Calling a cab to pick you up is more expensive because the meter starts running when the cab receives the call, but if you need to do it, call Alpha Taxis (☎ 01-53-60-63-50).

The initial fare for up to three passengers is 2.20€ ($3.50) and rises .85€ ($1.35) for each kilometer between 10 a.m. and 5 p.m. Between 5 p.m. and 10 a.m., the standing charge remains the same, but the per-kilometer charge rises to 1.10€ ($1.80). An additional fee of 1€ ($1.60) is imposed for luggage weighing more than 5kg (11 lb.) or for an extra bag. A fourth passenger incurs a 2.85€ ($4.55) charge.

Telephone/Telex/Fax

Public phone booths in Paris seem to be going the way of the dinosaur since the advent of cellphones. You might find a coin-operated phone in a cafe or restaurant, but most public phone booths are equipped to take *cartes à puces* (European credit cards or other cards with a microchip that are inserted directly into the phone) or *cartes à code* that have a code you enter into the phone before dialing a number. Those without a cellphone find *cartes à code* the most convenient because you can use the card on the phone in your hotel. *Cartes à code* start at 7.50€ ($12) for about an hour's worth of phone access and increase in price. You can buy them at any *tabac.* For directory assistance, dial ☎ 12. To make international calls, dial ☎ 00 (double zero) to access international lines.

To charge your call to a calling card or call collect, dial AT&T at ☎ 0-800-99-0011; MCI at ☎ 0-800-99-0019; or Sprint at ☎ 0-800-99-0087. To call the United States direct from Paris, dial 00 (wait for the dial tone), and then dial 1 followed by the area code and number.

For placing international calls from France, dial 00 and then the country code (for the United States and Canada, 1; for Britain, 44; for Ireland, 353; for Australia, 61; for New Zealand, 64), then the area or city code, and then the local number (for example, to call New York, dial 00 + 1 + 212 + 000-0000). To place a collect call to North America, dial ☎ 00-33-11, and an English-speaking operator will assist you. Dial ☎ 00-00-11 for an American AT&T operator; MCI ☎ 0800-99-00-19; and Sprint ☎ 0800-99-00-87.

For calling from Paris to anywhere else in France (the provinces, in other words, or *province*), the country is divided into five zones with prefixes beginning 01, 02, 03, 04, and 05; check a phone directory for the code of the city you're calling.

If you're calling France from the United States, the number you dial probably looks something like this: 011-33-(0)1-00-00-00-00. You must first dial the international prefix, 011; and then the country code for France (33); followed by city code and the rest of the number. When dialing from outside France, leave off the 0, which is often indicated in parentheses, in the city code.

Avoid making phone calls from your hotel room; many hotels charge at least .75€ (90¢) for local calls, and the markup on international calls can be staggering.

You can send telex and fax messages at the main post office in each arrondissement of Paris, but asking at your hotel or going to a neighborhood printer or copy shop is often cheaper.

Time Zone

Paris is six hours ahead of Eastern Standard Time; noon in New York is 6 p.m. in Paris.

Tipping

The custom is to tip the bellhop about 1€ coin per bag, more in expensive (splurge) hotels. If you have a lot of luggage, tip a bit more. Don't tip housekeepers unless you do something that requires extra work. Tip a few euro if a reception staff member performs extra services.

Although your _addition_ (restaurant bill) or _fiche_ (cafe check) bears the words _service compris_ (service charge included), always leave a small tip. Generally, 5 percent is considered acceptable.

Taxi drivers appreciate a tip of .50€ to 1€ (80¢–$1.60) or whatever it costs to round up the fare to the next euro. On longer journeys, when the fare exceeds 20€ ($32), a 5 percent to 10 percent tip is appropriate. At the theater and cinema, tip 1€ ($1.60) if an usher shows you to your seat. In public toilets, a fee for using the facilities often is posted. If not, the maintenance person will expect a tip of 1€ ($1.60). Put it in the basket or on the plate at the entrance.

Porters and cloakroom attendants are usually governed by set prices, which are displayed. If not, give a porter 1€ ($1.60) per suitcase, and a cloakroom attendant .50€ (80¢) per coat.

Transit Info

When taking a train on the national train system, you must validate your train ticket in the orange ticket _composteur_ on the platform or pay a fine. For information in English about Paris subways and buses (RATP) call ☎ 08-92-68-41-14.

Water

Tap water in Paris is perfectly safe, but if you're prone to stomach problems, you may prefer to drink mineral water.

Weather updates

Log on to the following Web sites:

http://europe.cnn.com/weather

www.weather.com

Toll-Free Numbers and Web Sites

Major airlines

Air Canada
☎ 888-247-2262
Air France
☎ 800-237-2747
www.airfrance.com

Air Tahiti Nui
☎ 877-824-4846
American Airlines
☎ 800-433-7300
www.aa.com

British Airways
☎ 800-247-9297
www.britishairways.com

Continental Airlines
☎ 800-784-4444
www.continental.com

Delta Air Lines
☎ 800-221-1212
www.delta.com

Iceland Air
☎ 800-223-5500
www.icelandair.com

Northwest/KLM
☎ 800-225-2525
www.nwa.com

United Airlines
☎ 800-864-8331
www.ual.com

US Airways
☎ 800-428-4322
www.usairways.com

Virgin Atlantic
☎ 800-862-8621
www.virgin-atlantic.com

Major car rental agencies in Paris

Avis
Gare d'Austerlitz, 13e
☎ 08-20-61-16-29 (.10€/20¢ per minute)
www.avis.com

Europcar
60 bd. Diderot, 12e
☎ 08-25-82-54-63
(.15€/25¢ per minute)
www.europcar.fr

Hertz France
Gare de l'Est, 10e
☎ 01-42-05-50-43
www.hertz.com

National
Gare de Lyon, 12e
☎ 01-40-04-90-04
www.nationalcar.com

Where to Get More Information

The information sources listed here are the best of the bunch; dig in before you go, and you'll be well prepared for your trip.

Tourist offices

For general information about France, contact an office of the **French Government Tourist Office** at one of the following addresses:

- ✔ **In the United States: The French Government Tourist Office,** 825 Third Ave., 29th floor, New York, NY 10022 France-on-call Hotline: ☎ 514 288-1904 (http://us.franceguide.com); Chicago ☎ 312-751-7800; Los Angeles 310-271-6665 (http://us.franceguide.com)

- ✔ **In Canada: Maison de la France/French Government Tourist Office,** 1800 McGill College, #1010, Montreal (QC) H3A 3J6 ☎ 514-876-9881 or ☎ 866-313-7262 (http://ca.franceguide.com)

- ✔ **In the United Kingdom: Maison de la France/French Government Tourist Office,** Lincoln House, 300 High Holborn, WC1V 7JH ☎ 09068-244-123 (60p per minute at all times) (http://uk.franceguide.com)

- ✔ **In Australia and New Zealand: Maison de la France Australia & New Zealand,** Level 13, 25 Bligh St. 2000 NSW, Sydney Australia ☎ 61-(0)2-9231-5244 (http://au.franceguide.com)

The city's **tourist information office,** L'Office du Tourisme et des Congrès de Paris (www.parisinfo.com), has two full-service welcome centers. The first, in Gare du Nord (Métro: Gare du Nord) beneath the glass roof, is open daily from 8 a.m. to 6 p.m. The second, the Opéra-Grands Magasins Welcome Center at 11 rue Scribe (Métro: Opéra or Chaussée d'Antin), is open Monday to Saturday from 9 a.m. to 6:30 p.m.

Several auxiliary offices, or welcome centers, are scattered throughout the city. The office in Gare de Lyon (Métro: Gare de Lyon) is open Monday through Saturday from 8 a.m. to 6 p.m. There are two offices in Montmartre, at 21 place du Tertre (Métro: Abbesses), open daily from 10 a.m. to 7 p.m., and on the median strip facing 72 bd. Rochechouart (Métro: Anvers), open daily from 10 a.m. to 6 p.m. The welcome center in the Louvre (Métro: Palais Royal or Musée du Louvre) is open daily from 10 a.m. to 6 p.m., while the nearby Pyramides office, 25 rue des Pyramides (Métro: Pyramides), is open daily from 9 a.m. to 7 p.m. from June 1 to October 31, 10 a.m. to 6 p.m. the rest of the year. Paris's convention center, Paris Expo (Métro: Porte de Versailles), has an information desk open 11 a.m. to 7 p.m. during trade fairs.

Surfing the Web

You can find plenty of excellent information about Paris on the Internet — the latest news, restaurant reviews, concert schedules, subway maps, and more.

- ✔ **Aeroports de Paris** (www.adp.fr): Click the American flag on this site's home page for an English version that provides transfer information into Paris and lists terminals, maps, airlines, boutiques, hotels, restaurants, and accessibility information for travelers with disabilities.

- ✔ **Bonjour Paris** (www.bonjourparis.com): This site should be one of the first you browse before your trip; it's just full of useful information about Paris. You can find everything from cultural differences to shopping to restaurant reviews, all written from an American expatriate point of view.

- ✔ **Café de la Soul** (www.cafedelasoul.com): A sleekly designed Web site for African-American travelers in Paris. The site features articles, travelogues, and links to resources in the City of Light.

- ✔ **French Government Tourist Office** (www.franceguide.com): Here you can find information on planning your trip to France and practical tips, family activities, events, and accommodations.

- ✔ **Google Maps** (http://maps.google.com): On the Google's map engine, typing in a Paris address with a zip code will bring up a detailed map of the surrounding area, including métro stops and any relevant information that Google can find on the business, including phone numbers, official Web pages, and business hours.

✔ **Paris Digest** (www.parisdigest.com): Paris Digest selects "the best sights in Paris" and provides photos and links to them and to restaurants with views and good décor, and information about shopping, hotels, and things to do.

✔ **Paris France Guide** (www.parisfranceguide.com): This site has plenty of useful information about Paris, with current nightlife, restaurant, music, theater, and events listings. This guide is brought to you by the publishers of the *Living in France, Study in France,* and *What's on in France* guides.

✔ **paris.org** (www.paris.org): So much information is on this site that you won't know where to begin. Lodging reviews are organized by area and the monuments standing nearby, and you can find photo tours, shop listings, and a map of attractions with details. Some of the information may be out of date.

✔ **Paris Tourist Office** (www.parisinfo.com): The official site of the Paris Tourist Office provides information on the year's events, museums, accommodations, nightlife, and restaurants.

✔ **Parler Paris** (www.parlerparis.com): This site should be among the first you browse before your trip, or sign up for the biweekly newsletter. Editor Adrian Leeds really knows Paris, and Parler Paris is a true insider's guide to visiting and living in Paris. Her insightful commentary covers everything from visits to hidden Paris places to delicious budget dining.

✔ **RATP (Paris Urban Transit;** www.ratp.fr): Find subway and bus line maps, timetables and information, and routes and times for Noctambus, Paris's night buses that run after the métro closes. Click on the word "English" for the English-language version.

✔ **SNCF** (French Rail; www.sncf.fr): The official Web site of the French railway system, this site sells seats online for trips through France. You can also find timetables and prices here. Click on the Union Jack on the upper-left corner of the screen for English.

Appendix B

A Glossary of French Words and Phrases

● ●

*W*hy *La Tour Eiffel* but *Le Tour de France?* Why *un cabinet* but une *cabine?* Simply put, in French and other Romance languages, nouns are assigned a gender. The article preceding the noun, such as *le* and *la* (which mean *the*) and *un* and *une* (which mean *a* or *one*), corresponds to that gender. *La* and *une* are feminine; *le* and *un* are masculine. Plural nouns are preceded by *les*. An extra letter is also added to the noun itself to signify feminine gender. So Brian Williams is *un journalist,* but Katie Couric is *une journaliste.* French schoolchildren spend years memorizing the gender of nouns; fortunately no one expects you to do the same!

Basic Vocabulary

English	French	Pronunciation
Yes/no	**Oui/non**	wee/nohn
Okay	**D'accord**	dah-*core*
Please	**S'il vous plaît**	see-voo-*play*
Thank you	**Merci**	mair-*see*
You're welcome	**De rien**	duh ree-*ehn*
Hello (during daylight hours)	**Bonjour**	bohn-*jhoor*
Good evening	**Bonsoir**	bohn-*swahr*
Goodbye	**Au revoir**	o ruh-*vwahr*
Police	**la police**	lah po-*leese*
What's your name?	**Comment vous appelez-vous?**	ko-mahn-voo-za-pel-ay-*voo*
My name is . . .	**Je m'appelle . . .**	jhuh ma-*pell*
Happy to meet you	**Enchanté(e)**	ohn-shahn-*tay*
Miss	**Mademoiselle**	mad mwa-*zel*
Mr.	**Monsieur**	muh-*syuh*

English	French	Pronunciation
Mrs.	**Madame**	ma-*dam*
How are you?	**Comment allez-vous?**	kuh-mahn-tahl-ay-*voo*
Fine, thank you, and you?	**Très bien, merci, et vous?**	tray bee-ehn, mare-see, ay *voo*
Very well, thank you	**Très bien, merci**	tray bee-ehn, mair-*see*
So-so	**Comme ci, comme ça**	kum-*see*, kum-*sah*
I'm sorry/excuse me	**Pardon**	pahr-*dohn*
I'm so very sorry	**Désolé(e)**	day-zoh-*lay*
Do you speak English?	**Parlez-vous anglais?**	Par-lay voo ahn-*glay*
I don't speak French	**Je ne parle pas français**	jhuh ne parl pah frahn-*say*
I don't understand	**Je ne comprends pas**	jhuh ne kohm-*prahn* pah
Could you speak more slowly?	**Pouvez-vous parler un peu plus lentement?**	poo-*vay* voo par-*lay* uh puh ploo lan-te-*ment*
Could you repeat that?	**Répetez, s'il vous plaît**	ray-peh-*tay*, see voo *play*
What is it?	**Qu'est-ce que c'est?**	kess-kuh-*say*
What time is it?	**Qu'elle heure est-il?**	kel uhr eh-*teel*
What?	**Quoi?**	kwah
Pardon?	**Pardon?**	par-*doh*
Help!	**Aidez-moi!**	*ay*-day moi!
How? *or* What did you say?	**Comment?**	ko-*mahn*
When?	**Quand?**	cohn
Where is . . . ?	**Où est . . . ?**	ooh-eh
Where are the toilets?	**Où sont les toilettes?**	ooh-sohn lay twah-*lets*
Who?	**Qui?**	kee
Why?	**Pourquoi?**	poor-*kwah*

(continued)

English	French	Pronunciation
Here/there	Ici/là	ee-*see*/lah
Left/right	à gauche/à droite	ah gohsh/ah drwaht
Straight ahead	Tout droit	too-drwah
I'm American/Canadian/ British	Je suis américain(e)/ canadien(e)/ anglais(e)	jhe swee a-may-ree-*cah (kehn)*/ canah-dee-*ahn (en)*/ahn-*glay (glaise)*
I'm going to . . .	Je vais à . . .	jhe vay ah
I want to get off at . . .	Je voudrais descendre à . . .	jhe voo-*dray* day-son-drah-ah

Health Terms

English	French	Pronunciation
I'm sick	Je suis malade	jhuh swee mal-*ahd*
I have a headache	J'ai mal à la tête	jhay mal ah la tet
I have a stomachache	J'ai mal au ventre	jhay mal oh *vahn*-trah
I would like to buy some aspirin	Je voudrais acheter des aspirines	jhe *voo*-dray *ash*-tay days as-peh-*reen*
Hospital	l'hôpital	low-pee-*tahl*
Insurance	les assurances	lez ah-sur-*ahns*

Travel Terms

English	French	Pronunciation
Airport	l'aéroport	lair-o-*por*
Bank	la banque	lah bahnk
Bridge	pont	pohn
Bus station	la gare routière	lah gar roo-tee-*air*
Bus stop	l'arrêt de bus	lah-*ray* duh boohss
By means of a bicycle	en vélo/par bicyclette	ahn *vay*-low/par bee-see-*clet*

English	French	Pronunciation
By means of a car	**en voiture**	ahn vwa-*toor*
Cashier	**la caisse**	lah *kess*
Driver's license	**permis de conduire**	per-*mee* duh con-*dweer*
Elevator	**l'ascenseur**	lah sahn *seuhr*
Entrance (to a building or a city)	**porte**	port
Exit (from a building or a freeway)	**une sortie**	oon sor-*tee*
Ground floor	**rez-de-chausée**	ray-duh-show-*say*
Highway to . . .	**la route pour . . .**	lah root por
Luggage storage	**consigne**	kohn-*seen*-yuh
A map of the city	**un plan de la ville**	uh plahn de la *veel*
Museum	**le musée**	luh mew-*zay*
No entry	**sens interdit**	sehns ahn-ter-*dee*
No smoking	**défense de fumer**	day-*fahns* duh fu-may
On foot	**à pied**	ah pee-*ay*
One-day pass	**ticket journalier**	tee-kay jhoor-nall-ee-*ay*
One-way ticket	**aller simple**	ah-*lay sam*-pluh
A phone card	**une carte téléphonique**	oon cart tay-lay-fone-*eek*
A postcard	**une carte postale**	oon carte pos-*tahl*
Round-trip ticket	**aller-retour**	ah-*lay* re-*toor*
Second floor	**premier étage**	prem-ee-*ay* ay-*taj*
Slow down	**ralentissez**	rah-lahn-tis-*ay*
Store	**le magasin**	luh ma-ga-*zehn*
Street	**la rue**	la roo
Suburb	**la banlieue**	lah bahn-*liew*
Subway	**le Métro**	luh may-tro

(continued)

English	French	Pronunciation
Telephone	**le téléphone**	luh tay-lay-*phun*
Ticket	**un billet**	uh *bee*-yay
Ticket office	**vente de billets**	vahnt duh bee-*yay*
Toilets	**les toilettes**	lay twa-*lets*
I'd like . . .	**Je voudrais . . .**	jhe voo-*dray*
a room	**une chambre**	oon *shahm*-bruh
the key	**la clé (la clef)**	lah clay

Shopping Terms

English	French	Pronunciation
How much does it cost?	**C'est combien?/Ça coûte combien?**	say comb-bee-*ehn?*/ sah coot comb-bee-*ehn*
That's expensive	**C'est cher/chère**	say share
That's inexpensive	**C'est raisonnable/ C'est bon marché**	say ray-son-*ahb*-bluh/say bohn mar-*shay*
Do you take credit cards?	**Est-ce que vous acceptez les cartes de credit?**	es-kuh voo zaksep-*tay* lay kart duh creh-*dee*
I'd like to buy . . .	**Je voudrais acheter . . .**	jhe voo-dray ahsh-*tay*
Aspirin	**des aspirines**	deyz ahs-peer-*eens*
Cigarettes	**des cigarettes**	day see-ga-*ret*
Condoms	**des préservatifs**	day pray-ser-va-*teefs*
Contraceptive suppositories	**des ovules contraceptives**	days oh-*vyules* kahn-trah-cep-*teef*
A dictionary	**un dictionnaire**	uh deek-see-oh-*nare*
A gift (for someone)	**un cadeau**	uh kah-*doe*
A handbag	**un sac à main**	uh sahk ah man

English	French	Pronunciation
A magazine	**une revue**	oon reh-*vu*
Matches	**des allumettes**	dayz a-loo-*met*
Lighter	**un briquet**	uh *bree*-kay
A newspaper	**un journal**	uh zhoor-*nahl*
A road map	**une carte routière**	oon cart roo-tee-*air*
Shoes	**des chaussures**	day show-*suhr*
Soap	**du savon**	dew sah-*vohn*
Socks	**des chaussettes**	day show-*set*
A stamp	**un timbre**	uh *tam*-bruh
Writing paper	**du papier à lettres**	dew pap-pee-*ay* a *let*-ruh

Elements of Time

English	French	Pronunciation
Sunday	**dimanche**	dee-*mahnsh*
Monday	**lundi**	luhn-*dee*
Tuesday	**mardi**	mahr-*dee*
Wednesday	**mercredi**	mair-kruh-*dee*
Thursday	**jeudi**	jheu-*dee*
Friday	**vendredi**	vawn-druh-*dee*
Saturday	**samedi**	sahm-*dee*
Yesterday	**hier**	ee-*air*
Today	**aujourd'hui**	o-jhord-*dwee*
This morning	**ce matin**	suh ma-*tan*
This afternoon	**cet après-midi**	set ah-preh mee-*dee*
Tonight	**ce soir**	suh *swahr*
Tomorrow	**demain**	de-*man*
Now	**maintenant**	mant-*naw*

Index

See also separate Accommodations and Restaurant indexes at the end of this index.

General Index

• A •

A La Cloche des Halles wine bar, 172
A La Mère de Famille, 266
A Priori Thé tea salon, 171
AARP, 62
Abracadabar, 314
Access-Able Travel Source, 64
Access America, 71
Accessible Journeys, 64
accommodations. *See also* Accommodations Index
 arrondissements, 105
 best rate, finding, 101–103
 best room, finding, 101–103
 breakfasts, 110
 budget planning, 43
 cost-cutting tips, 46
 criteria, 102–103
 descriptions of best picks, 12
 Disneyland Paris, 297
 Left Bank map, 108–109
 map of best picks, 106–109
 neighborhood index, 128
 online deals, 104
 options, 100–101
 price index, 128–129
 rates, 102–103
 reservations, 104–105
 Right Bank map, 106–107
 travel to, 81, 84, 86
Aeroports de Paris Web site, 343
agnès b, 256
Ai Nain Bleu, 270–271
Air Canada, 51, 341
Air France airline, 51, 52
Air France Holidays, 58
air show, 36–37
Air Tahiti Nui, 51, 341
Air Tickets Direct, 53

air travel
 airports, 51, 80–86
 best deal, finding, 52–53
 booking online, 53–54
 major airlines, 51–52, 341–342
 to Paris, 80–86
 security measures, 75
Alcazar, 320
alcohol, 134, 338
Alessi, 269
All Hotels, 104
Allo Maman Dépannage babysitting services, 61
Alpha Taxis, 96
American Airlines, 51
American Airlines Vacations, 58
American Express, 49, 50, 57, 334
American Foundation for the Blind, 64
Amnesia Café, 318
Ancient Rome architectural period, 20–21
andouillette, 26
Andy Whaloo lounge, 320
Angelina tea salon, 171
Anna Lowe discount store, 250–251
Annexe des Créateurs discount store, 251
Anthony Peto (store), 255
Antik Batik, 254
antiques shopping, 258
Antoine et Lili (store), 263
aparthotel, 101
Apartment Living in Paris, 100
apartment swaps, 101
apéritif, 134
Aquaboulevard, 213
Aquarium Tropical de la Porte Dorée, 207
Arc de Triomphe, 13–14, 186–187
arcade, 256–257
archaeological museum, 217
architecture, 20–22. *See also specific structures*

Accommodations Index

Restaurant Index